THE LIMITS OF DISSENT

Clement L. Vallandigham
& The Civil War

The University Press of Kentucky

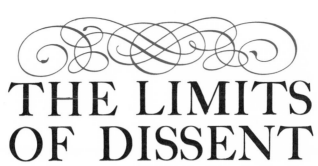

THE LIMITS
OF DISSENT

Frank L. Klement

The drawing of Vallandigham's arrest used on the title page spread is adapted from Frank Leslie's Illustrated Newspaper, May 23, 1863.

Standard Book Number 8131-1218-4
Library of Congress Catalog Card Number 71-111512

Editorial and Sales Offices: Lexington, Kentucky 40506

To the memory of

WILLIAM B. HESSELTINE

Contents

Illustrations

Acknowledgments

I am indebted for favors and assistance to many persons and several institutions. Dozens of librarians and curators gave excellent service in making research materials available and in answering queries. Mr. Gerald Shields, head of the Social Science Division of the Dayton and Montgomery County Public Library, and Mr. Conrad F. Weitzel, reference librarian of the Ohio Historical Society, exemplify those who gave help beyond the call of duty.

Three Daytonians deserve my special thanks. Mr. John Drake, president of the Montgomery County Historical Society, located the Vallandigham probate records in the catacombs of the county court house. Mr. Lloyd Ostendorf loaned some items from his excellent collection of Daytoniana. Mr. Carl M. Becker of the Wright State University shared with me an interest in Midwestern Copperheadism and offered friendly advice and encouragement.

Mr. William E. Van Horne of Columbus, Ohio, volunteered information concerning Vallandigham's return from exile and his relationship to the McGehan brothers. He also loaned an unpublished manuscript entitled "The Strange Deaths of Clement L. Vallandigham and Thomas McGehan."

Two Marquette University graduate students, serving as research assistants in the History Department, gave invaluable help in checking out scores of items in the *Congressional Globe*, the *Official Records of the Union and Confederate Armies*, and in various newspapers. Miss Sandra Collins served during the 1964-1965 academic year and Miss Edith Lechleitner during the 1965-1966 term.

Three grants subsidized research trips to various libraries and archives. A grant from the Graduate Research Committee of Marquette University enabled me to complete the gathering of notes in Dayton and Columbus. The Penrose Fund of the American Philosophical Society of Philadelphia subsidized a research trip into Canada as well as visits to libraries in Richmond, Philadelphia, New York City, Albany, Rochester, Buffalo, and Cleveland. And a grant by the Midwest Research Grants Committee (established jointly by the State Historical Society of Wisconsin and the History Department of the University of Wisconsin) covered some of the expenses of an extended stay in Washington, D.C., to examine materials in the National Archives and the Library of Congress, and limited stays in Madison and Chicago, as well as paying most of the typing costs of the first draft. The Graduate Research Committee of Marquette U. provided funds for typing the revised manuscript.

Editors of three historical quarterlies—*Journal of Southern History, Ohio History,* and *Journal of Negro History*—graciously granted permission to incorporate sentences from three of my articles into this book.

I am most indebted, of course, to my wife Laurel for encouragement and invaluable assistance—correcting, proofreading, indexing. During the last half-dozen years Clement L. Vallandigham has become almost a member of the family.

THE LIMITS OF DISSENT

INTRODUCTION

No figure of the Civil War era was more controversial than Clement L. Vallandigham. Republican party editors and orators denounced and detested him as a minion of Jeff Davis and a traitor. Self-styled "War Democrats" believed him devoid of patriotism and devoted to self-interest, playing a partisan fiddle while Rome burned. Most Midwestern Democrats, on the other hand, considered him their spokesman, able to put their thoughts, hopes, and fears into words. These Midwesterners, whether yeomen farmers of the backwoods area or workingmen of the cities, viewed him as their champion and endorsed his arguments against emancipation, his defense of states' rights, and his pleas for peace and compromise.

In opposing the changes brought by the Civil War, Vallandigham played the role of conservative. He recognized war as more than a military contest waged on far-flung battlefields. He recognized the revolution occurring within the Civil War, transforming the federal union into "a new nation," giving industry ascendancy over agriculture, extending rights to the black man, ending the upper Midwest's chance to play balance-of-power politics, and threatening civil rights and personal freedoms. As the spokesman for Western Democrats, "Valiant Val" popularized the slogan "The Constitution as it is, the Union as it was."

These Democratic critics of change and of the Lincoln administration came to be called "Copperheads." They tried to slow down and stop the revolution taking place within the war and they called for peace and compromise, not only to stop the slaughter, but to halt the changes which were an integral part of the conflict. Midwestern Democrats invariably applauded Vallandigham for defending the political and economic interests of their section and nodded in agreement when he said he was "inexorably hostile" to "Puritan domination in religion or morals or literature or politics."

Nationalist historians of the post-Civil War era have judged Vallandigham harshly, often accepting wartime political propaganda as fact. Because he opposed the will of the majority and the course of events, they have characterized him as obstructionist and traitor. Some have called him disloyal to his section and his country. Still others have furthered the legend that he was involved in the nefarious schemes of the Knights of the Golden Circle and linked to the conspiracy to establish a "Northwest Confederacy."

Conversely, his only biographer (a devoted and sympathetic brother) used the whitewash brush rather freely in *A Life of Clement L. Vallandigham,* published in Baltimore in 1872. Through omission and invention, James L. Vallandigham presented his brother as an heroic figure—a man of high intelligence and signal courage, devoted to principle and persecuted by fanatics and bigots.

Civil War historians who supposed that the truth about Vallandigham lay somewhere between the views expressed by the biographer-brother and the nationalist historians have long recognized the need for a scholarly and systematic study of the controversial Copperhead, since his activities involved such questions as civil rights, smear campaigns, white supremacy, subversive secret societies, Midwestern sectionalism, wartime politics, and, above all, the problem of dissent during war in a democracy. His role as the country's best-known exile and his activities in the Democratic National Convention of 1864 add to his importance as a historical figure. Even in the postwar years he played a major part in two important events, the Philadelphia Convention of 1866 and the presidential contest two years later.

The aspect of Vallandigham's life most meaningful to contemporary readers, however, concerns his role as a dissenter during the Civil War. Although protest against war was no new phenomenon in the United States, the limits of dissent were undefined and very vague, creating a special problem for the Lincoln administration and its chief critic. Clement L. Vallandigham, dissenter extraordinary, deserves an in-depth study so that some legends may be laid aside and his role as a Copperhead may be reassessed.

1

VALLANDIGHAM AND JOHN BROWN:
A STUDY IN CONTRASTS

BRILLIANT SUNSHINE greeted the west-bound Baltimore & Ohio train as it reached the red brick depot in Harpers Ferry, Virginia, at high noon on October 19, 1859. Many of the passengers alighted, some to stretch their legs in a stroll around the station, others to wait for a connecting train. Clement Laird Vallandigham, a second-term congressman from Dayton, Ohio, on his way home from Washington, was one of those who stepped down to the platform at the railroad junction. Natural beauty surrounded him. The town, located at the confluence of the Potomac and Shenandoah rivers, overlooked a picturesque gorge through which the waters plunged white with fury. The rugged slopes of the Blue Ridge Mountains held the village captive but rewarded the observer with a breathtaking view of hardwood trees in autumnal glory.

The brightness of the noonday sun was in contrast to the gloom encompassing the residents of the century-old village. Three days before, on October 16, John Brown and a band of raiders had captured the Harpers Ferry arsenal and seized a number of citizens as hostages. The next day local militia, aided by a company of U.S. marines commanded by Colonel Robert E. Lee, had recaptured the arsenal, killing ten of the defenders and making prisoner Brown and several survivors.

Vallandigham had first heard of the "insurrection" while awaiting his train in Baltimore and speculation about the incident furnished the chief subject of conversation for the passengers while their train puffed its way westward. The Dayton congressman decided to stop over in Harpers Ferry until the evening train to seek first-hand information about the historic event.

Filled with forebodings, Vallandigham wandered through the town inquiring about the raid and the capture of "Old Man"

Brown. He wished to learn if any Ohioans belonged to Brown's band and if any prominent Republicans from the state had furnished money for the ill-conceived enterprise. He found that two of Brown's sons had died while trying to repel the assault of the marines and that Brown and several wounded raiders were prisoners in the arsenal, where two rooms had been converted into a hospital.

The inquisitive congressman turned his steps toward the armory. Once he stopped to survey the railroad bridge and the magnificent scenery surrounding it. As he stood there in deep reflection, fearful of the country's future, Colonel Lee came by. The two strangers destined to become symbols of dramatic causes exchanged greetings; Lee offered to conduct Vallandigham into the presence of the wounded Brown. Eagerly the congressman followed his newly-found guide into the sixty-year-old structure and to the office of the army paymaster, where Brown lay suffering from saber and bayonet wounds.

Vallandigham thanked Lee for his services and joined a handful of men surrounding Brown. The group included reporters for the *Cincinnati Gazette* and the *New York Herald* as well as two well-known Virginians, Governor Henry A. Wise and United States Senator James M. Mason. In questioning Brown, Wise and Mason were trying to discover the motive for the raid.

Vallandigham noticed Brown's striking face disfigured with blood by a saber wound, the right cheek begrimed with powder and dirt. Brown's wounds appeared to be neatly dressed, but his disheveled hair and blood-matted, unkempt gray beard made him look like a grizzled man of seventy although he was but fifty-nine. Despite the pain of his wounds he was full of life, not at all dispirited, and even eager to talk. Since Vallandigham knew both Governor Wise and Senator Mason, he joined them in the interrogation, seeking answers which might incriminate Ohio Republicans and furnish ammunition which he could use politically against Governor Salmon P. Chase, abolitionist-minded congressman Joshua R. Giddings, and editor William F. "Deacon" Comly of the Republican-oriented *Dayton Journal*. Comly was a personal and political enemy for whom Vallandigham was developing an intense animosity. With a lawyer's talent for cross-examination, the Ohio congressman soon took over as chief examiner.

"Where did your men come from?" Vallandigham asked. "Did some of them come from Ohio?"

"Some of them," Brown answered as his eyes shifted toward his new interrogator.

"From the Western Reserve, of course? None came from southern Ohio?"

"Oh yes; I believe one came from below Steubenville, down not far from Wheeling."

"Have you been in Ohio this summer?" Vallandigham had earlier heard someone suppose that the insurrection had been planned at the Ohio State Fair in Zanesville the previous month.

"Yes, sir."

"How late?"

"I passed through to Pittsburgh on my way here in June," the wounded prisoner responded.

"Were you at any county or state fairs there?"

"I was not there since June."

"Were you ever in Dayton?" Vallandigham evidently hoped he could link some of his political enemies to the treasonable plot.

"No; a year or two since." The answer must have been disappointing. Perhaps, however, Vallandigham might get Brown to name some other Ohio Republicans.

Just then Senator Mason interrupted to ask the prisoner if talking annoyed or bothered him.

"Not in the least," Brown quickly retorted, and Vallandigham returned to his questions. Yes, Brown had spent some time in Cleveland and several days in Ashtabula County, the bailiwick of Joshua R. Giddings. Brown refused, however, to say anything that would implicate the congressman. Eager to link Giddings to the Harpers Ferry plot, Vallandigham tried again.

"Will you answer this question? Did you talk with Giddings about your expedition here?"

Brown was too alert to be caught on Vallandigham's baited hook. "No, sir, I won't answer that," he replied, "because a denial of it I would not make, and to make an affirmation of it I should be a great dunce."[1]

---

[1] *New York Herald*, 21 October 1859; *Cincinnati Daily Gazette*, 21 October 1859. The conversation, based on the account in the *Herald*, also appears in James L. Vallandigham, *A Life of Clement L. Vallandigham* (Baltimore, 1872), pp. 113-

Unable to get a firm statement from Brown, Vallandigham walked over to Aaron Stevens, one of Brown's companions, who lay nearby. Stevens groaned occasionally with the pain of his three gunshot wounds. His restless gray eyes wandered from one to another of those around him. Perhaps Stevens might give information which his leader had refused to divulge.

Vallandigham probed. "How recently did you leave Ashtabula County?"

"Some months ago," Stevens answered without hesitation. "I never lived there any length of time, but have often been through there."

"How far did you live from Jefferson?"

"Be very cautious, Stevens, about an answer to that," Brown broke in. "It might commit some friend. I would not answer it at all."[2] Stevens turned over with a groan and ignored those who had gathered about him. He was evidently suffering much from his wounds, although they seemed to have been well treated and skillfully dressed.

Vallandigham returned to Brown's side to ask, "Who were your advisers in this movement?"

Brown evaded a direct answer. "I have numerous sympathizers throughout the entire North."

"In northern Ohio?" The questioner was most persistent but Brown refused to be trapped. "No," he answered, "no more than anywhere else in all the Northern States."

Senator Mason and Governor Wise had a few more questions. Then, seeing the surgeon coming to dress the prisoners' wounds, Vallandigham turned his back on Brown, walked out of the door and headed toward the depot.[3]

The encounter with Brown lasted only twenty minutes, but it made an indelible impression upon Vallandigham. Later he described Brown as one of the most remarkable men he had

---

19 (hereafter cited as Vallandigham, *Vallandigham*). Dorothy E. Filing, "Ohio and John Brown's Raid at Harpers Ferry" (master's thesis, Ohio State University, 1944), contains information not found in the standard biographies of Brown. Mary Land, "John Brown's Ohio Environment," *Ohio State Archaeological and Historical Quarterly* 57 (January 1948): 24-47, throws additional light upon "Old Brown's" Ohio connections.

   2 Quoted in James Redpath, *The Public Life of Captain John Brown* (London, 1863), p. 201.

   3 *New York Herald*, 21 October 1859; Vallandigham, *Vallandigham*, p. 119.

ever met. Perhaps he sensed in Brown a spirit akin to his own—that of the uncompromising idealist who follows his chosen course regardless of consequences. Yet the two stood at opposite poles of the burning issue of their day, and sprang from vastly different origins.

Although John Brown came of "the best New England stock," his father was a restless soul who moved from place to place, job to job. His mother and sister, as well as an aunt and three cousins, had been adjudged insane. Brown's formal schooling was scanty and fragmentary. His business ventures brought failure and frustration. He moved about in Ohio, Pennsylvania, and Massachusetts, trying his hand as drover, tanner, stock grower, wool merchant, and farmer. He was a defendant in twenty-one lawsuits for failing to fulfill contracts or pay wages to men he hired, for failure to meet payments on promissory notes, and for neglecting to pay wool-growers whose product he had sold. Brown never ran for public office and the origin of his political views is shrouded in obscurity. He did not find his great mission—freeing the slaves by force—until he reached his fifties. He did not believe in evolutionary change; he said, "What is needed is action—action!" He believed that slavery must be destroyed through a bloody atonement. "I believe," he said at his trial, "that to have interfered as I have done—in behalf of his despised poor, was not wrong, but right."[4] Unrepentent to the end, Brown was hanged on December 2, 1859.

Clement L. Vallandigham, like Brown, was willing to don the martyr's cloak, albeit for a very different cause. He too could trace his ancestry back to a Van Lendegham who migrated from Flanders to Virginia in 1690. Several generations later one Michael Van Landegham changed his name to Vallandigham and moved to western Pennsylvania to farm, fight Indians, and speculate in land. His son George (grandfather of the congressman who interrogated Brown at Harpers Ferry) served as colonel in the Revolution, mixed law and farming, and condemned the "foolish and illegal" methods the "Whiskey rebels" used to achieve their ends.[5] George's second son, named Clement (C.L.V.'s

4 *Life, Trial and Execution of Captain John Brown known as "Old Brown of Ossawatomie," with a Full Account of the Attempted Insurrection at Harper's Ferry* (New York, 1859), p. 55.
5 Vallandigham, *Vallandigham*, p. 4.

father), attended Jefferson College in Washington, Pennsylvania, studied for the ministry, and married a neighboring Scotch-Irish lass named Rebecca Laird.

Several weeks after his ordination and marriage in 1807, the Reverend Clement Vallandigham moved to New Lisbon, Ohio, where he was installed as pastor of the Presbyterian church. He also assumed charge of congregations at Long's Run and Salem. He raised a family of seven children, preached Calvinist doctrine, and cultivated Puritan virtues. The serious-minded clergyman worshipped duty. "He was ever given to punctuality in his labors," wrote a friendly critic, "and frequently swam his horse through streams in order to make his appointments on time."[6] He raised his children in an atmosphere of zealous rectitude and most of them became impersonal, serious, ambitious, and strong-minded; duty and self-discipline rather than love and solicitude became basic traits of their character.

The Reverend Clement Vallandigham gave his third son, born on July 20, 1820, his own first name and his wife's family name. Clement Laird Vallandigham's mother, unlike John Brown's, typified strength, perseverance, and respectability.[7] Young Clem learned to read at his mother's knee, developed a love of books, and prepared for college in a school his father maintained in his home. He attended Jefferson College,[8] taught school in Snow Hill, Maryland, for two years, and studied law in the office of an older brother. He early appeared destined to enter law and politics, for he was bright, personable, self-assured, and eloquent. At twenty-one he represented his township at a county Democratic convention which adopted a series of resolutions espousing states' rights—a principle that dominated his life. Joining an older brother's law practice after admission to the

[6] Harold B. Barth, *History of Columbiana County, Ohio* (2 vols., Indianapolis, 1926), 1: 113.

[7] Most of the information about Clement L. Vallandigham's ancestry and family life comes from his brother's biography of him. Some additional information can be gleaned from the Vallandigham Papers, Western Reserve Historical Society, Cleveland. These papers contain 219 items, mostly letters which were written to C.L.V.'s paternal and maternal grandfathers.

[8] He entered the college as a junior, and completed one year before going off to Maryland to teach. He returned to Jefferson College but dropped out before the term's end, whether because of an argument with the president or because two professorial positions were unfilled is a debatable point. See Vallandigham, *Vallandigham*, pp. 24-25, and George S. Vallandigham to Rev. M. Brown (president of Jefferson College), 23 January 1841, Vallandigham Papers.

bar in 1842, he rose rapidly in law and politics. Keenly analytical and possessed of an eloquence envied by his rivals, the handsome attorney charmed juries or crowds at political rallies. Although he spoke easily and in resonant tones, his delivery seemed to imply that words were precious, for he closed his muscular lips tightly after each syllable as if doling out some treasure of thought in small coin.[9]

Vallandigham quickly became known as a Jacksonian Democrat with a strong states' rights bent and a conviction that the Union should not be split over slavery. He opposed abolitionism from the beginning and always denied the doctrine of the "irrepressible conflict," even saying, "In my considerate judgment, a confederacy made up of the slaveholding and non-slaveholding states is, in the nature of things, the strongest of all popular governments."[10] In the presidential campaign of 1844, which heralded the coming storm, it was natural for the aspiring young politician to favor James K. Polk. He spoke eloquently and passionately for Polk all over Columbiana County, and gloried in Polk's election.

Anticipating the sweets of political victory, Vallandigham sought a seat in the lower house of the state legislature, winning handily in the October 1845 election and again a year later. In the legislature he viewed himself as a representative of the common man and a defender of the public interest. Like a true Jacksonian, he criticized the banking and industrial interests. He campaigned futilely to abolish capital punishment. He supported what he thought were the wishes of the majority of Ohioans, voting for a measure which prohibited "people of color" from emigrating into the state. And he chided Whig legislators for opposing the Mexican War. Reciting a long list of grievances against Mexico, he declared the war both just and constitutional. The Democratic party, he said, gladly accepted the responsibility for this war. Whigs, he added, talked like "traitors." "Sirs," he declared, shaking his finger at the Whig critics of "Polk's War," "if ye will howl over its calamities in the name of the living, by the blood of its slain ye shall have

[9] William W. Armstrong, "Personal Recollections," published in *Cincinnati Daily Enquirer,* 20 March 1886. References to Vallandigham's early political activities are found in the *Ohio Patriot* (New Lisbon), 27 August 1841, 22 July and 5, 12, 19 August 1842.

[10] *Congressional Globe,* 37 Cong., 3 sess., "Appendix," p. 55.

no part in its glories."[11] Vallandigham's advocacy of war in 1846-1847, and the charge of treason he hurled at its critics, would come back to haunt him nearly twenty years later.

Friends Vallandigham had made in the legislature in Columbus urged him to move to Dayton with the lure of greener fields. Democratic leaders in Montgomery County wished to revitalize the *Dayton Western Empire* and sought a young and energetic editor. Thomas J. S. Smith, one of Ohio's elder statesmen, offered Vallandigham the newspaper and a print shop for $150, with permission to take his "own time for payment."[12] Smith put more bait on the hook, offering to share his law practice and offices with Vallandigham. The ambitious young man consulted with his wife of less than a year—he had married Miss Louisa A. McMahon[13] on August 27, 1846—and the two decided to accept the offer. Young Vallandigham believed New Lisbon to be a dying community and Dayton a dynamic one. Furthermore, Smith's offer seemed too good to be true.

The young couple moved to Dayton in August of 1847 and Clem Vallandigham's "Salutatory Address" appeared in the *Western Empire* of September 2.[14] He soon made the paper a paying venture and the voice of the Democracy of Montgomery County. His law practice grew fast, for his editorials, vigorous and partisan, endeared him to those who lived in the political house Jackson had built. He made a circle of friends. Since a hotel room was unsuitable quarters for a pregnant wife, he bought a fine two-story house at 323 First Street, a choice residential area. The long back lawn sloped down toward the levee which held the Great Miami River in bounds. Two houses away lived Robert C. Schenck, incumbent Whig congressman and one of Dayton's best-known citizens. It was but six blocks from 323 First Street to the office of the *Western Empire*.

Within two years Vallandigham tired of the demanding work of running a newspaper. His success in law drew heavily upon

---

11 *Journal of the House of Representatives of the State of Ohio, 1846* (Columbus, 1847), pp. 40-42.

12 *Dayton Daily Journal*, 26 September 1852.

13 She was the daughter of William McMahon of Cumberland, Maryland, and a sister of the well-known nonconformist John Van Lear McMahon of Baltimore. Clem Vallandigham met his wife-to-be when she was visiting a sister in New Lisbon.

14 *Dayton Western Empire*, 2 September 1847.

his time and he looked for a buyer to take over the flourishing paper. He did not like being chained to an editor's chair or having to fire offhand upon every passing question and have his thoughts pass away like cancelled checks. He preferred to read and study and ponder, so he felt restricted by newspaper work, with its schedules to be met and columns to be filled.[15]

The months which followed the sale of the *Western Empire* (the change in ownership brought a change in name to the *Dayton Empire*[16]) were perhaps the happiest of Vallandigham's life. No longer was he a prisoner in an editor's office. His wife appeared to have regained her health after the death of their month-old son. The earnings from his law practice enabled them to live comfortably. Politics had not yet become an obsession. He was relaxed and congenial, eager to cultivate friendships for friendship's sake. He enjoyed hikes through the woods, occasionally trying for bass or trout. He had money enough to add dozens of books to his ever-growing library and to spend long hours over the classics, history, biography, and law cases.[17]

Events, however, drew him inexorably back into politics. He felt obligated to support the Compromise of 1850, helping to organize a pro-Compromise rally in Dayton. He quarreled with the Comly brothers who edited the Whig-oriented *Dayton Journal* and espoused abolitionist doctrine. He made a bid for a county judgeship but lost out to a Whig candidate. The following year he sought his party's nomination for the lieutenant-governorship but that prize also eluded him. In 1852, after a Democratic legislature drew new lines for the congressional districts, he gained his party's nomination in the Third District, although a veteran politician seemed to have a better claim to the honor. But Vallandigham lost the election to Lewis D. Campbell, the incumbent congressman, who posed as a Whig but had become addicted to Know-Nothingism. The results were close, Campbell edging out the Democratic contender by 147 votes. Democrats had some cause to cheer, however, for Franklin Pierce won the

15 Armstrong, "Personal Recollections," *Cincinnati Daily Enquirer*, 20 March 1886.

16 *Dayton Tri-Weekly Bulletin*, 1 June, 2 July 1849. Vallandigham sold his share to William Ramsey of Wooster, Ohio, and the paper was then owned by Fitch & Ramsey. Ramsey became the new editor.

17 Francis T. Brown, "Recollections of C. L. Vallandigham," *St. Paul Pioneer*, 21 June 1871.

presidency and the right to dispense patronage through the party.

During the next several years Vallandigham added to his reputation as a lawyer. In the April 1855 term of the Court of Common Pleas he won four cases in one week. In one case, it is recorded that the jury's award to Vallandigham's client was so unexpected as to leave the judge gasping.[18] In law, as in politics, the ambitious barrister aligned himself on the side of the common man against the claims of the banker, the merchant, and the land speculator. Many of his clients were Irish-Americans and German-Americans, invariably Democrats, some of whom were able to pay only with pennies or prayers.

He did well enough at law, however, to pay off the mortgage on his home and set aside some money. He needed a good income to maintain the Vallandigham household, which now numbered five. His wife, rather temperamental, wished to live fashionably and believed that money was meant to be spent. His son Charlie, born in 1854, was oblivious to worldly things. His sister-in-law, Miss Belle McMahon, served as a lady-in-waiting to her less stable sister. A nephew, John A. McMahon, who read law in Vallandigham's office until his admission to the bar in 1854, also stayed at 323 First Street. Annually the entire entourage took a month-long trip to Cumberland, Maryland, to visit the in-laws. While the women gossiped and exchanged household hints, Vallandigham and his brilliant if eccentric brother-in-law, John Van Lear McMahon,[19] took a week-long outing in the Blue Ridge Mountains, communing with nature and hardening their muscles while discussing government, law, and politics.

Vallandigham also found time in Dayton to renew his interest in the militia, a favorite avenue for political advancement. He polished the colonel's insignia he had brought with him from

---

[18] *Dayton Daily Journal*, 20 April 1855; *Dayton Daily Empire*, 20, 27 April 1855. The judge, George B. Holt, had led the bolt which brought defeat to Vallandigham in his first bid for a seat in Congress.

[19] Newton D. Mereness, "John Van Lear McMahon," in *Dictionary of American Biography*, ed. Dumas Malone (20 vols., New York, 1933), 12: 137-38, characterized C.L.V.'s brother-in-law as a person possessed of "uncouth manners, unbridled temper and proud spirit." He was a great student of the law and a widely-known orator who repeatedly turned down chances to enter politics. His son, John A. McMahon, after being admitted to the bar in 1854, became the junior partner in the firm of Vallandigham & McMahon.

New Lisbon and organized several new companies, one composed entirely of German-Americans and another largely of Irish-Americans—an effective way to benefit both his law practice and his political ambitions.

Although military activity and occasional hunting and fishing excursions gave C.L.V. some satisfaction, his Calvinist background made him essentially a man of duty. He spent long hours in his law office or in his library at home. He read voraciously almost every book he owned or could borrow. He marched with Caesar's legions in Gaul, saw the French Revolution through Carlyle's eyes, and sympathized with the Dutch rebels through Motley. He especially relished biography, whether the subjects were Romans, Englishmen, or Americans. He was also entranced by political writings, especially those which reinforced his states' rights and law-and-order views. He read and reread Jefferson, combed Calhoun's *Disquisition on Government,* and devoured Burke's *Reflections on the French Revolution.* Burke seemed to be his favorite, for he had nine books by that English statesman in his library.[20] Both Burke and Vallandigham advocated conservative views, emphasizing law and order, stability, and social peace. While reading, Vallandigham copied down quotations from Burke, the Bible, the Greek and Roman classics, Shakespeare, and other literary figures, to be corporated into his speeches and lectures. Even his political enemies were impressed with the depth and breadth of his scholarship.

Although Vallandigham had failed in his first three bids for an elective office as a Daytonian, he decided to try again in 1854. He gained the nomination for Congress at his party's convention without much of a contest. Perhaps no other Democrat in the Third District was eager to take on Campbell, who had announced his intention to run again. In any case, Vallandigham and all Democratic congressional candidates in Ohio fared badly. Campbell defeated his Democratic opponent by 2,565 votes, a victory of landslide proportions. All eleven Democratic incumbents lost their seats. In all, the widespread reaction to

---

[20] Appraiser's report (*re* Clement L. Vallandigham), Probate Records (Packet No. 9875), Montgomery County Court House, Dayton. The inventory indicated that Vallandigham's personal library exceeded 1,200 books, with another 263 volumes in his own law library.

the Kansas-Nebraska Act cost every Democratic congressional candidate an office.[21]

The Democrats, defeated and dejected, looked toward the next presidential election with apprehension. Vallandigham, still mixing law and politics, attended the state Democratic convention of January 8, 1856, as a delegate from Montgomery County. He served on the resolutions committee and helped draft the planks which deplored radicalism and recommended the election of Democrats to check the tide of abolition and egocentric sectionalism. He was also named one of the four at-large delegates to the Democratic National Convention scheduled to meet in Cincinnati on June 2. Vallandigham appreciated the honor. It was an indication that he had come of age as an Ohio politician.[22]

At Cincinnati, C.L.V. helped James Buchanan secure the nomination over Stephen A. Douglas and Franklin Pierce. Douglas was still a rising star and Pierce's skirts were unclean, for he had flirted with Know-Nothingism. Since Vallandigham expected to run for Congress again, he was sure Buchanan would be more popular than Pierce with the Irish-Americans and the German-Catholics of his district. Douglas still suffered from the public reaction to the Kansas-Nebraska Act which he had pushed through Congress.

Vallandigham again bet on the right horse, and, in the closing hours of the convention, his fellow-delegates named him to membership on the Democratic National Committee as a tribute to his ability.

After returning home, Vallandigham set to work for Buchanan's election. He gave the main speech at the Dayton ratification meeting, praising Buchanan and predicting his election. Then he took to the hustings, partly to promote Buchanan and partly to enhance his own chances for the congressional nomination in the Third District in order to take on Lewis D. Campbell a third time.

After gaining the coveted honor at the Democratic district convention which met in Eaton on July 24, C.L.V. hit the cam-

---

[21] *Dayton Daily Journal*, 27 November 1854. The twenty-one victorious candidates included twelve Republicans, eight Whigs, and one Free Soiler.

[22] *Dayton Daily Empire*, 10, 12 January 1856. Vallandigham won the honor over such well-known Ohio Democrats as David Tod, Washington McLean, and Thomas W. Bentley.

paign trail with renewed energy, visiting nearly every village and picnic grove in the Third District. He spoke in his own behalf, praised Buchanan, criticized Republicanism and radicalism, and extolled the Democratic party's virtues. Bidding for the votes of the Irish-Americans and German-Catholics, he exposed Campbell's ties to Know-Nothingism. He also tried to frighten voters with the dire prediction that a Frémont and Republican victory would bring on a national crisis.

Campbell countered with charges that Vallandigham was a candidate of the slaveholders and slave-catchers, an unworthy opponent whose overweening ambition made him seek positions for which he was unqualified. Stung, the Democratic candidate charged the incumbent with being inconsistent, inept, and indecent. He delighted in reading derogatory statements made by Campbell's Republican rivals. He "nailed Campbell's hide to the fence" and threw tar at it with reckless abandon. It seemed as if the Third District congressional candidates were more interested in character assassination than in the issues of the day.[23]

In the elections of October and November 1856, Buchanan won the presidency and eight Democratic candidates wrested congressional seats from Republican contenders. But Clement L. Vallandigham lost again. It was close, 9,338 votes to 9,319—a margin of only 19. "The defeat of Mr. Vallandigham and the triumph of the trickster and shifting politician, Lewis D. Campbell," wrote one Democratic editor, "is about the only disagreeable event of the late elections."[24]

Vallandigham's friends urged him to contest the election, hopeful that a Democratic-controlled Congress might find an excuse to deny Campbell his seat. There seemed to be a valid case, for quite a number of "colored citizens" had cast Republican votes despite the fact that Ohio law expressly denied them the ballot. "The nigger has crawled out of the wood pile," wrote the editor of the *Dayton Empire*, "and slipped into a place where, under the Constitution, he has no business. We insist that this *colored* business shall be fully investigated."[25] "We rather think," added

[23] *Dayton Daily Journal*, 12, 15 September 1856; *Dayton Daily Empire*, 4 October 1856.
[24] *Cincinnati Daily Enquirer*, 18 October 1856.
[25] *Dayton Daily Empire*, 17 October 1856.

the racist-minded editor, "that a Democratic Congress will prefer the representative of the white men."[26]

The man who had failed at the polls in three bids for a congressional seat now took his case to the House of Representatives. The contest was protracted and exhausting. Vallandigham expected to get the vote of all Southern Democratic congressmen, but the issue was clouded and complicated by Know-Nothingism. Some Southerners, such as John A. Gilmer of North Carolina, were close personal friends of Campbell. Both belonged to the Know-Nothing hierarchy and fraternal loyalties transcended party lines. Furthermore, Douglas and President Buchanan had quarreled over bringing in Kansas under the Lecompton Constitution, and Douglas's friends in Congress feared that Vallandigham, if given a seat, might vote in support of the president's policy. Finally, on May 25, 1858, just two weeks before the end of the first session of the Thirty-fifth Congress, Vallandigham gained the contested seat by a narrow vote, and Lewis D. Campbell received a consolation prize in the form of a full year's salary. Then the two supposedly archenemies packed their bags and headed home, passengers on the same train. The ride gave them an opportunity to ease the enmity which the long and bitter contest over the Third District seat had engendered.[27]

Vallandigham also collected the full session's salary (a total of $4,200), but gained much more in intangible benefits. He had a chance to become acquainted with every member of the House, making close personal friends of some to whom he was greatly indebted. Highest on this list was Lucius Q. C. Lamar, Mississippi congressman and slaveholder.

Sixteen months later, homeward bound from Washington, where he had attended a meeting of the Democratic National Committee, Vallandigham stopped over in Harpers Ferry for his twenty-minute interview with John Brown. If the South was the incarnation of evil to Brown, the region was an object of high regard to Vallandigham. He traced his ancestry back to "Ole Virginy." Great uncles had migrated to Kentucky and

26 Ibid., 18 October 1856.
27 *Congressional Globe*, 35 Cong., 1 sess., pp. 2316, 2387; *Dayton Daily Empire*, 31 October, 13, 30 December 1856, 28 January, 17, 24 February, 31 March, 11 April, 7, 28 May 1858.

North Carolina.[28] His wife came from a slave state, although her father was a merchant rather than a slaveholder. Although he had earlier expressed the view that slavery was morally wrong,[29] he believed (like Lincoln in 1861) that slavery was sanctioned by the Constitution and that the national government had no right to touch that "domestic institution." More important perhaps than ties of kinship were the friendships Vallandigham had made with Southerners, such as Lamar of Mississippi and John C. Breckinridge of Kentucky, during the contest for the congressional seat. Although some Southern congressmen had procrastinated for months before giving him Campbell's seat, Vallandigham still owed them a debt of gratitude. Since the Dayton congressman had a reputation for being loyal to his friends, he resented the efforts of abolitionists to depict all Southerners as licentious, inhuman, and contemptible.

Vallandigham cherished his Southern ties, while John Brown spoke scornfully of white men who held black men in bondage. Although Vallandigham and Brown were both Ohioans, but for the dogmatism with which each cloaked his convictions, they were poles apart.

[28] James L. Vallandigham to George L. Vallandigham (a brother), 18 March 1837, Vallandigham Papers.

[29] Vallandigham to Stanley Matthews, 31 January 1850, transcribed letter in Stanley Matthews Papers, University of North Carolina Library, Chapel Hill.

2

VALLANDIGHAM AND DOUGLAS: AN EVOLVING ALLIANCE

ALTHOUGH CLEMENT L. VALLANDIGHAM and Stephen A. Douglas held similar views on most issues, they were slow to become allies. Both had supported Lewis Cass, the Democratic candidate for president in the election of 1848, and both seemed disposed to accept the "Cass doctrine"—that residents in a territory have the right to choose their own "domestic institutions"—as a means to lessen debate over slavery in Congress. Both opposed the Wilmot Proviso and both favored the Compromise of 1850—Douglas had been chief architect of the latter while Vallandigham tried to rally grass-roots support for the controversial measure. For both, law was destined to become only the handmaiden of political ambitions. And both possessed a self-confidence bordering on audacity.

Yet on the question of slavery they did not see eye to eye. Douglas refused to see it as a moral issue. To the "Little Giant," slavery was but an institution, tried and true. Douglas's first wife had inherited a Mississippi plantation and 150 slaves, and he seemed to feel no guilt in helping to keep human beings in bondage. Perhaps in time slavery would disappear; in the United States, geography and economics would stay its spread. Douglas simply refused to wrestle with the question of natural rights and the morality of slavery. Vallandigham, on the other hand, had put his views regarding slavery into print as early as 1850. He defined the institution as "a moral, social & political evil" and "deplored" its existence. At the same time, however, he considered slavery "a local institution" which could be erased within a state's borders only if the state so willed. The federal government dared not touch slavery in the states where it existed, for the Constitution gave the institution tacit approval. Although C.L.V. subscribed to the "Cass doctrine," he hoped the electorate of each new state would follow the example of California and write into its constitution an "emphatic edict" against the institution. Not only had he not put "one solitary *proslavery* sentiment" on paper, he wrote in 1850, but he had never "entertained one in his heart."[1]

Although Vallandigham opposed slavery, his respect for law and order made him detest abolitionists, who, he claimed, attempted to inflame the public mind and drive a wedge between the North and the South. C.L.V. occasionally brooded over the popularity of radicalism and egocentric sectionalism, and he predicted that the country would fall upon evil days unless moderation could push back the abolitionist tide.

The defeat of William Medill, incumbent Democratic governor of Ohio, by Salmon P. Chase in October 1855, spurred Vallandigham to make a public plea for law, order, and moderation. He spent long hours in his library, preparing a speech he intended to publish as a pamphlet. In it he surveyed the slavery question, historically and philosophically. It was "a peculiar institution," yet "sustained by the Constitution." Abolitionists were "Jacobins" and troublemakers, destroying the comity of sections and widening "the gulf of alienation." They assumed "a pretended responsibility" for "the sinfulness of slavery," and taught disrespect for laws and the Constitution. Clergymen should stay out of politics, he argued, and politicians should not interpret Christian doctrine. Politics and morals both had their "legitimate spheres." The public ought to accept Douglas's doctrine of popular sovereignty regarding the territories, adhere rigidly to the laws of the land, and recognize that abolitionism was dangerous doctrine. Congress must not meddle with slavery either in the states where it exists or in the territories![2]

Although Vallandigham readily accepted Douglas's principle of popular sovereignty, he was not ready to hitch his wagon to the young senator's rising star in 1855. He helped persuade some of his colleagues at the Democratic National Convention in Cincinnati to ignore Douglas's claims and he voted for Buchanan on each of the seventeen ballots.

[1] C.L.V. to Stanley Matthews (transcribed copy), 31 January 1850, Stanley Matthews Papers, University of North Carolina Library.

[2] *Dayton Daily Empire*, 30 October, 21 November 1855. Vallandigham's speech of 29 October 1855 in Dayton was later published as a pamphlet.

When Douglas broke with President Buchanan in 1857 because the administration sought to foist a slave constitution upon Kansas, C.L.V. had to choose which path he would follow. Douglas's widespread popularity in the upper Middle West made the choice easy, and Vallandigham tactfully grabbed hold of the Little Giant's coattails when campaigning for reelection to Congress from the Third District in 1858. In fact, the Democratic incumbent even begged Douglas to visit Dayton when he returned to Chicago from Washington. *"Don't fail,"* Vallandigham pleaded. "I have thrown out the hint [that you are coming] & you are expected."[3]

Douglas could not accommodate Vallandigham, but his reply was useful as a campaign document. C.L.V. usually read the letter at political rallies and public meetings to give the impression that the two were close friends and allies. Vallandigham, however, was cautious in his statements about Buchanan. As a member of the Democratic National Committee he had to walk a tightrope. His use of Douglas's letter, nevertheless, was proof of the direction in which he was heading. Perhaps the letter helped him win reelection, for it was another close race, with the incumbent netting 9,903 votes to Campbell's 9,715.

It mattered not that Vallandigham won by only 188 votes in that October 1858 election. The returns, he claimed, fully vindicated his right to Campbell's seat in Congress. Vallandigham's friends now held that Campbell's charge that he had been "cheated" out of a seat in the House of Representatives was "pure buncombe."[4] The Dayton Democrat could hold his head high when he returned to Washington, D.C., early in December to attend the second session of the Thirty-fifth Congress.

Vallandigham saw Douglas occasionally that winter in Washington. The second Mrs. Douglas was a great-niece of Dolly Madison and loved playing the gracious hostess. The Douglas residence in Washington dispensed a lavish hospitality, and congressmen flocked there in great numbers.

The winter of 1858-1859 witnessed a widening schism in

[3] C.L.V. to Douglas, 13 June 1858, Stephen A. Douglas Papers, University of Chicago Library.

[4] *Dayton Daily Journal,* 26 August 1858; *Dayton Daily Empire,* 14 October 1858.

the Democratic party. Buchanan had no use for Douglas and seldom missed an opportunity to refer to him in derogatory terms. The President's followers removed Douglas from the chairmanship of the Committee on the Territories. Douglas's support of a bill to purchase Cuba did not stop Southern Democrats from viewing him as a renegade bent upon breaking up the party. They fumed even more when Douglas, in a debate on the Senate floor with Jefferson Davis, stated adamantly his opposition to any active intervention by the federal government to protect slavery in the territories. He also denounced any attempt to reopen the African slave trade or to force the Northern wing of the Democratic party to be the servant of slavocracy.

Vallandigham, for his part, had decisions to make about thorny issues. He felt obligated to vote for Southern measures in return for being given Campbell's seat in Congress the previous spring. He therefore endorsed the annexation of Cuba. He also pleased his Southern friends when he voted against a proposal to enforce the laws against the African slave trade more vigorously.[5] Several times Vallandigham glibly stated that he regarded Negroes as inferior beings. Moreover, he repeatedly expressed his devotion to the principles of Jacksonian Democracy, fully aware that Jacksonian egalitarianism meant equality for the white man—not for the black man or the Indian.

Some Ohio Democrats urged Douglas to visit their state in 1859 to help them elect their gubernatorial candidate. Eyeing the Democratic presidential nomination, the ambitious senator readily assented and came into Ohio as the swashbuckling hero. He appeared in Columbus on September 7 and Vallandigham hustled over from Dayton to be seen at Douglas's side. Everywhere "the Little Giant" was greeted by "enthusiastic demonstrations of applause."[6] Vallandigham heard him denounce abolitionists as disunionists, defend popular sovereignty, and praise the Democratic party as the historic purveyor of law and order.

Vallandigham assured Douglas that Dayton Democrats were ready and eager to receive him and the next morning accompanied Douglas on the train to Dayton, where a "large assemblage

[5] *Congressional Globe*, 35 Cong., 2 sess., pp. 84-85, 234-36, 700-701; *Dayton Daily Journal*, 26 January, 7 February 1859.

[6] *New York Times*, 8 September 1859; *Daily Ohio Statesman* (Columbus), 8 September 1859.

of people" greeted Douglas at the depot. Efficient marshals transformed the huge crowd into a procession which followed Douglas's carriage to the Phillips House. There Vallandigham had the honor of introducing the noted guest to an appreciative audience, which responded with "deafening cheers." But Douglas was not physically able to do much more than acknowledge the cheers and applause. He was suffering from a bad cold and a sore throat, and his voice plainly corroborated this fact. Nevertheless, the people sent up "a tremendous shout as 'Little Doug' retired."[7] Although Dayton Democrats had no chance to hear their hero speak, they at least had a chance to see him and be inspired by his presence.

Douglas decided to stay over in Vallandigham's home town an extra day, trying to recover his voice and regain his health. Vallandigham called upon the bed-ridden patient several times, and the next day accompanied his party to Cincinnati. There he witnessed the warm welcome given the senator; a cannon boomed and the people shouted as Douglas stepped off the train and climbed into a waiting carriage. Vallandigham tagged along, accompanying the lion of the occasion to the Burnet House. That night he heard Douglas repeat much of what he had said several days before in Columbus. He discussed "the territorial question" and drew constant applause for his jibes at Republican "disunionists" and Buchanan's "Blacklegs."[8]

The next day C.L.V. returned to Dayton to go on a speaking tour for Rufus P. Ranney, the Democratic gubernatorial nominee. Arranged by the Democratic State Central Committee, the tour took the Dayton congressman from one end of the state to the other. He gave a major address in New Lisbon, returning to his birthplace as a local boy who had made good. On every platform he portrayed Republicans as "disunionists," using their own statements to convict them. Because it was difficult to defend President Buchanan's veto of the Homestead Bill, Vallandigham, like other Midwestern Democrats, tried to lessen the sting by pointing out that prominent New England Republi-

[7] Entry of 8 September 1859, Daniel L. Medlar, "Journal, September 1, 1859-April 30, 1862," Dayton and Montgomery County Public Library (hereafter cited as Medlar, "Journal"); *New York Times*, 8, 9 September 1859.

[8] *Cincinnati Daily Gazette*, 10 September 1859; *Cincinnati Daily Enquirer*, 8, 9 September 1859.

cans had voted against the bill. Even Vallandigham could not explain away the defalcation of John C. Breslin, the Democratic state treasurer, or allay the unrest and discontent caused by the Panic of 1857, which had stigmatized the party in power. In fact, he found it quite impossible to check Republicanism, spreading over the upper Midwest like a prairie fire.

The election returns of 1859 disappointed the Democrats. In Ohio the Republicans elected William Dennison, their gubernatorial candidate, won control over both houses of the state legislature, and carried forty-eight counties—five more than in 1857. Truly, it seemed that radicalism was in fashion. Dayton Republicans sponsored a noisy and spirited celebration, rubbing salt in Democratic wounds. "They [the Republicans] were very jubilant over their victory," one of Vallandigham's supporters wrote "and celebrated it . . . by the firing of cannons, very numerous and large bonfires, martial music, and marching around town in procession, with great enthusiasm, shouting and yelling most *horribly*—at least it sounds that way to us Democrats."[9]

Six weeks later Vallandigham again headed for Washington, this time to attend the first session of the Thirty-sixth Congress, scheduled to convene on December 5, 1859. The air was charged with tension, heightened by the hanging of John Brown three days earlier. Abolitionists spoke of his heroic death and his noble speech from the scaffold shortly before the trap was sprung. Ralph Waldo Emerson wrote that Brown's "martyrdom" would "make the gallows as glorious as the cross." Ohio abolitionists followed suit. The editor of the *Lebanon Western Star* predicted that history would "canonize" the "bearded patriarch" while the editor of the *Cleveland Leader* stated, "His death will illuminate history."[10]

These same Ohio abolitionists had earlier excoriated Vallandigham for interrogating Brown in the Harpers Ferry arsenal. One Republican editor had called the congressman "a dirty dog" who was guilty of asking "leading and tricky questions" to elicit answers he could "twist" for political gain. Another had referred to him as "a smelling committee of one," and his Cleve-

[9] Entry of 12 October 1859, Medlar, "Journal."
[10] Emerson, quoted in Ralph R. Rusk, *The Life of Ralph Waldo Emerson* (New York, 1949), p. 402; *Lebanon Western Star*, 5 December 1859; *Cleveland Leader*, 3 December 1859.

land colleague derided him as "a pettifogging inquisitor." The editor of the *Cincinnati Commercial* had contrasted "the steady manfulness of Brown" with the "demogogue" who had "probed among Brown's wounds for material with which to manufacture political capital."[11]

Vallandigham bitterly resented the abolitionists' efforts to canonize Brown. He rebuked Emerson for his "blasphemous" statements, and scorned abolitionists who predicted Brown's martyrdom as false prophets. He believed that Brown deserved the noose. A stable society, he maintained, could not be built in a state where people could invoke the "Higher Law" as a defense for murder, arson, and violence. "He perishes," Vallandigham had stated of Brown, "justly and miserably—an insurgent and a felon."[12]

While men on street corners, in pubs and parlors, and in the halls of Congress debated the question of Brown's sanctity and sanity, the clerk of the House of Representatives rapped his gavel for order, intent upon urging the members to elect their speaker. The Senate, of course, had no trouble effecting its organization, for Vice-President John C. Breckinridge had the prestige to secure the cooperation of most members, North and South. Stephen A. Douglas was also expected to add his voice to the cause of moderation, and the two hoped to keep the radicals in check.

In the House, on the other hand, the situation was much more explosive. The Harpers Ferry incident seemed to make Southern radicals more adamant and more quarrelsome, and the honors accorded Brown turned their indignation to anger. Those Southern ultras who had previously spoken of secession half apologetically now seemed more convinced that the slave states should have a confederacy of their own.

The situation in the House was complicated by the fact that neither the Republicans nor the Democrats had a clear majority; a handful of members of the American party held the balance of power. In the first ballot for Speaker, the Democrats voted

[11] *Ohio State Journal* (Columbus), 22 October 1859; *Cleveland Herald,* 24 October 1859; *Cleveland Leader,* 24 October 1859; *Cincinnati Daily Commercial,* 22 October 1859.

[12] C.L.V. to editor of the *Cincinnati Daily Enquirer,* 22 October 1859, published 29 October; entry of 3 December 1859, Medlar, "Journal."

down the line for Thomas Bocock of Virginia, Republicans split their votes between Galusha Grow of Pennsylvania and John Sherman of Ohio, and the Americans supported Alexander B. Boteler, another Virginian. The first tally read: Bocock, 86; Sherman, 66; Grow, 43; and Boteler, 14.[13]

Grow then withdrew his name from the list and the Republicans gave their full support to Sherman's candidacy. Southern Democrats attacked Sherman for previously endorsing Hinton R. Helper's book *The Impending Crisis and How To Meet It* (1857), quoting incendiary passages from the text which violently denounced slavery as well as Southern leaders. Other ballots followed, but no candidate could secure a majority. Democratic strategists dropped Bocock's name after the eleventh ballot and offered the names of other party leaders, but none of the various nominees could get the votes of the Americans and so walk off with the prize. Meanwhile, the Republicans stubbornly insisted that Sherman deserved the Speakership. The clerk continued to preside while the House remained unorganized, the members not yet sworn in.

Between ballots congressmen occasionally gave speeches intended for home consumption, or took time out to throw oil or water upon the smoldering fire, debating the merits of Helper's book, the question of slavery, abolitionism, and "all things on the earth and under the earth."[14]

Vallandigham sandwiched one of his best-known speeches between the fourth and fifth ballots for Speaker. In that reasoned address he warned extremists of the North and the South that there was a West and that its interests must be served. He condemned Republicans for organizing a political party along sectional lines and raising issues which widened the gap between North and South. The Northern radicals he excoriated for their contempt for the Constitution and their promulgation of a doctrine that abolitionist views were superior to law. Lawlessness, he stressed, only bred more lawlessness. It had evolved from a rivulet into a rushing stream. "Thirty years ago," he told his colleagues, "John Brown, hung like a felon, would have been buried like a dog."

[13] *Congressional Globe*, 35 Cong., 1 sess., p. 2.
[14] Ibid., p. 444.

Vallandigham asked the North not to be too greedy. New England industry, he suggested, asked for too much protection and imposed its views upon the Republican party. In its grasping for economic control, the Northeast had brought about the economic ills suffered by the West. Now that section must not only cease its exploitation of South and West, but it must also respect the constitutional rights of those two sections.

For a while he talked like a Western sectionalist and brazenly called himself one, averring he would remain dedicated to Western interests until his dying day. "I am as good a Western fire-eater," he crowed, "as the hottest salamander in this House."

He soon returned, however, to the subject of "national interest." Like Daniel Webster on an earlier occasion, he spoke out for one Constitution, one Union, one flag, and one destiny. That destiny, he warned, could not be fulfilled unless Westerners, Northerners, and Southerners subordinated sectional interests to the national welfare. This meant, he added, the immediate, total, and unconditional destruction of sectional Republicanism.[15]

It was a partisan speech. Perhaps he was but repaying Southern congressmen the debt he owed because they had given him Campbell's seat in Congress the previous year. There is no doubt, however, that he sincerely believed that both abolition and Republican sectionalism were evils, undermining constitutionalism and national unity. It was also the speech of a Westerner and a conservative. As a Western sectionalist he opposed the progress of the Industrial Revolution and he objected to New England industry making the upper Midwest both slave and servant. As a conservative, he regretted the ever-growing popularity of radicalism and the Natural Law doctrine used by abolitionists to justify their views. Vallandigham proved himself a disciple of Edmund Burke rather than John Locke in that he favored social order, toleration, and evolutionary change. Like Burke, Vallandigham blamed the radicals and revolutionaries for the nation's ills. Like Burke, he defined order in terms of individual freedom—free competition, free trade, and rewards for work and self-discipline. And like Burke, the Dayton congressman seemed to view political authority as an accountable trust

[15] Ibid., Appendix, pp. 42-47. Vallandigham gave his speech on 15 December 1859.

to pursue the common good—to heal the schism rather than destroy the comity of sections.

Vallandigham should have expected a partisan reaction to his speech. The abolition-minded editor of the *Cleveland Leader* accused him of "crawling on his belly" to "grovel at the feet of Southern slaveholders." Other Republican editors accused him of being a Southern stooge and a Northern traitor.[16] Democratic editors, on the other hand, rose to defend both the speaker and his speech. "There is a heartlessness evinced in the Abolition press in the abuse which must be very flattering," wrote one defender, "for it shows he is both hated and feared." "As to the speech itself," wrote another admirer, "it is quite unnecessary to speak. It is folly to paint the lily, or gild refined gold. It has all the essentials of a great speech; the conception and language are faultless; the sentiments, above all, are national and manly."[17]

While Ohio Democrats and Republicans continued to debate the merits of Vallandigham's speech, members of the House of Representatives continued to ballot for a Speaker. The stalemate lasted into January. The numerous roll-calls and the general despair frayed members' nerves; minor disagreements became major incidents. Once Vallandigham, failing to practice the moderation he had preached, disagreed over some parliamentary tactic with John Hickman of Pennsylvania. The Dayton Democrat taunted Hickman with lacking both brains and courage.[18] Southern ultras became more defiant as the weeks passed and still the Republicans stayed with Sherman. The Southerners bluntly declared Sherman's candidacy an "insult" to their section and there was even talk that his election might be the "initiatory step" toward secession.[19]

On some of the ballots, C.L.V. received complimentary votes.

[16] *Cleveland Leader*, 13, 29 December 1859; *Dayton Daily Journal*, 16 December 1859, 18 January 1860; *Dayton Daily Empire*, 4 January 1860.

[17] *Cleveland National Democrat* (n.d.), quoted in *Dayton Daily Empire*, 13 December 1859; anonymous letter, published in *Dayton Daily Empire*, 16 January 1860.

[18] *Congressional Globe.*, 36 Cong., 1 sess., p. 281.

[19] Ibid., pp. 226-33, 492-93, 546. Ollinger Crenshaw, "The Speakership Contest of 1859-1860," *Mississippi Valley Historical Review* 29 (December 1942): 323-38, contends that Sherman's candidacy stirred up the South and that his election might have resulted in a breakup of the Union.

On the twenty-sixth ballot he emerged as a serious candidate, getting 69 votes, though soon after, his name slipped out of contention.[20] Once (on the thirty-ninth ballot) it looked as if the House had named its Speaker, when William N. H. Smith of North Carolina received 116 votes, 1 more than necessary for election. Before the tally was officially announced, however, four Republicans changed their vote and announced they really favored John Sherman.[21]

Finally, on January 30, House Republicans realized that Sherman would never get the required majority and allowed him to withdraw his name. Two days later, after a backroom agreement, the Republicans joined forces with American party members to put William Pennington of New Jersey in the Speaker's chair.[22] A Know-Nothing who had voted for Sherman on every ballot, Pennington was, in fact, on the way to deserting his American party membership and becoming a Republican party regular. Although the Democrats were not overjoyed at his election, they could gain some satisfaction from the fact that they had defeated Sherman and also, in a sense, had repudiated Helper's *Impending Crisis*.

The first session of the Thirty-sixth Congress did nothing to promote the comity of sections, while it helped widen the breach in the Democratic party. In mid-March both the House and the Senate passed a bill providing virtually free farms for home-steaders. Vallandigham, Douglas, and all other Western Democrats voted for the measure,[23] but "Old Buck" vetoed the measure and made the party more vulnerable in the Western states. The controversy over the admission of Kansas under the proslavery Lecompton Constitution also widened the rift between Douglas and Buchanan. Vallandigham, like most Western Democrats, followed the Douglas line. The Dayton congressman said he would welcome Kansas into the Union with "open arms," but the would-be state had to present a constitution which had been framed by "a convention assembled and acting under a valid

[20] *Congressional Globe*, 36 Cong., 1 sess., pp. 338, 348.

[21] Ibid., p. 618; J. Henly Smith to Alexander H. Stephens, 30 January 1860, Alexander H. Stephens Papers, Library of Congress.

[22] *Congressional Globe*, 36 Cong., 1 sess., pp. 643, 650. The selection took place on the forty-fourth ballot, nearly two months after the session convened.

[23] Ibid., p. 1115; *Dayton Daily Empire*, 15 March 1859.

law of the territorial legislature" and ratified by an honest vote of the people. The Lecompton Constitution did not meet these conditions or qualifications. Neither did the Topeka Constitution, devised by the antislavery forces. Vallandigham, like Douglas, wanted the principle of popular sovereignty applied fairly and squarely in Kansas.[24]

The Utah question was another controversial issue. Utah Territory, which allowed the practice of polygamy, sought entrance into the Union. Some congressmen, encouraged by the clergy, introduced an antipolygamy bill. Vallandigham had no wish to defend polygamy, but he believed the bill contrary to the principle of popular sovereignty. It took considerable courage to contend that the bill, like the Lecompton Constitution, did not permit the people of the territory to control their destiny and their "domestic affairs."[25] Vallandigham's colleagues, however, had no intention of letting Utah enter the Union until she eradicated polygamy and served a lengthy apprenticeship as a territory.

The concerned Ohio congressman also put votes and voice into the record on several other issues, none of them partisan. He opposed limiting debate, when some members sought to speed up legislation by adopting a one-hour rule on "forensic eloquence." He also opposed abolishing the franking privilege for congressmen. He introduced a resolution declaring that Jews were entitled to the same rights given other United States citizens when traveling abroad, especially in Switzerland, and another instructing the Committee on Commerce to investigate and suppress cruelties practiced aboard American sailing ships.[26] Vallandigham, it seemed, was the congenital champion of the underdog—except where rights of black men were concerned.

Late in April 1860, the legislative machinery of Congress came to a halt when most Democrats headed for Charleston, South Carolina, site of the party's national convention. As secretary of the party's National Committee, Vallandigham left for Charleston several days before the convention was to be called

[24] Dayton Daily Empire, 2 April 1860; Congressional Globe, 36 Cong., 1 sess., pp. 1434, 1672.

[25] Congressional Globe, 36 Cong., 1 sess., pp. 1518, 1559.

[26] Ibid., p. 1359.

to order on April 23. He arrived in the city so proud of its colonial mansions, its shaded streets, and its azalea and magnolia gardens, to help set up committee headquarters at a convenient hotel, arrange for meeting rooms, and inspect the convention hall. While he was handing out lists of delegates to the press and conferring with the chairmen of rival delegations, visitors and accredited delegates streamed into committee headquarters, some to visit, some to complain, and some to make their gloomy predictions.

Vallandigham took time out from his duties to visit the head-quarters of some of the leading candidates. Douglas had re-mained in Washington, but his "reception rooms" in the Mills House, one of the city's finer hotels, were always crowded with his supporters. The Hon. William A. Richardson, Douglas's campaign manager, greeted every caller in his gruff voice, and the place was "as lively as a molasses barrel with flies."[27] Visitors found the rooms filled with tobacco smoke, the odor of whiskey, an assortment of rumors, and stacks of Sheahan's Life of Stephen A. Douglas.[28]

Vallandigham also visited the Charleston Hotel, where William L. Yancey, Alabama secessionist and prince of radicalism, had taken up residence. Earlier that year Yancey had bluntly told delegates attending a state convention that he saw no hope for the South to obtain justice "in the Union." "The events of the last quarter of a century," he added pessimistically, "are enough to blast hopes of every well-wisher of his country."[29] Yancey, who knew how to mix words and emotion convincingly, greeted callers, denounced Douglas, and dreamed of a Southern con-federacy. Fire-eaters such as Yancey and John Slidell of Louisiana were not the only delegates who distrusted Douglas. Jesse Bright of Indiana and William Bigler of Pennsylvania had naught but scorn for the ambitious senator from Illinois. Bright and Bigler, called "Doughfaces" by Douglas's supporters, expressed their contempt for Douglas wherever they went. It was reported that Bright had promised to stump Indiana, county by county and

[27] Murat Halstead, Caucuses of 1860 (Columbus, 1860), p. 15.

[28] Ibid. James W. Sheahan, editor of the Douglas-subsidized Chicago Post, wrote the campaign biography and had it published in his printing plant.

[29] William L. Yancey, Speech . . . Delivered in the Democratic State Conven-tion . . . 1860 (Charleston, 1860), p. 14.

township by township, against Douglas if he was nominated.[30]

Early developments seemed to favor Douglas, nevertheless, for his detractors could not agree upon a candidate. Robert M. T. Hunter of Virginia and James Guthrie of Kentucky had thrown their hats in the ring, but neither could corral much support. Both had established luxurious quarters and offered free drinks and free lunch to all comers. Hunter's friends dispensed free wine and free advice; Guthrie's used bonded whiskey and bland arguments. The failure of Douglas's enemies to rally behind any one candidate led some of his spokesmen to make extravagant claims, even calling his nomination "a sure thing." Douglas certainly was the pivotal individual at the convention. Every delegate was either for him or against him.[31] Vallandigham, of course, had known for several months that every one of the forty-six Ohio delegates was pledged to Stephen A. Douglas.[32]

Shortly before noon on April 23, the convention delegates began to gather in Institute Hall. It was a sultry day and the delegates, newspapermen, and visitors suffered in the ninety-five degree heat. An eleven o'clock shower failed to cool the city and only increased the humidity. Perspiration gathered on the foreheads of the many reporters who took places at tables, stacked high with pads of paper and dozens of sharpened pencils. Delegates strode into the large hall, stopping to chat with friends as they sought out their allotted seats.

Vallandigham had a place on the stage. He faced a sea of delegates, alternates, influence peddlers, and convention guests— perhaps more than 3,000 in all. Some of the delegates seemed more interested in exchanging greetings or arguing with other delegates than in taking the chairs provided for them. Judge David A. Smalley of Vermont, with gavel in hand, waited impatiently at the lectern to call the meeting to order so that the convention could be organized. Vallandigham knew that many plays and operas had been staged in Institute Hall in previous years. He could hardly have guessed that no drama would effect the course of American history more than the one unfolding.

---

[30] Halstead, *Caucuses of 1860,* pp. 15-61.
[31] Ibid.
[32] *Dayton Daily Journal,* 6 January 1860.

In time the Vermonter pounded his gavel menacingly, snarled for quiet, and then called the session to order. Vallandigham had helped to write the script, and events proceeded as pre-arranged. George W. McCook, a boyhood friend of the Dayton congressman, rose to nominate Francis B. Flourney as president *pro tem.* Flourney won the honor without contest, and several delegates escorted the impressive six-foot-two, 230-pound Arkansan to the platform. Then a local preacher, described as "a white-headed, red-faced, and gold-spectacled fellow," mumbled a prayer. Next a Virginia delegate, hand-picked by the National Committee, nominated a temporary secretary. Again the nominee had no competition and won by a voice vote. It was evident that Vallandigham's committee had planned the initial steps well.

The remainder of the first day's session was less orderly and tested the skills of the presiding officer and his parliamentarian. Members introduced resolutions, appealed to the chair, and raised points of order as Douglas's friends and foes matched tactics and maneuvers. Most of the afternoon's controversy concerned the seating of the New York State delegates; two rival slates claimed the right to the state's seats. Chairman Flourney repeatedly shouted for order, banged his gavel, and threaded his way through the parliamentary labyrinth. He closed the afternoon's session by reading the names of delegates selected for the usual convention committees.

The pro-Douglas men lost one skirmish and won another on the second day. The Committee on Organization selected and seated Caleb Cushing of Massachusetts as the permanent chairman of the convention. The "Doughfaces" considered Cushing's selection a tactical victory for their side. Douglas's men, however, scored a genuine victory when the Committee on Credentials recommended that "the regular delegation" from New York be given that state's seats.

The worst was yet to come. An impasse developed over the platform resolutions. Yancey's Southern ultras and Douglas's Northern supporters drew their cutlasses for a deadly struggle. The Southerners demanded a plank which would guarantee slavery in the territories. Such a plank could prevent Douglas from carrying a single Northern state in the presidential election in November. Even Vallandigham, feigning impartiality, knew that such a plank could drag him down to defeat in the congressional election. Douglas's supporters refused to budge. Yancey, whose voice had been compared to "silvery music," then presented the Southern ultimatum: the South must have equal rights in the territories! George E. Pugh, a close friend of Vallandigham and a United States Senator from Ohio, replied for Douglas. What Pugh lacked in polish and grace he made up in shrewdness, bluntness, and sincerity. Northern Democrats, he told Yancey and company, had worn themselves out defending Southern interests. Neither he nor his fellow Democrats of the North would give in to the ultimatum. "Gentlemen of the South," he thundered, "you mistake us—you mistake us— *we will never do it!*"[33]

Two dozen delegates sought the floor when Pugh, flushed with indignation and wet with perspiration, resumed his seat with the Ohio delegation. Some wanted to reply to Pugh or endorse his arguments. Others wanted to make a motion to adjourn so tempers might cool and a compromise might be contrived. Some "screamed like panthers," others "gesticulated like monkeys." Finally a Missouri delegate who had jumped on a table and outscreamed the others gained the chairman's attention and offered a resolution to adjourn. Cushing put the question to the noisy assemblage, ruled that the "ayes" carried the motion, pounded his gavel to signify that the day's session had come to an end, and walked off the platform.[34]

Gloom and despair hung over the meeting-rooms and cloak-rooms that evening. Vallandigham and a group of his friends gathered for dinner. Wine flowed freely and the diners offered toasts to party harmony. John A. Logan, a strong Douglas man from Illinois, still held hopes for a compromise, while Vallandigham, a realist this time, expressed only pessimism. With an air of gravity the Daytonian arose at the dinner table and posed as a prophet. "Gentlemen," he exclaimed in serious mien, "if the Democratic party is dissevered in this Charleston Convention, the result will be the disruption of the Union, and one of the bloodiest civil wars on record, the magnitude of which no

[33] Halstead, *Caucuses of 1860,* pp. 39-40.
[34] Ibid.

man can estimate. In the unity of the Democratic party, and in the Union, lies the hopes of the South and republican government." Most of the others at the table seemed to disagree, evidently thinking that the Ohio congressman had given way to despair. Logan, less imaginative and still optimistic, dissented audibly. "Sit down, Vallandigham," Logan advised, "and drink your wine. You are always prophesying." Before surrendering the floor, C.L.V. retorted, "I speak earnestly because I feel deeply impressed with the truth of what I have uttered."[35]

When the convention reconvened next morning, the debate over the platform continued with threats, pleas, and arguments. Dissension over parliamentary law, party and sectional aims, and national welfare continued. The presiding officer, Caleb Cushing, threatened to vacate the chair. Finally, late Saturday evening, the delegates agreed to put the platform (the minority report of the Committee on Resolutions) to a roll-call vote of the membership when the meeting reconvened on Monday.[36] To the uninitiated, it looked as if the Douglas delegates had walked off with a tactical victory.

Sunday was no day of rest for the politicians assembled in Charleston. Most of the delegates went to church, undoubtedly asking God to enlighten their enemies and sanction their own convictions. South Carolina and Alabama delegates agreed to walk out of the convention if the next day's roll-call vote approved the pro-Douglas platform.

Word of the agreement reached the hotel room where the Ohio delegation had its headquarters, casting disillusionment over these supporters of Douglas. Vallandigham, visiting the Ohio headquarters, must have thought that his prophesy, made several days earlier, would soon be fulfilled. Visitors who called found that the Ohio supply of whiskey had run out and no miracle refilled the empty barrel. Both the barrel and the apparent victory over the party platform must have sounded hollow to Douglas's Ohio supporters.

Tension reigned as the convention delegates gathered on Monday morning, April 30. The proceedings began with the

---

[35] Reported in the *Dayton Daily Herald*, 28 June 1871, shortly after Vallandigham's death.
[36] Halstead, *Caucuses of 1860*, pp. 52-61.

roll-call vote on the Douglas platform. The chairman announced the results of the poll: Douglas's delegates had won, 165 to 138 votes. Soon after, Southern delegations announced their withdrawal from the convention, and Vallandigham watched as Alabama and Mississippi led the way and the delegates of five other Southern states joined the exodus. The crowd quivered "as under a heavy blow" and tears of "heartfelt sorrow" flowed down many a cheek. Some, dry-eyed, let their faces express their "grim determination." But there were others who exhibited no sadness. William L. Yancey, who wanted the slave states to chart their own destiny, was "smiling like a bridegroom," having seen his hopes come to pass. He had helped to break up the Democratic party. Next he would help to break up the Union.[37]

Vallandigham and other Douglas supporters spent a sleepless night weighing the rumors and reports which made the rounds of the hotels. The "seceders" insisted that Douglas was a hollow shell and that his supporters were unprincipled, devoted unto death to a man and the spoils of office. The seceders also announced that they intended to hold their own convention next day in the Charleston Theatre.

The rump convention, mostly Douglas men, reconvened in Institute Hall next morning. They transacted little business and waited futilely for the return of the seceders. Unable to get the necessary two-thirds vote of the 303 delegates certified for the convention, the Douglas leaders agreed to adjourn and reconvene on June 18 in Baltimore.

Vallandigham hurried back to his hotel, packed his carpetbag, and caught the next train for Washington. It was difficult for Congress to get the wheels of legislation rolling again. Vallandigham spoke a few times during the remainder of the session, but no major measures dominated the docket. As a brigadier general in the Ohio militia, he made a determined effort to have Congress appropriate more money to state militia organizations. The effort ended in failure, but he was successful in securing some tariff protection for flaxseed producers in his district.[38]

The wheels of legislation again ground to a halt as Republican

[37] Ibid., pp. 68-87; *Richmond Dispatch*, 5 May 1860; entry of 2 May 1860, Medlar, "Journal."
[38] *Congressional Globe*, 36 Cong., 1 sess., pp. 1957-58, 1983.

members journeyed to Chicago to adopt a sectional platform for their party and nominate Abraham Lincoln as their presidential candidate. Vallandigham took a hurried trip home to appear as counsel in the celebrated Cooper Will case, to remind owners of flaxseed mills that he had served them well, to give the new editor of the *Dayton Empire* a pat on the back, and to express publicly his contempt for candidate Lincoln and all that the Republican party stood for. The Dayton congressman found little respect for Lincoln among his Democratic friends. Those who examined the latter's speeches, given in his debates with Douglas two years earlier, thought he had trimmed his sails too much, depending upon the sympathies or prejudices of his audiences. One of Vallandigham's supporters, who had read Lincoln's speeches with care, wrote, "Lincoln is a Janus-faced old chap. Honest Old Abe is! *and make no mistake.*"[39]

C.L.V. returned to Washington for the closing weeks of the congressional session. He took time out, however, to go to Baltimore to supervise the reconvening of the Democratic National Convention. In the end, there were two separate and rival Democratic conventions in Baltimore. Douglas delegates nominated their man at one convention and Southern Democrats nominated John C. Breckinridge at the other. The party was irrevocably divided, and the schism practically assured the defeat of both Democratic nominees.

The final count showed four contestants for the presidential prize in 1860. Two—Douglas and Breckinridge—represented sectional wings of the Democratic party, while Lincoln represented the Republican party, a conglomeration of ex-Whigs, Free Soil Democrats, Know-Nothingers, and Abolitionists. The fourth candidate was John Bell of Tennessee, who had been nominated by a convention called by some conservatives and some border state leaders. These men called their loosely-knit organization the Constitutional Union party, adopted the Constitution as their platform, and bid for the votes of men willing to close their eyes to the realities of the day.

When Congress finally adjourned on June 28, Vallandigham had to stay over in Washington for several days. Congressmen sympathetic to Douglas's candidacy had drafted the Dayton

[39] Entry of 14 June 1860, Medlar, "Journal."

Democrat to head the National Democratic Campaign Committee. As chairman, he had to help compose an address to the people, recommend speeches of his colleagues as campaign documents, and coordinate some phases of Douglas's campaign. His acceptance of the chairmanship was proof that his alliance with Douglas had been consummated. Early in the 1850s Vallandigham had been reluctant to accept Douglas's leadership; in 1860 the two walked the same road, putting up signs which read "caution" and "conservatism."

3

CAMPAIGNING FOR DOUGLAS

CLEMENT L. VALLANDIGHAM fretted in his Washington office in late June 1860 as he tried to transform the National Democratic Campaign Committee from a nonentity into an effective agency. As chairman of that committee, he had most of the responsibility for its activities. He was troubled because his committee lacked the money it needed, because Douglas's chances of gaining the presidency were slim, and because he was anxious to get home to Dayton.

Friends in Dayton had delayed the date of the Douglas ratification meeting until "Valiant Val" could get home from Washington to speak at the affair, scheduled for June 30. It was a well-planned party rally, for Dayton Democrats had made an extraordinary effort to put on a good show. A "magnificent bonfire illuminated the occasion," but it failed to bring a light of hope to the gloomy Democrats. Vallandigham received prolonged applause when he was introduced to the good-sized audience. He put up a good front, feigning optimism and pretending that Douglas had a good chance to gain the presidency. He developed the theme that all conservative men should vote for Douglas, lest a Northern sectionalist (Lincoln) or the candidate of the Southern radicals (Breckinridge) gain the White House. As he was emphasizing the need for action to save Douglas from defeat and the Union from destruction, a sudden squall visited the meeting place. Lightning and thunder, a heavy rain, and a strong wind dispersed the crowd and brought an early end to the rally. Vallandigham, slow to jump off the speakers' platform, was soaked to the skin as the torrential rain washed out the partisan program.[1] The storm was an omen of things to come.

The next day Vallandigham put on a new suit and headed for Columbus, site of the Democratic State Convention. He found little there to refurbish his hopes. The feud between

Buchanan and Douglas had divided the party in Ohio as the sectional controversy had wrecked it on the national level. Political realists knew that the schism was hopeless and that the odds therefore favored Lincoln, candidate of one of the sectional parties. Douglas's supporters could only hope that none of the three rival candidates would receive a majority of the electoral votes. The election would be thrown into the House of Representatives, then, and Douglas might emerge with the honors. Events would prove this ray of hope a false one.

Stepping to the fore as one of the state's leading Democrats, Vallandigham took a prominent part in the proceedings of the July 4 convention. He served on the Committee on Resolutions and helped to prepare the political potpourri presented as the party's platform. One of the resolutions, a gesture to conciliate the South, asked for "the acquisition" of Cuba "upon such terms" as would be honorable both to Spain and to the United States. Another reaffirmed Vallandigham's vote in the House of Representatives in opposing the reopening of the slave trade. One, which appealed to the racists, frankly stated that the laws of Ohio were for the "white man," implying that mulattoes and Negroes had no political rights. Another resolution reflected Vallandigham's states' rights views, for it affirmed "the absolute sovereignty of the states of the Union." The final resolution repudiated the "Higher Law" doctrine preached by some Republicans who had refused to accept the Fugitive Slave Act and the Dred Scott decision. Obedience to federal law, the resolution seemed to say, provided the basis for a stable society.[2]

After adopting the resolutions, the delegates selected their party's nominees for several state offices (supreme judge, attorney general, members of the Board of Public Works) and hand-picked a slate of presidential electors.

With the state convention out of the way, Vallandigham began his campaign for Douglas in earnest, speaking at the Douglas ratification meetings in Hamilton and Miamisburg. Always he had high praise for Douglas's qualities of leadership, his devotion to a conservative course, and his concern for Western interests. C.L.V. also attacked the Republicans for their sectional

---

[1] *Dayton Daily Empire*, 2 July 1860; *Dayton Daily Journal*, 2 July 1860.
[2] *Daily Ohio Statesman* (Columbus), 5 July 1860.

views, inimical to the national welfare. While he labeled the Republican party "the black and piratical craft of sectionalism," he viewed Southern sectionalism as simply the reaction to the "insane utterances" of Northern ultras. As a Westerner and conservative he was "inexorably opposed" to the extremists of both sections.[3]

While out in the field for Douglas, he secured his own renomination to the congressional seat he had wrested from Lewis D. Campbell two years earlier. Campbell would shortly desert the Republican party and endorse the candidacy of William Gunckle, running for congress on the Constitutional Union ticket. The Republican delegates, in convention in Germantown on August 8, shed few tears at Campbell's departure, and named Samuel Craighead, a former Whig, as their candidate to unseat Vallandigham.

When Dayton Republicans, full of liquor and enthusiasm, returned from Germantown at two o'clock in the morning, they did their best to awaken the townspeople and break the news of Craighead's nomination. With the Phoenix Band leading the way, they marched up and down the streets of Dayton, carrying their torches, singing party songs, and shouting for Craighead at the top of their voices. The nominee himself and other Dayton Republicans may have received the news with joy, but Democrats grumbled about the noise and the commotion. "They robbed me," complained one of Vallandigham's friends, "of two good hours of sleep."[4]

During the remaining days of August and September, the incumbent congressman visited every village and settlement in the Third District, speaking at party rallies, barbecues, and poleraisings. Vallandigham, who still thought of himself as a Jacksonian Democrat, noticed that hickory poles and hickory branches were most popular in the backwoods districts. Many Ohioans still spoke reverently of "Old Hickory," and at times it seemed as if Vallandigham called upon the ghost of Jackson more often than upon Divine Providence. The Jefferson Township rally, not far from Dayton, was one of the more interesting of the '60 campaign. There industrious Democrats, bent on outdoing

---

[3] *Dayton Daily Empire*, 11 July 1860.
[4] Entry of 9 August 1860, Medlar, "Journal."

others, raised a pole 165 feet high—"the tallest hickory pole in the state," it was claimed.[5]

On one of his speaking tours in the Third District, C.L.V. was away from home for nearly two weeks and spoke usually three times a day. Invariably defending his record as a congressman, he explained his antitariff views, gloated over his vote for the Homestead Bill, and tried to clarify his position on the complicated Kansas question. Republican speakers and Republican newspapers, on the other hand, sought to develop the conviction that, by refusing to bring in Kansas with the Topeka Constitution, Vallandigham was actually trying to make Kansas a slave state. Somewhat angry at Republican efforts to misrepresent him, he lashed out at the "liars" and the "falsehoods," and justified his "honest devotion" to the principle of popular sovereignty.[6] When Republicans raised the Homestead issue and claimed that President Buchanan, in league with Southern Democrats, had defeated the measure, Vallandigham pointed out that Hannibal Hamlin, Lincoln's running-mate, had voted against the Homestead Bill as a member of the Senate.[7]

Vallandigham again made an appeal to voters' fears and prejudices. He tried to frighten his listeners by stating that Lincoln's election would precipitate a crisis and bring on a war. He appealed to the anti-Negro prejudice so widespread among the poorer people of his district by claiming that Republicans favored emancipation and that free Negroes offered a threat to poor people's jobs and security. J. Frederick Bollmeyer, whom Vallandigham had brought to Dayton to edit the *Empire*, stated his own views more bluntly. Did white men want "stinking niggers" sitting next to them on workmen's benches or in jury boxes? Did they want their daughters to marry "black boys" and bear "black babies"?[8] It seemed to be good politics for Vallandigham to denounce John Brown, "negro equality," and "amalgamation" as he bid for reelection and tried to stem the Republican tide.

The Dayton Democrat also reminded his Catholic constituents that the Republic party bore the scarlet mark of Know-Nothing-

[5] *Dayton Daily Empire*, 6 August 1860.
[6] Ibid., 10 August 1860.
[7] *Dayton Daily Journal*, 21 May 1860.
[8] 9 January, 15 April, 15 September 1860.

ism. "When we consider that the mass of the Republican party were once in the Know-Nothing lodges, and there swore solemn, terrible, and proscriptive oaths against foreigners of every nation," wrote the editor of the *Empire*, "we may naturally presume that the present pretended affection which they profess for the German race grows out of nothing but an anxious and overweening desire for office."[9]

Republicans resented Vallandigham's appeals to racial prejudice and accused him of demagogic practices. "He is," wrote the Republican editor of the *Dayton Journal*, "an unscrupulous opponent, unfair in all his speeches, resorting to that dirty slang about negro equality, which for years has been his hobby and which has been nearly played out." And, in an appeal to emotion, he added: "It is still remembered how he interrogated old John Brown while he lay riddled with bullets in the Harpers Ferry Armory."[10] Perhaps it was just one more case of the pot and the kettle calling each other black.

Vallandigham found time in August to pay brief visits to two neighboring states to wave the flag for Douglas and buoy faltering Democratic hopes. He spoke in Richmond, Indiana, and several days later in Detroit, Michigan. Again he spoke out for conservatism and the Constitution. Conservative men must drive the fanatics back into their holes, and vote for Stephen A. Douglas to save the country from catastrophe. If the "flood of fanaticism" was not checked, a "devastating war" would drench the land with blood. Vallandigham evidently impressed his Detroit audience most favorably. The Democratic editor of the city's *Free Press* described the Ohio congressman as "one of the coming men of the country," a man "whose eloquence never fails to electrify an audience."[11]

While in Detroit, Vallandigham crossed the river and paid a brief visit to Windsor, Canada West, little dreaming that three years later he would spend nearly a year in that small city as an exile from his native land.

Dayton Democrats looked forward to Douglas's scheduled visit of September 23 as the highlight of the '60 presidential

[9] 5, 10 March 1860.
[10] 5 September 1860.
[11] 2 August 1860.

campaign. Vallandigham, as chairman of the "Douglas Reception Committee," helped to circulate thousands of flyers and post hundreds of handbills announcing the "gala event." The committee made an extraordinary effort to amass "a tremendous throng" and earn a compliment from "the Little Giant."

When all seemed in readiness, C.L.V. journeyed to Columbus to hear Douglas's speech in the state capital and to escort him to Dayton. Although Douglas's train was very late, Montgomery County Democrats turned out en masse to give him a rousing reception. Cannons belched a noisy welcome and four bands, each trying to play louder than the others, added to the din. Shouts and cheers from "twenty thousand throats" helped make the affair "one of the greatest demonstrations of enthusiasm" ever to occur in Vallandigham's home town.[12]

The crowd at the depot was so large that Vallandigham and Douglas had trouble making their way to the bedecked carriage waiting to take them to the Court House square. Eventually they reached the platform erected on the Court House steps, where thousands more had patiently awaited the arrival of their hero.

Douglas's voice was very hoarse, so he asked permission to limit his talk to ten minutes. He still had to make speaking stops in Hamilton and Cincinnati. The huge crowd, immersed in empathy, hung on every word and greeted each assertion "with cheer after cheer of the most enthusiastic kind."[13] Thousands followed the two political allies back to the depot, acting as an informal "guard of honor."

Vallandigham accompanied Douglas to Hamilton and Cincinnati before returning to his district to resume his speaking schedule. Douglas's visit had buoyed his hopes. Furthermore, Republicans were somewhat divided; some conservatives supported Gunckle although Craighead was the party's official nominee.

A successful "windup rally" also gave C.L.V. cause to be optimistic on the eve of the state election of October 8. A grand procession, featuring many floats and marching bands, drew "ohs" and "ahs" from the huge crowd lining the streets of

12 *Dayton Daily Empire*, 24 September 1860.
13 Ibid.; entry of 26 September 1860, Medlar, "Journal."

Dayton. After the parade the crowd gathered around the speakers' stand to hear Vallandigham give the best and longest of the three speeches. He found the audience most responsive to his thrusts at Republicanism in general and Lincoln, Gunckle, and Craighead in particular. "If the proud flesh of those insolent Republicans is not subject to irritation by the results of the elections . . .," predicted one of Vallandigham's loyal supporters, "then I do not read aright the signs of the times."[14]

The prediction was only partially right. Vallandigham edged out Craighead by 134 votes, but he gained reelection only because a third candidate competed for the ballots.[15] Elsewhere in Ohio most of the Democratic congressional candidates went down to defeat as the Republican trend swept the upper midwest.

After a brief rest and a chance to savor his victory, Vallandigham went forth to renew his campaign for Douglas's election. A cloud of gloom, evolving out of the October elections, hung heavily over the Douglas backers. Republicanism seemed to be on the upswing, a harbinger of the November elections.

Vallandigham's campaign trail took him to New York City, where he gave an address at the Cooper Institute—the same forum which had catapulted Lincoln into national prominence. The Ohioan found a sympathetic audience. Many were conservatives who deplored the radicalism of the hour and feared the consequences of Lincoln's election. Some were merchants who foresaw that secession might close their avenues of trade and their paths to profits. Others were Democrats unwilling to surrender the patronage positions they held from President Buchanan's hand. Most, of course, were the party faithful who had been led to believe that the Democratic party had a monopoly on virtue and wisdom.

It did not take C.L.V. long to win the favor of his New York audience. In Ohio he had learned to cater to the whims and prejudices of the common man. The audience repeatedly applauded him for his savage thrusts at radicalism, especially that with an abolitionist tinge. He blamed Northern radicalism,

[14] Entry of 8 October 1860, Medlar, "Journal."
[15] *Dayton Daily Journal*, 9 October 1860.

rather than Southern, for the nation's ills. He not only failed to denounce secession, he almost seemed to endorse it. If secession came, only "God and the great tribunal of History" had the right to judge "the sufficiency and justice" of such an act. Crawling out even further on the imaginary limb, he promised that he would never, as a member of Congress, *vote one dollar of money whereby one drop of American blood should be shed in a civil war.*" Evidently the enthralled audience endorsed his oratorical pledge, for it arose as one man to cheer and give him a "vehement and long-continued applause."[16]

Several days later, at a private dinner in the National Hotel in Washington, D.C., Vallandigham restated his determination to vote neither supplies nor men to coerce Southern states, and again he expressed his belief that Northern fanaticism was the nation's curse and secessionism but the Southern reaction to the abolition malady.[17]

Having expressed his anticoercion views twice, he returned to Dayton to cast his ballot for Stephen A. Douglas. He told one of his friends, a Democratic poll-worker, that he feared he had cast his last vote for a president "of the *United* States."[18]

In the days that followed, the telegraphic wires brought the news of Lincoln's victory and Douglas's defeat. Jubilant Dayton Republicans celebrated their victory with liquor in the grog shops, parades through the streets, and bonfires and speeches at the "jollification meetings." Secession rumors soon sobered the victorious Republicans and they haggled over the course their party ought to pursue. Horace Greeley, who had helped Lincoln achieve his victory, suggested that the administration should let "the erring sisters" go in peace.[19] Some abolitionists expressed the same sentiment, for they rationalized that the nation would be purer without slave states in it. In the Midwest, some Republican newspaper editors, such as those of the *Ohio State Journal* in Columbus and the *Indianapolis Journal*, en-

[16] *New York World*, 3 November 1860; *New York Tribune*, 3 November 1860; Vallandigham to editor of the *Cincinnati Enquirer*, 10 November 1860, published 13 November.

[17] *Washington Evening Star*, 6 November 1860.

[18] Quoted in Vallandigham, *Vallandigham*, p. 141.

[19] *New York Tribune*, 9 November 1860.

dorsed Greeley's suggestion. "If South Carolina, or any other state wants to secede," wrote one Republican editor, "let her in God's name go peacefully."[20]

Most Republican realists, however, expressed themselves in opposition to Greeley's let-them-go policy. They had won the election fairly and they wanted to enjoy the fruits of their victory. The editor of the *Dayton Journal,* William F. "Deacon" Comly, set himself firmly against secession. If it came, he would advocate coercion, whipping the South, if need be, "into a bloody submission." The Republican editor also took Vallandigham to task for stating he would refuse to vote money and men to coerce states that might secede. "In this he sets at naught all the powers of the Constitution, all the rights of the loyal States, all the obligations of law, and makes the national government a powerless, helpless, contemptible thing."[21]

Vallandigham ignored his Republican critics and continued to hope for peace. He deplored secession, but he preferred peaceable secession to civil war. He hoped President-elect Lincoln would listen to the voices of moderation—those advocating "peace, negotiation, concession." "At least, if he will forget the secession of the Ten Tribes," wrote Vallandigham, glancing backwards into history, "will he not remember and learn a lesson of wisdom from the secession of the Thirteen Colonies."[22]

[20] *Cairo City Gazette,* 6 December 1860.
[21] *Dayton Daily Journal,* 8 November 1860.
[22] Vallandigham to editor of the *Cincinnati Enquirer,* 10 November 1860, published in *Dayton Daily Empire,* 13 November.

4

EFFORTS AT COMPROMISE

REPUBLICANS SEEMED TO HAVE real reason to celebrate the results of the November 1860 elections. Many had feared that no candidate would receive a majority of the electoral vote. Lincoln's chance of being selected by the House of Representatives would have been practically nil, for only a minority in that body bore the Republican party label. Even the most optimistic prophets in the party did not predict such an overwhelming number of electoral votes, especially since their candidate polled only 39.9 percent of the popular vote. Ironically, Douglas, who received the second largest popular vote, came in fourth in the electoral vote tally.

After Republican celebrants emptied their casks and wore out their voices, they became seriously concerned with reports that Southern states were taking steps to secede. If the slave states left the Union it would be a hollow election victory indeed! Republican bigwigs exchanged views and discussed policy. Some gave a more positive endorsement to coercion with each passing week.[1] Several party regulars visited President-elect Lincoln in Springfield to strengthen his "backbone." Some Republican editors, on the other hand, still seemed to approve of peaceful secession, but the qualifications they added confused the issue. Although Horace Greeley changed his mind about letting the "erring sisters" go in peace, other editors still thought it would be in the best interests of the nation to get rid of South Carolina troublemakers. "If she [South Carolina] will," stated the editor of the *Chicago Tribune*, "let her go, and like a limb lopped from a healthy trunk, wilt and rot where she falls."[2]

Most Democrats continued to hope for some kind of compromise. Vallandigham stated his opposition to both secession and coercion, yet if he had to take one or the other, it would be peaceable secession.[3] Democrats hoped that they could force Republicans to accept some compromise plan and avert catastrophe. "With the United States Senate and the House of Representatives [in Democratic hands], and not less than one million of the majority of the popular vote against Lincoln," wrote one observant Democrat, "we hope to make him do right in spite of the fanatical creed of the party who elected him."[4]

When Vallandigham left for Washington early in December to attend the second session of the Thirty-sixth Congress, he felt a heavy weight upon his shoulders. Conservative Democrats, he believed, held the only hope for compromise and peace. Southern radicals talked of secession. Northern radicals talked more openly of coercion.

Vallandigham was sitting in his seat in the House of Representatives when the Speaker's gavel called that body to order at noon on December 3, 1860. He heard the white-haired chaplain, the Rev. Thomas H. Stockton, offer a solemn and impressive prayer. Then followed the calling of the roll, the swearing-in of a few new members, and adjournment. The rest of the afternoon was spent in speculation and in wondering what the future held.

Before he retired that evening, C.L.V. wrote a letter to his wife in which he expressed his fears and mentioned a duty he had assigned to himself. "I have just witnessed the assembling of the last Congress of the *United* States at its last session," he wrote with considerable feeling. "It was a solemn scene, although not appreciated as it will be viewed by posterity. Most of the Republicans look upon it as the beasts look upon the starry heavens—'with brute unconscious gaze.' All Southern men and Democrats sat with hearts full of gloom." He described the day as one of "tribulation and anguish," and concluded by stating, "When the secession has taken place, I shall do all in my power first to *restore* the Union, if it be possible; and failing in that, then to mitigate the evils of disruption."[5]

1 Entries of 13, 14, 18, 27 November 1860, Medlar, "Journal."
2 11 October 1860.
3 Entry of 14 November 1860, Medlar, "Journal."
4 Ibid., entry of 8 November 1860.
5 3 December 1860, published in part in Vallandigham, *Vallandigham*, p. 144. Although James L. Vallandigham's biography of his brother is a study in hero-worship, it is still invaluable because letters now lost or destroyed are frequently quoted or incorporated into the text.

Both the House and the Senate set up committees to consider "the perilous conditions of the country": the Senate, a Committee of Thirteen; the House, a special Committee of Thirty-three. Not a single Midwestern Democrat who had supported Douglas gained a place on either committee. John A. McClernand, a congressman from Illinois and a devoted disciple of Douglas, pointed out that discrimination had been practiced to sabotage compromise efforts. Vallandigham seconded McClernand's protest, insisting that "a most important segment" of the Democratic party had been ignored and insulted.[6]

A controversy developed over the appointment of a Florida congressman, George S. Hawkins, to the Committee of Thirty-three. Hawkins, a secessionist, begged to be excused; he said he expected no "fair and honest concessions" from the Republicans. The Speaker refused to accept Hawkins's request, and Vallandigham rose to express his opinion. It was wrong, he said, to force a man to serve against his will. Coercion should not be practiced in the House. The Speaker ignored Vallandigham's comments, still refusing to excuse Hawkins. The Florida congressman nevertheless nullified the appointment by failing to attend any of the committee sessions.[7]

While congressmen expressed opinions concerning compromise and coercion, Vallandigham took a hurried trip to Richmond, Virginia, to deliver an address at a forum sponsored by the Young Men's Christian Association. In Richmond he heard reports that South Carolina would soon secede. As a congressman from a Northern state, he knew that every word he uttered would be reported in the Virginia press. He used the occasion to speak out for compromise and to caution Virginians against precipitous action. Virginia blood flowed in his veins—it was the land of his fathers. He had "the fondest feelings of filial affection" for the state. Since fanatical men, North and South, had created the crisis, all sensible and conservative men must turn their energies to quash radicalism and effect a compromise. He hoped that Virginia, in the days ahead, would not "shut the doors

6 McClernand to Charles H. Lanphier, 10 December 1860, Charles H. Lanphier Papers, Illinois State Historical Library, Springfield; *Congressional Globe*, 36 Cong., 2 sess., p. 39.

7 *Congressional Globe*, 36 Cong., 2 sess., p. 36.

against her exiled children, or their descendents of her own kind and blood."[8]

After arriving back at his Washington hotel on December 18—two days before the secession of South Carolina—Vallandigham received a call to attend a meeting of the Ohio delegation to Congress. The Honorable Thomas Corwin, senior member of the state's congressional delegation and chairman of the Committee of Thirty-three, had called the caucus, hoping to solicit a strong antisecession statement. Vallandigham, tired from his trip to Richmond, showed little sympathy for Corwin's efforts or ideas. The two had often disagreed in previous years. While Vallandigham had earnestly supported the Mexican War in the Ohio legislature, Corwin had vigorously and rather vitriolicly opposed it as a United States senator. Most Democrats and many Whigs, in fact, had regarded Corwin's antiwar views as traitorous. Later, when Vallandigham had spoken out for the principle of popular sovereignty, Corwin had advocated the abolition of slavery in the territories. While Vallandigham had campaigned for Douglas, Corwin had spoken out for Lincoln.

When Vallandigham arrived at the meeting and learned its purpose, he declared it irrelevant and unnecessary. The seceding state, God, and history alone, he said, were qualified to judge whether a cause for secession existed. Several of Vallandigham's Democratic colleagues, including the ubiquitous George E. Pugh, rebuked him and thought he ought to speak out for the Union and against secession. But Vallandigham, tenacious once he had seized upon an idea, refused to retreat. As a congressman he would oppose coercion and civil war. Unrepentant and defiant, C.L.V. tossed all caution to the winds. No armed force heading south to suppress secession would march through the Third District except over his dead body![9] Then, to show his scorn for Corwin, and with his Democratic colleagues still gasping, he stalked out of the room and headed back to his hotel.

---

[8] *Richmond Daily Enquirer*, 18 December 1860. The editor of the *Enquirer* wrote: "The lecture was one of great ability and eloquence, and was received by the audience with evident satisfaction. There is no man in the Congress of the United States who has at all times and under all circumstances maintained the rights and interests of his own section with such full justice to all the rights of the South, as Mr. Vallandigham."

[9] *Dayton Daily Journal*, 22 December 1860.

Time would tell whether the threat was mere rhetoric, whether he exaggerated for effect, or whether he intended to implement his threat.

Two days later, the telegraph wires carried word of the secession of South Carolina. Moderates intensified their efforts for compromise. Corwin's Committee of Thirty-three found itself hamstrung by the extremists, North and South. Secessionist leaders, already committed to disunion, contended that compromise was hopeless and that the South could not expect justice from a Republican administration. Radical Republicans also took steps to block all schemes of conciliation—they dared not give way on the one plank (no slavery in the territories) which held the diverse factions of the Republican party together. Vallandigham, looking through partisan spectacles, blamed the Republicans rather than the Southern secessionists for lack of progress in the arena of compromise. "I see no hope of peace," he wrote to his wife in late December, "much less of adjustment of difficulties. Every day proves still more clearly that it is the fixed purpose of the Republican party not only to refuse all compromise, but to force a *civil war*."[10]

Vallandigham's supposition that Republicans intended to coerce states which had seceded or would, seemed to be borne out by House action on a measure introduced by the Hon. Roger Pryor, a representative from Virginia. Pryor, a close personal friend of the Ohioan, offered a resolution stating that it was both "impractical" and "destructive of republican liberty" to use force to restore the Union. Every Republican member of the House voted to table Pryor's resolution. Vallandigham was one of the fifty-five who voted in favor of the measure.[11]

In the Senate the venerable John J. Crittenden tried to don the mantle worn so long by Henry Clay. On December 18 he introduced a set of six propositions intended as amendments to the Constitution. The "Crittenden propositions" would restore the Missouri Compromise line and extend it, guarantee the protection of slavery in the District of Columbia against congressional action, prohibit Congress from touching slavery in the

[10] 24 December 1860, published in part in Vallandigham, *Vallandigham*, p. 150.
[11] *Congressional Globe*, 36 Cong., 2 sess., p. 220. The vote on the measure was 98 to 55.

states where it existed, and enhance enforcement of the Fugitive Slave Act of 1850.[12] Republican opposition to most of the compromise proposals caused Crittenden and Samuel S. Cox, one of Vallandigham's Ohio colleagues, to form a "committee" late in December to revise the six propositions in hopes of making them more palatable to Lincoln and his Republican cohorts. Crittenden and Cox spent a good portion of New Year's Day reworking the propositions, but could not satisfy the radicals of the two sections.[13] For his own part, Vallandigham favored the original Crittenden resolutions rather than the watered-down version, and he stated his views quite forthrightly on the floor of the House. "Anything less than a complete, final, and irrepealable adjustment, right now, of the question of slavery," stated the dogmatic Daytonian, "would be idle and mischievous."[14]

While congressmen quibbled over the wording of the Crittenden propositions, Ohio Democrats tried to create a grassroots movement for conciliation and compromise. Democrats in the state legislature, meeting in caucus, asked for a national convention to amend the Constitution and thus effect compromise.[15] Dayton Democrats circulated a petition which asked Congress to adopt the Crittenden propositions without further delay.[16] Samuel Medary, known as the "Old Wheelhorse of Ohio Politics," hitched himself to the compromise cause. He returned from Kansas, where he had served as territorial governor, to establish the *Crisis* in Columbus in order to shape Democratic policies, to work for "a peaceable solution," to war on Republicanism, and to save the country from the politicians. Medary feared "a fraternal war" and he believed the masses favored compromise and were entitled to have their say.[17]

[12] Ibid., p. 114.

[13] Samuel S. Cox, *Three Decades of Federal Legislation, 1855-1885: Personal and Historical Memories of Events* (New York, 1885), p. 28. Cox's role in the compromise game is ably treated in David Lindsey, " 'Sunset' Cox, Ohio's Champion of Compromise, in the Secession Crisis of 1860-1861," *Ohio State Archaeological and Historical Quarterly* 62 (October 1953): 348-67.

[14] *Congressional Globe*, 36 Cong., 2 sess., pp. 279-80.

[15] George S. Converse to Samuel S. Cox, 11 January 1861, Samuel S. Cox Papers (microfilm), Hayes Memorial Library, Fremont, Ohio. The original Cox Papers are in the Brown University Library, Providence, R.I.

[16] *Dayton Daily Journal*, 18 January 1861.

[17] *Crisis* (Columbus), 31 January 1861. Medary's role as editor and critic is treated in Clarence C. Broskney, "Samuel Medary, A Peace Democrat" (Master's

Efforts to stir Congress to action on the Crittenden propositions came to naught. The weeks of January passed in review. More Southern states seceded and their congressmen left Washington to return home. Republicans adamantly held to their party principles, pushing would-be compromisers back in line. Vallandigham still blamed the Republicans rather than the secessionists for the failure of compromise. He expressed his hopelessness to his wife. "I am able to do no good here—no man can," he wrote late in January, "so I sit, and am obliged to sit, quiet and sorrowful, as one who watches over the couch of his beloved mother slowly dying with consumption, to see my country perish by inches, and without power to save it."[18]

February 4 proved to be a fateful day in American history. On that day representatives of six Southern states met in Montgomery, Alabama, to organize their own confederacy. On that day, too, the Crittenden compromise proposal in Congress emitted a dying gasp. And on that day representatives of twenty-one states met in Washington at the call of Virginia. The so-called National Peace Convention sought to accomplish what Congress had failed to do—achieve reunion and peace. There was little likelihood, however, that the convention could breathe life into the compromise movement when old John Tyler pounded the gavel to bring the session to order. None of the states of the Deep South sent representatives. Three Northern states, firmly in Republican hands, refused to send delegates, and many "stiff-backed" Republican delegates had promised their governors they would not violate any plank of the party platform. Some of the delegates and many conservatives deceived themselves into thinking the convention was more than gesture.

Despite his apparent despair over the state of the nation, Vallandigham decided upon a new tack. Like John C. Calhoun, he devised a scheme to protect a minority section from the tyranny of the majority. The scheme took the form of three amendments to the Constitution, and he waited for an opportunity to lay his proposals before the House. The opportunity

---

thesis, Ohio State University, 1931), and Helen P. Dorm, "Samuel Medary: Politician, Statesman, and Journalist, 1801-1864" (Master's thesis, Miami University, Oxford, Ohio, 1938).

[18] 27 January 1861, published in part in Vallandigham, *Vallandigham*, p. 152.

came on February 7, a windy and wintry day. Having obtained the floor, he proposed his three amendments as the means to save the nation from civil war.

Vallandigham's proposed thirteenth amendment had its basis in Calhoun's "concurrent minority" doctrine, espoused in his "Discourse on the Constitution and Government of the United States," an essay found among his papers after his death. Calhoun believed that liberty could only be preserved under a government by "concurrent" rather than absolute majorities. There was need for an organic change to assure the "weaker section" protection from the stronger, for the equilibrium between sections had been permanently destroyed. This change could be effected through a constitutional amendment, such as one providing for a dual executive: two presidents, one elected by each section (North and South) and each president possessing a veto.

Vallandigham, however, went far beyond Calhoun in developing his own "concurrent minority" system. In the first place, his suggested thirteenth amendment listed four "geographical sections:" North, South, West, and Pacific. A majority of the electors *in each of the four sections* would be "necessary to the choice of the President and vice-President." The amendment also changed the president's term to six years with reelection possible only if the incumbent received a two-thirds majority of the electoral vote in each of the four sections. Furthermore, controversial measures introduced in Congress needed the approval of the majority of the senators of each of the four sections: "On demand of one-third of the Senators of any one of the sections on any bill, order, resolution or vote (except on questions of adjournment) . . . a vote shall be had by sections, and a majority of the Senators from each section voting shall be necessary to the passage of such bill, order, or resolution, and to the validity of every such vote."

Vallandigham's proposed fourteenth amendment sanctioned the principle of secession. No state could secede, however, unless every other state within its "geographical section" gave its approval. His final amendment ("Article XV") guaranteed equal rights in the territories to all citizens, Southern slaveholders as well as Northern freemen. The principle of popular sovereignty would govern territories seeking statehood; the people would decide whether they wanted slavery or not and would put their wishes into the state constitution they drafted.

The Dayton congressman asked his colleagues to be kind enough to read and consider his propositions "with candor." Since procedural rules did not give him an opportunity to present a prepared speech in defense of his proposed amendments, he stated he would speak at some later date.[19]

He had to wait until February 20 for the opportunity to explain his rather bizarre four-section scheme. It was evident that he had borrowed from Edmund Burke as well as Calhoun. The Daytonian, like Burke, believed in the organic nature of the state. It was constantly necessary to adapt institutions to circumstances, but change should be evolutionary rather than revolutionary. Again, like Burke, he stressed social order and toleration, and again he defined order in terms of individual freedom.

In that earnest appeal of February 20, Vallandigham asked his colleagues to face the hard facts of American life. A "great and terrible REVOLUTION" threatened to wreck the nation, bringing "a permanent dissolution." Again he laid much of the blame for the crisis upon the Republican party, built upon the tripod of sectionalism, antislavery, and intolerance. He scolded Republicans for speaking of a higher law than the Constitution and for developing the legend of "an irrepressible conflict."

Finished with his scolding, Vallandigham then recommended his four-section scheme as the solution for the times. His propositions, he insisted, looked solely toward the "restoration" and "maintenance" of the Union, now and forever.[20] These proposed amendments, he added, were intended "to maintain the existing Union, or 'nationality,' forever, by dividing or arranging the States into sections *within the Union, under the Constitution,*

---

[19] *Congressional Globe*, 36 Cong., 2 sess., pp. 794-97. Vallandigham offered his three proposals as an amendment to a resolution introduced by John Cochrane of New York. Cochrane's resolution asked for a popular referendum on the Crittenden compromise proposals. Vallandigham's controversial "Article XIV" read as follows: "No State shall secede without the consent of the Legislatures of the States of the section to which the State proposing to secede belongs. The President shall have power to adjust with seceding States all questions arising by reason of their secession; but the terms of adjustment shall be submitted to the Congress for their approval before the same shall be valid."

[20] Ibid., p. 1067 and Appendix, pp. 237-42.

for the purpose of voting in the Senate and electoral college."[21]

Republicans generally ridiculed and misrepresented Vallandigham's clumsy and unworkable four-section scheme. The garbled telegraphic reports that came out of Washington represented the proposal as a means to destroy rather than save the Union. Republican editors viewed the proposals as an attempt to set up four separate and independent confederacies, splitting one nation into four. Certainly it nullified the principle of majority rule practiced in a democracy. Horace Greeley thought it a device to plunge the country into civil war. William Dean Howells, then an editorial writer for the *Ohio State Journal*, branded it "pure and simple treason." William F. Comly of the *Dayton Journal* specialized in sarcasm and caustic comments. Yes, the so-called scheme was "the brightest idea of the age" and Vallandigham "the biggest fool in America." Would Vallandigham call the residents of his "four republics" "quarteroons"?[22]

Because of the confusing and dishonest telegraphic reports, even Vallandigham's Ohio friends misunderstood the scheme, believing it a four-republic proposal. The Dayton congressman therefore felt obligated to write long letters to editors to correct misimpressions and to reexplain his system.[23] But Republicans who read his explanations scorned them. Editor Comly, a master of editorial ridicule, blasted his neighbor with both barrels. "We think the explanation," wrote the sarcastic scribe, "more sensible than the thing explained." Perhaps Vallandigham believed the old legend that "the hair of the dog would cure his bite." And wouldn't it be reasonable for Vallandigham to give Irish names to each of his four sections? Did he borrow the idea from the ancient constitution of the Irish nation?[24]

While Vallandigham was still busy trying to explain his proposed amendments to his Ohio friends and foes, Republican congressmen took steps to discard all the compromise proposals and to widen the gap already existing between North and South.

[21] Vallandigham to editor of the *Cincinnati Daily Enquirer*, 18 December 1862, published 23 December.

[22] *New York Tribune*, 9 March 1861; *Ohio State Journal* (Columbus), 9 February 1861; *Dayton Daily Journal*, 9, 12 February 1861.

[23] Vallandigham to editor of the *Cincinnati Daily Enquirer*, 14 February 1861, published 19 February.

[24] *Dayton Daily Journal*, 22 February, 4, 23 March 1861.

By admitting Kansas as a free state, Republicans helped doom compromise efforts, and by advocating passage of the Morrill Tariff, a "new Bill of Abominations," they drove in the final wedges of separation.

Both Vallandigham and Douglas warned their colleagues that the "iniquitous tariff bill" affected all compromise measures adversely. It was sheer hypocrisy for a man to favor the high, high protective tariff and yet hope for compromise. Furthermore, the protective tariff policy enriched New England and robbed the West, basically an agricultural section. "Such oppressive taxation for the benefit of the few," wrote James J. Faran of the *Cincinnati Enquirer*, "is almost sufficient to drive any people into revolution"—Western as well as Southern. The pro-Western editor of the *Stark County Democrat* produced an editorial tirade against the Morrill Tariff, concluding with the supposition that "the crazy descendents of Plymouth Rock" were "as bloodless as the Rock."[25]

The protariff Republicans ignored the protests of Vallandigham, Douglas, and the border state congressmen. They seemed more willing to appease the manufacturing interests than to make concessions to the South, thereby driving a stiletto into the dying compromise hopes. On March 2, the last day of the second session of the Thirty-sixth Congress, the House of Representatives passed the tariff bill. The Dayton congressman cast one of the votes against the measure and announced, perhaps for political effect, that he intended to introduce a repeal proposal in the opening days of the next session.[26]

After Congress adjourned, most members tarried in Washington to witness the inauguration of the nation's first Republican president. Vallandigham also stayed over and joined the crowd on March 4 to hear Lincoln's inaugural address. Many Democrats, including Stephen A. Douglas, expressed satisfaction with the tone and contents of the president's speech. Neither Vallandigham nor Samuel Medary of the *Crisis*, on the other hand, found the message satisfactory. Medary said the message gave the president too much elbow room—to steer for any port. He

25 *Cincinnati Daily Enquirer*, 12 February 1861; *Stark County Democrat* (Canton), 9 January 1861; *Crisis*, 4, 28 April 1861.
26 *Congressional Globe*, 36 Cong., 2 sess., p. 4321.

would judge the new president by what he did rather than by what he said.[27] Vallandigham was even less kind. For him, the address lacked the direct and straightforward, statesmanlike language one had the right to expect from "the plain, blunt, honest man of the Northwest." Furthermore, Vallandigham added, the new president left thirty million people in doubt whether he wanted war or peace.[28]

Conservative Democrats were generally far more critical of Lincoln's selection of cabinet members than of his inaugural address. William H. Seward, the new secretary of state, had previously endorsed the "higher law doctrine," speaking occasionally like an abolitionist. Salmon P. Chase, newly named secretary of the treasury, had defied federal law when he was governor of Ohio. Simon Cameron, named secretary of war, was a Pennsylvanian who brazenly wore his radical stripe on his sleeve. Many Democrats perhaps expected to see Seward, Chase, and Cameron decide policy for the new president. Seward was an able man, a shrewd and experienced politician. He might well be the power behind the throne, perhaps greater than the throne itself.[29]

When Vallandigham returned to Dayton he found antiwar sentiment everywhere. His friend, J. Frederick Bollmeyer, who edited the *Dayton Empire* talked like a true peace man.[30] So did James J. Faran of the *Cincinnati Enquirer* and Samuel Medary of the *Crisis*. Even Douglas continued to plump for peace, advocating "an amicable settlement." Douglas gave a notable speech on March 15 in which he maintained his opposition to coercion and war: "War is disunion. War is final, eternal separation."[31] Clement L. Vallandigham shouted, "Amen!"

Ohioans' fears of a civil war had a half-dozen different bases. In the first place, ties of blood and friendship linked many "Buckeyes" to residents of the slave states. Mrs. Vallandigham's family, for example, lived in Cumberland, Maryland, and C.L.V.'s great-uncles had left Pennsylvania to live in North Carolina and

---

[27] *Crisis*, 14 March 1861.

[28] *Congressional Globe*, 37 Cong., 1 sess., p. 57.

[29] *Dayton Daily Empire*, 7 March 1861; entries of 4, 16 March 1861, Medlar, "Journal."

[30] *Dayton Daily Empire*, 28, 29 March 1861.

[31] Quoted in *Crisis*, 2 May 1861 and by Vallandigham in *Congressional Globe*, 37 Cong., 2 sess., pp. 1460-61.

Kentucky. Many of the so-called "Butternuts," residents of Ohio's backwoods area, had left behind many friends and relatives when they moved from the Southern uplands to find new homes in the upper Midwest.[32]

Economic ties also linked many Ohioans to the South. Hundreds of commercial houses had a vested interest in the Mississippi River trade. Southern bonds underwrote some of the paper money circulating in the upper Middle West. A portion of the farm surplus of Ohio moved southward, either to a consumers' market or to the New Orleans outlet. A dozen Cincinnati industries depended, in large measure, upon Southern buyers. Washington McLean, one of the owners of the *Cincinnati Enquirer*, also owned several boiler-plate factories which served the South. Small wonder then, that this friend of C.L.V. conducted a constant campaign for peace and compromise.[33]

Western sectionalists who feared the triumph of industrialism and the predominance of New England foresaw that a civil war could transform them into "slaves and serfs of New England."[34] They recognized that the closing of the competitive Mississippi River system would put them at the mercy of the Great Lakes shipping interests and the east-west railway trunk lines, owned mainly by New York and Boston capital. Some astute Midwesterners feared that New England industry and Northeastern capital would exploit their section through the Republican party.[35] The upper Midwest may have been partially bound to the Northeast by "hoops of steel," railroads and canals, as well as credit and culture, but Midwestern sectionalists still wished to play balance-of-power politics between the Northeast and the South.

[32] Richard L. Power, *Planting Corn Belt Culture: The Impress of the Upland Southerner and Yankee in the Old Northwest* (Indianapolis, 1953) is an admirable study. The student of Ohio migration trends should also consult: John D. Barnhart, "The Migration of Kentuckians across the Ohio River," *Filson Club Historical Quarterly* 25 (January 1951): 24-32; Henry C. Hubbart, "Pro-Southern Influences in the Free West, 1840-1865," *Mississippi Valley Historical Review* 20 (June 1933): 42-62; and David C. Schilling, "The Relation of Southern Ohio to the South during the Decade Preceding the Civil War," *Quarterly of the Historical and Philosophical Society of Ohio* 8 (January 1913): 3-19.

[33] *Cincinnati Daily Enquirer*, 28 December 1860, 29 January, 5, 12 February, 30 March 1861. The economic ties that bound Cincinnati and the South are explored in scholarly fashion in Charles R. Wilson, "Cincinnati, a Southern Outpost in 1860-61?" *M.V.H.R.* 24 (March 1938): 373-82.

[34] *Crisis*, 31 January, 2 April 1861.

[35] *Cincinnati Daily Enquirer*, 12 February 1861.

Vallandigham and Samuel Medary, both Western sectionalists and conservatives, frequently appealed to the nascent anti-New England sentiment which existed in many sections of the region lying north of the Ohio River.[36]

Western conservatives who preferred evolutionary change and compromise to revolutionary change and civil war spoke of the lessons of history. European civil wars had invariably ended in dictatorships: Oliver Cromwell had set up a military dictatorship at the close of the Puritan Revolution in England, while in France, Napoleon Bonaparte emerged as the end product of the French Revolution. Midwestern conservatives also saw a lesson in the change Louis Napoleon had effected in their own generation; he had transformed the Second French Republic into the Second Empire within a four-year period. A civil war in America might mean the end of representative government. "We are embarking upon a course," predicted James J. Faran of the *Cincinnati Enquirer,* "that will produce some Cromwell or Napoleon who will crush beneath his iron heel the Democratic legacy we have so long enjoyed."[37] Lincoln most surely was an unknown quantity, so conservatives in the upper Midwest felt they had reason to fear for the future. Adamantly against coercion, Vallandigham mistrusted both Lincoln and the future.

Midwestern conservatives noted that President Lincoln seemed to vacillate in his policy regarding Fort Sumter. In mid-March, when it looked as if he would withdraw federal troops from Sumter, they endorsed his course. Vallandigham and his Dayton friends favored the surrender of Forts Sumter and Pickens "as the best means to keep peace, avoid a civil war, and finally to bring back the seceded States, and upon just compromise, reconstruct the Union."[38] They deceived themselves with false hopes and wishful thinking, misjudging the force of the independence movement in the South and the intensity of Southern radicalism. Facing the past and fearing the future, however, Vallandigham reiterated Douglas's statement: "War is disunion. War is final, eternal separation."

[36] The "hoops of steel" metaphor appeared in the *New York Tribune,* 14 April 1861. Albert H. Kohlmeier, *The Old Northwest as the Arch of the American Federal Union: A Study in Commerce and Politics* (Bloomington, Ind., 1938) reveals the economic ties of the upper Midwest and the Northeast.

[37] 22 January 1861. Medary expressed a similar fear in *Crisis,* 31 January 1861.

[38] Entry of 16 March 1861, Medlar, "Journal."

5

AT THE CROSSROADS

A WARY SUN PEEKED over the horizon on April 12, 1861, its rays barely able to penetrate the smoke hanging over the Confederate batteries firing on Fort Sumter. Later that morning Major Robert Anderson, commanding the unfinished island fortress, hauled down the United States flag and ordered the white flag of surrender to take its place.

The news of Fort Sumter's surrender flashed over the telegraph wires, and a tidal wave of patriotism engulfed the North. Republican editors and politicians demanded revenge for the insult to the American flag, and many leading Democrats added their voices to the call for vengeance. "Let blood flow," cried one indignant Democratic editor, "until the past be atoned, and a long future secured to peace, prosperity, happiness and honor."[1]

President Lincoln called for 75,000 men and issued a series of proclamations as the Union's answer to Confederate action. The North seemed to arise as one man to answer Lincoln's call and to castigate the rebels. Democrats as well as Republicans rallied to the colors. "I am not deceived in my faith in the North," wrote Count Adam Gurowski from his observation post in Washington, D.C.; "The excitement, the wrath is terrible. Party lines burn, dissolved by the excitement. Now the people is fusion, as bronze."[2]

It was a time for soul searching. Democrats who had spoken out for compromise and against coercion had to decide what to do and say, or retreat to the shadows and hide themselves until the storm of passion passed by.

It was here that Stephen A. Douglas and Clement L. Vallandigham, allies for a dozen years, parted company. Douglas took the high road, where crowds cheered and emotion ran rampant. Vallandigham took the low road—the lonely road of the dissenter.

Those who knew Douglas must have expected him to take the high road. He had always been a Western nationalist, and he had always been a practical man, pragmatic in outlook. An apostle of manifest destiny, he did not want secession and civil war to destroy that dream. Immediately after the firing on Fort Sumter, Douglas called on President Lincoln to assure him of support. He also wrote a dispatch for the press, announcing his determination to sustain Lincoln in his efforts to preserve the Union. Then he journeyed into the Midwest to rally the country-side and urge Democrats to support the administration. "There are but two parties," he told his followers in Springfield, "the party of patriots and the party of traitors. We belong to the first."[3] Six weeks later, struck down by typhoid, Douglas lay on his deathbed. His last words were advice to his two sons: obey the laws and support the Constitution.

Those who knew Vallandigham well must have expected him to take the road of the dissenter. He was a Western sectionalist who feared that civil war would mean the ascendancy of New England and the triumph of industrialism. He was less inclined than Douglas to be practical because he had become too wedded to principle. As an advocate of states' rights, he was an out-and-out dogmatist. Once he had accepted a proposition, he hung on tenaciously. Once he had occupied a position, he was most reluctant to desert it. He regarded vacillation as a weakness and pussyfooting as cowardice. He chose to ignore expediency and he enjoyed courting controversy. He was introspective, self-conscious, and possessed of a sure sense of moral righteousness. He had tremendous ability and was especially well read. These factors led him to the certainty that he was right and others were wrong. Conscious of his own rectitude, he saw it as his duty to convince others. Since he detested abolitionism and blamed it for the crisis, since he mistrusted Lincoln, and since he believed war an irrational means to achieve an end, Vallandigham dissented.

He wasted little time in getting his antiwar views into print. Those who read the *Dayton Empire* knew that Editor J. Frederick Bollmeyer was Vallandigham's man Friday and that the views expressed therein would be those of the master. "Having taken

---

[1] *Wisconsin Daily Patriot* (Madison), 20 April 1861.

[2] Adam Gurowski, *Diary . . . from March 4, 1861 to November 10, 1864*, 3 vols. (Washington, D.C., 1862-1866), 1: 23.

[3] Douglas's emotion-filled Springfield speech was published in full in the *Illinois State Register* (Springfield), 27 April 1861.

our position in the beginning against the policy of coercion," Bollmeyer wrote the day after the surrender of Fort Sumter, "we intend to stand by it to the end. Whatever others may do, we stand firm and immovable against money and men for civil war."[4]

Convinced he was right and dismayed because many former anticoercionists were chanting "War! War!" Vallandigham prepared a letter to place his views on record. Although he addressed his letter to the "Editor of the Cincinnati *Enquirer*," he sent copies of the epistle to a dozen Democratic journals, including the *Dayton Empire* and the *Crisis*. He laid all the blame for the war at Lincoln's doorstep, restating the refrain that he opposed a coercive war, always had, and always would. If Ohio was invaded, he would, of course, hurry to her defense and help repulse the invaders. He would expect the people of Kentucky, Virginia, or Missouri to do the same. He expressed the belief that "the surging sea of madness" would ebb and that "the sober second thought of the people" would call out against Americans "butchering each other" in a civil war. He closed by expressing his contempt for the "cowardly slanderers" of the preachers of peace. He was unafraid, he said, and rumors that he had been arrested were the work of liars and libelers. He could be found daily at his home, in his law office, or upon the streets of Dayton.[5]

Governor William Dennison's call for troops in Ohio must have been somewhat embarrassing to Vallandigham, who held a brigadier general's commission in the Ohio militia and had a new uniform, with a well-polished star upon its epaulet, hanging in a closet. Some of the Dayton companies he had organized and which belonged to his brigade marched off to war. The brigade commander stayed home, sulking in his tent.[6]

Vallandigham and the handful of followers who had publicly stated their opposition to the war soon began to feel a deluge of hostility. Thomas H. Hodder, the editor of the *Marion Democratic Mirror*, who restated Vallandigham's contention that Lincoln had brought on the war and that Democrats should oppose

[4] 13 April 1861.
[5] Published in the *Cincinnati Daily Enquirer*, 20 April 1861. The letter also appears in Vallandigham, *Vallandigham*, pp. 159-60, but three sentences which put C.L.V. in a less favorable light are omitted.
[6] *Dayton Daily Journal*, 17 April 1861.

coercion, suffered for his views. Self-styled patriots assaulted him on the streets of Marion and threatened to hang him and burn his newspaper plant.[7] J. Frederick Bollmeyer received considerable abuse, being told bluntly that he ought to be on Jeff Davis's payroll. William F. Comly, a master of invective, used the editorial columns of his *Journal* to call Bollmeyer a dozen uncomplimentary names. When Bollmeyer hoisted an American flag over the *Empire* office building to prove his "loyalty," Comly flew into a rage and charged that use of the flag was a device "to hide treason most effectively." An impassioned editorial entitled "A Traitor Publishing Treason at Our Own Doors" aroused Dayton Republicans, who suggested mob action to burn the *Empire* building and to hang a perfidious editor.[8]

Vallandigham, of course, received a great amount of abuse. The *Dayton Journal* denounced him for uttering "treasonable sentiments" and compared Douglas's "laudable" course with Vallandigham's "dastardly treason." Had not Douglas said there could be only "patriots" and "traitors"? Vallandigham's efforts to make the war a "partisan issue," the paper suggested, brought disgrace and dishonor to the Third Congressional District. Since C.L.V. misrepresented his district, he ought to resign. "Could Jeff Davis desire a more faithful emissary than C. L. Vallandigham?" asked Comly. He ended his anti-Vallandigham editorial tirade with the query, "Shame, where is thy blush?"[9]

Most of Ohio's well-known Democrats followed Douglas's advice and came out for war. Samuel S. Cox made a patriotic speech in Columbus on April 22 and the venerable William Allen did the same in Greenville. David Tod and John Brough, still calling themselves Democrats, waved the flag vigorously. James J. Faran of the *Cincinnati Enquirer* wrote of the need to "sustain, protect, and defend the Federal Government without any reference whatever to the person who may administer it." George W. Manypenny, editor of the widely read *Ohio Statesman,* preached similar doctrine and thought the times called for

[7] Ibid., 23 April 1861.
[8] Ibid., 16 April 1861. On the day on which Comley's strong anti-Bollmeyer editorial appeared, he received word from Washington that he had been named Dayton's postmaster.
[9] Ibid., 22, 23 April 1861.

patriotism rather than partyism. After the editor of the *Hamilton Telegraph* had one copy of his newspaper returned with a rope around it and a note attached, he took the hint and said he would stand by the flag and support the war.[10]

A few Democrats refused to let the patriotic surge sweep them off their feet. George D. Prentice of the *Louisville Journal* defined Lincoln's call for 75,000 men as "utterly hair-brained and ruinous."[11] But then, Prentice was a Kentuckian and lived in a slave state. Samuel Medary of the *Crisis* wrote like a prophet of gloom and seemed much more critical of Lincoln than of Jefferson Davis. Despondently, he predicted that civil rights would be quashed and the country would disappear.[12] Dr. Edson B. Olds of the *Ohio Eagle* (Lancaster) preached partyism and bitterly condemned President Lincoln. John W. Kees of the *Circleville Watchman* was even less charitable; he viewed Lincoln as fool, fanatic, and figurehead rolled into one. Then, of course, there were Bollmeyer of the *Empire* and Vallandigham. Altogether, they were but a handful against the multitude.

In the weeks that followed the surrender of Fort Sumter, events of national importance occurred almost daily. The Baltimore riots, the Confederate seizure of Harpers Ferry, and the secession of Virginia all made headlines. Fear that a pro-Southern secret society might sieze the national capital warranted a congressional investigation. President Lincoln's war measures, some of questionable constitutionality, caused even some flag-waving Democrats to raise their eyebrows. Lincoln suspended the writ of habeas corpus in certain areas, declared a blockade of the Confederate States, and increased the size of the army and navy by presidential order. He ordered the letting of contracts for provisions and the tools of war, and he asked Congress to convene in extraordinary session on July 4, 1861.

Vallandigham feared that Lincoln's proclamations would help to transform the "armed peace" into an open conflict. Furthermore, he reasoned, the president had no right to usurp powers granted specifically to Congress by the Constitution. He hoped that Lincoln's extraordinary war measures would dampen the

[10] *Cincinnati Daily Enquirer,* 17, 24 April 1861; *Ohio Statesman* (Columbus), 23 April 1861; *Dayton Daily Journal,* 23 April 1861.
[11] 15 April 1861.
[12] *Crisis* (Columbus), 16, 18 April 1861.

patriotism expressed by some members of the Democracy, and tried therefore to unite Democrats in opposition to the war. He composed a circular letter suggesting that dissident Democrats meet in Chillicothe on May 15 to frame a cooperative protest against Lincoln's war measures, and sent it to twenty-five hand-picked party members. Most of the recipients turned their backs on the letter-writer. Only four even bothered to reply; three of the respondents favored such a conference and one advised against it. Vallandigham assumed that those who failed to reply opposed the scheme, and quickly and quietly dropped the conference idea.

Since party leaders in Ohio refused him a platform to state his antiwar views, Vallandigham composed another letter in an attempt to solicit subscribers for his views. Congress ought not to sanction Lincoln's war measures, he declared. He himself certainly would not. *"I will not vote to sustain or ratify—*NEVER," Vallandigham stated determinedly; "millions for defense, *not a dollar or a man* for aggressive and offensive civil war." Lincoln, in fact, deserved impeachment, he felt. Moreover, the rising national war debt would weigh down millions yet unborn. Easterners might desire war; Westerners certainly did not. This was his creed: "I am for the CONSTITUTION first, and at all hazards; for whatever can be saved by the UNION next; and for PEACE always as essential to the preservation of either." He closed his epistle with Douglas's statement: "War is final, eternal separation."[13]

Vallandigham also stated his antiwar views in personal letters not intended for publication. One such letter he wrote to the Rev. Mr. Sabin Hough, a clergyman whose antiwar views cost him his pulpit in the Second Presbyterian Church in Dayton. Vallandigham expressed disappointment that hysteria had invaded even the churches, mocked the Prince of Peace, and made ministers "thirst for blood." War might develop eternal separation not only of North and South, but also of West and East. "It is," he wrote pessimistically, "too late for anything except *peaceable separation.*" He expressed the hope that a reaction would set in to "the madness of the hour." Then he would step forward to lead

[13] C.L.V. to Richard K. Hendrickson, N. G. Oglesby, John McClellan, and Others, 13 May 1861, published in *Crisis*, 23 May 1861.

the forces for peace. "I shall watch for the first favorable chance," he added, "to move publicly for peace—and restoration [of the Union] if possible."[14]

Vallandigham's antiwar stand continued to draw a frontal attack by the Republican party press. Republican editors labeled him "traitor," "secessionist," and "champion of Jeff Davis." C.L.V., in turn, accused Republicans of conducting a smear campaign and wrote a rebuttal to impress his friends and defend his views. He claimed to be a constitutionalist and a conservative, standing up for order, law, and reason. "My sympathies are and ever have been," he wrote, "with my own home, my own State, and my own flag." He wanted peace—the war must be speedily brought to "an *honorable termination*." He opposed coercion. And as he was so often wont to do, he claimed that time would vindicate him.[15]

William F. Comly of the *Dayton Journal* recognized that Vallandigham had disassociated himself from the government and its war. Always a violent partisan, Comly suggested that Vallandigham resign his congressional seat. Certainly he did not represent the views of his constituents, the Republican editor declared. Time would not vindicate him, but blacken his name. "Be assured," Comly advised Vallandigham, "that 'Time the Avenger' will do justice. The lives of Arnold and Burr can testify how he deals with traitors."[16]

Friendships of long standing disintegrated as Daytonians argued the propriety of Lincoln's war measures. Each side cloaked its arguments with dogmatism. Vallandigham and Bollmeyer took the strongest possible stand against the war. Even though Southerners had fired the first shot at Fort Sumter, the two Democrats blamed Lincoln and the abolitionists for bringing on the crisis and the conflict. They also believed the Southern states could not be forced back into a Union they abhorred. A true nation must be built upon good-will and trust, not on force, distrust, and self-styled superiority. Coercion would only destroy the comity of sections; it would create hatreds and intolerance, both adverse to reunion. This would lead to "a complete, final,

[14] 26, 30 April 1861, published in *Dayton Daily Journal*, 18 September 1861.
[15] C.L.V., "The Public Arms," *Dayton Daily Empire*, 16 May 1861.
[16] 18 May 1861.

and eternal dissolution of the country." Yes, coercion and war would destroy and desolate a country once "fair and glorious."[17]

Some twenty or thirty Dayton Democrats gathered almost nightly in the editorial offices of the *Empire* to read the telegraphic dispatches, discuss events of the past, and conjecture about the crisis. They discussed the policy of the Lincoln administration and saw only evil on every hand. Believing that partisanship, not statesmanship, motivated Lincoln, they measured each act of the president by their own warped constitutional yardstick. By closing their eyes to reality, they could still see compromise as a solution to the crisis, even after the Fort Sumter affair had intensified the call for national vengeance. They denounced Dayton preachers who espoused abolition and prayed for vengeance. They wondered what effect a blockade of the Mississippi would have on the economy of the Midwest, and they conjectured as to who might inherit the mantle worn so majestically by Stephen A. Douglas.[18]

Bollmeyer generally served as the guiding genius and arbiter of the group. Vallandigham dropped in nearly every evening to take part in the discussions and to shape the opinions of the less informed Democrats. There was a tendency to give more weight to Vallandigham's views than they deserved, but there was a finality to his comments that convinced those seeking an answer. His ability to quote the classics, to call upon history as a witness, and to phrase opinions in scholarly terms impressed his audience and bolstered his ego. He quoted the Constitution at length—section and clause—and he also called upon Burke, Jefferson, and Calhoun to substantiate the views he expounded. As he recited Lincoln's "usurpations" nearly every night, he appeared to be trying to convince himself as well as his satellites. Moodily pessimistic and always dogmatic, he became impatient with those who refused to be as fatalistic and gloomy as he.[19]

Dayton Republicans, quite naturally, developed some suspicion of those who gathered almost nightly in the office of the *Empire*. Some believed they constituted "a band of traitors" who merited censure or arrest, while others supposed that the members of the clan belonged to a secret, pro-Southern society called the Knights

[17] Entry of 30 May 1861, Medlar, "Journal."
[18] Ibid., entry of 23 May 1861.
[19] Ibid.

of the Golden Circle—rumors about the ephemeral organization swept Ohio periodically. Dayton Republicans, of course, made Vallandigham the target of their scorn, ridicule, and hatred. The editor of the *Dayton Journal* warred upon the Democratic congressman in nearly every issue. He received able assistance from the editors of the *Cincinnati Gazette,* the *Cleveland Leader,* and the *Ohio State Journal.* "Vallandigham," the editor of the *Cleveland Leader* stated in one issue, "is a disgrace to the country and to the State he represents." Had he used the word "misrepresents" he would have been closer to the mark. Republican editors in Ohio, through their repeated attacks upon Vallandigham, made him the best known and most hated congressman in the nation.[20]

The beleaguered Vallandigham seized upon anything and everything to give validity to his views. He found considerable satisfaction in the decision Chief Justice Roger B. Taney handed down in *Ex Parte Merryman* late in May 1861. The decision was a severe rebuke to President Lincoln and a blow for civil liberties. It was the same decision Vallandigham would have given were he in Taney's stead.

The case had a Maryland setting. A Baltimore citizen of pro-Southern sympathies had been arrested by federal military authorities and imprisoned in Fort McHenry. No ground having been shown for his arrest, Chief Justice Taney, sitting in the Maryland circuit court, authorized a writ of habeas corpus in Merryman's behalf and commanded General George Cadwalader to deliver up the prisoner. Cadwalader, in turn, refused to give up Merryman and cited Lincoln's suspension of habeas corpus as his authority. Justice Taney then issued a writ of attachment for contempt against the general but Cadwalader refused to accept the writ and denied entrance to Fort McHenry to the marshal seeking to serve it. The chief justice then filed a long and learned opinion in Merryman's behalf and slapped Lincoln's hands resoundingly.

Interwoven with historical and constitutional arguments, Taney urged "extreme caution" in suspending the writ of habeas corpus. Furthermore, he pointed out, the right to suspend it belonged *only* to Congress; the president had no constitutional authority to effect such suspension himself. Since the civil courts were

[20] Ibid., entries of 23, 30 May 1861; *Cleveland Leader,* 26 June 1861; *Dayton Daily Journal,* 12, 19 June 1861.

open, Taney continued, the judicial process rather than arbitrary military practices should prevail. It was the president's sworn duty to maintain such constitutional decrees, not suppress them. In concluding, the chief justice strongly condemned Lincoln's "act of usurpation."[21]

Taney's notable decision won praise in some Democratic quarters. Nowhere was the applause louder than in the editorial offices of the *Dayton Empire*. There C.L.V., repeatedly denouncing Lincoln's sins, led the applause. Taney's decision must have bolstered Vallandigham's belief in his ability as a prophet.[22]

The approach of an economic recession also gave Vallandigham a chance to pose as a prophet—his gloom and apprehension seemed justified. After the blockade of the Mississippi River by presidential order, a depression slowly and surely began to envelop the upper Midwest. Avenues of trade disappeared and commercial firms along the Ohio River experienced hard times. Farmers also suffered, for the blockade cut off the Southern market for farm surpluses. Samuel Medary, who claimed to represent the agrarian interests, placed most of the blame for the developing depression on Lincoln and Republican policy. "It acts upon us," he wrote in the *Crisis*, "much like the man who bit his nose to spite his face."[23]

Vallandigham, who divided his time between his law office and the meeting rooms of the *Empire*, read Medary's pithy anti-Lincoln comments. He also noted Medary's opposition to the Union party movement, a political strategem devised by the Republicans to keep their party in the ascendancy. The *Crisis* editor wanted no Democrats to play ball with the fusionists. He characterized the Union party as a Republican cloak to hide their sins and transgressions. "We are opposed," Medary wrote with single-mindedness, "to the covering up of the monstrous inequities of the State Administration by a Union ticket."[24] Vallandigham, who believed party regularity a virtue, agreed.

Late in June 1861, Vallandigham put his affairs in Dayton in

---

[21] *Ex Parte Merryman*, 17 Federal Cases 144 (1861); *The War of the Rebellion: A Compilation of the Official Records of the Union and Confederate Armies*, 128 vols. (Washington, D.C., 1880-1901), ser. 2, 1: 576. (Hereafter cited as *Official Records*.)

[22] *Dayton Daily Empire*, 7 June 1861; *Dayton Daily Journal*, 10 June 1861.

[23] 13 June 1861.

[24] 13, 27 January 1861.

order so that he could attend the emergency session of the Thirty-seventh Congress. When he boarded the east-bound train he carried several boxes of clothes and a packet of books. He also took with him the knowledge that the Democratic party was more hopelessly divided than ever. Some wanted to join the Union party movement; others opposed it. Some wished to place patriotism above partyism; others viewed party loyalty as primary. Most Democrats obviously favored coercion of the seceded states, and only a handful opposed both the Lincoln administration and the war. Meanwhile, Douglas's death seemed to leave the northern wing of the Democracy leaderless and the party appeared to be disintegrating.

Most Democrats bowed to the wave of patriotic passion which swept the North in April, May, and June of 1861. George D. Prentice of the *Louisville Journal* typified those who talked like patriots, reversing his earlier position. He expected all of his Democratic colleagues to prove themselves worthy citizens. Any Democrat who opposed the war deserved castigation. Any congressman who would refuse to vote men and money to sustain the war deserved a string of epithets: "A TRAITOR, A MONSTER, A DISGRACE TO HIS ANCESTRY, A SHAME TO POSTERITY, A FOUL STAIN UPON HIS BIRTH."[25]

Vallandigham left for Washington, knowing that the tidal wave of patriotism, calling for vengeance and victory, would make the life of a dissenter most unpleasant. Yet he believed his anti-war views right and Lincoln's policy wrong. And those who knew Vallandigham best expected him to follow the course he believed right, regardless of the costs and consequences.

[25] Quoted in *Dayton Daily Journal*, 19 June 1861.

6

"WORSE THAN A JUDAS"

THE FOURTH OF JULY 1861 dawned bright and clear in Washington. A gentle breeze teased the flags which bedecked buildings and flagpoles, and the pleasant weather brought many of the city's residents and visitors into the streets.

Most of the congressmen, waiting for the opening of the Thirty-seventh Congress at noon, took to the streets to watch the parade and to attend the morning program. They saw President Lincoln and other notables sitting on a canopied platform erected between the White House and the street. They watched a dozen bands play martial music and twenty-six regiments of infantry march up Pennsylvania Avenue. Then some of them crowded around the platform to hear six short speeches, one by General Winfield Scott and another by President Lincoln. When the program was over, a military escort led the president to the Treasury grounds to hoist a huge flag up a 100-foot flagpole while a band played "The Star-Spangled Banner." As the ceremonies came to an end the highly emotional crowd gave nine cheers for "the grand old flag" and nine more for President Lincoln.[1]

Clement L. Vallandigham was among the congressmen who watched the proceedings. He noticed that the flag which Lincoln had hoisted skyward contained thirty-four stars. Perhaps Congress could take some measures to reunite the country and make that flag more than an empty symbol.

At noon the Senate and the House of Representatives met in response to Lincoln's special call. John W. Forney, clerk of the House, rapped his gavel, bringing to order the querulous congressmen and the crowded galleries, packed mostly with soldiers stationed in the many camps around the capital city. The Rev. Thomas H. Stockton read the opening prayer; he asked God to help right the "erroneous views" of the "southern brethren." Next Forney read President Lincoln's proclamation of April 15 which declared an "insurrection" in process and asked Congress to meet in special session at noon on July 4. Vallandigham was one of 159 congressmen who answered the roll call.[2] Two who claimed to represent the State of Virginia also answered when the clerk called the roll. Virginia thus seemed to have representatives in two congresses, one meeting in Washington, the other in Montgomery. Vallandigham was most interested in the complex problem, for Virginia was the land of his fathers.

It did not take the Dayton congressman long to make his presence known and to alienate several colleagues. He challenged the right of three (Francis P. Blair, Jr., of Missouri, Gilman Marston of New Hampshire, and Samuel R. Curtis of Iowa) to take their congressional oaths, claiming they held military commissions which disqualified them from sitting in the House.[3] He read aloud the sixth section of Article I of the Constitution, which specified that a person who held a commission in the United States Army could not serve in Congress. Vallandigham drew some boos from the galleries. Although the Constitution upheld his resolution, the Republican majority chose to ignore the protester and his contentions.

The House then turned to the task of electing its Speaker. The Hon. John P. Hickman of Pennsylvania, destined to become one of Vallandigham's most vehement critics, nominated Francis P. Blair, Jr., and complimented the Missourian on effective military action in his state—action which had kept Missouri in the Union and had "elicited the enthusiastic approbation of every loyal American."[4] Vallandigham winced as the galleries applauded and he immediately rose to protest. He did not want the galleries to affect debate and the course of events as they had during the French Revolution. Clearly, Vallandigham was out of step with the patriotic sentiment sweeping the country.

On the second ballot, the Republican majority elected Galusha Grow of Pennsylvania to serve as Speaker. Blair kept his congressional seat, turning down a brigadier generalship in order to avoid "political complications" in his state.

1 *National Intelligencer* (Washington), 6 July 1861; *Baltimore Evening Patriot*, 5 July 1861.
2 *Congressional Globe*, 37 Cong., 1 sess., pp. 1-2.
3 Ibid., p. 3; *Crisis* (Columbus), 11 July 1861.
4 *Congressional Globe*, 37 Cong., 1 sess., p. 4.

Speaker Grow began his tenure with a fervent and patriotic speech which galled Democratic members of the House. The country must be reunited by force "even though the waters of the Mississippi should be crimsoned with human gore, and every foot of American soil baptized in fire and blood. . . . If the republic is to be dismembered and the sun of liberty must go out in endless night," he continued, "let it set amid the roar of cannon and the din of battle, when there is no longer an arm to strike or a heart to bleed in its cause."[5] The galleries applauded again. Vallandigham, who wanted the Union restored by compromise rather than coercion, shook his head in disbelief. John Brown was dead, but his spirit permeated the land.

Vallandigham also disagreed with many parts of Lincoln's message, read by Forney in stentorian tones. He believed the president had failed to report on the state of the Union fully and impartially. He viewed the message as partisan and dishonest, "a labored and lawyerly vindication of his [Lincoln's] own course of policy." This partisan policy he believed had precipitated the nation into "a terrible and bloody revolution." Lincoln should not have blamed *only* Southern radicals for the distraught state of affairs, for Northern abolitionist and Northern radicals also deserved some of the blame—C.L.V. could recite their sins, too. Furthermore, had not Republican leaders repeatedly and consistently stymied all attempts at compromise?[6]

Routine business occupied most of the rest of the day. Although he was serving his third term in Congress, Vallandigham received only one minor committee assignment, to the Committee on Public Lands. Perhaps this was a part of the penalty for being a dissenter and a member of the minority party.

That evening Vallandigham attended a Democratic caucus session. Nearly all party members were there except congressmen from Kentucky and Maryland. Party spokesmen sought to establish some policy for the Democracy. Nearly everyone who arose to speak endorsed war as the only realistic road to reunion. Even the New York delegation favored supporting the government and suppressing the rebellion. Vallandigham alone spoke out against coercion and stated his antiwar views firmly

[5] Ibid., p. 5.
[6] Ibid., p. 57.

and frankly. Reunion, he argued, could be effected only by compromise and Northern concessions to the South. War, as Douglas said, could mean only "eternal, final separation." No other congressional Democrat supported Vallandigham's views. Evidently all had bowed to the passions and realities of the hour. He stood alone.[7]

Three days later Vallandigham called on some Ohio troops at an army camp outside Washington. It was a sunny Sunday and the Dayton congressman wanted to visit former friends who were both officers and constituents. Colonel Alexander McCook, an acquaintance from boyhood days in New Lisbon, accompanied Vallandigham and served as guide. Some soldiers belonging to a Cleveland regiment recognized C.L.V. as he passed their quarters and taunted him for his antiwar views. They called him "traitor" and "secessionist" and threatened to ride him out of camp on a rail. The visitor viewed the insults with disdain and replied tartly. Tempers flared and fisticuffs followed, but Colonel McCook and other officers intervened and rescued the congressman from the soldiers.

Indignant and undaunted, the Dayton congressman then visited the sector of the camp occupied by the soldiers of the Second Ohio Volunteer Regiment. Many of these soldiers were from Dayton and some were personal friends. He received a courteous welcome and spent several hours visiting or conveying messages he had in hand. The Cleveland soldiers, however, reported their "brush" with Vallandigham to a Republican newspaperman, who wrote up the "camp incident" for his paper and put it on the telegraphic wires. It made the rounds of the Republican press, with some editors exaggerating for effect. The New York Tribune told the wildest tale—it claimed that Vallandigham had lost his head when he passed an effigy of himself hanging from a tree and that he had been pelted with stones and chased out of the camp. The unfriendly papers also gave the impression that C.L.V.'s views were anathema to all soldiers. The Dayton congressman, on the other hand, supposed that a minor incident had been magnified and trimmed with lies so that it could be used against him at election time.[8]

[7] Baltimore Evening Patriot, 9 July 1861.
[8] Baltimore Clipper, 8 July 1861; New York Tribune, 8 July 1861.

Vallandigham contributed very little to the legislation enacted in the short, special session of the Thirty-seventh Congress. He was on his feet often, raising points of order and putting road-blocks in the way of legislation that President Lincoln desired. He frequently commented on procedure and Republican steam-roller tactics, and he exhibited a thorough knowledge of parliamentary law. His Republican colleagues usually treated him courteously even though some disdained the dissenter. They successfully sidetracked his motions and pigeon-holed his amendments as fast as he made them. They referred his proposal to repeal the Morrill Tariff and replace it with the Act of 1859 to the Committee of Ways and Means, where it died unattended and unmourned. They rejected his amendment to allow rabbis to serve as chaplains in the U.S. Army, and they successfully killed his motion to void the oath prescribed for all cadets attending West Point Academy. Vallandigham was even denied the right to speak on the controversial Military Academy Bill. Nevertheless, he shouted a few words of reproach. "Then, sir," he quipped sarcastically, "let it go down upon the record that this bill has been forced upon its passage without debate. I propose, sir, to discuss it in that GREAT HEREAFTER to which I have so often had occasion of late to deal."[9]

Vallandigham also carried on a futile fight against what he called "executive usurpation." On July 15 he introduced seven resolutions censuring Lincoln for "a series of unconstitutional acts." One cited the "illegal arrests" made by military authorities. Another challenged the suppression of freedom of speech and of the press. Others charged the chief executive with usurping Congressional prerogatives—declaring war, raising an army and navy, establishing a blockade, and suspending the writ of habeas corpus. He asked that his resolutions be made an early order of business and "referred to the Committee of the Whole." The Republican majority, impatient with Vallandigham's efforts to discredit Lincoln's war measures, disposed of the seven resolutions quickly, laying them "on the table" by a voice vote.[10]

[9] *Congressional Globe*, 37 Cong., 1 sess., pp. 23, 100, 348. Professor Bertram W. Korn had high praise for Vallandigham's effort to eliminate discrimination against rabbis in "Congressman Clement L. Vallandigham's Championship of the Jewish Chaplaincy in the Civil War," *American Jewish Historical Quarterly* 53 (December 1963): 188-91.
[10] *Congressional Globe*, 37 Cong., 1 sess., p. 130.

Despite his open antiwar views, the Dayton dissenter did vote for several war measures, much to the disappointment of Samuel Medary of the *Crisis*. He voted to pay the volunteers who had answered the president's call for 75,000 men, for he believed they had no motive "but supposed duty and patriotism" to move them. He also voted for the bill which authorized the president to call for 500,000 volunteers for "a period of not more than three years," justifying his action by the claim that they were needed "to protect and defend the Federal Government." On the other hand, he did not favor the use of the volunteer army to wage an aggressive war upon the South or "to invade states which had claimed that they had seceded."[11]

The Dayton congressman's only prepared speech of the thirty-three day session argued against war and for compromise. He criticized Lincoln's message to Congress as one-sided, and blamed the Republicans rather than the secessionists for producing the crisis and pushing the sections to the verge of war. Lincoln's "usurpations" nullified civil rights and threatened to transform the republic into a dictatorship. In some European countries, he suggested, such usurpations, would have cost sovereigns their heads. Peace and compromise were the means to reunion and the salvation of civil rights. Many Americans opposed coercion, but the emotional tide of the hour silenced some who would otherwise speak in protest. At a later date, Vallandigham predicted, time would vindicate him and praise those who preached the gospel of reunion through peace. "I am," he added "for *peace*—a speedy, immediate, honorable PEACE with all its blessings."[12]

The battle of Bull Run on July 21 made Vallandigham's peace proposals even more impractical and improbable. The rebel victory seemed to make more real the Confederates' dream of an independent nation. The North, with injured pride, girded the sword more securely to its side and prepared for a longer, bloodier contest. Vallandigham, failing to grasp the reality of the situation, still talked of peace when most Northerners wanted war and most Southerners wanted independence. He asked for concessions and compromise when most Northerners called for retribution and revenge. And he asked for charity and compas-

11 Ibid., pp. 59, 100, 130-32, 171, 332, 348.
12 Ibid., pp. 56-60. Medary printed the entire speech in the *Crisis*, 25 July 1861.

sion when the mood of the country nurtured distrust and hate.

Nevertheless, in the closing of the special session, C.L.V. made one more bid for compromise. He introduced a resolution asking for a "Convention of the States" to adjust "all controversies" and to amend the Constitution. The resolution and all hopes for negotiated peace died when the House adjourned *sine die* the next day.[13]

Most Republicans scorned Vallandigham's views on war and peace. One wondered aloud whether Vallandigham belonged in the Confederate congress rather than the one in which he held his seat. Another, Cyrus Aldrich of Minnesota, bluntly told the Dayton Democrat that he was "under a mental hallucination" and bent on making a nuisance of himself. Vallandigham, Aldrich added, had favored peace when he should have voted for war, opposed the government when he should have supported it, and preached partyism when he should have practiced patriotism.[14]

Republican editors, too, showed their contempt for Vallandigham and his views. The editor of the *Cincinnati Times* called C.L.V.'s speeches in Congress "treasonable stuff." The *New York Tribune* repeatedly accused him of treason and labeled him pro-secessionist in his sympathies. The *New York Herald* stated he was disloyal and "muddled and confused" as well. Even most of the Democratic newspapers in the North questioned the correctness and wisdom of his propeace pronouncements. The *Detroit Free Press,* for example, characterized his sentiments as "murky and impure," out of line with the wishes of the country. Most Democrats, like the Republicans, wanted the rebellion suppressed and the Union sustained.[15]

After Congress adjourned on August 6, Vallandigham took a leisurely trip home by way of Baltimore, Cumberland, and New Lisbon. In Baltimore he was the guest of Henry May, a Maryland congressman with pro-Southern sympathies. Vallandigham took two side trips, one in a carriage to May's country estate and another down the Potomac in May's celebrated yacht *Midge*. He also discussed politics with his famous brother-in-law, John

13 *Congressional Globe,* 37 Cong., 1 sess., pp. 440-44.
14 Ibid., pp. 93, 459.
15 *Cincinnati Times* (n.d.), quoted in *Dayton Daily Journal,* 18 July 1861; *New York Tribune,* 12-13 July 1861; *New York Herald,* 12 July 1861; *Detroit Free Press,* 18 July 1861.

Van Lear McMahon, who roomed at the Entau House. In Cumberland he visited with other in-laws and found that one of his nephews had marched off to join the Confederate army. In New Lisbon, he exchanged greetings with his mother, his brothers, and friends.

Vallandigham's short vacation in New Lisbon gave him a chance to rest, to sample public opinion, and to see rays of hope for the Ohio Democracy, which had turned its back on fusion. In a personal letter to a long-time political ally, he expressed his optimism:

> Light is beginning at last to break upon us. The vindication of free speech in Congress & the Battle of Manasses [sic]—the two great events of the age—are opening the eyes of the people to the true origin, character & magnitude of the war. The maintenance of the organization & integrity of the Democratic party gives us an ancient & still admirable machinery wherewith to rally the masses & to save the Constitution & public & private liberty, & I hope—it is the desire of my heart—to restore the Union, the Federal Union as it was forty years ago.[16]

After returning to Dayton, Vallandigham obtained some inside information on Democratic party activities. His friend and confidant, J. Frederick Bollmeyer of the *Empire,* reported on the in-fighting which had occurred at the State Democratic Convention, in session when Vallandigham was cultivating graciousness in Baltimore. The convention seemed to have endorsed Vallandigham's views; it had blamed "fanatical agitators, North as well as South" for the war, recommended the calling of a national convention, reprimanded President Lincoln for trespassing upon unconstitutional grounds, and placed civil rights and the Constitution on a pedestal.[17] The convention repudiated fusion (the Union party movement) and nominated Hugh J. Jewett as the Democratic candidate for the governorship. Vallandigham endorsed the state platform and was pleased that most Democrats rejected fusion. He was rather unhappy, nevertheless, with the nomination of Jewett, a rival within the party and a railroad man for whom Vallandigham had cultivated a personal animosity.

[16] C.L.V. to Alexander S. Boys, 13 August 1861, Alexander S. Boys Papers, Ohio Historical Society, Columbus.
[17] *Crisis,* 15 August 1861.

The returning congressman also reacquainted himself with the local political situation. County Democrats were badly split on the questions of the hour. Bollmeyer advocated Vallandigham's views in the *Empire*, where he favored compromise and peace, denounced Lincoln's war measures, and claimed civil rights must be respected. He received able support from Christian Gross, a German-American who had two sons serving in the Union army, and young Tom O. Lowe, a lawyer whose father commanded an Ohio regiment in the West Virginia campaigns. The antiwar Democrats had controlled the county convention of August 3 and had adopted antiwar and anti-Lincoln resolutions before electing peace men to the state convention.[18]

However, some sixty county Democrats who viewed Vallandigham's course as unpatriotic and Bollmeyer's editorials as unpardonable, had organized a convention of their own in order to give "an honorable direction" to their party. These "War Democrats" had supported fusion, had asked for vigorous prosecution of the war, had placed patriotism above partyism, and had repudiated Vallandigham's propeace views. Although some of these sixty were opportunists,[19] more interested in promoting their own than the country's welfare, others were solid citizens who had bowed to the patriotic surge of the day and believed antiwar resolutions were inimical to the country's welfare. Colonel Alexander McCook, once a close personal friend of Vallandigham, typified the "War Democrats" who denounced Bollmeyer's editorials and Vallandigham's views. Within Bollmeyer's hearing McCook had expressed his contempt for critics of the war. "*Yes, by G-d,*" he exclaimed as the editor of the *Empire* walked by, "*I say, d--n any man who is not for the Union, and d--n Vallandigham, too! He is worse than a Judas; he is a d----d traitor!*"[20]

The Democracy of Butler County, also in Vallandigham's congressional district, was as badly split as that of Montgomery County. Michael M. Maginnis of Hamilton, a disciple of Val-

---

[18] Lowe to "Dear Johnnie" [a brother], 24 August 1861, Thomas O. Lowe Papers, Dayton and Montgomery County Public Library; "Proceedings of the Democratic Mass Conventions, Montgomery County, August 3, 1861," *Dayton Daily Journal,* 7 August 1861.

[19] Entry of 8 August 1861, in Medlar, "Journal."

[20] Entry of 12 August 1861, in ibid.

landigham, led the antiwar faction, and the propeace and anti-Lincoln resolutions which he had foisted upon the county convention created a gaping party schism. In the days that followed, each faction subsidized its own newspaper, developed its own platform, and went its own way. The "War Democrats" supported fusion and learned to hate the "Peace Democrats" more than they hated the Republicans, once their detested adversaries.

Republicans, controlling the call for a "common ticket," developed the "Union movement" as a political stratagem. They usurped the Union party label for their county conventions and pulled the strings backstage. Patriotism served as a silent but effective partner, and prominent Democrats, such as David Tod and John Brough, cooperated with Republicans at the Union party convention of September 5, 1861. The fusionists named Tod as their gubernatorial nominee, asked for full support to suppress the rebellion, and prepared to carry the October elections.

Party-line Democrats viewed Tod as a renegade, an opportunist whom the Republicans had bought with thirty pieces of silver. They failed to understand that Tod's success in railroading and manufacturing made him more enamored of Republican party principles than of the antitariff and proagrarian principles preached by Ohio Democrats. Truly, Tod was out of place in a party which mechanics and workingmen regarded as their own. A year before the start of the war, Tod had drawn up "a conspiracy bill" which outlawed unions and strikes, and made workingmen who had struck for higher wages guilty of conspiracy and punishable as criminals. Perhaps Tod also felt out of place in a party which Samuel Medary of the *Crisis* wished to dominate. Years earlier the two had learned to hate and distrust each other. Medary's return to a place of influence in Democratic circles made Tod uneasy and he therefore looked for greener political pastures.[21]

While condemning Tod and Lincoln, Democratic editors saved

[21] Edgar A. Holt, "Party Politics in Ohio, 1840-1850," *Ohio State Archaeological and Historical Quarterly* 38 (January 1929): 108-9, states that Medary believed Tod had tricked him out of a consular appointment during Polk's presidency. Ruth Wood Gold, "The Attitude of Labor in the Ohio Valley toward the Civil War" (Master's thesis, Ohio State University, 1948), pp. 6-7, explains why Tod felt out of place in a party in which mechanics and workingmen predominated.

some of their sharpest barbs for the Union party movement. They appealed to public prejudice, calling the Union party "a mask to cover the deformities of Abolition." One might throw the lion's skin over "the same animal," they noted, but the ears would stick out.[22] They characterized the promoters of fusion as "Know-Nothing tricksters, Republican abolition leaders, and political trimmers generally." Other straight-line Democrats bragged that they were "neither for sale nor barter"—no matter what the price.[23]

As the election campaign became more intense in September, Vallandigham became more of an issue. Republicans hurled invectives in his direction and pretended that he held the Democratic party in the palm of his hand. They labeled him "an arch-traitor," an "unmitigated scoundrel," "a secessionist," and "the pliant tool of the rebel leaders." Concocting outright lies to tarnish his reputation, they charged, for example, that Confederates in Kentucky had named an army camp in Vallandigham's honor, and that he belonged to a pro-Southern secret society, the Knights of the Golden Circle, which intended to aid the Confederacy and bring about a rebellion in the North. "Every vote cast for Hugh J. Jewett for governor," asserted the Republican editor of the *Cleveland Leader,* "is a vote in favor of a dishonorable peace, in favor of the rebels, and in opposition to the Federal Government."[24] Some Republicans even held that Vallandigham "richly deserved the halter" because of his stand for peace and opposition to the war.[25]

The Republican campaign of villification against Vallandigham paid dividends. Independents, unburdened by party ties, refused to vote for the party in which C.L.V. held membership. Republicans, gathering grapes in the political vineyards, worked harder to defeat "Vallandigham and Jewett." In some places in Dayton it was not even safe to speak a word in C.L.V.'s defense. "There is no denying the fact now," wrote a sympathetic

22 *Daily Ohio Statesman* (Columbus), 1 August 1861.
23 *Stark County Democrat* (Canton), 10 July 1861; *Crisis,* 15 August 1861; *Dayton Daily Journal,* 29 August 1861.
24 *Cleveland Leader,* 4 October 1861; *Dayton Daily Journal,* 28 August, 24 September 1861; *Cincinnati Daily Gazette* (n.d.), quoted in *Crisis,* 5 September 1861.
25 Entry of 19 August 1861, Medlar, "Journal."

Dayton observer, "that he is the most unpopular man in the north, and that here in his own district, he has but a minority of the people with him."[26]

Vallandigham was not one to be intimidated or bow to pressure. Indeed, the insults hurled his way and the efforts to intimidate him only made him more defiant and self-righteous. He walked the streets of Dayton openly, with head held high and opinions unyielding. Occasional incidents caused tempers to flare. Once a Republican grocer whom the Vallandighams had patronized for years told the congressman he would give him no more credit—that as a scoundrel and traitor he deserved no consideration. Vallandigham answered heatedly, threatening to thrash his accuser on the spot. The grocer then picked up a pistol and threatened to use it, upon which Vallandigham beat a hasty retreat. In his hurry to get outside, he stumbled over the doorsill, "fell on all fours" on the flagstones, and scrambled into the millinery store next door for safety. He injured only his pride, however, while Republicans generally found the incident amusing. Their hatred of Vallandigham blinded them to the seriousness of the incident and the threat it offered to personal rights and safety.[27]

Actually, Vallandigham took only a very small part in the Democratic campaign to put Jewett into the governor's chair. Because of the personal antagonism existing between the two, Jewett did not care to have Vallandigham speak in his behalf. At the nominee's request, the Democratic State Central Committee gave the Dayton congressman not a single speaking engagement. Jewett's friends discouraged county and city leaders from extending C.L.V. an invitation to speak in their communities as if he were anathema to the party. Vallandigham gave only one speech during the entire campaign, and that in Dayton on the eve of the election. That speech, as everyone expected, turned into a severe indictment of the Lincoln administration.[28]

Although Vallandigham appeared to be a drag on the wheel of the party bandwagon, Ohio Democrats seemed to have some things going for them. They could point out that "Mr. Lincoln's

[26] Thomas O. Lowe to "Dear Johnnie," 24 August 1861, Lowe Papers.
[27] *Dayton Daily Journal*, 31 August, 2 September 1861.
[28] Entry of 8 October 1861, Medlar, "Journal."

Army" had met defeat at Bull Run because the chief executive ordered the army into battle before it was ready for action, thus laying the debacle at the president's door. Then, too, the economic depression which engulfed the upper Mississippi Valley seemed to worsen with each passing month. The bottom dropped out of the farmers' market basket; in some parts of Ohio farmers sold their corn for seven cents a bushel, while others used it for fuel. Some businessmen in Ohio river cities cursed Lincoln even though they had voted for him a year earlier. "Matters look blue enough here," reported a Democrat visiting Cincinnati. "Business men have long faces and short money receipts. One Jim Brown & Co. say they have lost $40,000 since the election [1860] by depreciation in stock. There are three of them and they each voted for Lincoln 'God & Liberty,' and say now they 'wish Lincoln and all political parties were in hell.' "[29]

Both Republicans and Democrats expressed apprehension as the campaign passed through its final weeks. When October 8 arrived, however, Republican concern had changed to a quiet confidence. Rampant patriotism, feeding on the Republican campaign against "treason," gave Tod and the Union party the edge.

The election passed off quietly enough in Dayton, with the exception of a few incidents in two of the city's wards. In the Sixth Ward a "Vallandighamer" openly declared that he would rather live under Jeff Davis than Abe Lincoln. Some "patriot" knocked him down on the spot. Arising slowly, the Democrat eyed his tormentor, then decided to run off, but not before a hearty kick sent him scampering across the commons. Another foolish fellow, also a defender of Vallandigham, made a statement endorsing secession and condemning President Lincoln. When a "patriot" threatened to whip him, he pulled a pistol out of a pocket, but bystanders quickly overpowered him, dragged him down to the canal and thoroughly ducked him. After he promised to behave, he was released, going home wetter if not wiser. In the Fifth Ward an Irish poll-worker named Dennis Dwyer argued heatedly with Republicans who accused him of

---

[29] Matt Marion to Samuel S. Cox, 3 December 1861, Samuel S. Cox Papers (microfilm), Hayes Memorial Library, Fremont, Ohio.

working to elect "a secessionist." A fight occurred and Dwyer, badly outnumbered, was seriously injured. No one made an effort to intimidate or attack Vallandigham on election day. He spent the entire day, from sunrise to sunset, around the polls of his ward, badgering acquaintances to renounce the fusion movement by voting the straight Democratic ticket.[30]

After the bruises were counted and the votes tabulated, officials reported that David Tod had carried Dayton, Montgomery County, and the state of Ohio by handsome margins. Republicans gloried in the election returns and held a series of party jollifications. The Republican editor of the *Dayton Journal* thanked God that virtue, patriotism, and Tod had triumphed. His headline must have galled Vallandigham: "TREASON DEAD AND BURIED! Vallandigham and His Traitorous Crew Squelched!"[31]

Some members of the state Democratic organization, seeking a scapegoat, held Vallandigham in part responsible for the defeat of their ticket. They viewed him as a millstone around Jewett's neck, and claimed that his imprudent remarks had cast a cloud over the Democratic party, making it vulnerable to charges of treason.

Those Republicans who had centered their campaign fire on Vallandigham thought it proper to view the election returns as a repudiation of the Dayton congressman and his policies. "Since Vallandigham's traitorism has been so effectively rebuked by the voters of his District," the editor of the *Dayton Journal* proclaimed, "he must, if he has the least respect for their expressed will, resign his position as their elected representative."[32]

Vallandigham, always self-righteous, had no inclination nor intention to resign. He still believed he was right and the voters wrong. He spent considerable time in his law offices, doing occasional favors for indigent Irish or German-American constituents. He also put the election returns out of his mind by immersing himself in the books which occupied so many shelves in his study. He sought justification for his views in the works of Burke, Macaulay, Hume, Jefferson, and John Adams. In a

---

[30] Entry of 8 October 1861, Medlar, "Journal"; *Dayton Daily Journal*, 8, 9 October 1861.
[31] 9 October 1861.
[32] 10 October 1861.

sense, he was preparing himself for the second session of the Thirty-seventh Congress, scheduled to convene on December 2. In that session Vallandigham was destined to impress his contempt of abolitionists, his hatred of radicals, his antipathy for New England, and his distrust of President Lincoln deeper into the record.

7

GADFLY

LINCOLN'S FRIENDS and foes alike found his message to Congress of December 1, 1861, disappointing. Abolitionists especially felt frustrated because the president failed to endorse emancipation. His suggestion that the United States recognize "the Negro republic" of Haiti was but "a tub thrown to the Abolition whale."[1] His failure to say anything about the *Trent* affair upset Americans afflicted with Anglophobia, especially the Irish-Americans. In fact, most of the important issues of the day were not even mentioned.[2]

Democrats, without even trying, found much to criticize in Lincoln's message. Many, including Vallandigham, did not intend to vote for any measure recognizing Haiti or advancing abolition. Since most Irish-Americans of his district voted the Democratic ticket, Vallandigham decided to use the *Trent* affair for personal gain. He also realized that events linked to that incident gave him a chance to chide the Lincoln administration.

The roots of the *Trent* controversy dated back to November 8, when an American warship, the *San Jacinto*, stopped a British mail steamer, the *Trent*, and seized two Confederate agents, James M. Mason and John Slidell. Britain promptly asked for an overt apology, demanded the immediate release of Mason and Slidell, and began preparations for war. Misguided patriots, aided by Democrats such as Clement L. Vallandigham, complicated the touchy problem by adopting a House resolution which applauded the captain of the *San Jacinto* for his "brave, adroit, and patriotic conduct." Another resolution, even more absurd, pledged the same treatment for Confederate commissioner Mason as that received by Colonel Michael Corcoran, supposedly confined in a felon's cell after falling into enemy hands at First Bull Run.[3]

When rumors circulated in the halls of Congress that President Lincoln intended to release Mason and Slidell and apologize for their seizure, C.L.V. decided to exploit the issue, embarrass Lincoln, and pose as a prophet. He introduced a resolution instructing the president to stand firm and defy the British demands. "We have heard the first growl of the British lion," the Dayton congressman exclaimed seriously, "and now let us see who will cower." He added that the purpose of the resolution was "to expose the shallow but blustering and cowardly statesmanship of the Abolition party in the House. . . . These men [Mason and Slidell]," he said as he looked into his crystal ball, "will be surrendered before three months in the face of a threat. I make that prediction here today."[4]

Events proved Vallandigham to be an excellent prophet. The administration "cheerfully liberated" Mason and Slidell and admitted the seizure to have been an error. The Dayton congressman seized upon "the surrender" as an excuse to condemn the Lincoln administration, labelling its action "a calamity, . . . tenfold more disastrous than a five years' war with Great Britain." He also reminded his listeners that he had predicted the surrender of the two Confederates within three months, amidst Republican denials. They had, in fact, been surrendered within three weeks. "For the first time," the grumpy gadfly moaned, "the American eagle has been made to cower before the British lion."[5]

A few of Vallandigham's friends praised him for trying publicly to embarrass the administration. A few even reiterated that he was a prophet—"a true prophet."[6] The Republican editor of the *Dayton Journal* fumed at the *Empire's* efforts to portray Vallandigham as a man of courage and vision. He was a prophet all right, but "Jeff Davis' prophet." The angry editor added, "He is a prophet of evil, speaking with a lying tongue. He is a prophet without honor in his own, or any other country, save 'Secessia,' where his predictions of evil to our Government are hailed with delight, and his name is enrolled in the calendar of secessionist saints."[7]

1 *Cincinnati Daily Gazette*, 4 December 1861.
2 Entry of 3 December 1861, Medlar, "Journal."
3 *Congressional Globe*, 37 Cong., 2 sess., p. 5.
4 Ibid., pp. 101, 120.
5 Ibid., pp. 210-12.
6 *Dayton Daily Empire*, 3, 9 January 1862.
7 *Dayton Daily Journal*, 4 January 1862.

Vallandigham also twitted Lincoln for the way military control was extended in the border states, especially Kentucky and Maryland. Arbitrary arrests had been most numerous in those states and the blanket of military authority had even extended into the states north of the Ohio River. Vallandigham endorsed George H. Pendleton's scorching attack upon Lincoln for suspending the writ of habeas corpus without congressional sanction. The doughty congressman shocked even his Democratic colleagues by introducing a bill providing for the president's arrest and imprisonment if he should cause any more persons to be arrested arbitrarily, in either the border states or the loyal states.[8] Republicans gasped and promptly shelved the resolution. They believed Vallandigham's sole purpose was to embarrass the administration, and some questioned his sincerity and sanity. "In war time," wrote "Deacon" William F. Comly of the *Dayton Journal*, "it is the duty of legislators to strengthen the hands of the government, and not to weaken them, even when their views do not coincide with its policy."[9] A few Democrats were pleased with Vallandigham's boldness and his apparent bid for notoriety. Others suspected he was using the resolution merely as a means of calling the country's attention to the many arbitrary arrests already made—offering the administration some of its own bitter medicine. "His friends had better admonish him," wrote one concerned Democrat, "that if he does not desire to be expelled, he should not get so sarcastically funny."[10]

The congressman from Dayton also joined the Democratic minority in its efforts to stay the course of abolition. These Democrats voted against a resolution proposed by Thaddeus Stevens which blamed slavery for the war and endorsed emancipation. They also voted against Thomas D. Eliot's measure to authorize generals in command of military districts or departments to free the slaves of rebels within their jurisdiction. And they opposed, en masse, a bill to abolish slavery in the District of Columbia and a second measure to abolish it in the western territories. They spoke out against the Confiscation Bill because it gave Lincoln a lever to attack slavery in the Confederate states.

[8] *Congressional Globe*, 37 Cong., 2 sess., pp. 40, 67, 92.
[9] 20 December 1861.
[10] John W. Kees to Samuel S. Cox, 20 December 1861, Samuel S. Cox Papers (microfilm), Hayes Memorial Library, Fremont, Ohio.

They objected to the assignment of a consul or ambassador to "the Negro republic of Haiti." They opposed the repeal of an act forbidding Negroes to serve as stagecoach drivers or to carry the United States mail. Finally, they opposed Lincoln's efforts of March and April 1862 to promote compensated emancipation in the border states—admitting thereby that he could no longer resist the abolition pressure.

Occasionally C.L.V. was able to get the floor to object to some abolition measure or speak briefly against it. He had a chance, for example, to enumerate his objections to the bill voiding slavery in the District of Columbia. He argued that the measure would prolong the war and nullify future attempts at reunion through compromise.[11] He also abhorred all of the other abolition measures which took long hours of congressional time. His views were quite like those of another Democrat, who wrote:

> Congress has the negro-phobia. It is nigger in the Senate, and nigger in the House. It is nigger in the forenoon and nigger in the afternoon. It is nigger in motions and nigger in speeches. It was nigger the first day and it has been nigger every day. Nigger is in every man's eye, and nigger in every man's mouth. It's nigger in the lobby and nigger in the hall. . . . The nigger vapor is a moral pestilence that blunts the sense of duty to the Constitution and destroys the instinct of obedience to the law.[12]

Vallandigham interpreted the abolitionists' attack upon slavery as a revolutionary measure. It was an attack not only upon a socioeconomic institution, but upon states' rights, as well. The administration's war measures centralized the government, causing the ship of state to founder upon unconstitutional shoals and change the nature of the federal union. He advocated "the Constitution as it is, the Union as it was"—the prewar union with states' rights dominant and with slavery still intact. He believed that Jeffersonian principles must be maintained at all hazards, that eternal vigilance was the price of liberty, and that time would immortalize those who resist revolution and abolition, "the twin madnesses of the moment." "We are in the throes of

[11] *Congressional Globe*, 37 Cong., 2 sess., pp. 5-6, 1589-90, 1698, 1767, 1788, 1819-20, 2359-60, 2363, 2560-61; entry of 7 March 1862, Medlar, "Journal."

[12] *Macomb Eagle* (n.d.), quoted in *Indianapolis State Sentinel*, 23 December 1861.

a revolution," he wrote to one of his political allies, "and I cannot see what the issue is yet; but I dread the worst."[13] He revealed his own self-righteousness and his faith in "Time the Great Avenger" in a note to ex-President Franklin Pierce. "The time will come," he predicted confidently, ". . . when *all* men who have stood firm and true to their principles and to the real interests of the country will be remembered with gratitude and honor."[14] In a sense, the Dayton congressman was offering evidence that he was a conservative, rooted to the past and fearful of the future.

In addition to opposing all the abolition measures introduced in Congress, Vallandigham also voted "nay" on many other Republican-sponsored bills. Some were measures to enact planks from the Republican platform into law. He voted against the Pacific Railway Bill, which provided a federal land subsidy for the construction of a transcontinental railroad over the plains and across the Rockies. He objected to new tariff levies. He objected to the Illinois Ship Canal Bill, denying that it had any relevance to military needs. He argued against the Treasury Note Bill (providing for the issue of $150 million of greenbacks as legal tender), saying that "forced federal currency" would bring "depreciation" and then "a final explosion." He told Republicans to their faces that they were guilty of "fiscal irresponsibility" and "financial contrivances." He saw the burdens of war weighing heavily upon a worn populace, for continued war meant heavier taxation. Those who wanted to continue the war, he warned, must be willing to levy the taxes and suffer the political consequences. Fancy schemes to evade that responsibility merited only censure. "Taxation, heavy taxation, but upon a sound principle and in the right way," asserted the self-styled watchdog of the Treasury, "can alone save us now."[15]

The Dayton congressman did not vote for any of the army appropriation bills introduced in the second session of the Thirty-seventh Congress—nor did he vote against them. When the Army Deficiency Bill reached the House, he asked several em-

[13] Vallandigham to Alexander S. Boys, 27 January 1862, Alexander S. Boys Papers, Ohio Historical Society, Columbus.

[14] 11 April 1862, Franklin Pierce Papers, Library of Congress.

[15] *Congressional Globe*, 37 Cong., 2 sess., pp. 168-70, 198-99, 345, 523, 526-27, 593-94, 614-15, 618, 638, 640, 665, 680, 689, 693-95, 874, 887, 1589, 1659, 1682-83, 1971, 2906, 3031.

barrassing questions. He slurred the War Department and the administration by asking if it were a discrepancy rather than a deficiency bill—was it a means to hide a $30 million defalcation in the War Department? Nor did he give any support to the Army Bill, which appropriated $422 million for the year ending June 30, 1863. He remained noticeably silent during the debate on this major bill and conveniently refrained from voting, so that Republicans could not use his vote against him in the '62 election campaign.[16]

Vallandigham's self-asserted role as critic and gadfly led to verbal encounters with a couple of Republican congressmen. One of those with whom he crossed swords was John P. Hickman of Pennsylvania. The two had tangled once before and Hickman bore a grudge because he had been badly bested. The Pennsylvanian's bluntness, combined with a swaggering self-assurance, had led him into "engagements" with other congressmen. Once Hickman had wrestled with two Virginia representatives at the top of the Capitol steps, and before the fight was over the three had rolled down to the bottom, punching, tugging, and kicking each other.

On February 19, 1862, Hickman threw down the gauntlet. Having secured the floor, he looked directly at Vallandigham and impugned his loyalty before the overflowing galleries. In his right hand he held a copy of the *Baltimore Clipper;* he gesticulated with his left, often pointing in the direction of the Dayton congressman. He read selections from an editorial which charged Vallandigham with harboring traitorous designs, claimed that the Democrat had referred to the South as "bleeding Dixie," and accused him of tainting his oath to support the government and the Constitution. Then, without differentiating between an editor's lie-filled charges and the facts of the case, the representative from Pennsylvania introduced a resolution instructing the Committee on the Judiciary "to inquire into the truth of certain charges of disloyalty" made against Vallandigham.

Feigning composure though seething with indignation, Vallandigham rose immediately to refute the charges, contradicting

---

[16] *Ibid.*, pp. 569, 576, 579, 907-8, 1309. Vallandigham's congressional record is reviewed in a cursory and confusing fashion in Christena M. Wahl, "The Congressional Career of Clement Laird Vallandigham" (master's thesis, Ohio State University, 1938).

every sentence in the scurrilous article. He denied ever having used the term "bleeding Dixie." He had *never* gone into the so-called Confederate states to meet with rebel leaders as the article charged—indeed, he had not been south of the Mason-Dixon line since the start of hostilities. Moreover, he denied that he had ever sent an article on politics to *any* Baltimore newspaper.

Taken aback by Vallandigham's refutation, Hickman countered weakly. Had not Kentucky rebels named a camp in Vallandigham's honor? Had not other newspapers also questioned Vallandigham's loyalty?

The accused congressman answered every question forthrightly. He had never heard of a Camp Vallandigham in Kentucky, but he knew of a city named Hickman in that border state. The camp story, like others, was evidently invented by lying newspapermen, probably for political effect. Republican newspapers had circulated countless lies and made numerous charges, many libelous. Republican editors repeatedly misrepresented his views and concocted new tales as fast as he could deny the old. Sarcastically, Vallandigham suggested that an intelligent gentleman ought not to give currency to newspaper slander already denounced as false and unfair.[17]

Bested in the exchange, Hickman raised the white flag. He meekly withdrew the resolution he had earlier introduced, and Vallandigham was complimented by some of his Democratic friends for making Hickman look like a simpleton. Even some Republican congressmen, disgusted with Hickman's overbearing manner and roughhouse tactics, commended Vallandigham for besting the Pennsylvanian. Vallandigham, known for his assertiveness and self-assurance, enjoyed his triumph. He expressed his satisfaction with the outcome to his wife: "I was never more gratified in my life with any result. . . . It was a signal triumph. . . . They will let me alone bye-and-bye."[18]

Benjamin F. Wade, one of the United States senators from Ohio, was the next prominent member of Congress to attack Vallandigham. Friends had told "Bluff Ben" that the Dayton congressman coveted his Senate seat, and they urged him to

---

[17] *Congressional Globe*, 37 Cong., 2 sess., pp. 879-81; *Indianapolis State Sentinel*, 1 March 1862.

[18] 20 February 1862, published in part in Vallandigham, *Vallandigham*, p. 192.

discredit the would-be competitor by stamping the traitor's brand upon his forehead.[19] Once, outside the halls of Congress, Wade characterized Vallandigham as "a man who never had any sympathy with the Republic, but whose every breath is devoted to its destruction, just as far as his heart dare permit him to go."[20] Later, on the Senate floor, Wade made a frontal assault upon the Democratic party in general and Vallandigham in particular. He accused Democrats of trying to intimidate and discredit patriots, "men who boldly stand forth in defense of their country." Some treason-tainted Democrats, he claimed, belonged to a subversive secret society, the Knights of the Golden Circle, and tried to use that serpentine organization to reconstruct the Democratic party. He stated that Vallandigham belonged to this association, that the Dayton congressman had tried to discredit and crucify Stephen A. Douglas and was now trying to lead the Democratic party down the road to treason.[21]

After Wade's remarks appeared in the *Congressional Globe*, Vallandigham sought the floor of the House for his reply. Holding a copy of the *Globe* in his hand, he read Wade's slanderous charges to an attentive audience. Then, rising on tip-toe and raising his voice, he discarded his decorum and usual temperance. "Now, sir," he shouted, "here in my place in the House and as a Representative, I denounce—and I speak it advisedly—the author of that speech as *a liar, a scoundrel, and a coward*—His name is BENJAMIN F. WADE!"[22]

The presiding officer, of course, called Vallandigham to order. One of Wade's friends quickly introduced a resolution to censure Vallandigham for his intemperate remarks and personal attack upon the senator. But Vallandigham escaped censure, partly through his knowledge of parliamentary law. Then, too, congressmen were reluctant to interfere in a personal feud in which both parties had overstepped the bounds of propriety.[23]

Others joined Wade and Hickman in trying to discredit Vallandigham. John A. Gurley and Samuel Shellabarger, congress-

[19] John H. Geiger to Wade, 20 February 1862, and Peter Zinn to Wade, 5 February 1862, Benjamin F. Wade Papers, Library of Congress.

[20] Quoted in Vallandigham, *Vallandigham*, p. 193.

[21] *Congressional Globe*, 37 Cong., 2 sess., p. 1736.

[22] Ibid., pp. 1828-29.

[23] Ibid., pp. 1828-31, 1833; *Crisis*, (Columbus), 7 May 1862.

men from Ohio, presented petitions from their districts asking for Vallandigham's expulsion from the House as "a traitor and a disgrace to the State." Since the petitions had not come from Vallandigham's own congressional district, and since there was no evidence offered that he was guilty of treason or had disgraced Ohio, a House committee shelved the batch of petitions.

Republican constituents occasionally wrote to their congressmen to excoriate Vallandigham and sometimes to urge his expulsion. "I look upon him [Vallandigham] as one of the *blackest traitors* in either the Senate or the House," wrote a Michigander who thought he could read the minds of voters in a neighboring state, "and I am confident I speak the sentiments of 7/8 of the Democrats of Ohio when I say their wishes are that he might in some way be expelled."[24] The expulsion of Jesse Bright of Indiana from the Senate in February 1862 tempted some to suggest the same medicine for C.L.V. "If justice were done," wrote one such critic, "Vallandigham would be kicked from the House as Bright was from the Senate."[25]

Republican editors made an art of abusing Vallandigham. John W. Forney, editor of the *Philadelphia Press* and a confidant of President Lincoln, set the pattern and the pace. He asserted that Vallandigham and Jeff Davis belonged in the same bed and that Vallandigham's stand on the *Trent* affair and other measures gave hope and encouragement to the enemy.[26] "His record for the past four months," wrote another Republican editor in January of 1862, "is sufficient to render him infamous for life, and will in all probability, unless he seeks absolution in sackcloth and ashes."[27] Occasionally Republican editors put their villification of Vallandigham into rhyme. One wrote:

> Vile traitor to the blood our fathers spilt for thee,
> And dark inheritor of Arnold's infamy;
> List to the hiss of moral serpents in thy breast,
> Lapping their forky tongues of treason from their nest,
> And spawning in thy heart's tartarian cell,
> New gems to make thee worthy of a hell;

24 L. A. Pierce to Zachariah Chandler, 6 December 1861, Zachariah Chandler Papers, Library of Congress.
25 *Dayton Daily Journal,* 7 February 1862.
26 *Philadelphia Press* (n.d.), quoted in *Dayton Daily Journal,* 17 January 1862.
27 *Dayton Daily Journal,* 16 January 1862.

Damnation's seal is set upon thy rebel name—
In blackest brand, thou moral vagabond, in same,
Go forth, a traitor to thy country, and thy God:
Hearing afar the voice of Lyon's; and Ellsworth's blood
Asking sweet vengeance for thy festering crime,
Making thee hissed and hated through all coming time.[28]

When occasional compliments of Vallandigham appeared in Southern newspapers, Republican editors in Northern states viewed them as evidence that the Dayton congressman deserved to be expelled from Congress, arrested promptly, and tried for treason. Republican strategists, such as Benjamin Wade or Horace Greeley, recognized that a treason campaign against Vallandigham would affect his political future and stigmatize the Democratic party. "We have the monster [Vallandigham] branded with the traitor's mark," croaked one Republican in mid-April of 1862, "and it is treason on the part of our friends to *let up* the impure and damnable party that has held its organization above the interest of the country."[29] Some Republicans were so partisan in their approach to all problems that they even thought it treasonable for a Democrat to wear his own party's emblem, be it a butternut, a hickory branch, the head of Liberty, or a picture of Jefferson.[30]

Vallandigham was so busy serving as gadfly and quarreling with Republicans that he did not take time to return to Dayton to vote in the April 1862 elections, even though a close personal friend, William H. Gillespie, sought the mayor's office. Since the Republican newspaper in Dayton had questioned Vallandigham's loyalty, he chose to view the election returns as an endorsement of his course and his cause. Not only was Gillespie elected, but a Democratic resurgence seemed to be in process in most parts of the upper Midwest.[31]

The April election returns offered proof, Vallandigham believed, that the people were beginning to repudiate the Lincoln administration. "Gloomy as the prospect is," he wrote to ex-

---

[28] *San Francisco Bee* (n.d.), reprinted in *Dayton Daily Journal*, 5 March 1862.

[29] Peter Zinn to Benjamin F. Wade, 15 April 1861, Wade Papers.

[30] O. T. Fishback to Thomas O. Lowe, 22 April 1862, Thomas O. Lowe Papers, Dayton and Montgomery County Public Library; *Dayton Daily Journal*, 5 April 1862.

[31] *Dayton Daily Journal*, 4, 5 April 1862; *Crisis*, 16 April, 7 May 1862; entry of 9 April 1862, Medlar, "Journal."

President Pierce, "there is yet hope. The Democratic party was not dead; it only slept; but it is now stirring itself as the strong man rousing himself from his slumbers. Its success is our only hope. Yes, it is amazing that our people—Americans proud, boastful and free—should have submitted to usurpation and despotism which would have roused Greece even to resistance after two thousand years of servitude . . . . But, thank God, the regenerating spirit breathes again upon this people and we are young enough to recover all: *and we will*—I mean our public and private liberties. I hope for more."[32]

Encouraged, Vallandigham tried to rally his party and revive its prewar principles. Trying to step into the leadership void created in the party by Douglas's death, the Dayton congressman wrote a "call to action," and got thirty-five other congressional Democrats to sign the call and agree to a meeting date. Next he formed an ad hoc committee to prepare a statement of Democratic faith and tried to impose his antiwar views upon the other members. Some of the self-styled War Democrats, however, fully aware that Vallandigham's reputation as an antiwar man hurt rather than helped the party, used delaying tactics to nullify his leadership. Peeved and impenitent, Vallandigham then wrote a statement in collaboration with William A. Richardson of Illinois, tacked on the names of most Midwestern Democrats, and published it under the title "Address of the Democratic Members of the Congress to the Democracy of the United States." The document urged conciliation and compromises, recommended use of the ballot box to change the direction of events in the country, and asserted that states alone had the right to touch slavery ("domestic institutions"). The Vallandigham-Richardson address emphasized the worthiness of states' rights doctrine, restating the views of Jefferson and Calhoun. It tied the Democratic party to the past, promising to reconstruct the Union upon prewar ideas and with prewar institutions. It was further proof of Vallandigham's conservatism, uncomfortable with the revolution which was modifying the country's institutions. The document tried to foist the slogan "The Constitution as it is, the Union as it was" upon the Democratic party.[33]

Vallandigham's action helped to widen the schism already

[32] 11 April 1862, Pierce Papers.
[33] Published in the *Washington Intelligencer*, 8 May 1862.

existing within the Democratic party. Some of those whose names had been attached to the address were incensed or embarrassed. "I think no document ought to have been sent out," wrote one who found his name listed as a sponsor, "which was not acceptable to the majority of our party."[34] Astute Democrats like Manton Marble of the *New York World* recognized the weaknesses of the abortive document. It abounded with "uncandid aspersions" and failed to condemn the Southern rebels. Marble viewed the latter as inexcusable. He also recognized that the document was "a monstrous anachronism." "Its spirit," he asserted, "belongs not to the present but to the past."[35]

Republicans, wont to criticize Vallandigham at every opportunity, attacked the document with glee. Horace Greeley condemned it as a poisonous potion composed of "old party catchwords and phrases, . . . half-truths," and rank partisanship. "Slavery, imperilled by her own treason in the Slave States," Greeley wrote, "summons her trusty servitors in the Free States to the rescue."[36]

The hostile Washington atmosphere proved wearing to Vallandigham, affecting his disposition and making him long to be home again. "I wish I could get away from here," he wrote to his mother in mid-June, adding, "I am weary, very weary of it." Although worn and tired, he still nurtured the hope that peace and prosperity would revisit his war-torn and unhappy country. "I am still hopeful of the future," he insisted, "even amidst the darkness that surrounds us, and the evil and wickedness I see on every side." But thoughts of his "victories" over Benjamin F. Wade and John P. Hickman buoyed his spirits. "God has been very good to me in the midst of sore persecution," he wrote in closing, "and has delivered me out of the hands of my enemies, and given me the victory over them in every assault."[37]

Early in July, Vallandigham found an excuse to escape Washington's pressure-laden atmosphere. He left for Columbus to attend the Democratic State Convention. There he found many

[34] James A. Cravens to William H. English, 25 June 1862, William H. English Papers, Indiana State Historical Society, Indiana State Library, Indianapolis.

[35] *New York World*, 9, 13 May 1862.

[36] *New York Tribune*, 9 May 1862.

[37] Vallandigham to his mother, 14 June 1862, published in Vallandigham, *Vallandigham*, p. 211.

delegates optimistic about the future of the Democratic party. Indeed, it seemed as if a Democratic revival was in progress. The April election returns served as a stimulant. The failure of McClellan's peninsular campaign cost the Lincoln administration prestige. The economic depression of 1861-1862, affecting the Midwest brutally, touched many pocketbooks and caused some to transpose their economic grievances into political discontent. Democratic partisanship had become fashionable again.

Dayton delegates such as Bollmeyer of the *Empire* and Mayor Gillespie, two of Vallandigham's closest friends, gave him a warm welcome when he arrived at his hotel in Columbus late on July 3. That evening a crowd gathered in front of his hotel, gave him three cheers, and called for a speech. It was good for C.L.V.'s ego to feel wanted again. He lit into the Lincoln administration and the crowd repeatedly applauded his oratorical sallies. *144075*

The next morning he gave one of the principal addresses at the convention. He emphasized two themes, attacking abolitionism and "arbitrary government." The recent congressional session, he asserted, had done more for the cause of secessionism in six months "than Beauregard, and Lee, and Johnson, and all the Southern generals combined, had been able to accomplish in one year." He denounced arbitrary arrests, especially those of Ohio Democrats. The audience response emboldened him; he closed by asking Ohio Democrats to demand their rights and to maintain them at all hazards. Perhaps the nation needed a Runnymede or a John Hampton! It was a speech which breathed defiance and he received a tremendous ovation, proof that he had regained some of his lost luster and that his views had become more popular in Democratic circles. "He rises from persecution," wrote a sympathetic Democratic editor, "and attracts public notice and approbation from abuse."[38]

Vallandigham also served on the Committee on Resolutions, where he found the membership badly split on the question of war and peace. One faction, led by Samuel Medary of the *Crisis*, believed that the Union "was gone for good," that the army should be withdrawn from the South and an armistice arranged.

[38] *Crisis*, 9 July 1862; *Daily Ohio Statesman* (Columbus), 7 July 1862; *Ohio Patriot* (New Lisbon), 8 August 1862.

Medary argued that Lincoln ought to be impeached, either for violating the Constitution or for incompetence and idiocy. He even berated Vallandigham for failing to vote against all military bills or army appropriation measures. The "War Democrats," on the other hand, led by George W. Manypenny of the *Ohio Statesman*, believed that all efforts should be subordinated to two basic issues: defeating the rebels and restoring the Union. Army officers wearing Democratic buttons and on leave from their field assignments gave support to Manypenny's arguments. Vallandigham occupied a middle position. He believed that the Union might still be restored by compromise—that it was not lost forever. The Southern states, he felt, might still be enticed back into the Union by reasonable promises and concessions. The West, he warned, could never allow "a foreign power" to control the lower section of the Mississippi. He detested abolitionism. President Lincoln's many unconstitutional acts merited censure. His slogan was still "The Constitution as it is, the Union as it was."[39]

In time, the Committee on Resolutions hammered out its planks, taking strong stands against arbitrary arrests, "the abolition heresy," and Lincoln's "unconstitutional acts." The Democratic party had a monopoly on virtue, Republicans on vice.[40] In short, the resolutions seemed to restate the preachments which Vallandigham had earlier helped write into the "Address of the Democratic Members of Congress to the Democracy of the United States."

After the convention adjourned (1862 was not a gubernatorial election year in Ohio), most of the delegates took trains for home. Some of the delegates and visitors, however, spent the evening of "the glorious Fourth" in Columbus, drinking Democratic toasts. A crowd of celebrants visited Vallandigham's hotel and called for him to say a few words. He answered their calls by stepping out on the balcony, lighting into Lincoln and abolitionists, and appealing to political prejudices. The crowd loved it. This was his third speech in Columbus within twenty-four

[39] John D. Martin to Philip Ewing, 9 July 1862, Thomas Ewing Papers, Ohio Historical Society; *Crisis*, 12 December 1861; *Daily Ohio Statesman*, 7 July 1862; *Ohio State Journal* (Columbus), 8 July 1862.

[40] "Report of the Democratic State Convention, 1862," 4 July 1862, in Samuel Medary Papers, Ohio Historical Society.

hours, and each had been "a crowd-pleaser."[41] He may have been physically exhausted, but he was light at heart.

Vallandigham did not return to Washington for the closing weeks of Congress, which remained in session until July 17. Instead, he took the train to Dayton to be reunited with his family, to visit his friends, and to dispose of some business in his law office. He also wanted to take the necessary steps to insure his reelection to Congress. Events at the State Democratic Convention had renewed his conviction that he was right and the Republican congressmen wrong. No longer was he a voice crying in the wilderness, for growing dissatisfaction with the Lincoln administration and the war made some Democrats who had been most critical of him the previous summer stand at his side and pay him homage. He could again pose as a prophet and glory in the change of public opinion.

[41] *Crisis*, 9, 16 July 1862; *Daily Ohio Statesman*, 9, 16 July 1862.

8

DEFEATING THE DISSENTER

HEARTENED BY THE RESURGENCE of the Democratic party, as revealed at the state convention, C.L.V. was eager to begin his campaign for reelection. Yet he knew that the odds were against him because earlier that year a Republican-dominated state legislature had redrawn district lines, dropping Preble County from the Third District and adding Warren, with the express purpose of defeating him.[1] Preble County held about an equal number of Republicans and Democrats, whereas Warren was strong Republican country. Most of its voters (at least three-fourths) had been Whigs and the antislavery movement had prospered there. Since Vallandigham had gained reelection in 1860 by a very narrow margin, he had a Herculean task upon his hands.

The Dayton congressman got off to a good start in his bid for renomination and reelection. Dayton friends, including Mayor Gillespie and editor Bollmeyer, arranged for a Democratic rally and engaged the city's largest hall. The *Empire's* editorials and party posters brought in an overflow crowd and the smiling sponsors moved the meeting to the Courthouse grounds. In time the presiding officer called Vallandigham to the platform and the Democratic audience gave him thunderous applause.[2]

He began his speech moderately enough, advising his listeners to follow dual roads: vote the Democratic ticket and obey the laws. "Whosoever should be drafted, should a draft be ordered according to the Constitution and the law," said Vallandigham, "is duty bound . . . to . . . go; he has no right to resist and none to run away."[3] He did not advise his fellow Ohioans to defy the enrolling officers, to destroy the machinery of the draft, or to resist the authorities. As a well-trained lawyer, he had respect for the law. He would even take time out to make some speeches to help raise troop quotas assigned to Ohio, and he always advised malcontents to obey the laws.[4]

After paying his respects to law and order, he turned to the business of excoriating the Lincoln administration. He blamed the president's party for high taxes, depreciated currency, and bad economic conditions. Then he lashed out at the abolition measures passed during the last session of congress and Republican calls for more and more of the same; he drove the spit into Abolition, burning it to a crisp with his fiery ridicule. He also spent some time condemning Lincoln's suspension of the writ of habeas corpus and the arbitrary arrests perpetrated in Ohio. He restated his views on compromise, asking for a restoration of the Union with a Constitution untarnished and with civil rights fully revived. He wanted "the dear old flag" to fly again in every state and "honored once again in every land and upon every sea." He ended, however, with a show of defiance, demanding every civil right guaranteed in the Constitution. He would not bow to threat of arrest nor the intimidation of Republican rowdies. Even the menacing knife of the assassin could not change his convictions. He was willing to be a martyr for his political views. He had been born a freeman and he proposed to die one![5]

Vallandigham had no trouble in securing the Democratic nomination at the Third District convention of September 4 in Hamilton. No one else sought the honor, all recognizing that the "gerrymander bill" had given the Republicans an edge in the district. Yet at the Hamilton meeting there was plenty of enthusiasm and some false optimism. The Democratic resurgence and Vallandigham's apparent popularity plagued Republican editors. "Of course it [Vallandigham's nomination] was very enthusiastically done," wrote the resentful editor of the *Dayton Journal*, "for such a political trickster pulls the wires to suit himself. He has determined to ride rough shod over every principle of true Democracy, and has given ample evidence that he will stickle at no means of self-aggrandizement."[6]

Vallandigham did not have to wait long to learn who his

---

1 William G. Beggs to Samuel S. Cox, 25 March 1862, Samuel S. Cox Papers (microfilm), Hayes Memorial Library, Fremont, Ohio; *Crisis* (Columbus), 30 April 1862.

2 *Dayton Daily Empire*, 4 August 1862; *Dayton Daily Journal*, 4 August 1862.

3 *Dayton Daily Empire*, 4 August 1862.

4 Thomas O. Lowe to his brother William, 6 September 1862, Thomas O. Lowe Papers, Dayton and Montgomery County Public Library.

5 *Dayton Daily Empire*, 4 August 1862; *Crisis*, 13 August 1862.

6 *Dayton Daily Journal*, 5 September 1962.

Republican opponent would be. He had hoped it would be Lewis D. Campbell or Samuel Craighead, both of whom he had defeated in earlier contests. Republicans, including President Lincoln and Secretary of the Treasury Salmon P. Chase, wanted Vallandigham retired from Congress, and both took a hand in pushing General Robert C. Schenck into the congressional race.

Schenck was a well-known Ohioan. As a Whig he had served four terms in the House of Representatives (1843-1851), gaining there the friendship and confidence of Congressman Abraham Lincoln. Later, 1851-1853, he had served as minister to Brazil, his mission terminating when a Democratic president took office following the election of 1852. In time he became a strong antislavery man, a respected lawyer, and an effective orator. With the coming of the war, Schenck raised a regiment, President Lincoln favored him with an appointment as brigadier general, and he marched off to war.

To friends who urged him to run for congress against Vallandigham, Schenck turned a deaf ear. Then, as if fate had intervened, an incident occurred on the battlefield at Second Bull Run. Late on the afternoon of August 30, while Schenck was gallantly rallying his troops, a fragment of grapeshot struck his right hand. The shot tore an ugly hole just above the wrist and knocked Schenck's sword to the ground. A plucky aide retrieved the sword and bandaged the wound, and the courageous general urged his troops forward, waving the weapon in his left hand. In time, Brigadier-General Schenck was led to the rear, hustled off to Washington, and quartered in Willard's Hotel. Next morning a doctor examined the wound, found bones broken and tendons severed, and reported that it would be several months before the anxious general could regain the use of his right hand and return to the front lines.

While Schenck lay in his hotel room cursing his luck, some notable visitors called. Edwin M. Stanton, the secretary of war, paid his respects and the two reminisced about their earlier Ohio days. Chase, who kept his hand deeply immersed in the muddied waters of Ohio politics, also called. He recognized that Schenck's ill-fortune on the battlefield might be turned into good fortune in the political arena, and urged Schenck to run for Congress in the Third District, saying, "You are the only man who can beat that traitor Vallandigham."[7]

President Lincoln also called upon Schenck, trying to convince him that he could do a greater service by sidetracking Vallandigham than by leading a brigade on the battlefield. Furthermore, the president assured Schenck that a major general's commission would soon be his. Schenck, although Vallandigham's neighbor in Dayton, bowed to the pressure exerted by Chase and Lincoln. The Republicans subsequently named him their congressional candidate at "a Union convention" in Middletown on September 9, praising him as a man "wise in council and brave in battle."[8]

Vallandigham, recognizing that the nomination of Schenck raised the odds against his reelection, nevertheless rode forth bravely into battle. The Democrats had some strange allies during the fall election campaign. Union military failures enabled critics to question Lincoln's competency as commander-in-chief. Robert E. Lee and "Stonewall" Jackson soundly whipped the Army of the Potomac at Second Bull Run on August 29-30, inflicting heavy losses on the Union troops and giving General John Pope a lesson in strategy and tactics. Less than a month later, the Army of the Potomac checked Lee's first invasion of the North at Antietam Creek on September 17, but the long, long Union casualty rolls prevented Lincoln from claiming a true victory. Events in the West were equally discouraging. Confederate General Braxton Bragg conducted a spectacular flanking movement against General Don Carlos Buell's troops, causing the Union army to fall back all the way from northern Alabama to Louisville. Confederates scored a political coup by installing a secessionist governor in Frankfort, Kentucky. Overall, the Union status in the West was considerably worse than it had been a year earlier. Defeatism began to undermine Union morale and Democratic critics of the Lincoln administration stood to reap the harvest.

The economic recession of 1861-1862, especially in the upper Midwest, also served as a Democratic ally. The war boom had not yet fully counteracted the devastating effects of the agricultural, commercial, and banking slump produced by the closing of the Mississippi River and the secession of the Southern states. Sky-high freight rates charged by the east-west railroad lines prevented Midwest farmers from benefitting from the European demands for American foodstuffs. These high rates also gave Western sectionalists such as Vallandigham and Samuel Medary a chance to denounce Eastern capital and New England manufacturers. The editor of the *Crisis* repeatedly reminded his readers that the selfish Northeast had driven Southern states out of the Union and now tried to make the West its "slave and servant." New England capital and Northeastern manufacturing extended "their tentacles" westward, imposing a heavy penalty upon a Midwest which had once held the balance of power in the national capital. Vallandigham, like Medary, appealed to sectional prejudice whenever he saw a chance to get more votes.[9]

Vallandigham also knew how to appeal to racial prejudice. Six of the resolutions which had been adopted on July 4 at the State Democratic Convention had condemned abolition. Democratic editors also catered to the anti-Negro prejudice of the working man. "If the laboring men of this State do not desire their places occupied by negroes," wrote one Democratic editor, "they will vote for the nominees of the Democratic ticket."[10] Another, in an editorial entitled "Abolition, the Worst Enemy of the Free White Laborers," ended with a call to action: "Workmen! Be careful! Organize yourself against this element which threatens your impoverishment and annihilation."[11] One of Vallandigham's Dayton apostles revised the Democratic slogan to show his racial prejudice: "The Constitution as it is, the Union as it was, *and the Niggers where they are.*"[12]

Anti-Negro prejudice underwrote race riots in two Ohio cities during the summer of 1862. One broke out in Toledo, where employers hired "contrabands" (Negroes freed by the war) as

[9] Frank L. Klement, "Economic Aspects of Middle Western Copperheadism," *The Historian* 14 (Autumn 1951): 27-44; and idem, "Middle Western Copperheadism and the Genesis of the Granger Movement," *Mississippi Valley Historical Review* 38 (March 1952): 679-94; both articles explore the relationship between economics and politics in the upper Mississippi Valley.

[10] *Cincinnati Daily Enquirer*, 4 August 1862.

[11] *See-Bote* (Milwaukee), 23 April 1862.

[12] Thomas O. Lowe to his brother William, 2 July 1862, Lowe Papers.

strike-breakers and "scab labor." The Cincinnati riot was even
more serious; it extended over several days and ended in the
burning of many homes in Shantytown, the Negro sector of
Cincinnati.[13]

Lincoln's preliminary proclamation of emancipation of September 22, 1862, issued during the election campaign, furnished
more arguments for Vallandigham and other Democrats to stir
the anti-Negro prejudices of Midwesterners. "This is another
step in the nigger business," wrote one of Vallandigham's supporters, "and another advance in the Robespierrian highway of
tyranny and anarchy."[14] Vallandigham, who had predicted that
the president would bow to abolition pressure and add a new
dimension to the war, pointed with scorn to Lincoln's proclamation and shouted, "I told you so!"[15]

Vallandigham's antiabolition and anti-New England arguments
had a strong appeal to three elements of the Midwest's population. The Irish-Americans in the cities feared that abolition
would release a flood of "cheap labor" to compete for the crumbs
on their tables. Irish stevedores in Toledo and Irish boathands in
Cincinnati instigated the anti-Negro riots in those cities in July
of 1862. In addition, Irish-Americans had little respect for
Puritanism, which they associated with New England. They
objected to New England's efforts to impose temperance upon
the country and they detested the holier-than-thou attitudes
expressed by the Yankees. Furthermore, the Republican party
was tainted with Know-Nothingism. Irish Catholics, under the
prompting of Democrats like Vallandigham, learned to detest
abolition and New England, voted the straight Democratic ticket,
and became the backbone of the "Copperhead" movement in
the cities.[16]

Many German-Americans, especially those of the Catholic

[13] *Cincinnati Daily Commercial*, 11, 16-17 July 1862. William H. Lofton,
"Northern Labor and the Negro during the Civil War," *Journal of Negro History*
39 (July 1949): 251-73; Frank L. Klement, "Midwestern Opposition to Lincoln's
Emancipation Policy," *Journal of Negro History* 49 (July 1964): 169-83; V.
Jacque Voegeli, *Free but Not Equal* (Chicago, 1967); all deal with the subject
of racism and politics.

[14] *Stark County Democrat* (Canton), 24 September 1862.

[15] *Dayton Daily Journal*, 14 October 1862.

[16] Frank L. Klement, *The Copperheads in the Middle West* (Chicago, 1960)
examines the socio-economic base for Democratic opposition to the Lincoln administration.

faith, formed the second important element in the Democratic party. They had the same reasons for hating abolitionists, New Englanders, and Republicans as the Irish-Americans had. "The jealousy of the low Germans and Irish against the free negro," wrote a foreign newspaper correspondent, "was sufficient to set them against the war which would have brought four million of their black rivals into competition for that hard and dirty work which American freedom bestows upon them."[17]

Upland Southerners who crossed the Ohio River to preempt the poorer soils of Ohio, Indiana, and Illinois formed the third element of the Midwest's population who readily accepted anti-abolition or anti-New England preachments. They brought their anti-Negro prejudices with them and supported state laws which denied the black man citizenship rights. They became the "Butternuts" of the backcountry, known for hating Negroes, liking "corn licker," and voting the Democratic ticket. The areas where they lived were characterized by poorer soils, smaller homesteads, and more widespread illiteracy. They mistrusted the sons and scions of New England who wanted to refashion the cultural practices of others in line with the Yankee image. They became "the unterrified, unwashed Democracy," applauding those speakers most adept at abusing abolition and upbraiding New England. Vallandigham developed a rapport with these backwoods settlers, catering to their prejudices and building a bond of affection. They turned out en masse to hear him, and he came to regard himself as their champion and spokesman, the representative of the common man.[18]

Vallandigham had no difficulty in convincing Irish-Americans, German Catholics, and Butternuts that they should hate abolitionists and New Englanders. It was more difficult to convince them that Lincoln's suspension of the writ of habeas corpus and arbitrary arrests should raise their ire. After a number of Ohioans were arrested and carted off to prison, it was easier for the

---

[17] *London Times*, 1 December 1863. The correspondent was that noted English observer, William H. Russell.

[18] John L. Stipp put the historical microscope upon the Democratic areas of Ohio in his excellent doctoral dissertation, "Economic and Political Aspects of Western Copperheadism" (Ohio State University, 1942). The conflict of Southern and Yankee culture is admirably treated in Richard L. Power, *Planting Corn Belt Culture: The Impress of the Upland Southerner and Yankee in the Old Northwest* (Indianapolis, 1953).

Dayton congressman to make the point that civil rights were vanishing and a despotism developing. John W. Kees of the *Circleville Watchman* and Dr. Edson B. Olds of the *Ohio Eagle* in Lancaster found themselves behind bars for speaking too critically of the Lincoln administration. Several other arrests struck closer to home. Taylor Webster, a law student in Dayton and son of one of Vallandigham's closest friends, was imprisoned for contending that abolitionists had brought on the war and that Democrats ought not to help Republicans coerce the South. Two Presbyterian clergymen, guests in Vallandigham's home in late July, were arrested in early August in Cincinnati and accused of spying for the Confederacy—rather ridiculous charges. The officials who arrested the clergymen found no evidence that the two belonged to "an association of traitor spies to furnish information for the Southern army"; the searchers did find several of Vallandigham's congressional speeches in the prisoners' carpet bags. Although embarrassed officials apologized to the two clergymen, released them, and sent them on their way to Loveland, Ohio, the incident aroused Vallandigham. They had been, said the indignant congressman, arrested "without accusation or legal authority, . . . incarcerated like felons" and searched "like criminals." Vallandigham, therefore, joined other Democrats in demanding that the voters rebuke the administration for violating citizens' rights and ignoring constitutional guarantees.[19]

Republicans tried to stem the Democratic resurgence by appealing to patriotism, and to cover President Lincoln's transgressions by waving the flag vigorously. Democratic critics of the administration were accused of opposing the government—in Republican parlance the two were one and the same. Vallandigham, of course, received much of the Republican fire. The editors of the *Dayton Journal* and the *Cincinnati Gazette* led the Republican effort to discredit the controversial congressman. They depicted him as "a contemptible traitor," "a de-

[19] Vallandigham, quoted in *Dayton Daily Journal*, 4 August 1862; *Ohio Eagle* (Lancaster), 8 January 1863. Also see "Report of the Select Committee on Military Arrests," in *Journal of the House of Representatives of the State of Ohio* (Columbus, 1863). Elden R. Young, "Arbitrary Arrests during the Civil War" (master's thesis, Ohio State University, 1924), has too little on arrests of 1862 in Ohio; and Dean Sprague, *Freedom under Lincoln* (Boston, 1965) does not even mention the arrest of Rev. James H. Brooks, Rev. Robert Hoyt, and Taylor Webster.

fender of secession," "a pro-slavery apologist," and "a friend of Jeff Davis." They made name-calling an art, and claimed that a vote for Vallandigham was a vote to prolong the war, to put Jefferson Davis in the White House, and to institute a conscription system. "Let the infamous Vallandigham, whose *votes* convict him of no sympathy for the Union [and] whose *speeches* convict him of being in the full confidence of the conspirators," wrote one Republican propagandist, ". . . retire from public life as one of the infamous trinity—*Arnold, Burr,* and *Vallandigham.*"[20]

Republican editors often took Vallandigham's statements out of context, misdated and misquoted his speeches and statements, and even attributed letters to his pen which he had never written. On the eve of the election the Republican press published a forged letter, supposedly written by Vallandigham to a Southern congressman, indicating that he sympathized with secession and supported the rebel cause. Some papers published it on the morning of election day, so that the man maligned would have no chance to repudiate the document before voters marched to the polls.

Republican newspapers also circulated the rumor that Vallandigham had been arrested and evidence unearthed which proved he was guilty of "disloyalty" and had been involved in "treasonable plots." The story, devised in the telegraph office in Dayton, reached even the New York newspapers. Vallandigham, learning that "the lie" had been sent as a "special" to the *New York Herald,* rushed a denial to James Gordon Bennett: "Sir— I thank you for your former courtesies and am sorry to trouble you again. But persistent lying demands continual contradiction. The statement that I was 'arrested' and that I was implicated in 'treasonable plots,' or in any other thing 'disloyal' is an imprudent fabrication of the anonymous scoundrel who telegraphed it. How long is the telegraph to be prostituted to such infamous falsehoods?"[21] Although Bennett's *New York Herald* published Vallandigham's denial, most Republican newspapers in Ohio played a different game. They published the rumors and lies

20 Pamphlet (author unknown), "The Secession Record of C. L. Vallandigham" (Dayton, 1862). The document probably came off the presses of the *Dayton Journal.*
21 *New York Herald,* 5 August 1862.

but ignored Vallandigham's repudiation of them, for they wanted the rumors to make the rounds and influence the election.

Another outright lie which circulated in the Republican press linked Vallandigham to the Knights of the Golden Circle, a supposedly subversive and secret pro-Southern society with castles in the upper Middle West.[22] It was even asserted that "the wily one" was the head of that organization, believed to be involved in a grand plan to take the upper Midwest out of the Union.

Republicans seemed to invent stories and lies about Vallandigham faster than he could deny them. "I know," wrote one of the Dayton congressman's disciples, "that almost every charge brought against him has no foundation than the most unscrupulous lying."[23] Perhaps it was proof of the axiom that all is fair in love, war, and politics.

The Republican campaign to unseat Vallandigham received an assist from Lincoln. He made Vallandigham's opponent a major general and endorsed his heroics at Second Bull Run. Republicans sought to influence voters by discussing Schenck's wound, and, of course, they compared his patriotic course with that of Vallandigham, a brigadier general (in the Ohio militia) who stayed home to light a fire in the rear.[24]

On October 14, a gray autumnal day, Ohioans marched to the polls and Vallandigham lost his bid for reelection as Schenck carried the Third District by more than 600 votes. C.L.V. even trailed the Democratic state slate by 400 votes in his own district in a year when Democrats gained ground everywhere in the Midwest. Democrats in Ohio helped their party's resurgence; they won fourteen of nineteen congressional seats and elected their slate of state officers. The incumbent congressman from Dayton lost a battle while Democrats were winning a war. Two neighboring states, Indiana and Pennsylvania, also rebuked President Lincoln in October elections, and other states, includ-

---

[22] The Golden Circle legend is debunked in part in Klement, *Copperheads in the Middle West*, pp. 134-49, 244-45, and in a series of articles by the same author appearing in state historical quarterlies, for example, "Carrington and the Golden Circle Legend in Indiana during the Civil War," *Indiana Magazine of History* 61 (March 1965): 31-52.

[23] Thomas O. Lowe to his brother William, 6 September 1862, Lowe Papers.

[24] *Dayton Daily Journal*, 6-8, 10, 13 October 1862.

ing Illinois and New York, did the same in November. Democrats offered the election returns as proof that the people rejected emancipation, arbitrary arrest, and military incompetency.[25]

Vallandigham's friends rejoiced in the anti-Republican trend, but expressed disappointment in his defeat at the hands of Schenck. "The loss the Democracy have sustained in the defeat of the Hon. C. L. Vallandigham," wrote one dejected supporter, "is a national calamity."[26]

Friends offered a variety of reasons for his defeat. Some admitted that the treason campaign against him had paid dividends. Supporters in earlier years had turned their backs upon him in 1862. His friends might defend him, but they could not deny that some of the statements he had made had been used against him, endangering his own political future and damaging the cause of the Democratic party.

Then, of course, there was the gerrymandering—substituting Warren County for Preble County in the redistricting. The incumbent received a 1,320-vote margin in Montgomery and Butler counties, but Warren County, where Schenck carried every township, tipped the scales to defeat Vallandigham. Samuel Medary suggested the real reason for Vallandigham's defeat in the *Crisis:* "The abolitionists have only this satisfaction," he wrote. "They beat him by *legislation,* not by voting."[27]

Republicans, who found very little in the '62 election returns to cheer about, therefore made much of Vallandigham's defeat, calling it "glory enough for one day."[28] After he finished serving in the lame-duck session, he would "no longer pollute the national capitol."[29] The editor of the *Buckeye State,* published in New Lisbon, where Vallandigham had been born and grown to man-

[25] Many historians have dealt with the theme that the 1862 election returns repudiated Lincolnian policy. See, for example, Harry E. Pratt, "The Repudiation of Lincoln's War Policy—the Stuart-Swett Congressional Campaign," *Journal of the Illinois State Historical Society* 24 (April 1931): 129-40; and Winfred A. Harbison, "The Election of 1862 as a Want of Confidence in President Lincoln," *Papers of the Michigan Academy of Sciences, Arts, and Letters,* 1930, pp. 499-513.

[26] Arthur T. Goodman to Alexander Long, 28 October 1862, Alexander Long Papers, Cincinnati Historical Society.

[27] *Crisis,* 22 October 1862. Early in 1862 the editor of the *Daily Ohio Statesman* (Columbus) (issue of 9 May 1862) labeled the redistricting bill "an infamous swindle." The charge was grossly partisan, but there was a deliberate effort to change the Third District lines to bring about Vallandigham's defeat.

[28] *Ohio State Journal* (Columbus), 16 October 1862.

[29] *Cleveland Leader,* 17 October 1862.

hood, wrote an editorial thanking God for the fellow's defeat, claiming he was an agent of Satan rather than the spokesman for many Ohio Democrats:

> Let Union men all over the country rejoice, and let the heart of the nation be exceedingly glad! That arch-traitor and chief of Copperheads—that pimp of Jeff. Davis and standing disgrace to his State, Clem Vallandigham, is laid out cold and stark in the embrace of political death. No longer will the presence of this renegade miscreant in the legislative halls of the nation, outrage the loyal men of our State, nor his name be accounted a tower of strength to the enemies of the Republic. The people have sealed his doom, and given him the *coup de grace*. He is dead, dead, dead —and a loyal people will bury him so deep in the mire of his own infamy, that the stench from his putrid carcass will never offend the nostrils of good men, nor the recollection of his treason and perfidy tarnish the fair fame of the State he has so long mis-represented and dishonored. To the good cause of Union, his defeat more than counterbalances all that is lost in the defeat of our State ticket, and to the butternuts his loss is utterly irrepar-able. Let the friends of the Union thank God and take courage.[30]

Vallandigham, abused in defeat as he had been during the campaign, did not openly show his disappointment. Instead, he made the rounds of Democratic jollifications, telling his audiences that the election results repudiated Lincoln and ad-ministration policies, including emancipation and arbitrary ar-rests. He spoke at party "celebrations" in Dayton, Mount Vernon, Hamilton, Hillsborough, and Centreville, Indiana. He always claimed that the election results made Democratic principles respectable again, and never failed to add that he still supported the tenet "The Constitution as it is, the Union as it was." He always developed a rapport with his audience, repeatedly bring-ing forth "wild and enthusiastic applause." This emotional response served as an intoxicant for which he developed an insatiable craving. Often he spoke for three hours, and the more he talked the more he convinced himself of the rectitude of his views and that the Lincoln administration, backed by abolitionists and revolutionaries, was leading the country down the road to ruin. And members of his audience, seeking endorse-ment of their prejudices, cheered him when he denounced aboli-

[30] 28 October 1862.

tionists, Republicans, and Negroes. Their applause encouraged him to practice partyism and racism.[31]

Late in October, C.L.V. took the train to New Lisbon to keep a speaking engagement, to give the lie to editorials in the *Buckeye State,* and to visit his brothers and his aging mother. Democrats arranged an impressive homecoming which featured a parade and a mass meeting. Vallandigham rode in a bedecked carriage at the head of the two-mile-long procession and gave a rousing speech at the enormous rally. New Lisbon paid tribute to her son, even though he had been defeated in the October 14 election.

Several days later, while he was relaxing at his mother's home, word of a Dayton tragedy reached him via the telegraph wires. J. Frederick Bollmeyer, whom C.L.V. had brought to Dayton to edit the *Empire,* had been shot by a Republican neighbor during a personal argument. Vallandigham hurried back to Dayton to help bury his friend and to make political capital out of the tragedy. He chose to interpret the shooting as "a political assassination" rather than a personal quarrel. It was, he said, "abolition revenge" for the defeats suffered in the Ohio elections. Bollmeyer had paid for his political principles with his life, and his death was but the opening incident in a campaign to deprive Democrats of their lives and their freedoms.[32] Vallandigham talked like a demagogue, trying to whip up passions and indignation. He talked himself into a corner, in fact, emerging as less than the self-disciplined gentleman he imagined himself to be.

After Bollmeyer was buried and affairs in his law office were in order, Vallandigham prepared to leave for Washington to attend the lame-duck session of the Thirty-seventh Congress. Dayton friends organized a "handsome entertainment" in the home of Judge William Morris as a farewell tribute. Thomas O. Lowe, on behalf of the ladies of the city, presented his political patron with a gold-headed cane, suitably inscribed. His friends assured C.L.V. that his views still were those of the Ohio Democ-

31 *Crisis,* 12 November 1862; *Dayton Daily Empire,* 20, 24, 29 October 1862.

32 *Hamilton True Telegraph,* 6, 13 November 1862; *Ohio State Journal,* 7 November 1862; *Crisis,* 26 November 1862; *Cincinnati Daily Enquirer,* 4 November 1862; Carl M. Becker, "The Death of J. F. Bollmeyer: Murder Most Foul?" *Bulletin of the Cincinnati Historical Society* 24 (July 1966): 249-69.

racy, that the country still opposed emancipation and arbitrary arrests and still looked toward compromise rather than war as a means to restore the Union. Some also assured him that they wanted him to be the state's next governor.[33]

With the cheers of his friends still ringing in his ears, Vallandigham entrained for Washington via Philadelphia. He stayed overnight at the Continental Hotel in the City of Brotherly Love. Philadelphia Democrats knew of his presence in their city and hundreds called upon the congressman from Dayton to pay their respects. They made him feel like a hero rather than a politician defeated in the recent elections. Some encouraged him to organize a crusade for peace. Others lionized him because they believed him a victim of Republican-sponsored hysteria. It was salve for a sore heart.

Next morning Vallandigham departed for Washington to resume his role of Gadfly. He was also destined to be the instigator of a peace crusade—to become a symbol as well as a congressman.

[33] Lowe's speech is given in Vallandigham, *Vallandigham*, pp. 218-21.

9

APOSTLE FOR PEACE

THE FINAL SESSION of the Thirty-seventh Congress convened at noon on Monday, December 1, 1862. Vallandigham
sat at his desk, smiling at friends and foes. "Old Thad" Stevens,
the fiery radical whip who bore his seventy winters well,
hobbled down the aisle. The smiling face of Schuyler Colfax
beamed at his friends, nodded to his enemies. The sturdy form
of Elihu B. Washburne, reputed to be in the confidence of President Lincoln, cast a long shadow, even at noontime. John P. Hickman, the Pennsylvanian whom Vallandigham had twice bested
in House encounters, fumed at his desk, awaiting a chance for
revenge. The Republicans controlled the machinery of legislation, so Vallandigham and the Democrats would be able to
do little more than cast minority votes.[1]

After the usual preliminaries, the House listened to the reading
of President Lincoln's message. Two things in it disturbed
Vallandigham and other conservatives. The president refused to
retract his emancipation proclamation, despite the fact that the
fall elections in the upper midwest had apparently repudiated
that policy. "The tenacity with which Mr. Lincoln holds on
to his emancipation proclivities," wrote one conservative Democrat, "cannot fail, I think, to alarm the friends of the Union
and of Constitutional liberty throughout our land."[2]

The conservatives' second concern was with some rather radical
statements in the message. "The dogmas of the quiet past," the
message stated in one place, "are inadequate to the stormy
present . . . . As our case is new, we must think anew. We must
disenthrall our selves and then we shall save our country."[3] Did
Lincoln have some new radical measures up his sleeve? Conservatives thought of the French Revolution and shuddered.

When Justin A. Morrill of Vermont moved to have President
Lincoln's message printed, Vallandigham rose to ask for a debate.
He wanted a public opportunity to express his displeasure with

certain sections of the message and with presidential policy. But Morrill refused to yield the floor to the congressman from Ohio, so the gadfly missed an opportunity to harass the administration.

Soon afterwards, Vallandigham introduced a resolution to investigate the postmaster general's practice of closing the mails to some Democratic newspapers, especially those most critical of the Lincoln administration. He was pleased that the resolution won House approval, perhaps because some radical Republicans never missed an opportunity to kick Postmaster General Montgomery Blair in the shins.[4]

Vallandigham was less successful, however, in helping other recalcitrant Democrats secure the passage of two partisan resolutions. One requested a report from the president on arbitrary arrests; the other accused Lincoln of usurping authority and violating the Constitution. Administration forces closed ranks and tabled both resolutions.[5]

Several days later C.L.V. was back at his old game of trying to discredit Lincoln and his policies—acting as gadfly and obstructionist. On December 6 he introduced a package of six resolutions which accused the president of "attempting to establish a dictatorship," reprimanded him for interfering with "established institutions" (that is, slavery), and instructed him to refuse any peace or compromise which would recognize the independence of the Confederacy.

As these resolutions indicated, Vallandigham was not yet a peace-at-any-price man. Reports had circulated in the lobbies and cloakrooms that Secretary of State Seward intended to negotiate a "peace" which would acquiesce in Southern independence. As a Westerner, Vallandigham could never permit a foreign power, whether England or the Confederate States of America, to control the lower half of the Mississippi River.

---

[1] Washington correspondent, in *Ohio State Journal* (Columbus), 2 December 1862; *New York Independent*, 4 December 1862.

[2] Thomas Dudley to John J. Crittenden, 8 December 1862, John J. Crittenden Papers, Library of Congress.

[3] Lincoln, "Annual Message to Congress," 1 December 1862, in James D. Richardson, ed., *A Compilation of the Messages and Papers of the Presidents*, 10 vols. (New York, 1896-1899), 8: 3343.

[4] *Congressional Globe*, 37 Cong., 3 sess., pp. 2-3.

[5] Ibid., p. 3.

Fearful that the rumors were actually a trial balloon of the administration, the Dayton congressman put his opposition into the record. From the very first, he had desired peace *and reunion,* not peace and separation. Needless to say, the Republican majority in the House of Representatives quickly disposed of the six resolutions, tabling them by a strict party vote of 79 to 50.[6]

Vallandigham next joined Samuel S. Cox in trying to obtain freedom for Dr. Edson B. Olds, an Ohio citizen being held in solitary confinement in Fort Lafayette in the national capital. Cox, who represented the Columbus district in Congress, and Vallandigham both knew Dr. Olds as a longtime, respected Democrat from Lancaster and as editor of the outspoken *Ohio Eagle.* Vallandigham's friendship dated back to the years when the two served in the Ohio legislature, defending "Polk's War" against Whig onslaughts. Later Dr. Olds served three terms as a congressman, winning a reputation for criticizing abolitionists and radicals who put themselves above the law. After the Civil War started, Dr. Olds wrote strong anti-Lincoln editorials for the *Ohio Eagle* and denounced the administration from the lecture platforms. In 1862 he directed much of his criticism at "the Kentucky situation," where Union soldiers engaged in nightly marauding and Union generals imposed a military dictatorship. Olds contended that the high-handed tactics of the generals and troops changed Kentucky Unionists into secessionists.

Some Republicans in Lancaster convinced Secretary of War Edwin M. Stanton that Dr. Olds's pen should be stilled and his tongue silenced. During the night of August 12, 1862, three federal agents broke into his home and arrested him, treating him like a criminal rather than a well-known Ohio citizen.[7] Vallandigham, Cox, and a dozen other prominent Ohio Democrats had formulated a protest, drafting a petition to President Lincoln that asked him to intercede in behalf of simple justice for Dr. Olds. Lincoln chose to ignore that petition.[8] In mid-December Vallandigham joined other Democratic congressmen

6 Ibid.
7 Olds's detailed account of his arrest and imprisonment is included in John A. Marshall, *American Bastile: A History of Illegal Arrests and Imprisonments of American Citizens during the Late Civil War* (Philadelphia, 1878), pp. 586-605.
8 *Dayton Daily Empire,* 17 December 1862; Olds to Cox, 5 December 1862, Samuel S. Cox Papers (microfilm), Hayes Memorial Library, Fremont, Ohio.

in the bid to gain Dr. Olds's release, but the wheels of justice moved slowly—seemed, in fact, to be at a standstill. While the prisoner languished in a felon's cell, the death of a state senator in Dr. Olds's district created a vacancy and necessitated a special election. Olds's friends, viewing him as a martyr, nominated the incarcerated Democrat for the legislative post, which he won by 2500 votes over a Republican opponent. It was the largest vote ever given to a candidate in Fairfield County. Dr. Olds's resounding election victory embarrassed the administration, and the secretary of war ordered his quiet release on December 20. Olds's friends then prepared a gala homecoming reception for the ex-prisoner, and the shouts and cheers reverberated all the way to Washington, giving heart to Clement L. Vallandigham. The Dayton congressman noted that Dr. Olds's arrest seemed to have made him a hero—a martyr for the principle of free speech. It brought Olds publicity and political rewards. The lesson made a deep impression upon Vallandigham.

Democratic contentions that President Lincoln's emergency measures had violated the Constitution prompted Republican leaders to try to put a blanket of approval over them. Thaddeus Stevens drafted a bill to expiate "the President and other persons for suspending the writ of habeas corpus." This so-called Indemnity Bill met Democratic resistance in the House. Vallandigham, in his turn, arose to challenge the bill and stated his unequivocal opposition to it. He again offered the six resolutions he had introduced on December 5 as a substitute for the sections of the Indemnity Bill. By mutual consent, the House members postponed the consideration of Stevens's resolutions and Vallandigham's amendments until "the first Monday of January, 1863."[9]

Vallandigham took a firm stand against two other Republican-sponsored measures which were debated in the House in the closing weeks of December 1862. One was a bill to welcome West Virginia into the Union, thereby sanctioning the president's use of "military force and political puppets" to create a new state out of a portion of an old one. C.L.V., like other Democrats, believed Lincoln's action in bringing the new state into being unconstitutional and based upon pretense rather than fact.

[9] *Congressional Globe*, 37 Cong., 2 sess., pp. 14, 20, 22, 104.

The Republican majority ignored the carping criticism of conservative Democrats and by a 96 to 55 vote added a new star to the flag.[10] The action put the stamp of approval on the questionable tactics which had carved Virginia in two; it also increased the Republican majority in Congress and contributed to offsetting Democratic gains in the '62 congressional elections.

The second measure concerned Lincoln's efforts to free the slaves by proclamation. Democratic congressmen, especially those from the border states, still criticized the preliminary emancipation proclamation of September 22 and still sought to dissuade the president from issuing the definitive one on January 1, 1863. A Kentucky congressman, therefore, introduced a resolution which characterized the proclamation as an ill-timed, illegal, and intolerable transaction. Vallandigham too believed presidential emancipation unwarranted, unnecessary, devisive, and unconstitutional. He believed it would discourage enlistments, breed discontent in the border states, unite the South to a man, and dampen the war effort in the North. It would make peace, compromise, and reunion more difficult to achieve. After tabling the antiemancipation resolution by an 81 to 53 vote, Republicans countered by bringing forth a statement which endorsed Lincoln's emancipation policy; the president's policy, it declared, was "well adopted to hasten the restoration of peace, well chosen as a war measure, and had proper regard for the rights of citizens and the prosperity of a free government." The resolution carried, 78 to 51. Vallandigham cast one of the votes against it.[11]

The Dayton congressman left Washington only once in December. In the company of George H. Pendleton, another Democratic congressman from Ohio, he took a hurried trip to New York to visit the Wood brothers and speak at a rally which they had organized. The Wood brothers, who controlled the *New York News,* also tried to control the city's Democratic organization. Fernando Wood, previously a three-term mayor of New York City, had won a congressional seat in the 1862 election. Although he had given the war qualified support in 1861-1862, he became disillusioned with administration policy and began to view Vallandigham as a statesman and prophet. His brother

10 Ibid., pp. 51, 59.
11 Ibid., pp. 76, 92, 130; *New York Independent,* 18 December 1862.

Benjamin, who sat in the Thirty-seventh Congress in a seat near Vallandigham's, developed considerable respect for the Dayton representative and their mutual respect evolved into a personal friendship. The brothers promised Vallandigham and Pendleton a serenade and a chance to speak if they would visit their fair city.

Soon after the two Ohioans, in the company of Congressman Fernando Wood, arrived at their New York hotel, "Dodsworth's Band" serenaded them and a crowd gathered. Calls from the crowd brought Vallandigham and Pendleton out on the balcony. The Daytonian, grabbing at the opportunity to speak first, lit into the Lincoln administration and soon had the crowd in a responsive mood. He listed and elaborated upon Lincoln's many "crimes," saving his harshest comments for the arbitrary arrests perpetrated in a supposedly free country. He would not seek his own safety, he said defiantly, by paying compliments to a chief executive undeserving of any. He did not fear the handcuffs carried by Lincoln's agents nor the knives or guns carried by assassins. His assassination had been bluntly suggested in a hostile press. The editor of the *Wheeling Intelligencer*, for example, had written, "Brutus slew a man for treason in the capital whose lowest characteristics would ennoble Vallandigham."[12] "The traitors," stated another radical, pointing a finger at the Dayton congressman, "have only two rights—the right to be hanged and the right to be damned."[13]

After an hour, C.L.V. finally got around to the subject of peace, the desirability of compromise and reunion. The public demand for peace, he said, was growing louder and longer. Humanity called out for peace; charity would underwrite the compromise. If the Democratic party regained political ascendancy, compromise could be achieved and the Union restored. When Vallandigham finally finished, he received a prolonged applause. The enthusiastic audience evidently approved of his views.[14]

George H. Pendleton, playing second fiddle, then had his chance to offer an antiadministration tune. His speech was

[12] *Wheeling Intelligencer* (n.d.), quoted in *Cleveland Leader*, 2 November 1862.
[13] William G. "Parson" Brownlow, quoted in *Cleveland Leader*, 31 October 1862.
[14] *New York Times*, 13 December 1862.

brief, however, for the hour was very late. The informal program ended shortly after midnight, and the two Ohio congressmen retired to their rooms. The alacrity with which the New York listeners accepted pleas for peace impressed Vallandigham. The mood of the country was changing. No longer was he a prophet in the wilderness. Many, maybe millions, were ready to applaud peace doctrines. It seemed as if all the country needed was a bold leader to step forward and transform the latent peace sentiment into an open crusade.

The defeat of General Ambrose E. Burnside and the Army of the Potomac at Chancellorsville on December 13 nurtured defeatism and seemed to give validity to Vallandigham's contention that the South could not be conquered. Democrats also gained a hearing for their claim that the multiplication of unconstitutional acts presaged the establishment of a military dictatorship. The intensity of defeatism and the fear of despotism furnished fertile ground for the spread of propeace sentiment. On December 22, three days before the birthday of the Prince of Peace, Vallandigham introduced a resolution in Congress proposing "an immediate cessation of hostilities." He said that such action might revive negotiations for peace and effect reunion. The North should devise some amendments to the Constitution in order to secure "the rights of the several States and sections within the Union."[15] The Republican majority, led by Thaddeus Stevens and Schuyler Colfax, quickly quashed Vallandigham's public bid for peace. Republican congressmen might be able to sidetrack his demand for "an immediate cessation of hostilities," but they could not eradicate the peace sentiment pervading the hearts of the people and prevailing in many sections of the upper Midwest.

The year 1862 ended on a gloomy note. Statisticians totaled the Union casualties at Chancellorsville, and the figures passed the 13,000 mark. Prophets of gloom gained popularity in certain circles. There was widespread disgust with Lincoln's emancipation measures in Democratic quarters. "The year 1862," Samuel Medary wrote in the *Crisis*, "has been a year of blood and plunder, of carnage and conflagration . . . of falsehood and cor-

---

[15] *Congressional Globe*, 37 Cong., 3 sess., p. 165.

ruption . . . of defeat, desolation, and death."[16] William T. Logan, whom Vallandigham had helped select to edit the Democratic daily in Dayton, the *Empire,* wrote in the same gloomy vain: "Civil War stalks the land. The earth is crimson with the blood of brave men. Desolation, ruin, and suffering follow the march of contending armies. . . . In almost every house there is a mourner, and in almost every heart a vacant place. The ferry man on the river Styx has done a heavy freighting business during the last twelve-month."[17]

Over the Christmas holidays, Vallandigham, who stayed in Washington, decided that he would try to crystalize the peace sentiment so prevalent on every hand, and would seek recognition as the apostle of peace. He prepared a formal, propeace oration to be given at the earliest opportunity after Congress ended its holiday recess. "Next week or the following," he wrote on New Year's Day, "I shall speak at length on peace, war, and the present state of the Union—also the future."[18]

Vallandigham received the opportunity to give his carefully prepared speech on the afternoon of January 14, when Stevens's Indemnity Bill (with the Dayton congressman's amendatory resolutions) again became the official business of the House. He had let some of his colleagues and some newspapermen know that he had a major speech ready and that he hoped to give it on the fourteenth.

After gaining the floor, Vallandigham left his seat on the extreme left and moved to the center of the opposition benches. Members of the House noticed his action and laid aside their newspapers or put down their pens, for reports had circulated that he had "a speech worth listening to." Veteran congressmen, quite immune to oratory, moved into empty seats nearer the speaker. "Old Thad" Stevens, wearing his snuff-colored wig, braced himself in his chair and grimly eyed Vallandigham, shuffling his papers only a few feet away. Owen Lovejoy, the abolitionist congressman from Illinois, hitched his chair forward and raised his hand to his ear to catch the opening sentences.

[16] *Crisis* (Columbus), 31 December 1862.
[17] *Dayton Weekly Empire,* 3 January 1863.
[18] Vallandigham to "My dear Sir" [recipient unknown], 1 January 1863, Ford Collection, Pierpont Morgan Library, New York City.

Charles W. Wickliffe, a gout-ridden representative from Kentucky, used both a crutch and a cane to hobble down the aisle and seat himself at C.L.V.'s elbow. Schuyler Colfax, smiling as always, turned in his chair, brushed back his locks, and gave his rapt attention. The ladies and soldiers in the overcrowded galleries ceased their chatter as they impatiently awaited the opening words. Calm and self-confident, Vallandigham looked his audience in the eye, seeking complete silence and full attention.[19]

He began mildly enough, reviewing the events leading to the war. He gathered fire as he blamed the Republican party, rather than the fire-eaters of the South, for the crisis of 1860-1861. He reproached President Lincoln for foisting a policy of coercion upon a reluctant populace. He saw Southern radicalism as but a natural reaction to the rantings of the abolitionists and the dogma of the Higher Law advocates. The Fort Sumter affair, Vallandigham continued, unleashed a torrent of hysteria upon the country, sweeping all before it: "The gospel of love perished; hate sat enthroned; and the sacrifices of blood smoked at every altar."

Vallandigham next discussed the series of Lincolnian proclamations which, he said, violated the Constitution and eroded congressional power. A wave of arbitrary arrests alarmed defenders of "the inviolate rights of the citizens." The administration heaped corruption atop corruption and taxes atop taxes, threatening the nation's survival. An alert electorate, reacting to the incompetence of the administration and concerned with saving civil rights, repudiated Lincoln and the Republicans in the fall elections of 1862. The administration, despite having all the resources—men, money, materials, and public confidence—had failed "utterly, signally, and disastrously." The people of the North had given their wealth, confidence, and lives in vain; excessive taxes, a menacing national debt, mangled bodies, thousands of graves, and military defeats were "the true trophies of war." President Lincoln had turned to emancipation as a means to divert attention from his own failures and the country's frustrations. The war ought not to continue another day or another hour. The country, and especially the upper Midwest,

[19] Washington correspondent, in *Cincinnati Daily Gazette*, 15 January 1863; *Boston Herald* (n.d.), quoted in *Dayton Daily Empire*, 31 January 1863.

wanted compromise, conciliation, and peace. "The people of the West," said the conservative and sectionalist, "demand peace, and they begin to more than suspect that New England is in the way." Eastern disunionists had driven the South out of the Union; they might also cause the Northwest to go its own way.

"The experiment of war," Vallandigham continued, "has been tried long enough." It was time to turn to a peace policy. He proposed, therefore, "an informal, practical recognition" of the Confederacy, mediation by a friendly foreign power, and concessions aimed at eventual reunion. He asked for an armistice—not a formal treaty—and the withdrawal of Northern armies from the seceded states. Then, as steps to reunion, the two sections should declare an "absolute free trade between the North and South," restore travel and communication, open up the railroads, and give all the natural and artificial forces which tend to reunite "the fullest sway." "Let time," he added, "do his office—drying tears, dispelling sorrows, mellowing passions, and making herb and grass and tree grow again upon the hundred battlefields of this terrible war. Let passions have time to cool, and reason to resume sway." This program of armistice, aimed at rebuilding the comity of the two sections, would bring "eventual reunion" and "the ultimate achievement of the nation's destiny."[20]

He preached his gospel of peace for an hour without interruption. Some of his colleagues occasionally nodded approvingly; others shook their heads now and then to show their dissent. The crowds in the galleries, even the many uniformed soldiers, sat silent and spellbound. The speech was Clement L. Vallandigham's formal bid to lead the peace crusade.

Although the Dayton congressman spoke with an earnestness which was convincing, his plan of reunion was really quite vague and impractical. Southern rebels wanted no peace except that which promised them independence and the chance to go their own way. Nor did most Northerners believe that all was lost; they recognized that their advantages in population, production, and capital would give them an eventual military victory. Northern morale had not yet fully crumbled and there still existed a fatalistic faith in the future.

Vallandigham also erred in believing that the federal union

[20] *Congressional Globe*, 37 Cong., 2 sess., Appendix, pp. 52-60.

of prewar days could be restored. The nation and government had already changed. Industrialism held the reins. Furthermore, the Emancipation Proclamation was irrevocable; Lincoln could not put back into slavery men whom he had declared to be free. Vallandigham simply misjudged both the temper of the North and the goals of the South. He spoke more like a dreamer than the practical man he claimed to be.[21]

Four colleagues, including one Democrat, secured the floor to answer Vallandigham and put their disapproval of his recommendations into the record. John A. Bingham of Ohio, who viewed himself as a radical Republican, denied most of what Vallandigham had said. He insisted that the rebels rather than the Republicans had brought on the war. The president was duty bound to suppress the insurrection. Vallandigham was a defeatist; the North could and would raise more men, money, and materials to win the war. Furthermore, Vallandigham was a false prophet, guilty of ignoring some basic facts and perverting others. Next James M. Ashley of Ohio reprimanded the Dayton congressman for failing to vote for the army appropriation bills. "When our flag is dishonored and our sons murdered," he stated, pointing his finger at Vallandigham, "you sit here and refuse to devote a dollar to defend our institutions." Ashley then reminded Vallandigham that he had failed of reelection—had been repudiated by his constituents. Bah! Vallandigham did not represent the wishes of the people of Ohio nor the upper Midwest. Time would reward and honor those who had the courage and the will to carry on the war to crush treason, both in the South and on the home front.[22]

Owen Lovejoy of Illinois and Samuel C. Fessenden of Maine endorsed Ashley's critical comments. Lovejoy bluntly assured his colleagues that Vallandigham did not speak for the Midwest —he was a misguided apostle preaching falsehood rather than truth. Fessenden defended New England and rebuked Vallandigham for stirring up sectional spirit, which affected national unity adversely.[23]

[21] Alexander Stephens to his brother Linton, 18, 22, 29 January 1863, quoted in part in Richard M. Johnston and William H. Browne, *Life of Alexander H. Stephens* (Philadelphia, 1878), pp. 431-32, 435.
[22] Ibid., pp. 314-18.
[23] Ibid., pp. 345-46.

Henrick B. Wright of Pennsylvania was the lone Democrat to rise and deny Vallandigham's contentions. Wright said he still had full faith in the eventual triumph of Northern arms, and he curtly told Vallandigham that he had deceived himself as to the Southern mind. Men who want independence are not interested in compromise and reunion. The president was guilty of errors of judgment, but such blunders did not excuse citizens from supporting their flag and their country. "Demagogues cannot corrupt the people," Wright said as he looked straight at Vallandigham, "and woe to the men who deceive them."[24]

Vallandigham tried to get the floor to answer his critics. He stood in the aisle and sought the Speaker's attention. But Speaker Galusha A. Grow ignored him and soon directed the business of the House in another direction. Evidently he felt that Vallandigham had already had too much of a hearing.

Although many Republican newspapers made no mention of Vallandigham's peace speech, those that did commented on it adversely. Some called its author a traitor and defined his speech as "a treasonable production." "The people of the Northwest spurn him," wrote Isaac Jackson Allen of the *Ohio State Journal*, "and spit upon his detestable dogma."[25] One resentful Republican suggested they hang Vallandigham first and apologize afterward.[26] He was "a hyena" who ought to be hunted down and shot, "a secession toad" who ought to be "punctured with the spear of Ithuriel." He was as much an enemy of the country as the rebels of the South—neither should be tolerated; both must be whipped.[27]

A considerable number of Ohio Democrats joined the Republicans in criticizing Vallandigham's speech of January 14. Some thought it would hurt the Democracy, giving Republicans a chance to stigmatize the party. He had drunk from the cup of defeatism, they said, and had forfeited the right to speak for the party. Samuel S. Cox, for example, repudiated the idea of an armistice. Hugh J. Jewett, already at odds with Vallandigham,

24 Ibid., pp. 318-21.
25 20, 26 January 1863.
26 Edwin B. Morgan to Elihu B. Washburne, 31 January 1863, Elihu B. Washburne Papers, Library of Congress.
27 *Chillicothe Advertiser* (n.d.), *Eaton Register* (n.d.), *Cincinnati Commercial* (n.d.), and *New York Independent* (n.d.), all quoted in *Dayton Daily Empire*, 7 February 1863.

used the propeace speech as an excuse to sever personal relations. Some who had befriended him earlier backed away, mumbling about leprosy. "He has at last revealed to the country his true position," wrote a former friend. "He is a rebel, and I will henceforth treat him as such."[28]

On the other hand, many of Vallandigham's defenders praised him for his bold step forward. John T. Logan of the *Dayton Empire* called the apostle of peace "the greatest living American statesman" and described his exposition as "one of the ablest ever delivered in the halls of Congress."[29] "It is a speech," wrote James J. Faran in the *Cincinnati Enquirer*, "which would add to the fame of a Clay, or a Webster, or a Burke, or a Chatham."[30] Samuel Medary of the *Crisis* cheered. At last the Dayton congressman had joined his camp of extremists. He therefore paid Vallandigham one compliment after another. "This is no ordinary speech—made by no ordinary man," wrote the Columbus curmudgeon, "and under circumstances the most remarkable which ever overtook any nation or people. It may be well if this nation ponders seriously and with judgment over the words of wisdom and burning eloquence which run through every paragraph, sentence, and line."[31]

Praise for Vallandigham came from other quarters. The Wood brothers, using the editorial page of the *New York Daily News*, designated the Ohio congressman as the leader of the peace crusade.[32] The *Boston Courier* endorsed Vallandigham's peace sentiments. So did scores of lesser known papers, as a groundswell for peace and compromise swept over the land. The multitudes began to see him as a prophet and to put their faith in him. He expressed sentiments held in their hearts, once suppressed by the surge of patriotism. " 'Peace' is on a million lips," wrote John W. McElwee of the *Hamilton True Telegraph*, "and it will thunder, ere long, in the ears of our rulers like an Alpine storm."[33] Vallandigham's propeace speech, entitled *The Great Civil War in America* and published as a pamphlet, sold like hotcakes at five cents a copy. "The Vallandigham Polka," described

---

[28] *Ohio State Journal*, 28 January 1863; *New York Independent*, 22 January 1863.
[29] 24 January 1863.
[30] 20 January 1863.
[31] 21 January 1863.
[32] 20, 23, 27 January 1863.
[33] 29 January 1863.

as a "spirited piece of music,"[34] gained popularity at the backwoods dances and at party rallies. A new book entitled *The Record of Hon. C. L. Vallandigham on Abolition, the Union, and the Civil War* experienced a widespread sale in Democratic circles.[35] Intended to help him gain the governor's chair, the book impressed Vallandigham's old friends and won new ones. "Those who have been accustomed to denounce Mr. VALLANDIGHAM as a traitor and disunionist," wrote the partisan publisher, "will not take a favorable interest in this *Record*, for they will find their slanderous accusations nailed to the wall, and hung up to the gaze of the public."[36] The widespread desire for peace rehabilitated Vallandigham's reputation in many quarters.

As he regained popularity in certain circles, Vallandigham received many invitations to speak at Democratic rallies. His commitment to his congressional duties allowed him to accept very few. Perhaps the most pressing invitation came from the Democratic Association of Newark, New Jersey. Since he had some admirers there, he accepted an engagement for the evening of February 14, just a month after he had dropped his "peace bomb" in the House of Representatives.

James W. Wall and other Newark Democrats provided an overflow crowd in Concert Hall and an impressive setting. Nehemiah Perry presided at the session, and three "guests of honor" sat on the stage. Each of the guests was well known to the crowd, for each had been arbitrarily arrested, confined in a federal prison for a time, and later released without any charges ever being filed. Each of the three guests was presented "as living testimony" that the Lincoln administration had violated the Constitution, crushed freedom of speech and press, and intimidated Democrats. The clever sponsors wanted to draw a comparison between the *lettres de cachet* of Louis XVI's day and the arbitrary practices of the Lincoln administration.

Dennis A. Mahony, onetime editor of the *Dubuque Herald*, occupied "the chair of honor" nearest Vallandigham and at his right. Mahony had spent three months in "Old Capitol Prison" in Washington for writing editorials too critical of the Lincoln

---

[34] *Dayton Daily Empire*, 9, 23 December 1862.

[35] Ibid., 17 February 1863.

[36] Jefferson A. Walter, "Publishers' Notice," in *The Record of Hon. C. L. Vallandigham on Abolition, the Union, and the Civil War* (Columbus, 1863), p. 4.

administration. After his release he began a manuscript stating his side of the case and relating his experiences as a prisoner of state. He happened to be in New York helping to get his manuscript ready for the publisher when the Newark Democrats invited him down to occupy a chair of honor on the stage while Vallandigham was speaking.[37]

James A. McMaster, who occupied the second chair of honor, had spent six months in a federal prison for his bold and imprudent criticism of President Lincoln in the *Freeman's Journal* of New York. Unrepentant, McMaster developed a genuine mistrust of Lincoln, believing he wished to establish a despotism. If anything he was more defiant and churlish after his release than before his incarceration.

The third chair of honor was occupied by Henry Reeves who had edited the *Republican Watchman* of Greenport, Long Island. His intense partisanship led him to defend slavery, oppose the war, eulogize Jefferson Davis, and abuse President Lincoln. In time federal authorities seized him and put him behind bars in Fort Lafayette. After a month he gained his release, more contrite than either McMaster or Mahony.

After each of the three guests of honor was introduced, Nehemiah Perry turned the platform over to Vallandigham, who devoted considerable time to flaying the arbitrary arrests made by the Lincoln administration. He viewed the fall elections of 1862 as a repudiation of "despotism" and as a means of opening the doors of Lincoln's bastilles. He denounced William H. Seward, "a mere twaddle of a man," reputed to be organizing a coalition of conservatives and a new political party. He spent most of the hour and a half, however, pleading for peace, compromise, and reunion. Northern peace men and Southern peace men, he said, should cooperate in giving reality to the slogan "The Constitution as it is, the Union as it was." He prayed that God would favor his people so they could be led through the Red Sea of war and into the promised land of peace. He was willing to assume the leadership of the peace movement; he was

[37] Mahony's indictment of the Lincoln administration appeared under the title *The Prisoner of State* (New York, 1863). Mahony's career as a Copperhead has been treated in a number of studies, including: Herbert W. Wubben, "Dennis Mahony and the Dubuque *Herald*, 1860-1863," *Journal of Iowa History* 56 (October 1958): 289-320; and Roger B. Sullivan, "Mahony the Unterrified" (A.B. thesis, Loras College, Dubuque, 1938).

willing to be the guide with the "nerves of steel" and "strength of will" which the occasion demanded.[38]

A deafening applause followed when the Dayton congressman concluded his remarks, bowed gracefully, and sought his chair. Perry, the presiding officer, rushed over to grab Vallandigham's hand, and the three guests of honor added their compliments. The applause continued for a full four minutes, satiating Vallandigham's soul and encouraging him to believe that the country wanted peace and that Lincoln and Company misrepresented the people.

When he returned to his desk in Congress, Vallandigham continued his opposition to most administration measures. In his effort to prevent the Conscription Bill from having "any advantages" in the procedural labyrinth, he made rather barbed comments against both Abram B. Olin and James B. Campbell. Olin had introduced the Conscription Bill in the House on February 20, and Campbell had implied that all Democrats were pure and simple traitors. Before proceeding with his prepared speech against the Conscription Bill, Vallandigham expressed contempt for Campbell's remarks impugning the loyalty of Democratic critics. Looking straight at the Pennsylvania Republican, Vallandigham scornfully declared: "His threat I hurl back with defiance into his teeth. I spurn it. I spit upon it."[39]

Pretending innocence, Campbell said that he had no particular person in mind when he denounced traitors, but if the shoe fit, Vallandigham could put it on. "That's enough" retorted the Ohio congressman, visibly angry. Campbell politely tried to interrupt, begging, "One moment." "Not a moment after that!" retorted Vallandigham. "I yielded the floor in the spirit of a gentleman and not to be met in the manner of a blackguard!" "The member from Ohio is a blackguard!" Campbell barked back as the galleries applauded the Pennsylvanian and hissed Vallandigham.[40]

His feathers ruffled, the comely cock from Ohio turned from exchanging personal insults to discussing the Conscription Bill. He found many sections of the proposal unpalatable, even re-

[38] *New York Times*, 15 February 1863; *Dayton Daily Empire*, 20 February 1863; *Crisis*, 25 February 1863; *Hillsborough Weekly Gazette*, 5 March 1863.
[39] *Congressional Globe*, 37 Cong., 3 sess., Appendix, p. 172.
[40] Ibid.

pulsive. The provost marshal system for which the bill provided, would put the fate of civil rights in the hands of partisan federal agents, swarming over the land like locusts. That section of the bill which authorized the provost marshals "to inquire into and report . . . all treasonable practices" threatened the liberties of citizens. The courts, not single-minded provost marshals, should have the right to decide what "treasonable practices" were. The provost marshal system should not usurp the functions of the courts.

After finishing his thorough and effectual examination of each section of the Conscription Bill (which was later revised in line with some of Vallandigham's objections) the Dayton Democrat digressed into partisan pastures. He reminded Republicans that they had been repudiated in the 1862 elections. And when Republicans claimed that there was a need for "forceful conscription," he declared, they confessed that the people had lost faith in Lincoln, in the administration, and in coercion as a means to an end. Still, he could not resist the opportunity to put in a plug for peace.[41]

Even before Vallandigham had taken his seat, James M. Ashley asked for the floor to reply to the Democratic dissenter. Ashley, who liked to badger Vallandigham, called his speech "a ruse" to protect rebels, draft dodgers, and traitors—none of whom merited any defense. Vallandigham, who believed Ashley was persecuting him, tried to rebuke his Republican colleague from Ohio, but the Speaker ignored his calls for attention. Daniel W. Voorhees of Indiana rushed to Vallandigham's defense, gaining the floor to praise the anti-Conscription Bill speech and chide Ashley for his "offensive speeches." Voorhees agreed with every criticism made of the measure, he said, and he characterized Vallandigham's speech as "a spellbound worthy argument." Ashley, who feared Voorhees's sharp tongue, did not reply and settled in his seat. He had put "the traitor's brand" upon Vallandigham again, and he knew that he would later enjoy the toasts and praise of his friends.[42]

Before the Conscription Bill came to a vote,[43] Vallandigham

[41] Ibid., pp. 172-77.
[42] Ibid., pp. 1227-28, 1230.
[43] The vote in the House came on 25 February 1862, and the bill carried by a 115 to 48 vote. Vallandigham gave one of the "nay" votes.

was accused several times more of being an obstructionist and a traitor. Once Thaddeus Stevens made the charge, reading a summary of Vallandigham's Newark speech from a Republican newspaper. He then questioned the Ohioan's integrity and patriotism. This time the Speaker gave the Dayton congressman a chance to reply. Vallandigham had "a corrected newspaper version" on his desk and he read what he had actually said, not what a partisan newspaper had accused him of saying. He had a few unkind words for editors who distorted and misrepresented in order to smear him with Republican mud.[44]

Several days later, an old nemesis, John A. Bingham, arose to reprimand Vallandigham for his pro-Southern views and his unpatriotic practices. He even questioned his Ohio colleague's honesty and intelligence. He too misrepresented Vallandigham's views in his disorganized discourse, and once more charged that the four-section scheme which he had proposed two years earlier was no more than an attempt to set up four separate confederacies. The Speaker again gave Vallandigham time to correct Bingham's misstatements and to deny that he sympathized with the rebels. He repeated his oft-uttered contention that the four-section proposal was intended to prevent the Union from breaking up. "My object—the sole motive by which I have been guided from the beginning of this most fatal revolution," said the oft-abused congressman, "is to maintain the Union and not destroy it."[45]

The third critic to enter the lists against Vallandigham was another Republican congressman from Ohio, Harrison G. T. Blake. This detractor reminded the Dayton congressman that he had called himself a Western sectionalist and "fire-eater" several years before the war, and then accused him of identifying himself with the South rather than the North during the war years. Blake not only questioned Vallandigham's patriotism but implied he was a traitor who should be so branded. Again Vallandigham arose to defend himself and again he tried to explain his views to critics who tended to see any opposition to administration measures as treason.[46] His rebuttal was lost on men in whose hearts a narrow patriotism burned and whose minds equated Republican doctrine with truth and justice.

[44] Congressional Globe, 37 Cong., 3 sess., p. 1292.
[45] Ibid., pp. 1402-4.
[46] Ibid., pp. 1408-9.

During the closing hours of the final session of the Thirty-seventh Congress, Vallandigham gave his brief valedictory speech. In a sense it was a plea for fairness on the part of Republicans bent upon abusing Democrats who expressed dissenting views. It was wrong and unfair to label dissident Democrats "traitors" or "secessionists," he declared. Patriotism would not be served by name-calling, nor unity by misrepresentation. Truth would not bend before the wrath of blind partisanship, and those who let passion dislodge reason would live to regret their over-indulgence.[47]

Before returning to Dayton after Congress adjourned, C.L.V. took a trip into the Northeast to seek new converts for the cause of peace, reconciliation, and reunion. He made a one-night stop in Philadelphia and spoke to a good-sized crowd collected by antiwar Democrats. He catered to the anti-Negro prejudices of the city's Irish-Americans, who made up the bulk of his appreciative audience, denouncing the administration's emancipation measures. Then he sermonized on the subject of peace. He recommended a national convention as a means to reunion. Had not the fall elections repudiated the policies of the Lincoln administration, including emancipation and coercion? The country wanted peace, and a national convention seemed to be the best way to make the hopes of the people a reality. The apostle found new converts for his cause in the "City of Brotherly Love." His Philadelphia experience proved to be "exceedingly gratifying."[48]

In New York City the Wood brothers, assisted by James A. McMaster, made arrangements for the peace crusader to address the Democratic Union Association. Since most members of the audience read and approved the antiwar editorials in the New York Daily News, Vallandigham had to do more interpolating than converting. His central theme was that the liberties of the people could be saved only by the cession of the war, which had eroded the civil rights of citizens—the arbitrary arrests were proof of that. Those rights could still be saved if compromise and reunion were substituted for coercion and subjugation. He ended with several threats of his own. If Lincoln and "his

[47] Ibid., pp. 1415-16.
[48] Philadelphia Inquirer, 7 March 1863; Dayton Daily Empire, 13 March 1863; Vallandigham, Vallandigham, pp. 231-33.

minions" knew that Democrats would defend their liberties with their lives, those who held the scepter and brandished the sword would not trifle with men's rights. If Lincoln, "surrounded by the parasites of power," failed to heed the wishes of the people, a revolution might visit America as in earlier years revolutions had visited overseas countries.[49]

The next day Vallandigham noticed that the *New York Times* had credited to him things he had not said and views he did not hold. This issue of the *Times* reached Lincoln's desk, and the president did not know that he was being misled. Furthermore, a *Times* editorial added to the misrepresentation with the assertion: "He [Vallandigham] opposed the war, advocated immediate peace, denounced our Conscription Act as ten times worse than that of Poland."

The apostle of peace, indignant because the *Times* had falsified what he had said, felt compelled to write a letter to editor Caleb C. Norvell. His letter was brief and summarized his views on questions of law, order, and revolution:

> Allow me to say that the statement of your reporter that I denied any allegiance to the Conscription Act, and your own that I counseled resistance to it by the people of the North, are both incorrect. On the contrary, I expressly counseled the trial of all questions of law before the judicial courts, and all questions of politics before the tribunal of the ballot-box. I AM FOR OBEDIENCE TO ALL LAWS—obedience by the people and by the men in power also. I am for a free discussion of all measures and laws whatsoever, as in former times; but FORCIBLE RESISTANCE TO NONE. The ballot-box, and not the cartridge-box is the instrument of reform and revolution. . . .[50]

After his brief stay in the New York City, Vallandigham took the train to Albany and a conference with Governor Horatio Seymour. Samuel S. Cox and William Bigler, ex-governor of Pennsylvania, were also there and the four discussed party welfare. Vallandigham and Bigler took an antiwar stand, whereas Cox and Seymour took a more moderate view. Governor Seymour made his points well as he discussed the party's future, and the two antiwar men agreed to qualify their opposition to the war.

---

49 *New York Times*, 8 March 1863; *Dayton Daily Empire*, 27 March 1863; Vallandigham, *Vallandigham*, pp. 231-33.
50 8 March 1863, published in *New York Times*, 10 March.

"Mr. Vallandigham," one writer noted, "has agreed to abate his hostility to the war for the sake of the party."[51]

From Albany Vallandigham went into Connecticut to give several antiwar speeches. He seemed less the antiwar crusader now than before his trip to Albany. Still, however, he spoke out for a national peace convention and still he believed compromise a better means to reunion than coercion.

The Dayton congressman then turned his face toward the Midwest, Ohio, and home. He knew that peace sentiment was widespread in the upper Midwest, much more extensive than in New England. He knew that Kentucky had tried to promote a national peace convention; the state legislature had discussed the desirability of appointing commissioners to meet with representatives of Ohio, Indiana, Illinois, Missouri, Pennsylvania, and New York to "counsel upon the state of the country."[52] Vallandigham also knew that the Democratic-controlled legislatures in Indiana and Illinois had tried to cooperate with Kentucky in promoting a national peace convention, but in each case Republican governors had prevented formal action.

Ohio had a dozen Democratic editors who regarded themselves as out-and-out peace men. Editor Thomas Beer of the *Crawford County Forum* fit that category. "Every dollar spent for the persecution [*sic*] of this infamous war," he wrote in despair, "is uselessly wasted—and every life lost in it is an abominable sacrifice, a murder, the responsibility of which will rest upon Abraham Lincoln and his advisors. The man who does not wash his hands of all participation in such a war, shares the guilt of those by whom it is persecuted [*sic*]. Support of this war and hostility to it show the dividing line between the enemies and friends of the Union. *He who supports the war is against the Union.*" The Bucyrus editor developed the argument that only disunionists, North and South, favored the war. Unionists, therefore, must advocate peace and reunion. Beer wanted a six-month armistice during which delegates from the North and the South would meet to settle major differences and restore the Union.[53]

---

[51] Samuel S. Cox to Erastus Corning, 13 March 1863, Horatio Seymour Papers, New York State Library, Albany; *Dayton Daily Journal*, 16 March 1863.

[52] John W. Finnell to John J. Crittenden, 9 February 1863, Crittenden Papers.

[53] *Crawford County Forum* (Bucyrus), 30 January, 6 March 1863. Beer's contributions to the antiwar crusade are well presented in Thomas H. Smith, "The

Young Thomas O. Lowe, a Dayton disciple of Vallandigham, also wanted to push the Democratic party toward all-out peace goals. Lowe stated his views in a well-written treatise published in the *Dayton Empire:* "We are always for peace when war will do us more harm than good, or when war can be honorably avoided. [Emerich de] Vattel says 'War is so dreadful a scourge that nothing less than manifest justice, joined to necessity, can authorize it or exempt it from reproach.' We believe this war could have been honorably avoided by the North . . . and that there is no possibility of its resulting in anything but evil, and therefore we are for peace."[54]

The doubting Thomases, Beer and Lowe, were but two of many Ohioans chanting "Peace! Peace! Peace!" As an apostle of peace, Clement L. Vallandigham was anxious to organize and lead the movement in his home state. He was also anxious to gain his party's gubernatorial nomination and continue his public career. In March 1863, it seemed as if his propeace crusade might make him Ohio's most popular figure and push him toward the governor's chair. Opportunity seemed to be knocking, and a key labeled "Peace" might unlock the door.

Peace Democratic Movement in Crawford County, Ohio, 1860-1865" (master's thesis, Ohio State University, 1962), and "Crawford County 'Ez Trooly Dimecratic,'" *Ohio History* 76 (1967): 33-53.

[54] Lowe used the pseudonym "Hampton," in the *Dayton Daily Empire,* 7 February 1863. Lowe's views are presented admirably in Carl M. Becker, "Picture of a Young Copperhead," *Ohio History* 72 (January 1962): 3-23.

10

SEEKING OFFICE AND MARTYRDOM

CLEMENT L. VALLANDIGHAM was never one to sit in a corner and daydream while others played games or directed affairs. He was essentially a man of action, one who enjoyed argumentation, controversy, and challenge. He had endless confidence in his own ability, and he raised his sights as time passed. He liked attention and he liked the spotlight. He gained great satisfaction in developing rapport with an audience and applause was essential to his ego. Politics enamored him, making him prisoner and patron. He looked forward to the excitement of an election campaign. He was Sir Galahad, entering the lists against the champions of evil, error, and incompetence.

His defeat at the hands of Robert C. Schenck in October 1862 did not shake his confidence in himself. He did not feel that the electorate of the Third District had repudiated him, for he believed he had been defeated by political trickery. He was both pleased and flattered, therefore, when friends suggested he seek Benjamin F. Wade's seat in the United States Senate or cast an eye in the direction of the governor's chair, then occupied by David Tod.

Vallandigham decided to seek Tod's chair. His first step was to prepare a compilation of his speeches for publication, and a publisher-friend in Columbus brought out the book, entitled *The Record of Hon. C. L. Vallandigham on Abolition, the Union, and the Civil War*, early in 1863. The book made no mention of Vallandigham's ambition, cloaking it with indirection: "The object [of the compilation] is to furnish the means of forming a correct judgment in relation to a man who, through malignant assaults of his enemies, and the esteem of his friends, has become one of the most generally talked of men of these times."[1]

On his way home from Connecticut, C.L.V. stopped in Cleveland and Columbus to promote his candidacy for the governorship. In Columbus he called on William W. Armstrong, an old boyhood friend whom the Democratic tide of late 1862 had swept into the office of secretary of state in Ohio. Vallandigham told Armstrong that he intended to seek the Democratic gubernatorial nomination. Then, bluntly he said that he expected Armstrong's full and open support for the office. "But Colonel," replied the secretary of state, "this is not your time to run for Governor. I think Hugh J. Jewett ought to be nominated."[2]

Vallandigham gritted his teeth, then expressed his displeasure that an old and trusted friend should choose a rival over him. Armstrong in turn justified his views. Party usage dictated that Jewett should be given the nomination if he wanted it. He had accepted the responsibility in 1861, had conducted an honorable campaign—his letters and speeches had been patriotic and conservative—had met defeat, and deserved a second chance. Previous Democratic gubernatorial candidates, defeated in their first try, had always been given a second opportunity. Armstrong also explained that Jewett's stand on most issues had been more moderate than Vallandigham's; it would be more difficult for Republicans to defeat Jewett, for they would have more trouble misrepresenting his views. Armstrong told Vallandigham in confidence that Democratic party leaders deplored his entry into the race. They also feared that a furious fight for the nomination between Jewett and Vallandigham would split the party and "bring defeat and disaster to the Democracy." The growing personal animosity between Jewett and Vallandigham would only help the Republicans. For the sake of the party Vallandigham could well shelve his ambitions.[3]

The Dayton curmudgeon shunted Armstrong's arguments aside, for he had made up his mind that he wanted the prize. Jewett's defeat in 1861 did not necessarily give him a claim to the nomination in 1863. Even if the Democratic party chieftains opposed him, he would make a bid for the nomination. He believed the people wanted him even if the leaders did not. His hat was definitely and determinedly in the ring. The argument, frank and friendly, ended in an impasse.

Vallandigham then asked Armstrong to accompany him to

---

1 Jefferson A. Walter, "Publishers' Notice," p. 3.
2 William W. Armstrong, "Personal Recollections," published in the *Cincinnati Daily Enquirer*, 20 March 1863.
3 Ibid.

the halls where the state legislature was still in session. As the two passed through the rotunda of the state capitol, Vallandigham stopped and looked up toward the rounded ceiling. He pointed toward the state seal, depicted in a mosaic high in the dome. Using a portion of a quotation attributed to Lincoln, Vallandigham said in all seriousness, "We will own, occupy, and possess these premises, you as Secretary of State and I as Governor, next January."[4]

Armstrong said nothing although he wrote much later that he questioned the truth of Vallandigham's self-serving prophecy. The two then walked onto the floor of the House of Representatives, the lower house of the Ohio legislature. Vallandigham met old friends, exchanging greetings and shaking hands often, but said nothing more about his gnawing ambition.[5]

The next day C.L.V. took the train for Dayton and home, knowing full well that he had little chance of walking off with the gubernatorial honors at the Democratic State Convention of June 11. All prominent men in the party supported Jewett's candidacy and even friends like Armstrong wanted him to step aside. Perhaps he could learn a lesson from the story of Dr. Olds, whose arbitrary arrest had made him a hero and martyr and had won him a seat in the state senate. Could the same thing happen to Clement L. Vallandigham?

Dayton Democrats knew the hour and day of Vallandigham's scheduled arrival.[6] In fact, he had tarried in Columbus and taken the afternoon train so his friends could stage a noisy and noteworthy homecoming. It was evident to the experienced eye that the affair was carefully planned, intended to get Vallandigham's bid for his party's gubernatorial nomination off to a raucous start.

The crowd began to gather at the Dayton railway depot long before "the four-thirty" was due to arrive from Columbus. The promoters of the rally fired a cannon periodically, attempting to attract the curious to the station. Two brass bands enlivened the occasion, taking turns playing as loudly as they could. David A. Houk, a personal friend and political ally, paced to and fro;

[4] Ibid.
[5] Ibid.
[6] *Dayton Daily Empire*, 9, 10, 11, 12 March 1863.

he was giving shape to his thoughts, for he had the responsibility of delivering the welcoming speech. The excitement reached a peak as the Columbus train roared into Dayton and screeched to a halt near the depot.

When Vallandigham alighted he received an impressive ovation. An outdated cannon boomed a thunderous welcome. Both bands played, but the blare of the trumpets and the clash of the cymbals could scarcely be heard above the cheers and the shouts. Women waved white handkerchiefs, reports said, gracing the occasion with their fair faces and enjoying the excitement of the homecoming rally. The crowd surged forward, mixing calls and applause in disorganized fashion.

The members of the welcoming committee, headed by Houk, greeted C.L.V. as a hero and had to protect him from the crushing crowd. They had difficulty in opening an avenue through the huge throng so they could get to the waiting carriages. Finally some lifted him up on strong shoulders and ploughed through, while Vallandigham waved to strangers and called friends by name.

After the cannoneers fired twenty-four rounds, parade marshals transformed the milling mob into an organized procession which headed for the courthouse. A regimental band led the way. A group of friends, carrying huge signs and banners, came next. Then came the well-decorated carriage, bearing Vallandigham and Houk. Mayor William H. Gillespie and Dr. Jefferson A. Walter, two of Vallandigham's closest friends and disciples, occupied the second carriage. A dozen other carriages, wheels rumbling over the brick pavement, followed. The Salem Band separated the carriages from the thousands who trudged on foot in the procession. The sidewalks were crowded with bystanders all the way from the depot to the courthouse square, and they cheered and waved as the procession passed by.

In time, members of the procession fanned out into an audience, surrounding the platform erected on the courthouse steps. Mayor Gillespie called the meeting to order, expressed his appreciation for Vallandigham, and turned the duty of giving the welcoming speech over to Houk, at one time the ex-congressman's law partner. Houk gave Vallandigham a glowing tribute, characterizing him as "a faithful sentinel upon the watchtower of public liberty." He praised the "homecoming hero" for preaching the gospel of peace and putting into words the hopes resting in the heavy hearts of the people. And he praised Vallandigham for his boldness, his willingness to speak defiantly despite "the frowns of tyrants and usurpers." Vallandigham would not turn his back upon the people, and he would speak out for truth and justice despite the vicious vituperation of "an abusive and venal press."[7] Then he asked Vallandigham to address the crowd.

The "honored guest" thanked Houk for his compliments and the audience for its warm welcome. It was good to be among friends again. Then he turned to a discussion of "the struggle" taking place between "despotic power" and "liberty." The Democratic party, Vallandigham asserted, would never let the Lincoln administration trample upon the rights of the people. The ballot-box and free speech would be retained "at all hazards!"

After discussing the need for liberty and peace, Vallandigham turned his attention to the Conscription Act. Of all his votes in Congress, he was proudest of the one he had cast against the Conscription Bill, for the conscript laws of Russia and Austria were lenitive compared to the one forced through Congress by the Republicans. He wanted its validity and its constitutionality tested in the courts. He called the $300 commutation clause discriminatory and undemocratic. The rich man could buy his way out of army service; the poor man would be forced to go. Yes, the price of blood was $300; it was as if the Lincoln administration had said, "Three hundred dollars or your life." He suggested that the city council of Dayton appropriate enough funds to pay the commutation money of all citizens too poor to pay it themselves. Although he opposed the Conscription Act, he made it clear, he would not counsel disobedience. The laws of the land should be obeyed, but people could use their votes to change them.

Vallandigham closed with a touching allusion to J. Frederick Bollmeyer, late editor of the *Empire*. Bollmeyer was really "the first martyr in the cause of constitutional liberty." Vallandigham continued to dip his hand in Bollmeyer's blood and sprinkle it over the crowd.[8]

[7] Ibid., 14 March 1863.
[8] *Dayton Daily Journal*, 14 March 1863; *Dayton Daily Empire*, 14 March 1863.

When Vallandigham concluded his speech he received a long and noisy applause, for he had touched the hearts of his people; he stood as their champion. Houk escorted him to the carriage, and the procession re-formed and followed the carriage down Main Street, then along First Street. The carriage stopped in front of his modest home at 323 First Street, and friends carried "the hero" on their shoulders to his very door and set him down as gently as they could. After giving three cheers, the crowd dispersed and the ex-congressman had a chance to greet his wife, his ten-year-old son Charlie and his sister-in-law.

William T. Logan, who had taken over the editorship of the *Dayton Empire* and was one of the sponsors of the gala homecoming, revelled in the spontaneity and success of the affair. As far as he could recall, it was "by far the most hearty and enthusiastic welcome ever extended to anyone" in Dayton. Logan assured his subscribers that Vallandigham deserved the honors and accolades heaped upon him. "He has passed through the furnace of persecution," Logan added, "with not even the smell of gunpowder upon his garments."[9]

Vallandigham found antiadministration sentiment widespread in the Dayton area. Fear of federal conscription underwrote apprehension in the backwoods areas and in the poorer sections of the cities. It was reported that large numbers of citizens were arming, getting ready to resist enrollment for the draft.[10] In Noble County, efforts to arrest a deserter and his friend evolved into the so-called "Hoskinsville Rebellion"—lots of smoke and little fire. It became necessary to send a company of soldiers into the disaffected area to arrest the deserter and intimidate the aroused residents. Republicans magnified the backwoods incident for political effect. "If such scrapes are to be gotten up to make Abolition votes in Ohio," Samuel Medary wrote in the *Crisis*, "it will be a dear electioneering campaign for taxpayers."[11]

Democratic apprehension and discontent stemmed from more than the threat of enrollment and conscription. Republican

---

[9] *Dayton Daily Empire*, 14 March 1863.
[10] *Cleveland Leader*, 28 March 1863.
[11] 1 April 1863. Wayne Jordan, "The Hoskinsville Rebellion," *Ohio State Archaeological and Historical Quarterly* 47 (October 1943): 319-54, debunks the incident in Noble County most effectively, burying another Civil War myth.

editors conducted a smear campaign against Democratic party spokesmen, comparing them with the poisonous copperhead snake. Preaching the dogma that the Lincoln administration and the government were one, Republicans tended to view all Democratic criticism of Lincoln or his administration as "disloyalty" and "a hindrance to the war effort." Some Republican superpatriots denied that the "Copperheads" had any rights at all. The narrow-minded editor of the *Cleveland Leader* wrote, "Treat Copperheads as assassins; as men who, if they would not aim the knife at your breast, would, at least, not move a finger to arrest the blow. They are assassins; they are traitors; and that last word is the sum of everything vile."[12]

Such preachments prompted Republican ruffians to intimidate Democrats or to mob Democratic newspaper offices. On March 5 about a hundred soldiers, armed with sabers and revolvers, descended upon the office of the *Crisis* during a blinding snowstorm. They did "a thorough job" of wrecking the editor's quarters before retreating to Camp Chase outside Columbus. Most of the mobsters belonged to the Second Ohio Cavalry, recruited in the Western Reserve and exposed to the doctrine of intolerance preached by the editors of the *Cleveland Leader* and the *Ashtabula Sentinel*.[13]

Other Democratic editors besides Medary felt the hand of the mob. The editor of the *Marietta Democrat* was continually harassed, and finally a mob demolished his printing plant.[14]

Mob action threatened the rights of spokesmen of the minority party and gave meaning to Vallandigham's charges that civil rights were in danger of being trampled in the dust. Threats only made Vallandigham more defiant and prompted some Democrats to preach the law of reprisal. "For every Democratic printing office destroyed by a mob," suggested William T. Logan of the *Dayton Empire*, "let an Abolition one be destroyed in turn. For every drop of blood spilled by Abolition mobites [*sic*], let theirs flow in retaliation."[15] Editor Logan also let

[12] N.d., quoted in *Dayton Weekly Empire*, 4 April 1863.

[13] *Ohio State Journal* (Columbus), 7 March 1863; *Crisis*, 11, 18 March 1863. Eugene H. Roseboom, "The Mobbing of the *Crisis*," *Ohio State Archaeological and Historical Quarterly* 59 (April 1950): 150-53, gives a brief but scholarly account of the incident.

[14] *Cleveland Leader*, 28 March 1863.

[15] *Dayton Weekly Empire*, 14 March 1863.

Republicans know that Democrats intended to keep their rights at all costs. "The spirit of Patrick Henry," he wrote, "which gave utterance to the undying words of freedom—'Give me Liberty or give me death'—still lives in the hearts of the American people."[16] Republicans, believing they had a monopoly on virtue and truth, responded by waving the flag more vigorously and demanding unconditional loyalty, which they defined according to their political prejudices.

Republicans made Vallandigham the special target of their antitreason campaign. Republican editors seemed to take particular delight in publishing soldiers' letters which condemned the Dayton ex-congressman or which intimated that he would not live long if he visited their quarters.[17] The editor of the *Cincinnati Commercial,* who vied with the editor of the *Cincinnati Gazette* in nailing Vallandigham's hide to the wall, repeatedly called him names. "The fellow," he wrote, "is a dastard —a cold-blooded, mean-spirited coward."[18] Some Republican editor blamed Vallandigham for the "Hoskinsville Rebellion," saying that the affair was the work of "misguided men" merely carrying out "the doctrine of opposition" which Vallandigham preached.[19]

Even Colonel Henry B. Carrington, commanding the District of Indiana, cast aspersions at Vallandigham and helped to develop the legend that the backcountry seethed with treason. Carrington, stationed in Indianapolis, wrote to Lincoln that "the popular daring of Vallandigham" made him "so mischievous" that either he or General John Hunt Morgan, the bold Confederate cavalry commander, "could raise an army of 20,000 traitors in Indiana." Carrington asked the president if he might arrest Vallandigham should he set foot in Indiana to counsel "resistance or defiance to any U.S. statute."[20]

Vallandigham had even less respect for Carrington than Carrington had for Vallandigham. The incompetent colonel, seeking a brigadier general's star and serving as Governor Morton's man

16 Ibid., 7 March 1863.
17 Letter of A. N. Patterson (Company E, 90th Ohio Volunteer Regiment), 5 March 1863, published in *Cleveland Leader,* 12 March.
18 *Cincinnati Daily Commercial,* 13 March 1863.
19 *Morgan Herald,* 1 May 1863.
20 Carrington, "Memorandum of Conditions of Public Affairs in Indiana," 19 March 1863, Robert Todd Lincoln Papers, Library of Congress.

Friday, groped for evidence to justify his high-handed practices. He had sent a squad of soldiers to New Richmond to seize a lot of twenty-four pistols when he heard they were being sold to Democrats. He had sent two sergeants outside his jurisdiction and after they were arrested by the sheriff of an Illinois county, sent in a trainload of troops to liberate them and arrest the Democratic judge hearing their case.[21] Worse than that, the officious colonel issued a proclamation denying the right to Hoosiers to keep and bear arms—a blatant violation of the Constitution.

In a speech in the courthouse yard in Hamilton, Ohio, Vallandigham fired away at both Lincoln and Carrington. He read Carrington's officious proclamation, "General Orders, No. 15," which forbade residents within his military district to secure and bear arms. C.L.V.'s wry comments and witty ridicule made the pompous colonel look like a midget. He told an appreciative audience that he based his opposition to Carrington's "general orders" upon "General Orders, No. 1," the Constitution of the United States. He read aloud the second amendment, and for effect repeated, "The right of the people to keep and bear arms shall not be infringed." Carrington had the right to issue an order to his regiment, Vallandigham averred, but he had no right to deny constitutional privileges to people who were not in military service. Carrington's decree was no more than "military insolence." He ended with the query, "Is the man deranged?"

Vallandigham followed his criticism of Carrington with a double-edged plea for law and order: "Try every question of law in your courts, and every question of politics before the people and through the ballot-box; make no resistance to law; but meet and repel all mobs and mob violence by force and arms on the spot." Republican reporters said that he preached a revolutionary doctrine and that he drew people into the hellhole of treason. Some selected sentences out of context in order to present him in a more unfavorable light. Their patriotism and partisanship prompted them to defend Carrington when he was wrong and condemn Vallandigham even when he was right.[22]

21 Carrington's bungling tactics are exposed in Frank L. Klement, "Carrington and the Golden Circle Legend in Indiana during the Civil War," *Indiana Magazine of History* 61 (March 1965): 31-52.

22 *Dayton Daily Empire*, 23 March 1863; *Dayton Daily Journal*, 24 March 1863; *Hamilton True Telegraph*, 26 March 1863.

Vallandigham, again in demand as a speaker, made three more speeches before the voters went to the polls on the first Tuesday of April 1863. In Dayton, the elections passed off with a minimum of violence. Despondent Democrats, who feared that Republicans would use troops to screen voters at the polls, choked on their false prophecies.

Dayton Democrats had cause to cheer after the tally-clerks tabulated the votes, and Vallandigham found considerable personal satisfaction in the election returns. William H. Gillespie, his close friend, won reelection to the mayoralty and carried the entire Democratic city slate to victory. Each of the four Ohio cities in which Vallandigham had given a preelection speech elected its Democratic slate of candidates. Furthermore, the Republican editor of the *Dayton Journal* had to eat crow—he had made much of his contention that each vote for the Democratic ticket was really a vote for Vallandigham and "infamy."[23]

In their postelection celebration, Dayton Democrats gave Vallandigham "special honors." After the last votes were counted and a Democratic victory was assured, party workers lighted a huge bonfire in front of the *Empire* building, rolled out "the old baby-waker" stored in the office, and fired thirty-four rounds in honor of the victory. By the time the cannon had boomed for the twenty-fourth time, a crowd of 2000 had gathered. Marshals formed the crowd into "lines" and the procession headed for 323 First Street. Repeated cheers brought Vallandigham out of his house to make "a few pertinent remarks." After giving the pleased politician cheers to the number "three times three," the procession re-formed, marched to the home of Mayor Gillespie, and accorded him the same honor given Vallandigham. After voices became hoarse and excitement drained the physical stamina of the participants, they returned to their homes or to the bars.[24] Perhaps the tribute paid him by the party faithful of Dayton reaffirmed Vallandigham's decision to seek the governorship. Certainly Dayton Democrats did not view the ex-congressman as an obstructionist, renegade, or traitor.

If Vallandigham interpreted the Democratic victory in Dayton as proof of a national trend, he was mistaken. Such Democratic strongholds in Ohio as Cincinnati and Sandusky witnessed Re-

---

[23] *Dayton Daily Journal*, 6 April 1863; *Dayton Daily Empire*, 11 April 1863.
[24] *Dayton Daily Empire*, 11, 18 April 1863.

publican victories. Elsewhere throughout the North, Republicans began to regain the ascendancy and roll back the Democratic tide which had crested in the fall elections of 1862. It was not chance that helped Republicans gain the political offensive. They had deliberately solicited and publicized patriotic letters from the soldiery. They had organized the Union League as an adjunct of their party and used it as a means "to educate" the electorate. They had conducted an antitreason campaign in the press, seeking to stigmatize the proponents of peace. They had erected the Knights of the Golden Circle as a straw-man and tried to link this mythical subversive society to Vallandigham and dissident Democrats. They had developed soldier voting-in-the-field as a political stratagem, and had generated nationalism and popularized the doctrine that the Lincoln administration and the government were one.

Republicans expressed pleasure that the tide had turned in their favor again. One credited the Union Leagues, devised by Republicans to promote patriotism and influence public opinion, with being a political dike. "Our *Union* organization is perfect," wrote one Republican strategist, "and we have good reason to be proud of the result of our first effort."[25] They expected to do even better in the fall elections. "The great sandhedrim [sic] of the Copperheads and the Knights of the Golden Circle," wrote one with obvious reference to Vallandigham, "can no more stop this swelling tide of popular feeling and loyal sentiment than they can stop the rising tide of the ocean."[26]

While Republicans and Democrats argued over the meaning of the April election returns, Major General Ambrose E. Burnside became acquainted with his new duties as commander of the Department of the Ohio, with headquarters in Cincinnati. His defeat at Fredericksburg the previous December still rankled him, affecting his disposition as well as his reputation. Colonel Carrington apprised Burnside of discontent in Indiana and told fanciful tales to cover his errors of judgment. Indeed, Ohio and Illinois seemed to be on the edge of a volcano. Democratic editors, irate because the soldiers who had destroyed the editorial offices of the *Crisis* went unpunished—in fact were treated as

25 George W. O'Brien to Gov. Samuel J. Kirkwood, 7 April 1863, Samuel J. Kirkwood Papers, Iowa State Department of History and Archives, Des Moines.
26 *Ohio State Journal,* 8 April 1863.

heroes—began to talk again about "the law of reprisals." "For every dime of your property destroyed," wrote William T. Logan in the *Empire*, "destroy a dollar's worth in return." Democrats, he said, deserved to lose their rights if they stood by submissively while administration representatives took them away. "If we are cowards, unworthy the freedom our forefathers wrested from tyrants' heads," Logan wrote defiantly "then we will meekly wear, and deservedly too, the chains which abolition despots are forging for our hands."[27] It was evident that Logan was a fire-brand, willing to fight and die for his rights.

General Burnside had no understanding of the reasons for the widespread disaffection in the upper Midwest. As a general, and a discredited one at that, he understood only the law of force. He read the editorials and news stories in the *Cincinnati Gazette* and the *Cincinnati Commercial*, but was incapable of recognizing their partisan slant. He accepted the Republican-sponsored interpretation that James J. Faran of the *Cincinnati Enquirer*, Logan of the *Dayton Empire* and Samuel Medary of the *Crisis* played a traitorous game. He believed they sowed the dragon's teeth of discontent, aided the rebels of the South, and discouraged enlistments in the North.

Thus Burnside, in a rash moment, issued "General Orders, No. 38" on April 13, 1863. It was a military edict intended to intimidate Democratic critics of President Lincoln and the war. The "habit of declaring sympathy for the enemy," Burnside stated, would no longer be tolerated in the Department of the Ohio; persons "committing such offenses" would be arrested and subject to military procedures—that is, be denied rights in the civil courts.[28] The indiscreet general thus set himself up as a censor to draw the fine line between criticism and treason and decide when a speaker or an editor gave aid and comfort to the enemy. He set up his own will as superior to the civil courts, usurping for the military the right to define and judge, to decide the limits of dissent. Worse than that, his proclamation implied that criticism of the administration, in any form, was treason and that civil officials and civil courts had failed to do their duty by not eliminating it.

Speaking at a Republican political rally in Hamilton, halfway

[27] *Dayton Daily Empire*, 6 March 1863.
[28] *Official Records*, ser. 1, 23, pt. 2: 147.

between Dayton and Cincinnati, Burnside gave clear evidence of his poor judgment. To the applause of partisans, he declared that he had the authority to define and suppress treason.[29] Inadvertently, he was taking steps which would help Clement L. Vallandigham gain martyrdom and the Democratic gubernatorial nomination.

Late in April, Vallandigham entrained for Columbus for a three-day stay, intending to further his hopes for the governorship. He attended the Democratic State Convention of April 28, but found little to give him cheer. The skies wept during the entire day and the moon failed to shine at night. The band music sounded like a funeral dirge. Party leaders treated him rather coldly, letting him know that they believed Jewett merited the gubernatorial nomination, that Vallandigham was an unwelcome guest. Jewett, who thought Vallandigham too aggressive and self-serving, expressed his contempt in the cloakrooms and the two aspirants avoided each other. Vallandigham insisted that he be given a chance to speak, and finally talked briefly, but wasted his allotted time in berating the *Ohio State Journal* for calling him a "traitor" and for suggesting that he be arrested.[30]

The hostile attitude of party leaders led Vallandigham to the conclusion that his only hope of getting the nomination was to get himself arrested and ride the public reaction into office. His friends encouraged him to play the game.[31] They knew that Burnside would read the *Ohio State Journal's* suggestion for his arrest. After all, Francis Hurtt, one of the copublishers of that Republican newspaper, was serving as Burnside's quartermaster in Cincinnati, and he surely would endorse the suggestion of his editor, Isaac Jackson Allen. It was even conceivable that the editorial suggestion had originated in Cincinnati, where Hurtt and Burnside saw each other repeatedly. Neither had any use for the Dayton dissenter, and both believed it was time to teach Democrats and would-be traitors a lesson.

Columbus friends, including Samuel Medary of the *Crisis*,

29 *Ohio State Journal*, 21 April 1863.
30 Ibid., 29 April 1863; *Crisis*, 29 April 1863; *Daily Ohio Statesman* (Columbus), 29, 30 April 1863.
31 James A. Garfield, "Diary," entry of 28 January 1877, James A. Garfield Papers, Library of Congress. The entry, in part, reads: ". . . and Thurman stated what I had never heard before, that Vallandigham's [sic] arrest was procured in order to make him candidate for governor, and this was done by his friends."

organized a Democratic rally on April 30 to give Vallandigham a chance to bait Burnside. The man who wanted to be a martyr, therefore, spoke before a "tolerably large" crowd under starlit skies. He made "a bold and manly defense of the right of the people to assemble in times of peace and war, to discuss and hear discussed the policy of any administration, and to approve or condemn the official acts of any one in civil or military authority." He alternately ridiculed and denounced "General Orders, No. 38," boasting somewhat arrogantly of the contempt in which he held that edict. He even challenged Burnside's right to use courts-martial to try citizens who might be arrested for violating "No. 38" or other military decrees. He was daring the general to make good his threat.[32]

Next morning Vallandigham returned to Dayton. Telegraphic dispatches brought reports that General Milo S. Hascall, who had tentatively replaced Carrington, had issued an order quite like Burnside's. Hascall's "General Orders, No. 9" stated that "all newspaper [editors] and public speakers that endeavor to bring the war policy of the Government into disrepute" would be considered "as having violated General Burnside's Order No. 38" and would be "treated accordingly."

Vallandigham fumed. He stated his indignation publicly and in a letter to ex-President Franklin Pierce. Men merited freedom only if they possessed the courage and determination to have it. He reminded the former president of the scornful exclamation of Tiberius regarding the degraded and servile Roman Senate centuries earlier: *"O Homines ad Servitutem paratos!"*[33]

In the *Dayton Empire*, William T. Logan lashed out at Generals Hascall and Burnside and their military decrees; a few suspected that Vallandigham wrote some of the editorials. "Does Mr. Lincoln or his satraps and minions," Logan asked, "suppose for a moment that they can by any power at their command wrest from the freemen of this country that most sacred inheritance of our revolutionary fathers—freedom of speech and of the press?" His closing paragraph expressed open defiance: "Away with your impotent threats of imprisonment in dungeons and bastiles.

[32] *Ohio State Journal,* 2, 4 May 1863; *Daily Ohio Statesman,* 2 May 1863; *Crisis,* 6 May 1863.
[33] Vallandigham to Franklin Pierce (photostatic copy), 11 April 1863, Franklin Pierce Papers, Library of Congress.

Freemen scorn them as 'the tempest scorns a chain.' Prison bars and bolts have no terrors for a freeman in the conscientious discharge of his duty. Fortified behind the Constitution, he can bid defiance to the impotent threats of usurpers and would-be despots."[34]

Burnside's ears burned. He resented the scorn and ridicule of Logan and Vallandigham. The link between his quartermaster, Francis Hurtt, and the editor of the *Ohio State Journal*, Isaac Jackson Allen, insured that paper's endorsement of the arrest of Logan or Vallandigham or both.[35] Burnside needed little prompting to carry out his threats. Vallandigham had thrown down the gauntlet, and the doughty general, with a reputation for rashness, dared not ignore it.

Burnside soon learned that Vallandigham would appear in Mount Vernon on May 1 at a rally of the Democracy of Knox County. He anticipated that the Dayton Democrat would again ridicule "General Orders, No. 38" and denounce the Lincoln administration. Burnside therefore sent to Mount Vernon a party of "observers," consisting of ten Cincinnati citizens and two captains from his own staff in civilian clothes. He instructed the two members of his staff to "observe" the affair and "take notes." One of Vallandigham's friends in Columbus discovered Burnside's intentions and promptly informed the would-be martyr. So the stage was set, and Vallandigham, needing martyrdom to gain his goals, intended to make the most of his opportunity.[36]

Early on the morning of May 1, 1863, the party faithful began to pour into Mount Vernon for the county Democratic rally. They came in carriages, in wagons, on horseback, and even afoot. Delegations from some of the outlying districts and rural villages came in procession, carrying banners, flags, and hickory branches. Backcountry folk, wearing jeans and linseys and belonging to the "unterrified, unwashed Democracy," came in disorganized fashion. Party members, serving as marshals for the day, directed all new arrivals to areas assigned to each

[34] *Dayton Daily Empire,* 1 May 1863. It is likely that this editorial came from Vallandigham's pen.

[35] *Mount Vernon Democratic Banner,* 9 May 1863. The link between the *Ohio State Journal* and General Burnside is also revealed in John Y. Simon, ed., "Reminiscences of Isaac Jackson Allen," *Ohio History* 73 (Autumn 1964): 207-38.

[36] Armstrong, "Personal Recollections," in *Cincinnati Daily Enquirer,* 20 March 1886.

township. Union flags, with all their stars, flew from the numerous hickory poles erected especially for the rally.

Almost all Democrats who came into Mount Vernon to re-affirm their faith in their principles took part in the "grand parade." The procession, estimated to be four or five miles long, numbered nearly five hundred wagons, many bearing Democratic slogans or pointed statements, and took two hours to pass any point along the route. Many of those who watched the procession or marched in it wore "Butternut" badges or "Copperhead" pins to indicate they were proud of their politics and contemptuous of their political opponents.

After the parade, the participants gathered around the several speakers' stands erected for the occasion; the crowd was much too large for all to be within hearing distance of the principal stand. Messrs. Clement L. Vallandigham, Samuel S. Cox, and George H. Pendleton sat in chairs on the main stand, which was decked with flags, banners, emblems, and hickory branches.

Lecky Harper, editor of the *Mount Vernon Democratic Banner*, called the meeting to order. He read off the list of vice-presidents and secretaries, one for each township represented. He next announced the membership of the various committees. While committee members marched off to meetingplaces, Harper intro-duced Vallandigham as the first of the three speakers.

As Vallandigham arose he received a burst of applause "as fairly made the welkin ring." After the shouts and the clapping ceased, the speaker began his discourse with an allusion to the American flags which bedecked the platform. These flags sym-bolized the Constitution of the country, made sacred by Demo-cratic presidents. He revered the flag and he abided by the Constitution—he expected others to do likewise. He remarked that the flags had thirty-four stars and added that all states would still be united if it were not for Republican perfidy—or if his four-section scheme had been adopted as a constitutional amendment.

Then he turned to the discussion of his rights as "a freeman." He did not have to ask Abraham Lincoln or David Tod or Ambrose E. Burnside for the right to speak as he was doing! The audience interrupted with applause, appreciative of his daring and insolence. Intoxicated by the adulation and aware that two of Burnside's agents were taking notes—he noticed one leaning on the platform scribbling in a little black book—Vallandigham fired both barrels. His right to speak was based upon a document which antedated and superceded "General Orders, No. 38." Burnside's military edict was no more than "a bane usurpation of arbitrary power." He could spit upon it and stamp it under foot. His right to speak and criticize was based upon "General Orders, No. 1," the Constitution of the United States. Then he reminded his hearers that oppression and tyranny developed in direct proportion to the servility of a people—their submissiveness, cowardice, and lack of desire to be free. "The sooner the people inform the minions of usurped power," he stated defiantly, "that they will not submit to such restrictions upon their liberties, the better."

The Dayton dissenter continued for nearly two hours more, most inconsiderate of the two well-known men waiting impatiently to follow him on the central stand. He finally closed with the assertion that "the remedy" for all "the evils" was at the polling places and through "the ballot-box." Citizens who valued their rights would use "the ballot-box" to hurl "King Lincoln" from his throne. He added his standard statement that he loved the Union and wished to see it restored by compromise.[37]

Thunderous applause rent the air when Vallandigham finished his bid for martyrdom. The echoes reached Cincinnati and grated upon the sensitive ears of General Burnside. Having crawled out on a limb, he did not dare turn back lest he be accused of indecision or faint-heartedness. After hearing the reports of his two agents, he ordered the arrest of Clement L. Vallandigham. First, of course, he had to ascertain that the dissenter would be at home when the posse, charged with seizing him, arrived in Dayton.

A "gentleman" from Dayton, a Republican who had urged that Vallandigham's tongue be silenced, happened to visit Burnside's headquarters on May 4. He agreed to return to Dayton, ascertain if Vallandigham was at home, and send a telegraphic

[37] Vallandigham's speech can be reconstructed from the account recorded in the *Mount Vernon Democratic Banner*, 9 May 1863, and the report of James T. Irvine, one of the secretaries of the convention, which appears in Vallandigham, *Vallandigham*, pp. 248-59. The accounts of Burnside's two agents appear in "Proceedings of a Military Commission, Convened in Cincinnati, May 6, 1863," Citizens' File, 1861-1865, War Department Collection of Confederate Records, National Archives.

message at exactly eight o'clock that evening. Shortly before eight, General Burnside and his aide walked to the telegraph office to await word from Dayton. Exactly on the hour the noisy receiving instrument tapped out the message "All is well."[38]

Burnside and his aide hurried back to headquarters to sketch out plans for the arrest. They commandeered a special train, ordering the engineers and crew to be ready to leave Cincinnati for Dayton at midnight. Burnside selected his aide-de-camp, Captain Charles G. Hutton, to lead the expedition charged with arresting Vallandigham, and he ordered him to take his entire company of sixty-seven men to help him carry out that assignment. Captain Hutton accepted the orders "to succeed at all hazards" and to return to Cincinnati with his prisoner before daylight.[39]

Vallandigham felt he had outmaneuvered General Burnside and forced his hand. After issuing his rather imprudent military decree and sending agents to take notes at Mount Vernon, the self-righteous general had no choice but to arrest Dayton's best-known politician.

[38] Entry of 5 May 1863, Daniel Read Larned, "Journal," Daniel Read Larned Papers, Library of Congress.
[39] *Official Records,* ser. 2, 5: 555.

11

ARREST AND TRIAL

RUMORS THAT Vallandigham would be arrested had made the rounds of Dayton for more than a year. As early as October 1861, some Dayton Republicans had suggested it to silence his "dastardly influence."[1] Several Republicans revived the idea after his gala homecoming of March 13, 1863. The rumors became rather routine in the days that followed, prompting friends to offer to stand watch and foil attempts to seize him. Vallandigham waived the kind offers, for he needed notoriety to bolster his sagging political fortunes.

On the evening of May 4 Vallandigham retired early. He had returned to Dayton from another out-of-town speaking engagement, and, after a brief visit to the office of the *Empire*, sought the comforts of home. The Vallandigham household now numbered five. Besides his wife and ten-year old son, a sister-in-law and a nephew lived at 323 First Street. The sister-in-law, Miss Belle McMahon, doubled as companion and helpmate to Mrs. Vallandigham, whose nervousness and stability fluctuated with her health, moods, and anxiety. The nephew, John A. McMahon, had read law in Vallandigham's office and in 1861 had formed a partnership with George A. Houk. Young McMahon, exceedingly capable, served as the man-about-the-house when his uncle was away in Washington or pursuing the campaign trail.

About two hours after midnight, when the Vallandigham residence was enshrouded in darkness, a special train from Cincinnati rolled silently into the Dayton station. Captain Charles G. Hutton, in charge of the extraordinary expedition, detailed a handful of men to watch the train while he led the rest of his company quietly through the town to 323 First Street. The captain threw a cordon around the Vallandigham residence, as if fearing that those inside might try to escape. Then Hutton, with a dozen soldiers at his side, rang the doorbell. Vallandigham appeared at an upstairs bedroom window and looked down upon the front steps. He could see the dark shapes of a cluster of men below. He could also see flashlights gleaming amidst the shrubbery and the glittering of bayonets, for the gas-light on the nearby street corner penetrated the darkness. He could hear the muffled voices of the officers, the whispering of the soldiers directly below, and the footsteps of some other armed men.

Vallandigham asked his callers what they wanted. Captain Hutton replied that he had been sent by General Burnside to make an arrest and suggested that Vallandigham come down and surrender. The defiant Democrat answered that he would not— no army officer had the right to arrest him. Nor did Burnside have the right to issue an order for his arrest. Captain Hutton repeated his request, again saying he had an order from General Burnside. The mention of the general's name seemed to infuriate Vallandigham, and he snarled rather scornfully, "If Burnside wants me, let him come up and take me!" Then, leaning out of the bedroom window, he called loudly for the police, as if he expected them to come to his aid. Captain Hutton, very properly, then made his third request for Vallandigham to come down and surrender; he added that Vallandigham might as well stop shouting and that if he would not come down the soldiers would be forced to break down the door. Vallandigham replied that he was not dressed. The captain, in turn, assured him that he would be given time to dress. Vallandigham, instead, redoubled his shouts to the police. Captain Hutton then ordered his men to force the front door and the obedient soldiers attacked it with bars and axes. While the soldiers were pounding and pushing, Vallandigham returned to the front window with a pistol and fired three shots into the air, evidently hoping to alert his Dayton friends.

Vallandigham's shouts, the three pistol shots, and the banging on the front door awakened the rest of the household. Mrs. Vallandigham, nearly crazed with terror, and her excited sister shrieked out of their bedroom windows for the police. Vallandigham, meanwhile, sat down on the edge of the bed to dress himself, his pistol nearby.

The heavy front door refused to yield to the soldiers and
1 Petition (undated), signed by F. J. Tytus and Jacob Morris, addressed to

William H. Seward, in *Official Records*, ser. 2, 2: 128-29.

their implements, so a half dozen went around to the rear to try the back door. In time the rear door gave way and a dozen soldiers, with guns in hand, crowded through and felt their way in the darkness toward the front of the house and the stairway leading to the second floor. Captain Hutton stopped for a moment at the foot of the stairs and again called for Mr. Vallandigham to come down and surrender—he emphasized the third rather than the second syllable of the surname.

"My name is not Vallandigham," replied the man whom Captain Hutton had come to arrest.

"I don't care how you pronounce it," replied the captain, "that's the way we spell it and you are 'my man.' "

The defiant Copperhead refused to obey the order to come downstairs, and the soldiers, led by Captain Hutton, felt their way up the stairway. Meanwhile, Vallandigham locked the door of his bedroom, returned to the front window, and gave a shrill, peculiar whistle which was answered by someone in the distance. As the soldiers started to pound upon his bedroom door, Vallandigham stepped into an adjacent bedroom and locked that door too—putting two locked doors between himself and the soldiery. Using the butts of their muskets, the soldiers knocked out the panels of both doors and stepped through to corner their quarry. Someone had brought a light, and its rays revealed Vallandigham standing in the middle of the room, with his wife and sister-in-law standing and shrieking behind him. The two sisters, in their nightdresses, berated the soldiers for invading their privacy and called them beasts for violating their rights as citizens. Although Vallandigham had put his pistol in his trouser pocket, he did not use the weapon in self-defense. Half a dozen muskets, with bristling bayonets, were pointed at him. He surrendered to Captain Hutton, saying somewhat sarcastically, "You have now broken open my house and overpowered me by superior force, and I am obliged to surrender."[2]

The soldiers lowered their muskets and Captain Hutton asked

---

[2] Entry of 5 May 1863, Daniel Read Larned, "Journal," Daniel Read Larned Papers, Library of Congress; *Cincinnati Daily Gazette*, 5, 6 May 1863; *Cincinnati Daily Enquirer*, 6 May 1863; *Nashville Daily Union*, 26 May 1863; *Richmond* (Va.) *Sentinel*, 13 May 1863; Vallandigham, *Vallandigham*, pp. 255-57. Vallandigham related the account of his arrest at a Democratic rally on 10 October 1867, and it was reported in the *Dayton Daily Ledger*, 30 October 1867.

Vallandigham to lead the way downstairs. The prisoner gave his sobbing, hysterical wife a brief hug and stepped through the shattered panels of the two bedroom doors. The soldiers followed and Vallandigham led them down the stairs and out the front door.

The soldiers stationed in the yard reported that they had heard the ringing of fire bells, several pistol or musket shots, and some shouts or calls in the distance. But only a few Dayton citizens appeared and they gave no trouble. Captain Hutton asked his troops to reassemble, and a bugler sounded recall. As Vallandigham stepped into the street, Captain Hutton moved to his side. Surrounded by soldiers, Hutton and Vallandigham walked toward the railway depot. They boarded the waiting train, with its locomotive belching smoke and emitting steam. As soon as all were aboard, the train started for Cincinnati. Captain Hutton had performed his chore most expeditiously. Not more than thirty minutes elapsed between the arrival of the special train in Dayton and its departure for Cincinnati with the prisoner aboard. The train arrived in Cincinnati just before daybreak, and Captain Hutton conducted his celebrated prisoner to Kemper Barracks, a military post near Cincinnati, where he placed him in a cell as if he were a common criminal.

Vallandigham spent the early morning in his rough cell, awaiting a call from his Dayton friends and preparing a statement for the press. The address, entitled "To the Democracy of Ohio," portrayed its author as "a martyr" whose only crime was love of his party, his country and its Constitution, and civil rights. He intended to give the document to his Dayton friends when they came to call and he hoped the press would broadcast it over Ohio and the entire North.

About mid-morning General Burnside ordered his prominent prisoner transferred to a luxurious room in the Burnet House, the best-known hotel in the entire Midwest. The general also ordered that Vallandigham be served a good lunch, courtesy of the United States government.

Later in the morning a delegation from Dayton arrived to make inquiries of General Burnside and consult with his prisoner. The group included Mayor William H. Gillespie and Vallandigham's nephew, John A. McMahon. The grim general informed his callers that he intended to convene a military commission as soon as possible and give his political prisoner a speedy trial. Burnside then gave them permission to visit Vallandigham. It was a brief visit, closely supervised by several of Burnside's aides. The conferees decided to ask George E. Pugh, George H. Pendleton, and Edward A. Ferguson to serve as Vallandigham's counsel. Pugh and Pendleton were prominent Democratic politicians, and Ferguson was a respected Cincinnati lawyer. Vallandigham, of course, denied that a military commission had any right to try him, but his Dayton friends decided to seek counsel anyway. Before his callers left, Vallandigham "passed" to his nephew his address to the Democracy of Ohio and a note to his wife.

Rumors that Dayton Democrats might invade Cincinnati and demand the prisoner's release or rescue him "by overpowering the guard" caused Burnside to order Vallandigham returned to Kemper Barracks. Still fearful that a rescue operation might be successful, the wary general then transferred his captive to Newport Barracks, across the river and in the midst of an armed camp. There the prisoner, still believing that "Time the Avenger" would "set all things even," was locked up for the night.[3]

Dayton Democrats replied to Burnside's arrest of Vallandigham with a first-class riot. Many Daytonians expressed indignation when they learned that soldiers had battered down the doors of Vallandigham's house and carted him off to Cincinnati. They gathered on street corners, forming "crowds of excited men." Some talked of rescuing Vallandigham; others, embittered, vented their wrath upon President Lincoln, General Burnside, and prominent Dayton Republicans. Supporters of the Lincoln administration went into hiding lest they become the targets of Democratic displeasure.

John T. Logan of the *Dayton Empire* fanned the flames of discontent with an inflammatory editorial. The headlines read:

VALLANDIGHAM KIDNAPPED

A DASTARDLY OUTRAGE!!!

WILL FREE MEN SUBMIT?

THE HOUR FOR ACTION HAS ARRIVED

The editorial mixed innuendo and direct accusation; it cursed the "cowardly, scoundrelly abolitionists" of Dayton and blamed

---

[3] *Cincinnati Daily Enquirer*, 5, 6 May 1863; entry of 5 May 1863, Larned "Journal."

them for advocating the arrest. It suggested that Democrats employ "blood and carnage" to save their "endangered liberties." It characterized Vallandigham's arrest "a hellish outrage," and served to incite readers to revenge.[4]

Logan's ill-advised editorial and liquor from the grog shops helped transform angry men into a mob which gathered in front of the *Empire* building, evidently seeking solace from that bastion of Democratic dogma. Across the corner, at 110 Main Street, stood the *Journal* building, housing the editorial offices and printing plant of the Republican newspaper which had criticized Vallandigham so unmercifully. The *Journal* building symbolized Vallandigham's arrest, the impending draft, and "Black Republicanism." Some members of the mob hurled choice epithets at the *Journal* building, while a few bolder spirits threw stones at the windows. Several rash rascals made balls of pitch, applied a match, and tossed their flaming missiles across the street. One such "turpentine ball" landed among some newspapers in the editorial office of the *Journal* and "in an incredibly short space of time, flames burst from the roof."[5] The misguided malcontents cheered. Another bastille was being destroyed! Democratic hotheads of Dayton thus gave a devilish answer to Burnside's arrest of an ex-congressman seeking to refurbish his political influence.[6]

The fire spread to adjacent buildings, consuming nearly half a block and destroying buildings worth $89,000—a sacrifice to the god of vengeance. The Dayton fire department had trouble checking the spread of the flames, for mob members interfered with the work of the red-helmeted firemen.

Fearing a riot, some perceptive Republicans had earlier asked General Burnside to detail some troops to Dayton. Their arrival brought quick suppression of the riot. One soldier shot a rioter cutting a water hose, the mob dispersed, and the firemen then performed heroically. At the suggestion of Republicans, General Burnside suspended the publication of the *Empire,* arrested editor Logan, and put Montgomery County under martial law.[7]

[4] *Dayton Daily Empire,* 5 May 1863; *Dayton Daily Journal,* 6 May 1863.

[5] Thomas O. Lowe to his brother William, 11 May 1863, Thomas O. Lowe Papers, Dayton and Montgomery County Public Library.

[6] Ibid.; *Dayton Journal,* 6 May 1863; *Cincinnati Daily Commercial,* 7 May 1863.

[7] Burnside, "Special Orders, No. 164," published in the *Dayton Daily Journal,* 7 May 1863. The *Empire* property was auctioned off on May 23. Nine Vallandighamers arrested during the riot were released in Cincinnati three weeks later,

No sober Dayton Democrat endorsed the action of the mob. Most recognized that Logan's editorial of May 5 had encouraged an angry people to open defiance, and they blamed his "crazy article" as much as they blamed Burnside's "General Orders, No. 38" for the riot. It was still another case of imprudent acts producing unfortunate results.[8] Thomas O. Lowe, recognized in Democratic circles as a disciple of Vallandigham, wrote an "open letter" to allay the excitement and ask for a return to reason, law, and order. After stating that "mobocracy" and "democracy" had opposite meanings, young Lowe told his readers that he believed in the right of revolution, but other means of expressing a grievance still existed.

> Whenever people are crushed beneath the heel of despotism, and have no other means left them of obtaining the inalienable rights of man [wrote Vallandigham's disciple] it is their sacred right after long suffering to arise in their might against their oppressors. *The circumstances justifying revolution do not exist in our country now.* Although in my judgment, there have been many unwise, arbitrary and cruel things done by the present administration towards their political opponents in the North, we have still left us the great remedy for all political wrongs, the ballot box. As long as there is any alternate besides absolute slavery, an appeal to arms is a high crime against God and humanity.[9]

It was the advice of a moderate reacting to mob violence and the threat of anarchy. Young Lowe, like his mentor, was much more a student of Edmund Burke than of John Locke.

The same telegraphic wires which carried the story of Vallandigham's arrest and the Dayton riot also broadcast the details of the dramatic defeat of General Joseph Hooker's army in the Battle of Chancellorsville. Union casualties totaled more than 17,000 as the Army of the Potomac suffered another stunning defeat. If Vallandigham had expected that the story of his arrest would give him headlines and widespread sympathy, he was somewhat mistaken. Editors, both Democratic and Republican,

---

after swearing anew allegiance to the government. Dayton Democrats revived the *Empire* on August 6, 1863, importing George Barber (one-time editor of the *Nashville Republican Banner*) as the new editor.

[8] Thomas O. Lowe to his brother William, 11 May 1863, Lowe Papers.

[9] Thomas O. Lowe to editors of the *Dayton Journal*, 6 May 1863, manuscript in the Lowe Papers, printed in *Dayton Daily Journal* on 7 May 1863.

headlined the Battle of Chancellorsville, and Vallandigham's arrest seemed of secondary importance.

Nevertheless, the arrest drew fire from many quarters. Dr. John McElwee of the *Hamilton True Telegraph*, regarding himself as a personal friend of Burnside's prisoner, wrote of "the most atrocious outrage ever perpetrated in any civilized land."[10] Samuel Medary not only called Burnside's act "a great blunder," but warned the Lincoln administration that civil war might visit the Midwest if rights were trampled upon any more.[11] Lecky Harper applied the old quotation "The blood of the martyrs is the seed of the Church" to Vallandigham's arrest, wrote of the "Reign of Terror" which had visited his country, and predicted that history would accord him honors.[12] Perhaps Vallandigham was disappointed because James J. Faran of the *Cincinnati Enquirer* protested so mildly, but General Burnside had intimidated him, too. On the day that he ordered Vallandigham's arrest, he called in Faran and S. B. Wiley McLean, editors and proprietors of the *Enquirer,* and ordered them to play the part of patriots unless they too wanted to look out through the iron bars of a prisoner's cell.[13]

Nearly every Democratic newspaper published Vallandigham's address "To the Democracy of Ohio" which McMahon had smuggled out of the prisoner's room in Cincinnati. After it appeared in one Democratic newspaper, other editors republished it and gave it nation-wide circulation. The address read:

> *To the Democracy of Ohio:* I am here in a military bastile for no other offense than my political opinions, and the defense of them and the rights of the people, and of your constitutional liberties. Speeches made in the hearing of thousands of you, in denunciation of the usurpation of power, infractions of the Constitution and the laws, and of military despotism, were the causes of my arrest and imprisonment. I am a Democrat; for Constitution, for law, for Union, for liberty; this is my only crime. For no disobedience to the Constitution, for no violation of law, for no word, sign or gesture of sympathy with the men of the South, who are for disunion and Southern independence, but in obedience to their demand, as well as the demand of Northern Abolition disunionists and traitors, I am here today in bonds, but

10 *Hamilton True Telegraph*, 11 June 1863.
11 *Crisis* (Columbus), 13 May 1863.
12 *Mount Vernon Democratic Banner*, 9, 16, 23 May 1863.
13 Entry of 6 May 1863, Larned "Journal."

'Time, at last, sets all things even.'
Meanwhile, Democrats of Ohio, of the Northwest, of the United States, be firm, be true to your principles, to the Constitution, to the Union, and all will yet be well. As for myself, I adhere to every principle, and will make good, through imprisonment and life itself, every pledge and declaration which I ever made, uttered or maintained from the beginning. To you, to the whole people, to time, I again appeal. Stand firm! Falter not an instant!

C. L. Vallandigham[14]

Although some moderate Republicans expressed concern over General Burnside's precipitous action, most of the influential editors of the party endorsed the arrest. Isaac Jackson Allen of the *Ohio State Journal* did not disappoint General Burnside or his quartermaster and top aide, Francis Hurtt. Both the *Cincinnati Gazette* and the *Cincinnati Commercial* endorsed the arrest and wrote of the need to crush traitors in the North. The *Dayton Journal,* which had earlier recommended Vallandigham's arrest, neither condemned nor defended Burnside. Dayton Republicans tried to resurrect the *Journal* from the ashes; it reappeared in reduced size and was printed on another press for a week.[15]

While Republicans and Democrats in Ohio debated the necessity and desirability of Vallandigham's arrest, General Burnside took steps to set the wheels of a court-martial in motion. There was precedent for such arbitrary action, for early in the war Major General John C. Frémont, commanding the Department of the West, had arrested Edmund J. Ellis, a Missouri editor. Frémont had convened a court-martial, which found editor Ellis guilty on every charge and sentenced him to be exiled "out of Missouri." The Ellis case came to the attention of Simon Cameron, Secretary of War, in 1861; he not only approved the summary action, but said he would follow the same procedure in other departments of the army.[16]

---

[14] *Crisis*, 13 May 1863. The address also appears in Vallandigham, *Vallandigham,* pp. 260-61.

[15] The *Journal* appeared as a 12″x18″ tabloid and was printed on presses which printed the Brethren (Mennonite) Church weekly. Daytonians, meanwhile, raised $6,000 to reestablish the *Journal* and invited William D. Bickham (aide-de-camp on the staff of Maj. Gen. William S. Rosecrans) to become editor. Bickham accepted the invitation and assumed control of the *Journal* on 11 May, six days after the riot. Bickham made the *Journal* into one of Ohio's best-known newspapers.

[16] The Ellis case receives rather cursory treatment in Dean Sprague, *Freedom*

Furthermore, General Burnside must have known that no jury in a civil or criminal court in Ohio would find Vallandigham guilty either of violating "General Orders, No. 38" or of treason. Having a bird in the hand, the headstrong general had no intention of letting it return to the bush. He therefore selected a panel of eight army officers, all his subordinates and servants, to try the case. He set ten o'clock the next morning (May 6) as the starting time for the trial.

Vallandigham awakened early on the morning of the sixth in his heavily-barred room in the Newport Barracks. From his window he witnessed the roll call after reveille and saw "Old Glory" revealing its stars and stripes on the nearby flagpole. He heard the regimental band playing "Hail Columbia, Happy Land" while he awaited word regarding his trial. Later in the morning, a squad of soldiers carrying loaded rifles and glistening bayonets called at Vallandigham's cell to escort him across the river to the room where the military commission had convened, with Brigadier General Robert B. Potter presiding and Captain James M. Cutts serving as judge advocate.[17]

After the prisoner was escorted into the room, the judge advocate read General Burnside's order appointing the members of the military commission. Next he asked the prisoner if he had any objection to offer against any of the eight members of the commission. Vallandigham scanned the faces of the eight members confronting him. No, he was not acquainted with any of them, so he had no objection to any individual. At the time the prisoner did not know that only one of the eight was a citizen of Ohio, one was "an unnaturalized foreign adventurer," and another had once been convicted for keeping "a disreputable house." Nor did he know then that Judge Advocate James M. Cutts would soon afterwards be apprehended while standing on a chair peaking through a transom into a lady's bedchamber in the Burnet House.[18]

Vallandigham next turned to the presiding officer, Brig. Gen. Robert B. Potter, to protest that the military commission had no authority to try him. He belonged to neither the land nor the

---

under *Lincoln* (Boston, 1965), p. 230. Despite its title, Sprague's book is concerned in the main with only the first year of the war.

[17] Vallandigham's account, in *Dayton Daily Ledger,* 30 October 1867.

[18] Ibid.; *Crisis,* 30 October 1867.

naval forces of the United States, nor the militia in actual service, so he was only under the civil courts of the land. General Potter shrugged his shoulders, then shook his head. He seemed perplexed by the legal language which Vallandigham employed. Judge Advocate Cutts ignored the prisoner's protest and read the charges against him: "Publicly expressing, in violation of 'General Orders, No. 38' . . . sympathies for those in arms against the Government of the United States, declaring disloyal sentiments and opinions, with the object and purpose of weakening the power of the Government in its effort to suppress the unlawful rebellion." Next the judge advocate read the specification which stated when, where, and how the prisoner had violated "General Orders, No. 38," after which he asked the prisoner "what his plea was." Vallandigham refused to enter a plea and continued to insist that the military court had no right to try him. The presiding officer interrupted Vallandigham's argument, ordering a plea of "Not Guilty" entered upon the record.[19]

The court then offered Vallandigham a chance to consult his counsel, recessing for that purpose until 1:30 P.M. First, however, the prisoner asked for a delay in the trial in order to subpoena Fernando Wood of New York City as a witness. The presiding officer consulted the judge advocate and they decided against any delay—they believed the prisoner was using stalling tactics.

When the court reconvened, General Potter asked Vallandigham if he desired to have his counsel present for the proceedings. Feeling that he would be sanctioning the trial if his counsel was invited into the courtroom, Vallandigham answered no. So Messrs. Pugh, Pendleton, and Ferguson remained in an adjoining room.

Judge Advocate Cutts then called his first witness, Captain Harrington R. Hill, who testified that he had attended the Democratic rally at Mount Vernon on May 1 and had heard Vallandigham's speech from beginning to end. He had occupied a spot near the end of the platform, a scant six feet from the speaker. He referred constantly to his copious notes and recon-

19 "Proceedings of a Military Commission, Convened in Cincinnati, May 6, 1863," Citizens' File, 1861-1865, War Department Collection of Confederate Records, National Archives.

structed Vallandigham's speech rather extensively. Several times the attentive prisoner interrupted Captain Hill, either to make a minor correction or to offer words of explanation. After Hill, prodded by Cutts, completed his account, Vallandigham cross-examined him. He was still interrogating Captain Hill when the clock showed 3:30. Brigadier General Potter then adjourned the trial until the next morning.

The second day's trial began with a review of the previous day's proceedings and testimony. The judge advocate again called Captain Hill to the stand, and Vallandigham probed all corners. Next, Captain John A. Means was called to the stand; he was the second of the two aides who had been sent to Mount Vernon to take notes on Vallandigham's speech. He had occupied a position directly in front of the stand, about ten feet from Vallandigham, and had heard "the whole of the speech." His testimony corroborated most of what Captain Hill had said earlier. Vallandigham, still acting as his own lawyer, cross-examined Means. The prisoner limited his second cross-examination to twenty minutes. The judge advocate rested his evidence.

Vallandigham asked the presiding officer to recess the trial for fifteen minutes so that he could consult his counsel. The prisoner returned to the courtroom with the Hon. Samuel S. Cox, who had hurried down to the Queen City to testify in Vallandigham's behalf. General Potter decided to let Cox testify, and he took the witness stand. The Columbus congressman stated that he had heard Vallandigham's entire speech, paying close attention, since he was scheduled to speak next. Cox steadfastly denied that Vallandigham had applied any epithet to General Burnside, as the other witnesses claimed he had. Cox also stated that the Dayton Democrat had denounced military orders generally, not "General Orders, No. 38" specifically. Furthermore, Cox affirmed, Vallandigham had not counseled resistance to the laws. He, as well as other speakers at Mount Vernon, had denounced the perversion of the original objectives of the war and had decried the move to bring about peace by recognizing the independence of the Confederacy. Vallandigham, he declared, still wanted peace and reunion.

The judge advocate admitted that it seemed feasible that Vallandigham had denounced military orders generally and not

"General Orders, No. 38" specifically. The prisoner then dropped his request to call other witnesses and asked for time to prepare a written defense. The court reluctantly acquiesced, recessing for half an hour while he wrote his report or protest.

When the military commission reconvened at 5:00 P.M., Vallandigham asked that Cox's testimony be read aloud. The judge advocate consented, confident that the court would return a verdict favorable to Burnside. The defendant concluded the court session by reading aloud his own statement. It challenged the legality of the arrest and trial, emphasizing that military courts had no jurisdiction over him. He insisted upon a civil trial according to due process of law. Citizens certainly had the right to criticize public policy and public servants. And he closed by avowing that he had never counseled disobedience to the Constitution, nor resistance to law or lawful authority.[20]

After Vallandigham read his written protest, the judge advocate asked that the room be cleared "for deliberation." The commission members dared not challenge their superior's action. Thus they found the prisoner "Guilty" of the charge and the specifications, with the exception of one of the thirteen items listed. The members had more trouble agreeing on what penalty to impose. They discussed exiling the prisoner to the Confederacy. Shooting him, they concluded would be exceedingly extreme and would make him a martyr. Eventually they agreed upon imprisonment.

The presiding officer called Vallandigham before him to hear the sentence read. He would be "placed in close confinement in some fortress of the United States, to be designated by the commanding officer of the Department, there to be kept during the continuance of the war." General Burnside, after approving the findings of his hand-picked military commission, selected Fort Warren in Boston Harbor as the place of "confinement."[21]

Two days after the military commission brought forth its verdict, the Hon. George E. Pugh moved for a writ of habeas corpus on behalf of Mr. Vallandigham before Judge Humphrey H. Leavitt of the United States Court for the Southern District

[20] Ibid.
[21] Ibid. The proceedings of the military commission were later published in *Official Records*, ser. 2, 5: 633-46, and in Vallandigham, *Vallandigham*, pp. 262-84.

of Ohio. Although Congress (by act of March 3, 1863) had authorized "the President . . . to suspend the privilege of the writ," he had not done so in Ohio. Furthermore, Pugh and Vallandigham believed Taney's decision in *Ex Parte Merryman* had repudiated such earlier action in the Washington sector. Judge Leavitt, leaning backward to cooperate with the military, asked that notice of Pugh's application be given to Burnside. The impulsive general, in turn, prepared a forthright defense of his authority and his actions. He claimed a legal and constitutional right, as commander of the Department of the Ohio, to arrest and try Vallandigham. Evidently Burnside regarded the states north of the Ohio River as "a vast army camp" in which every soldier and civilian was subject to military authority.[22] Pugh, arguing in Vallandigham's behalf, countered with able and convincing arguments in behalf of habeas corpus action, citing English and American precedents. He contended that civil rights were paramount, not subject to the whims of military men.

Pugh was followed by Benjamin F. Perry, a capable Cincinnati lawyer, who defended Burnside's summary action. He appealed to patriotic passion, praised the grand old flag, and endorsed "the doctrine of necessity." Pugh arose to challenge Perry's arguments, speaking with even greater eloquence than he had before. He made an impassioned plea for civil rights, sacred and essential in all but dictatorships. "We cannot move a single step," Pugh properly asserted, "but we do not see with what jealous care our fathers handcuffed military power."[23] At the conclusion of Pugh's plea, Judge Leavitt took the case under advisement, expressing the hope that he might be able to render a decision in about a week.

Vallandigham spent the week in Room 246 of the Burnet House; General Burnside had him transferred to these more comfortable quarters from the barren and barred room in the Newport Barracks. The new room was well guarded, however, and the guards had instructions to shoot to kill in case of an attempted escape or rescue.[24] Vallandigham had quite a few visitors from Dayton, with Mayor Gillespie, Dr. Jefferson A.

[22] 28 Federal Cases 923 (1863).
[23] Ibid.; *Cincinnati Daily Gazette*, 16 May 1863.
[24] Vallandigham, quoted in *Dayton Daily Ledger*, 30 October 1867.

Walter, his nephew, and David Houk repeatedly stopping to buoy his hopes. George H. Pendleton, congressman from Cincinnati, and Washington McLean, Democratic "boss" of Hamilton County, came every day for an extended visit. George Pugh also spent most of his spare hours with Vallandigham.

The prominent prisoner found time to write a dozen letters, and his Dayton callers smuggled them out of Room 246. His letters to his wife indicated concern for her health; he tried to build up her faith in the future and instructed her to avoid a nervous breakdown. He assured her that time would right all wrongs and bring them "days of prosperity, happiness, and exultation." "I depend on you to be self-possessed and patient," he stated in one letter, "no matter what happens to me." This was an indication that he did not expect a favorable ruling from Judge Leavitt. Vallandigham still retained his defiant spirit. "Remember me to my friends," he added once, ". . . enemies I will remember myself."[25]

The impenitent prisoner also wrote two letters to Manton Marble, the influential editor of the New York World. In the first Vallandigham thanked Marble for his "noble articles" denouncing Burnside's high-handed practices. The second anticipated that Judge Leavitt would surrender principle and bow to expediency. In fact, he thought Judge Leavitt seemed to be "in league with Burnside." Vallandigham predicted that posterity would link Leavitt to "Empson & Dudley & Jeffries [sic], . . . the basest & most servile judges of the worst periods of English Tyranny." He asked Marble "to open up on him [Leavitt] till his infamy becomes historic."[26]

While the public awaited Judge Leavitt's decision, rumors concerning the disposition of Vallandigham, if he was not freed by the writ, made the rounds of the newspapers. Speculation begot rumors, and rumors enhanced the speculation. It was reported, for example, that Burnside's preference had been a death sentence—execution by a firing squad. Another report had Vallandigham being sent to the Dry Tortugas, a group of ten coral keys some seventy miles west of the southermost tip of

[25] Vallandigham to "My Very, Very Dear, Dear Wife," 14 May 1863, published in Vallandigham, Vallandigham, pp. 284-85.
[26] 12, 15 May 1863, Manton Marble Papers, Library of Congress.

Florida. Since the military commission which had tried Vallandigham had considered exiling him to the Confederacy, reports that he might be exiled also made the rounds. Then of course there was speculation as to what prison might be selected by General Burnside if Vallandigham was confined to a felon's cell.[27]

After consulting with General Burnside, Judge Leavitt ruled against the writ of habeas corpus sought in Vallandigham's behalf. He chose to ignore Marshall's decision in *United States vs. Burr* and Taney's decision in *Ex Parte Merryman*. Since he had weak grounds for his refusal, he turned to the concept of "moral guilt." There was a type of treason, Leavitt argued, not covered by the law or the Constitution. This was "moral guilt." Those who live under the protection and enjoy the benefits of the benign government "must learn that they cannot stab its vitals with impunity." Those who criticize a government in time of crisis "should expect" to be treated arbitrarily, for necessity is the law of self-preservation. "The sole question," Judge Leavitt stated, "is whether the arrest was legal; . . . its legality depends on the necessity which existed for making it, and of that necessity . . . this Court cannot judiciously determine."[28]

Aware that General Burnside would ignore a writ of habeas corpus if it was issued in Vallandigham's behalf, Judge Leavitt bowed to expediency and the will of the military. In effect, he allowed the general to intimidate him. He allowed practicality and his own political predilections to twist the law. "Not since the days of Empson, Dudley, or Jeffrey[s]," Vallandigham said four years later, "has such servility to executive power been exhibited."[29]

Two days after Judge Leavitt ruled in the case, Burnside announced that he had selected Fort Warren for the confinement of his prisoner.[30] Vallandigham, of course, hoped that the summary treatment accorded him would make him a hero and

---

[27] *Washington* (D.C.) *Chronicle,* 14 May 1863; *Richmond Sentinel,* 19 May 1863; Vallandigham's speech of 24 October 1867, published in *Crisis,* 30 October 1867. "Pendleton telegraphed you this afternoon," Vallandigham once wrote to his wife, "that the absurd Tortugas story was denied by authorities." Vallandigham, *Vallandigham,* pp. 284-85.

[28] 28 Federal Cases 923 (1863).

[29] *Crisis,* 30 October 1867.

[30] *Official Records,* ser. 2, 5: 657.

martyr in the eyes of those who loved liberty and glorified civil rights. He dreamed that a public reaction would cause the bastilles to crumble and give him the governorship of Ohio and recognition in history. He could repeat Richard Lovelace's famous quotation: "Stone walls do not a prison make, Nor iron bars a cage."

12

LINCOLN VS. VALLANDIGHAM: CONTENTION FOR PUBLIC OPINION

ABRAHAM LINCOLN and Clement L. Vallandigham had several things in common. Both were successful lawyers possessing the typical barrister's high regard for property rights and law and order. Both served their political apprenticeships in the arena of state politics; Lincoln served four terms in the state legislature, Vallandigham but two. Both served in Congress, Lincoln one term and Vallandigham three. Both cultivated their political ambitions; neither could resist the siren song of "Dame Politics." Political campaigns exhilarated both, for they found matching wits with clever and capable antagonists a stimulating challenge. Both possessed the ability to develop rapport with an audience, learning to blend wit, sincerity, and argumentation into an effective formula. Both associated themselves with the common man, shunning sophistry and pretense. Yet neither had the vices of the common man of the upper Midwest; neither smoked, cursed, or drank whiskey, though at one time Lincoln had tended a still.

Although Lincoln and Vallandigham held common views regarding slavery in 1850, believing it "a domestic institution which was morally wrong, yet protected by the Constitution," the two went in opposite directions in the years that followed. Vallandigham repressed the belief that slavery was morally wrong into the recesses of his mind and came close in later years to defending that "peculiar institution." Even at the time of his arrest he still dreamed of a federal union *with slavery.* Lincoln, on the other hand, discarded his inaugural pledge that he would not and dared not "touch" slavery. His proclamations of emancipation, which Vallandigham bitterly opposed, proved that the president had changed his views and shifted his ground.

Actually Lincoln and Vallandigham were unlike in more ways

than they were alike. Lincoln, like Douglas, was a Western nationalist; Vallandigham called himself a Western sectionalist. Lincoln became a servant of New England and industrialism; Vallandigham resented the efforts of New England to impose her cultural patterns, social ideas, and economic domination upon the West. From his earliest days in politics Vallandigham advocated states' rights, opposed banks and tariffs, and imagined he was promoting Jacksonian Democracy. States' rights evolved from an abstraction into an integral part of Vallandigham's philosophy, becoming a political dogma. Lincoln, from the first, moved in an opposite direction. As a young man he memorized Clay's speeches, accepted Clay's ideas about the national welfare, and followed Clay into the Whig party. As a Democrat in the Ohio legislature, Vallandigham gave his full support to the Mexican War; as a Whig in Congress, Lincoln opposed "Polk's War." Vallandigham came to accept Douglas's doctrine of "popular sovereignty" for the territories; Lincoln took a positive stand against it.

Vallandigham read all the standard works in the field of political economy and considered himself a disciple of Edmund Burke. He developed a rigidity in his political ideas, and was prone to believe his views right and those of others wrong. He could not shift his ground, so he revered the past and worried about the future. Lincoln, on the other hand, had a limited knowledge of political theory; he gained his knowledge of politics from the newspapers and by active involvement. In fact, he was a political pragmatist, less intransigent than Vallandigham and willing to adopt "new views" as soon as he regarded them to be "true views." Lincoln knew how to bow graciously to pressure, and he could retreat from a position without qualms of conscience. Yet there were some basic principles he would never surrender. He believed slavery morally wrong and he held tightly to the no-slavery-in-the-territories doctrine. He believed in democratic government—"of the people, by the people, and for the people." He regarded states' rights doctrine as a political heresy, and believed in the destiny of the nation. And as a pragmatist, he convinced himself that coercion was the most realistic road to reunion.

Partisanship, practiced by both Lincoln and Vallandigham,

drove the two farther apart. Vallandigham blamed the Republicans for the failure of the Crittenden Compromise and became one of the most outspoken critics of the extraordinary measures Lincoln believed essential to the prosecution of the war. Lincoln's emancipation measure widened the rift, and so did Vallandigham's role as a gadfly in Congress. When the Dayton congressman, on January 14, 1863, took steps to assume the leadership of the ill-organized peace crusade, the two became more than partisan enemies. To complicate matters, Lincoln believed what he read about Vallandigham in the Republican newspapers, failing to allow for the distortion and misrepresentations in their anti-Vallandigham campaign. The *New York Times* report of Vallandigham's Newark speech exemplified irresponsible reporting and misled Lincoln as to what Vallandigham had really said. Lincoln's views of Vallandigham were also shaped by the statements of prominent men in Lincoln's confidence. Horace Greeley believed Vallandigham "a moral traitor" if not a legal one. Benjamin F. Wade, influential chairman of the Joint Committee on the Conduct of the War, bluntly called Vallandigham a traitor in his public speeches, as did United States Senator Zachariah Chandler. Salmon P. Chase and Edwin M. Stanton, members of Lincoln's cabinet, also believed that Vallandigham gave aid and encouragement to the enemy.

Lincoln found himself on the horns of a dilemma when General Burnside arrested Vallandigham early on the morning of May 6, for Lincoln was reluctant to interfere with freedom of speech and press in the republic, even in time of war. From the first, General Burnside had acted high-handedly. He had failed to report his action immediately to his superiors, so President Lincoln, Secretary of War Stanton, and Maj. Gen. Henry W. Halleck knew only what they read in the newspapers. Lincoln and Stanton wondered if the rash general had jumped into water way over his head, and they feared that his summary action might bring public wrath down upon the administration.

After Lincoln read of Vallandigham's arrest, he telegraphed Burnside to ask if the newspaper stories were correct. At the same time he assured the general that he would give his full support to the maintenance of law and order. Burnside replied promptly, "Your dispatch just rec'd. I thank you for your kind assurance of support & beg to say that all possible effort will be made on my part to sustain the Gov't of the United States in its fullest authority."[1] The reply, however, made no mention of Vallandigham's arrest nor of his plans for a speedy military trial.

Lincoln still had to rely on newspaper reports for information about events in Cincinnati. General Burnside sent no official report on the arrest or trial to Washington. "Gen'l B. [Burnside] has acted without any special instructions from me or the Scty of War," General Halleck complained as late as May 18, "and as far as I know, he has made no official report of the charges, trial, or sentence."[2]

Burnside's solitary course, plus rumors that Judge Noah H. Swayne might hear Vallandigham's application for a writ of habeas corpus, worried Lincoln and Stanton. Judge Swayne, sitting in the U.S. Circuit Court for Ohio, had been purged by the state's Republicans five years earlier, and Stanton therefore feared that he might render a pro-Vallandigham decision, repeating the story of *Ex Parte Merryman*. In an effort to forestall such a decision, Stanton prepared an order suspending the writ in Vallandigham's case and drafted an accompanying dispatch to General Burnside. He put the two documents on Lincoln's desk for his consideration and signature. Lincoln solicited advice from William H. Seward and Salmon P. Chase. Both warned him that such special action would stir the Ohio beehive even more and both advised him against Stanton's proposal. Chase also reported that he had heard Vallandigham's plea would be made in Judge Leavitt's court, not Swayne's. When newspaper reports verified this, Lincoln and his cabinet members breathed easier. They evidently expected Judge Leavitt to give a decision favorable to Burnside and the federal government. Stanton's special proclamation, therefore, never received Lincoln's signature.[3]

Although he had not yet had an official report from General Burnside, Lincoln took up the Vallandigham case at a cabinet

---

[1] Telegram, 8 May 1863, Robert Todd Lincoln Papers, Library of Congress. Lincoln's inquiry seems to be a lost item.

[2] Halleck to Francis Lieber, 18 May 1863, Francis Lieber Papers, Huntington Library.

[3] Lincoln to Stanton, 13 May 1863, Edwin M. Stanton Papers, Library of Congress. The two documents which Stanton drafted are in the Robert Todd Lincoln Papers.

meeting on May 19. The secretary of the navy, Gideon Welles, bluntly called Burnside's summary action a grave "error"—it had embarrassed the administration. The other cabinet members seemed to agree, most doubting that there was a real necessity for it. But, since it had been done, all favored giving the government's support to the ill-advised general. Someone suggested it would be more judicious to exile Vallandigham to the Confederacy than to confine him to a cell in Fort Warren, and the rest of the cabinet endorsed the proposal. Imprisonment might make him a martyr, whereas exile to the Confederacy might carry the implication that he was among friends. Lincoln liked the suggestion. He therefore changed the sentence from imprisonment to banishment and instructed his secretary of war to send Vallandigham "beyond the lines."[4]

Stanton took immediate steps to carry out the president's directive. First, he inquired of Burnside where Vallandigham was at the moment. Burnside replied that the prisoner was "under guard" and still in Cincinnati. Stanton then ordered the prisoner sent to General Rosecrans, "to be put" by him "beyond the lines." Stanton also sent a letter to Rosecrans, instructing him to "receive" Vallandigham and keep him in "close custody" until he was turned over to the Confederates. If the prisoner returned, he should be rearrested, and Rosecrans should then await further orders.[5]

Before taking steps to carry out his orders, Burnside appealed to his superiors not to change the sentence. "In making up a verdict in the case," Burnside argued, "the sentence to send the prisoner South was . . . fully discussed and decided against." Would not some view the change in sentence as a challenge to the validity of the military trial? Judge Leavitt's decision, in a sense, gave approval to the summary action and it was best to leave well enough alone.[6] Lincoln, however, having a better grasp of factors affecting public opinion, refused to give in to

4 Howard K. Beale, ed., *Diary of Gideon Wells*, 3 vols. (New York, 1960), 1: 306; idem, ed., *The Diary of Edward Bates, 1859-1866* (New York, 1933), p. 306; telegram (in cypher), Lincoln to Burnside, 29 May 1863, Special Collections Division, Brown University Library, Providence; telegrams, Stanton to Burnside, both dated 19 May 1863, in *Official Records*, ser. 2, 5: 656-57.

5 Telegrams, Stanton to Burnside and Burnside to Stanton, both 19 May 1863, and letter, Stanton to Rosecrans, 19 May 1863, in *Official Records*, ser. 2, 5: 656-57.

6 Burnside to Stanton, 20 May 1863, *Official Records*, ser. 2, 5: 665.

Burnside's request. He asked that the reluctant general carry out his instructions "without delay."[7]

Even before Lincoln instructed his secretary of war to send Vallandigham beyond the lines, the contest for public opinion had begun in earnest. Burnside's summary action had caused a storm of protest. Lincoln and his cabinet felt the gusts in Washington as winds of remonstrance swept the prestige of the administration to an all-time low. The Union defeat at Chancellorsville, of course, also helped undermine public confidence. So did the ever-intensifying spirit of defeatism which nurtured the peace movement. Greenbacks slipped in value, reflecting dwindling confidence in eventual success. Copperheads grew in number and boldness. The movement reached high tide in May and June of 1863. Gloom settled over Washington as public opinion swung against the administration.

Democratic editors led the blistering attack upon Burnside and Lincoln. They recognized that the general's action was a threat to their rights as well as to Vallandigham's. "For when his right goes down," stated one editor who had no special love for Vallandigham, "there goes down with it my right, and yours, and every man's."[8] Some Democratic editors declared the prisoner both hero and martyr. The editor of the *Iowa City State Press*, for example, wrote: "Noble Vallandigham! Doubly noble in your imprisonment! When this wild storm of fanaticism shall have spent itself, the people—chastized into the exercise of their 'sober second thought'—will do justice to your motives and your actions."[9] John J. Jacobs of the *Ashland Union* expressed his indignation in strong language in dozens of editorials, including one entitled "The Reign of Terror"; he predicted that the Democratic press would be silenced, elections controlled by the bayonet, and a dictatorship established in Washington.[10] Samuel Medary of the *Crisis* ranted and raved against both Burnside and the Lincoln administration. "Would to God," he wrote with great feeling, "that the authorities were fully sensible to the great blunder they have made [and] of the slumbering

---

[7] E. R. S. Canby to Burnside, 20 May 1863, *Official Records*, ser. 2, 5: 666.
[8] *Detroit Free Press*, 8, 26 May, 7 June 1863; *Hamilton True Telegraph*, 11 June 1863.
[9] 9 May 1863.
[10] 20 May 1863.

volcano underneath."[11] Impolitic editors coined new epithets for Lincoln and refurbished old ones: "usurper," "flat-boat tyrant," "demagogue," "dictator," "fool," "Caesar," "bumblehead," "despot," and "a mere doll, worked by strings."[12]

Democrats who expected the *Dubuque Herald* to excoriate Burnside and Lincoln were not disappointed. The editor had a reputation for using a stiletto effectively. "A crime," the editor wrote, "has been committed against the most vital right of the poor and the rich, and humble and the exalted—the right to think, to speak, to live. When this thing is consummated, then plainly before the American people does Abraham Lincoln stand—the murderer of the nation. The plea of military or governmental necessity is a flimsy screen that will command no respect. No necessity can justify the monstrous outrage."[13] No one, perhaps, summed up the case as succinctly as Henry N. Walker of the *Detroit Free Press.* "Vallandigham was arrested for no crime known to law," he wrote, "tried by no tribunal recognized as having any cognizance of crimes committed by man in civilized life, sentenced to a punishment never heard of in any free country, and arbitrarily changed by the President to one not recognized in the Constitution."[14]

Even Democratic editors who had disapproved of Vallandigham's antiwar views joined the chorus of protesters. Manton Marble of the *New York World,* for example, wrote several strong articles condemning General Burnside's high-handed tactics. Furthermore, Marble viewed Burnside's defense of his action as both ridiculous and execrable.[15]

Democratic orators joined the party's editors in attacking Burnside and criticizing Lincoln. Party chieftains sponsored protest rallies or indignation meetings to intensify public reaction to the arrest of a civilian by army authorities and to his trial in a military court. Nearly every city in the North witnessed

---

[11] 13 May 1863.

[12] *Chatfield Democrat,* 23 May 1863; *LaCrosse Democrat,* 16, 23, 30 May 1863; *See-Bote* (Milwaukee), 13 May 1863; *St. Paul Pioneer and Democrat,* 26 June, 3 July 1863; *Hamilton True Telegraph,* 18 June 1863; *Detroit Free Press,* 8, 26 May 1863.

[13] *Dubuque Herald,* 14 May 1863.

[14] 26 August 1863.

[15] Vallandigham to Manton Marble, 12, 15 May 1863, Manton Marble Papers, Library of Congress.

such a meeting. The Detroit protest meeting of May 25 typified these well-organized affairs. Orators took turns depicting Vallandingham as hero or martyr and flaying Burnside and the Lincoln administration. An emotionalized audience gave three lusty cheers for the man who had dared defy military proclamations, and its "resounding approval" to resolutions which denounced the arrest, glorified civil rights, and arraigned the administration for backing Burnside.[16]

The Indianapolis indignation rally attracted national attention because of the size of the crowd and the remarkable speech of Daniel W. Voorhees, one of the finest orators in the Midwest. Voorhees repeatedly referred to Vallandigham as his "friend"; he eulogized liberty and deplored the demise of "the first and most sacred right of the citizen." "A man can die for a cause like this without grief or sorrow," cried the impassioned speaker, "but to prolong life at the expense of liberty our proud race cannot and will not do."[17]

The protest meeting sponsored by Fernando and Benjamin Wood in New York City also attracted considerable attention. The *New York News* and the *New York World*, at odds on most issues, both urged that Democrats turn out *en masse* to express their displeasure with Burnside's repressive action. The "immense attendance" startled Republicans and heartened Democratic critics. An imposing array of speakers took turns at the four different outdoor stands to abuse President Lincoln, General Burnside, and Judge Leavitt. One of the spirited speakers imagined he was the Patrick Henry of his day. "Let us remind Lincoln," he said with a show of emotion, "that Caesar had his Brutus and Charles the First his Cromwell. Let us also remind the George the Third of the present day that he, too, may have his Cromwell or his Brutus."[18] The crowd cheered lustily and the sound waves reached Washington.

In the light of later developments, the protest meeting held in Albany on May 16 was the most important of all. That rally, in the hands of conservative Democrats such as Erastus Corning, took a remarkably strong stand against the summary treatment of Vallandigham. Loyal Democrats wanted to know if the war

[16] *Detroit Free Press*, 26 May 1863.
[17] *Indianapolis State Sentinel*, 21 May 1863.
[18] Quoted in *New York Herald*, 19 May 1863.

was being waged to put down rebellion in the South or "to destroy free institutions at the North."[19] After several able addresses, the audience ratified the "Albany Resolves," ten resolutions which stated the case against the Lincoln administration: Liberties of the citizen must be honored and constitutional government maintained at all hazards; arbitrary arrests by misguided military commanders and the use of courts-martial to try citizens violated time-tested principles of democratic governments; Vallandigham had been arrested and tried by an illegal commission "for no other reason than words addressed to a public meeting"; the president "must" be "true" to the Constitution, and must "maintain the rights of the States and the liberties of the citizens."[20] After the meeting, the presiding officer, Erastus Corning, sent the "Albany Resolves" to President Lincoln with an accompanying letter which asked the president's "earnest consideration" of the resolutions.[21]

The popular reaction to Vallandigham's arrest and trial caused even some prominent Republicans to speak out against Burnside, for he had scarred their party. The misguided general had been rash and impolitic. The *Anti-Slavery Standard* of New York characterized Vallandigham's arrest and trial as "a blunder," and the influential *New York Independent* labeled it "a great mistake." "The Union can survive the assaults of all the armed and disarmed Vallandighams of the South and North," wrote the clever and perceptive editor of the *New York Sun*, "but it cannot long exist without free speech and free press."[22] Noticing Vallandigham's new prestige, one astute Republican editor summed up the situation with true discernment. "Vallandigham was fast talking himself into the deepest political grave ever dug," he noted in an editorial, "when Burnside resurrected him."[23]

Vallandigham's Democratic friends expressed satisfaction with

[19] The query was included in Horatio Seymour's letter to the convention. (He did not attend.) Although the letter was read to the assembled convention, it was really a statement prepared for the press and published by nearly every Democratic newspaper in the North. See, for example, *Cincinnati Daily Enquirer*, 23 May 1863.

[20] The "Albany Resolves" were published in Edward McPherson, *The Political History of the United States . . . during the Great Rebellion* (Washington, D.C., 1864), p. 163, and in [Appleton's] *Annual Cyclopedia and Register of Important Events . . . 1863*, pp. 799-800.

[21] Corning to Lincoln, 19 May 1863, Robert Todd Lincoln Papers.

[22] N.d., all quoted in *Crisis*, 27 May 1863.

[23] *Harper's Weekly*, 30 May 1863.

the wave of reaction sweeping all before it. He did not come out the scheming politician resorting to a stratagem to refurbish a fading career in politics. Instead, public reaction transformed him into a martyr—the champion of civil rights and the symbol of free speech. Vallandigham's friends assured him, before he was exiled to the Confederacy, that the Democratic gubernatorial nomination was his for the asking. They predicted that public indignation would also gain him the governorship of Ohio. Some visionaries even supposed that the wave might carry him into the White House.[24]

President Lincoln, always aware of public opinion, recognized that Vallandigham's newly won popularity threatened his own political future, the future of the Republican party, and the future of the country. He realized that Burnside's impetuous action had bruised the Republican party and evoked a Democratic revival. It harmed unity on the home front and affected the war effort.

Erastus Corning's letter and the "Albany Resolves" gave Lincoln a chance to put his side of the controversy before the public. He therefore prepared a long and carefully-worded reply. It was much more than a letter to "Hon. Erastus Corning & others"; it was a well-reasoned rebuttal, a state paper, intended for publication and extensive circulation. Moreover, it constituted a deliberate effort to check the rising tide of public indignation caused by Vallandigham's arrest, trial, and exile.

Lincoln's long, long "open letter" stated that the enemies of the government were seeking to destroy the Constitution while relying upon its guarantee to protect them. The civil courts had proved most inadequate ("utterly incompetent") in dealing with the serious threat posed by the insurgents and their Northern sympathizers. (It was evident that the president believed the partisan charges made by the Republican press.) Arbitrary arrests which had been made, he argued, were "preventative" rather than "vindictive. . . . I think the time not unlikely to come," Lincoln wrote with all seriousness, "when I shall be blamed for having made too few arrests rather than too many."[25]

[24] *Hamilton True Telegraph,* 31 May 1863; *Copperhead* (New York, n.d.), quoted in *Mount Vernon Democratic Banner,* 23 May 1863; *London Times,* 24 July 1863.
[25] 12 June 1863, published in *New York Tribune,* 15 June. The autographed

As for Vallandigham, his crime was not merely the "words addressed to a public meeting." He had been arrested, the president maintained, because of his "open hostility" to the war for the Union. "He was not arrested," Lincoln insisted, "because he was damaging the political prospects of the administration, or the personal interests of the commanding general; but because he was damaging the army, upon the existence of which, the life of the nation depends." Then, with a stroke of genius, Lincoln asked that famous question which Democrats found quite impossible to answer: "Must I shoot a simple-minded soldier boy who deserts, while I must not touch a hair of the wiley [sic] agitator who induces him to desert?"[26]

Lincoln's contention that he endorsed only that action which was necessary for the public safety seemed more valid after he revoked General Burnside's suppression of the *Chicago Times*. On June 1, 1863, at the very time the president was struggling with his long answer to the "Albany Resolves," Burnside ordered the *Times* suppressed and two days later sent soldiers to occupy the plant, stop publication, and put the premises under guard. Noting the consternation caused by the action and needing to regain prestige lost as a result of Vallandigham's arrest, the shrewd president promptly revoked General Burnside's order. Thus, with the stroke of his pen, he regained some of the favor he had lost earlier by endorsing Burnside's summary action in the Vallandigham case.

While Lincoln wrestled with the problems which General Burnside created, Ohio Democrats took steps to elect delegates to their party's state convention, scheduled to meet in Columbus on June 11. Vallandigham's name was on nearly every lip, party leaders damning him and his friends shouting his praises. All of the party leaders favored Hugh J. Jewett's candidacy for the governorship; he had carried the party's banner two years earlier and merited a second chance—party tradition so dictated. Leaders such as Samuel S. Cox and George W. Manypenny of the *Ohio Statesman* believed that Vallandigham's nomination would "ruin" the party, and that it would provide Republicans

---

draft in the Robert Todd Lincoln Papers was somewhat revised before being released to the press.
[26] Ibid.

a chance to make a patriotic or emotional appeal for their candidate.[27]

Members of the Democratic State Central Committee, all favoring Jewett's nomination, let affairs slip out of control. Many delegates, anxious to repudiate Burnside and Lincoln, favored Vallandigham because he was a "martyr." Other delegates, impressed with the widespread sentiment for peace, believed that Vallandigham symbolized the peace movement. The two forces gathered momentum, and, like a snowball rolling down a mountainside, turned into an avalanche.

When Jewett recognized that the pro-Vallandigham boom would push him aside, he offered to withdraw from the canvass and let the nomination go to Vallandigham by default. Cox and Manypenny then pulled the name of General George B. McClellan out of the hat and urged him to become a candidate for the governorship; it was a desperate effort to sidetrack Vallandigham. But McClellan still thought President Lincoln might call him back to reorganize the defeated and demoralized Army of the Potomac, so he refused "to let his name be put forth" as a gubernatorial candidate. Cox and Manypenny then urged Jewett to stay in the race, hoping that in some mysterious way the pro-Vallandigham forces might still be checked. But the groundswell for Vallandigham and the zeal of his supporters (one radical can always be counted on to do more work than ten moderates) assured Vallandigham's nomination even before the convention met on June 11.

Delegates and would-be spectators began to arrive in Columbus the day before the convention. The large number of "interested observers" indicated the convention could become more a mass meeting than a deliberative session. A tone of defiance prevailed in many quarters, and it was evident that Vallandigham's supporters might disrupt the convention if "Valiant Val" failed to gain the prize. Delegates and visitors, especially those representing "the great unwashed Democracy" of the backwoods area, spoke excitedly of events of the past and of their expectations while drinking toasts to "the martyr."[28]

[27] Cox to Manton Marble, 1 June 1863, Marble Papers; *Toledo Blade,* 8 June 1863; *Cleveland Leader,* 8 June 1863.

[28] William W. Armstrong, "Personal Recollections," published in *Cincinnati Daily Enquirer,* 20 March 1886.

Delegations continued to pour into Columbus early on the morning of convention day. Many brought their own bands and banners and loads of hickory branches. The streets were filled with wagons, buggies, men on horseback, and many men carrying walking sticks. The sidewalks were crowded with excited men, as if it were a pentecost of politics. Delegates jostled in long lines when they registered.[29]

It was soon evident to those in charge that no hall in Columbus was large enough to hold a tenth of those who wanted to attend. They decided therefore to hold the convention on "the east front of the State-House." Since most of the "spectators" happened to be Vallandighamers, those in charge inadvertently changed a convention into a Vallandigham rally.[30]

Jewett's supporters succeeded in getting William Medill elected as "permanent chairman," despite the fact that some Vallandigham men favored George E. Pugh. After accepting the chairmanship, Medill bowed to the inevitable. In his acceptance speech he intimated that "public sentiment" decreed who the standard-bearer would be—the convention could do no less than endorse Clement L. Vallandigham. Bedlam reigned, with Vallandigham supporters giving cheer after cheer. The pro-Jewett delegates groaned or sat stunned and silent.

In time the permanent chairman restored order, appointed the usual committees, and called for nominations. Judge William C. James of Muskingum County nominated Vallandigham, setting off a "noisy demonstration." When Henry B. Payne nominated Jewett, boos and jeers by Vallandighamers drowned out the applause of Jewett's supporters. During the roll call, the pro-Vallandigham "spectators" cheered when county delegations cast their votes for their hero, booed when votes were cast for Jewett. One county delegation after another, bowing to pressure from the "galleries," jumped on the Vallandigham bandwagon. It proved to be a one-sided victory. Jewett received only eleven votes.[31] It was proof that public reaction to Vallandigham's arrest had emotionalized Ohio, sweeping conservative Democrats aside. Vallandigham, in seeking arrest, had taken a calculated risk. Events of June 11 proved that the gamble paid off.

29 Ibid.
30 *Daily Ohio State Journal* (Columbus), 12 June 1863.
31 Ibid.

After the totals were announced, the delegates followed the usual procedure of making the nomination unanimous. The convention then named George E. Pugh as Democratic candidate for lieutenant-governor, entrusting him to do most of the campaigning while Vallandigham was in exile.

The delegates also gave their resounding approval to "Twenty-three Resolutions." The first stated that free government, endangered by military decrees and presidential proclamations, really rested upon "the will of the people." The second assailed the Emancipation Proclamation and the suspension of the writ of habeas corpus. Others denounced abolitionism and radicalism, condemned the arrest of Vallandigham, and criticized Governor David Tod. The so-called "peace resolution" stated that the return of the seceded states would be "hailed with delight" and recommended "a convention of the States" to provide against future wars. The final resolution called for the appointment of "a Committee of Nineteen," one representative from each of the state's congressional districts, to call upon President Lincoln, present the resolutions, state the case against him, and demand the release of Vallandigham.[32] Perhaps the mood of the convention was best reflected in the statement of an articulate farmer who said, "In Vallandigham my rights have been violated, and in Vallandigham my rights shall be vindicated."[33]

The following week the Union Party Convention met in Columbus, with Republican strategists again pulling the strings. The fact that some conservative Democrats expressed their displeasure with Vallandigham's nomination heartened Republicans. They drummed up a good attendance for the convention and put on a spirited show. Although David Tod sought renomination, the wire-pullers pushed him aside and secured "Honest John" Brough, also a former Democrat, as their candidate. While Vallandigham's nomination had its basis in a grass-roots movement, Brough's was a shrewdly calculated and carefully planned affair.[34]

32 *Crisis*, 13 June 1863; *Cincinnati Daily Gazette*, 13 June 1863.
33 Quoted in *Daily Ohio Statesman* (Columbus), 1 July 1863.
34 R. H. Stephenson to William Henry Smith, 16 August 1863, William Henry Smith Papers, Ohio Historical Society; A. Denny to John Sherman, 25 April 1863, and James J. James to Sherman, 18 June 1863, John Sherman Papers, Library of Congress; *Cleveland Leader*, 17 June 1863; *Daily Ohio State Journal*, 16 June 1863.

On June 22, fifteen members of the Committee of Nineteen, named at the Democratic State Convention, gathered in the Neil House in Columbus to discuss their proposed meeting with President Lincoln. Twelve of the fifteen were either congressmen or congressmen-elect. They chose Judge Mathias Birchard, formerly a member of the Ohio State Supreme Court, as their chairman, and decided to entrain the next day for Washington, D.C., to seek an appointment with the president.[35]

The committee members arrived in Washington on the evening of June 24, and the chairman took steps to arrange a meeting with the president. When Secretary of the Treasury Salmon P. Chase heard that Lincoln had scheduled an appointment with the Committee of Nineteen, he wrote a note of admonition: "What is said to them or replied to them should be only in writing."[36]

President Lincoln held a brief meeting with Birchard's committee on the morning of June 25. He already knew several of them and shook hands with the others as if he was happy to see them. But before they had a chance to make an oral request for Vallandigham's "release," Lincoln, heeding Chase's advice, asked them to put their supplication in writing.

Later that day President Lincoln took up the Vallandigham question at a meeting of his cabinet. Gideon Welles expressed the opinion that members of the Committee of Nineteen were more interested in manufacturing factious party propaganda than anything else. Most of those who spoke out opposed pardoning Vallandigham. Montgomery Blair thought it was politic to let the exile return to the United States—he would damage his own friends and his party more than the administration. The president stated he had no special objection to Vallandigham's return, but he feared that a pardon might have an adverse effect upon

[35] *Crisis*, 24 June 1863. The members appointed to the Committee of Nineteen were: Mathias Birchard, David A. Houk (of Dayton), Thomas W. Bartley (an ex-governor of Ohio), William J. Gordon (a wealthy merchant from Cleveland), John O'Neill (president *pro tem* of the state senate in the previous legislative session), Louis Schaefer (of Canton), and Congressman George Bliss, Abner L. Backus, George H. Pendleton, Chilton A. White, Warren P. Noble, Wells A. Hutchins, Francis C. LeBlond, William C. Finck, Alexander Long, Joseph W. White, John F. McKinney, James R. Morris, and George L. Converse. Samuel S. Cox was one of the original nineteen appointed, but he refused to attend the organizational meeting, so Converse was named in his stead.

[36] Chase to Lincoln, 24 June 1863, Robert Todd Lincoln Papers.

army discipline. It might also antagonize "patriotic sentiment."[37]

On the morning of June 26, Judge Birchard delivered the long epistle of the Committee of Nineteen to President Lincoln. It listed, in abridged form, the twenty-three resolutions adopted at the Democratic State Convention of Ohio on June 11. Another section of it countered some of Lincoln's "answer" to the "Albany Resolves." Several sentences reminded Lincoln that, as a congressman and citizen, he had opposed the Mexican War. Now, as president, he and his "agents" denied to others the same rights and freedoms he had practiced then. General Burnside and others had been guilty of violating basic rights of American citizens. Ohio citizens could no longer put up with intimidation and suppression—the administration should be aware of the slumbering volcano. Justice demanded that the order banishing Vallandigham be revoked, the military commission's verdict reversed, and all of the other rights restored. "The undersigned assure your Excellency," one line of the epistle read, ". . . that the public safety will be far more endangered by continuing Mr. Vallandigham in exile than by releasing him."[38]

The president spent a good part of the next several days working on his reply to the Committee of Nineteen. He was aware that he was writing another state paper; he also recognized that his reply would be a Republican campaign document, used to counter and undermine the popular reaction to Vallandigham's arrest, trial, and exile. Lincoln went so far as to convene his cabinet on Sunday, June 28, at ten o'clock, to read his reply and to solicit suggestions for its improvement. The cabinet members approved of the carefully-worded statement; Gideon Welles considered it well written and well conceived. Neither Lincoln nor his cabinet members favored giving "the graceless traitor" the "notoriety and office" which he sought.[39]

The president's reply resurveyed some of the ground he had covered seventeen days earlier in his long response to the "Albany Resolves." He stated again that he did not want "the public safety" to suffer because of the irresponsible acts of individuals. Democrats erred, Lincoln added, in reserving for themselves the

[37] Entry of 26 June 1863, *Diary of Gideon Welles*, 1: 344.

[38] Mathias Birchard and others to Lincoln, 26 June 1863, Robert Todd Lincoln Papers.

[39] Entry of 28 June 1863, *Diary of Gideon Welles*, 1: 347.

right to decide what the Constitution meant, nor did they have the right to twist facts in their favor. Somewhat sardonically he expressed a willingness to "release" Vallandigham, paroling him to the Committee of Nineteen if its members would keep him from infringing upon the public safety.[40]

Judge Birchard wrote a rejoinder to Lincoln's "reply" on behalf of the Committee of Nineteen, expressing surprise that the president impugned the loyalty of those who did not agree with him or who opposed administration measures. Loyalty should be to the Constitution rather than an administration. Clement L. Vallandigham was entitled to his rights—they were not a favor held in the hands of the president.[41]

Lincoln chose not to answer Birchard's rejoinder. He knew he had defended the administration ably in his two "open letters" —his responses to the "Albany Resolves" and to the epistle of the Committee of Nineteen. Both were well-reasoned documents, which would help to roll back the high tide of Copperheadism.

Lincoln's effort to hold the dikes against pro-Vallandigham sentiment received an assist from General Ulysses S. Grant and George B. Meade. Meade commanded the Army of the Potomac when it turned back Lee's army at Gettysburg in a memorable battle on July 1-3, 1863. Grant captured Vicksburg and a beleaguered Confederate army on July 4. These two Union victories did more than shatter the dreams of Southern leaders. No longer could Copperhead critics say the war was a failure. Defeatism began to retreat, too, and Copperheadism to ebb. Perhaps Gettysburg and Vicksburg did more to nullify the arguments in the "Albany Resolves" and the epistle of the Committee of Nineteen than President Lincoln's excellent answers.

[40] Lincoln to M. Birchard and others 29 June 1863, Robert Todd Lincoln Papers; *New York Tribune*, 9 July 1863. Lincoln dated his reply 28 June; John Nicolay, one of Lincoln's private secretaries, changed the date to 29 June.
[41] Birchard and others to Lincoln, 1 July 1863, Robert Todd Lincoln Papers.

13

A PRISONER BECOMES AN EXILE

GENERAL BURNSIDE DISAPPROVED of President Lincoln's change of sentence for Vallandigham from imprisonment to exile. But when his protests came to naught, he reluctantly took steps to convey his famous prisoner to Maj. Gen. William S. Rosecrans, commanding the Army of the Cumberland. Burnside asked Captain Alexander M. Pennock of the Mississippi Squadron to lend him one of the gunboats tied to the Cincinnati docks. Since Rosecrans had asked Burnside to effect the transfer with "the greatest secrecy," lest the prisoner be shot by some "lawless person,"[1] Captain Pennock was given no reason for the loan of a gunboat. It was therefore ironic that Pennock loaned out a gunboat named the *Exchange.* Since the *Exchange* had not as yet received her armament, General Burnside placed a battery and "a small guard" aboard the borrowed boat "for temporary purposes."[2]

Shortly after midnight on May 19, General Burnside's aides led Vallandigham from his room in the Newport Barracks to the wharves and onto the *Exchange,* commanded by Captain John Sebastian. Burnside kept the borrowed gunboat at the dock for several days, evidently still hoping Lincoln would come around to his point of view and send the prisoner to Fort Warren.

Vallandigham and Captain Sebastian had a chance to get acquainted while awaiting orders to proceed down the river. Captain Sebastian, always courteous, treated Vallandigham as a gentleman rather than a convicted criminal. In fact, the erudite captain seemed to sympathize with his famous prisoner, and a friendship developed between the two which lasted into the postwar years.[3]

While waiting in his room on the *Exchange,* Vallandigham spent considerable time at a table which doubled as a desk. He wrote several letters to his wife. She definitely was not well, still suffering from the shock of seeing her husband led off by soldiers armed with guns and bayonets. He also wrote again to Manton Marble to tell the editor of the *New York World* that he appreciated the firm stand which he and the New York Democracy had taken against Burnside's summary action. He hoped that "a united Democratic party" might still save "the Constitution, the Union, and liberty." Also, he assured Marble that he had an ace up his sleeve; he would "foil and counteract" Mr. Lincoln's plan to degrade and stigmatize him.[4] Vallandigham also composed another address "To the Democracy of Ohio." He hoped to swell the wave of indignation which lapped Ohio's shores, transforming a prisoner into a hero and bringing the Democratic gubernatorial nomination within reach.

In this address C.L.V. depicted himself as a martyr to free speech and a knight-errant fighting "an arbitrary and tyrannic power." Whether imprisoned or banished, he wrote, nothing could affect his allegiance to his state and his country. He still loved his country, respected the Constitution, and revered the rights which it conferred upon all citizens. He ended his discourse with the hope that the people of Ohio would not cower before the threats of arbitrary power, and would prove themselves "worthy to be called freemen."[5]

After procrastinating for several days, Burnside finally ordered the *Exchange* to begin its downriver journey. The general's aides called upon Vallandigham early on the morning of May 22 to tell him his sentence. Had Vallandigham been given a choice, he would unhesitatingly have chosen imprisonment—it fitted the martyr concept much better than banishment, which could be claimed to put him among his "friends."[6]

At eleven o'clock, Captain Sebastian ordered the *Exchange* untied from the dock, and the cumbersome gunboat began its

---

[1] Rosecrans to Burnside, 19 May 1863, published in *Official Records,* ser. 2, 5: 658.

[2] Report, Captain Alexander M. Pennock, dated 26 May 1863, *Official Records of the Union and Confederate Navies in the War of the Rebellion,* 26 vols. (Washington, D.C., 1894-1922), ser. 1, 25: 140.

[3] Vallandigham, *Vallandigham,* p. 295.

[4] 21 May 1863, Manton Marble Papers, Library of Congress.

[5] This address, dated 22 May 1863, is in the Samuel L. M. Barlow Papers, Henry E. Huntington Library, San Marino, California.

[6] George E. Pugh, Vallandigham's counsel during the trial, said that Val would have chosen imprisonment if given a choice. See Pugh's speech of 11 June 1863, published in the *Ohio State Journal* (Columbus), 11 June 1863.

journey downriver to Louisville. It must have been an emotional moment for the prisoner to look back upon the Ohio shoreline and wonder when and how he would return. If his heart beat faster and his throat was dry, he did not show it. He appeared calm as if confident that all things would end well. His friends had earlier apprised him of the public reaction to his arrest and trial, a reaction which they hoped might put him in the governor's chair. Then Lincoln would have to retract his sentence and eat humble pie.

All things considered, the trip down the river was a pleasant one. The weather was ideal and Captain Sebastian was a gracious host. Captain Alexander Murray, in charge of handing Vallandigham over to General Rosecrans, joined in the conversation while his detail of soldiers played cards at the other end of the deck. William S. Furay of the *Cincinnati Gazette* contributed to the discussion of a dozen questions, many of them irrelevant. Furay was the only newspaperman with the party, going "loosely and *ad libitum*."[7] Captain Murray gave his prisoner considerable latitude; at times it seemed as if the would-be exile was a guest rather than a prisoner.

As the gunboat neared Louisville, Vallandigham asked permission to write another note to his wife. Some newspapers had reported that she had lapsed into insanity. He was pleased to read that she was better in the latest issue of the *Cincinnati Enquirer*,[8] brought on deck just before the *Exchange* started on its downriver journey. His note was brief and to the point—he was "in fine spirits and enjoying excellent health." He asked his wife to persevere and trust the future. There was little more he could say.[9]

The stay in Louisville was brief indeed. After the *Exchange* docked, Captain Murray and C.L.V. stepped off the boat together, and started for the railroad depot. The squad of soldiers served as a "strong guard." Newspaperman Furay tagged along behind. Citizens in the streets ignored the soldiers and the prisoner; details of soldiers were a common sight in Louisville, and no one recognized the would-be exile. When the party

[7] *Cincinnati Daily Gazette*, 29 May 1863.
[8] *Cincinnati Daily Enquirer*, 21 May 1863.
[9] 23 May 1863, published in part in Vallandigham, *Vallandigham*, p. 297.

arrived at the depot, Captain Murray conducted Vallandigham to a special train, waiting on a spur nearby, to start on its journey to Nashville.

It was less than 180 miles from Louisville to Nashville, but it was a tiring, drawn-out trip. Trains carrying provisions and reinforcements for Rosecrans's army clogged the railroad, so the special train carrying Vallandigham spent as much time on side-tracks as on the main line. All heaved a sigh of relief when the train finally pulled into the railway depot in the capital city of Tennessee.

Although General Rosecrans had asked Burnside to effect the transfer with "the greatest secrecy," a fair-sized crowd was on hand to witness the arrival of the well-known prisoner. Somehow, reports or rumors had brought an inquisitive audience to the depot. The curious saw little. Vallandigham was hurried aboard a bus and driven across town to the Chattanooga depot, where another special train waited to convey him to Murfreesboro. This segment of the trip passed without much delay and the special train arrived at the Murfreesboro depot "a little past 10 o'clock" on Sunday evening, May 24. None save those on General Rosecrans's staff knew of Vallandigham's arrival.

Rosecrans sent his provost marshal general, Major William M. Wiles, and several other aides to meet the special train. Wiles brought along a small open-spring carriage. He boarded the train as soon as it came to a complete stop, introduced himself to Captain Murray, and said he had been instructed to conduct the party to General Rosecrans's headquarters. After all had detrained, Major Wiles invited Vallandigham, Captain Murray, and newsman Furay to ride in the carriage. They bounced along the dusty and well-worn streets, though the darkness blanketed some of the dust. There was little conversation, for all were very tired and the situation discouraged levity.

Major Wiles directed the party to the house of Charles Ready, once a congressman and Vallandigham's colleague in Washington. Wiles had promptly preempted this fine building as his headquarters—after all, he was Rosecrans's provost marshal general and deserving of the better things in life. In the presence of General Rosecrans and one of his aides, Colonel Joseph C. McKibbin, Vallandigham was officially transferred from the Department of the Ohio to the Department of the Cumberland. Captain Murray, representing General Burnside, turned over his prisoner to Major Wiles, representing General Rosecrans. The battered lantern and the flickering candles cast light upon the strange scene which occurred but slightly more than an hour before midnight.[10]

After Rosecrans greeted Vallandigham, the prisoner renewed his acquaintance with Colonel McKibbin. Vallandigham recognized McKibbin as a one-time friend; the two had first met during the sessions of the Thirty-fifth Congress, when Vallandigham contested Lewis D. Campbell's seat and McKibbin was a Democratic congressman from California. McKibbin voted with the majority to give Vallandigham Campbell's seat. After the start of the Civil War he sought a colonelcy and happened to be one of the first six cavalry officers appointed by President Lincoln. The hand of fate placed him in the Charles Ready house in Murfreesboro when Rosecrans and Vallandigham met for the first time shortly before midnight on May 24.

Although the hour was late, General Rosecrans's curiosity prompted him to visit with Vallandigham, probing reasons for his views and actions. Colonel McKibbin and Major Wiles also joined in the discussion. It was a strange interview, and, considering the circumstances, much more agreeable than could have been expected. Rosecrans, always rather self-righteous, turned the discussion to the question of war aims and disloyalty. As a friendly favor he tried to lecture Vallandigham concerning his opposition to the war. The prisoner argued back in a friendly, polite, and dignified manner, and his line of reasoning soon put the articulate general in a corner. "Why, sir," Rosecrans said by way of extricating himself from an untenable position, "do you know that, unless I protect you with a guard, my soldiers will tear you to pieces in an instant?"

"That, sir," replied Vallandigham quickly and tartly, "is because they are just as prejudiced and ignorant of my character and career as yourself." Then, to prove that he meant what he said he made a proposition to General Rosecrans: "Draw your soldiers

10 Furay in *Cincinnati Daily Gazette*, 29 May 1863; *Nashville Dispatch*, 26 May 1863; Vallandigham, in speech of 24 October 1867, published in *Crisis*, 30 October 1867.

up in a hollow square tomorrow morning, and announce to them that Vallandigham wishes to vindicate himself, and I will guarantee that when they have heard me through, they will be more willing to tear Lincoln and yourself to pieces than they will Vallandigham." He still believed in his own righteousness and still had confidence in his ability to practice the art of political persuasion which he had developed through the years.

General Rosecrans heard Vallandigham's proposition with interest and good nature. He shook his head, saying he had too much respect for the life of the prisoner to try it. Soon after, the conversation became less personal. The prisoner's congenial manner completely disarmed Rosecrans, and the interview evolved into a convivial session. Before the discussion ended it became quite apparent that Rosecrans regretted having to perform the duty of enforcing the penalty against his prisoner.

Long after midnight Rosecrans arose to take leave of Vallandigham. Laying his hand on the prisoner's shoulder, Rosecrans turned toward Colonel McKibbin and asked, "He don't look a bit like a traitor, now does he, Joe?" Then, warmly shaking the prisoner's hand, the general took leave and departed into the night.[11]

Major Wiles now began preparations to conduct the prisoner into the Confederate lines. The clatter of hoofs indicated that a company of cavalrymen, assigned to accompany Vallandigham to the front lines, had arrived. The major went outside to check whether "the conveyance" and the troops were fully ready for the assignment. When he came back into the room he informed C.L.V. that all was in readiness—his "journeying" would be resumed. Newspaper correspondent Furay looked at his watch. It was two o'clock—still several hours before daylight—when the prisoner stepped through the door of the Ready house into the darkness outside. Major Wiles escorted Vallandigham to the same open-spring carriage which had met him at the Murfreesboro railway depot about four hours earlier. Just as Vallandigham got ready to step up into the conveyance he turned to Colonel

---

[11] Furay's account of the interview appeared in the *Cincinnati Daily Gazette*, 29 May 1863. The conversation is also reported in Vallandigham, *Vallandigham*, pp. 298-99, and Henry Howe, *Historical Collections of Ohio: An Encyclopedia of the State*, 2 vols. (Norwalk, O., 1898), 1: 444. The event, as reconstructed and related by Vallandigham, also appeared in *Crisis*, 30 October 1867.

McKibbin and said in a jocular vein, "Colonel, this is worse than Lecompton." He evidently referred to the prewar days when he and McKibbin, as fellow congressmen, had contested President Buchanan's efforts to foist a proslavery constitution upon Kansas.

It was a strange party that moved off into the night, heading southward on the Shelbyville pike toward the Union outposts. A company of cavalry led the way, raising dust which the nostrils could feel but the eyes could not see. Next came the wagon bearing the prisoner; Lieutenant Colonel Arthur C. Ducat sat on the front seat with the driver, while Vallandigham and Colonel McKibbin sat in back. Then came a second small wagon, carrying Major Wiles, correspondent Furay, Captain John C. Goodwin, an assistant provost marshal, and the prisoner's trunk. Another company of cavalry followed, serving as escort and rear-guard.[12]

The strange procession passed along the dusty road through the quiet and slumbering army camp and down, down the Shelbyville road toward the fringe of rebellious Dixie. It passed guard after guard, picket after picket, and sentinel after sentinel. The magic counter-signs opened the gates in the wall of living men. Those on guard gazed in silent wonder at the unwonted spectacle, barely discernible, fully unaware that "the most notorious Copperhead in the North" rode by silently and unknown.

Vallandigham and Colonel McKibbin exchanged differing opinions and observations freely, and the other two riders in the lead wagon occasionally joined in the discussion. The prisoner proved most talkative, exhilarated perhaps by the excitement of the occasion. He explained his views on the war and his scheme for restoring the Union. He avowed himself as firm a Union man as any in America. He did not believe in the efficacy of war as a means to settle sectional disputes, allied and related as the South and the North were. He said that while in exile he would not lift his voice or raise his arm against the Federal Union. Someone in the party asked Vallandigham if his criticism of the Lincoln administration had not weakened the arm of the government. After all, the government had chosen war and the people had sustained that choice—congressional action endorsed administration policy. The prisoner replied that, as he understood it,

[12] *Cincinnati Daily Gazette*, 29 May 1863.

the war was being prosecuted in vindication of the free principles of the Constitution. These principles had been violated in his arrest, and if the war meant the "sacrificing" of "rights and liberties," it was not worthy of support. He did admit, however, that if the government was to be restored by a war calling for the full use of all physical force, the government could tolerate no opposition, and all "rights and liberties" might disappear in the process. Vallandigham, however, again stated his earlier contention that constitutional guidelines must be respected and revered. He evidently still believed that his proposal of "compromise and concession" would restore the Union ultimately, at the same time conserving and preserving basic constitutional rights and liberties.[13]

After crossing the Stone River, the procession continued its southward journey for several more miles. Just as the first faint light of dawn appeared in the east, the cavalcade stopped at a farmhouse to wait for daylight. Colonel McKibbin and Major Wiles advanced to the front door of the well-kept house to awaken the occupants, who came downstairs to meet their uninvited guests. Members of the household stared at the prisoner and the army officers, and then made haste to prepare whatever conveniences they could in order to give the courteous intruders "an hour's repose." Considerable time, however, was spent in conversation. Again Vallandigham talked freely and frankly, discussing dispassionately the circumstances of his arrest and trial. He seemed to manifest no bitter feeling whatsover, either toward the government, General Burnside, or those who were conducting him into exile. Even such a prejudiced partisan as William S. Furay, whose newspaper had abused Vallandigham relentlessly, developed sympathy and respect for the prisoner, who was always self-confident, sincere, and decorous. Vallandigham's self-confidence and self-righteousness underwrote his martyr complex and convinced him that time would vindicate him.

As the conversation lapsed, the principals made an effort to obtain a little sleep. Just after Vallandigham dozed off, Colonel McKibbin came over to awaken him; it was daylight and time

[13] Ibid.

to resume the journey. Some poetical remark having been made about the morning, the sleepy-eyed prisoner raised himself upon his right elbow and said dramatically:

Night's candles are burnt out, and jocund day
Stands tiptoe on the misty mountain tops.

He paused, his mind evidently failing to tap his memory for the remaining line of the quotation. Newspaperman Furay came to the rescue: "I must be gone and live, or stay and die." The closing line seemed so applicable to Vallandigham's case that it startled everyone, even the prisoner himself. An embarrassing silence settled upon those present, and little more was said until the cavalcade was set in motion again.[14]

Just as the first rays of the sun tinted the leaves of the trees on the western hills with gold, the procession reached the remotest outposts of the Union army. Major William M. Wiles stopped and instructed Lt. Col. Ducat to take charge of the prisoner while he and Colonel McKibbin advanced toward the Confederate lines to make arrangements for the transfer of the prisoner. Wiles and McKibbin, astride their nervous horses and carrying a flag of truce, then trotted off toward the Confederate vedettes, half a mile or more down the Shelbyville pike.

Lt. Col. Ducat, charged with keeping the prisoner, led him toward the nearest farmhouse, the home of a Mr. Alexander, and asked if the ladies would serve breakfast to the "guests." The Alexanders avowed they could and seated Ducat, Furay, and Vallandigham at the dining room table. The officer in charge then informed Mrs. Alexander that one of the gentlemen before her—he pointed to his prisoner—was Clement L. Vallandigham of Ohio. Mrs. Alexander, quite excited, exclaimed, "Can it be possible? Mr. Vallandigham!" Turning toward the prisoner she said, "Why I was reading only last night of your wonderful doings! I must introduce you to the old man, shure."[15]

Soon Mrs. Alexander reappeared with her husband and a "not remarkably handsome daughter." The three gave Vallandigham a warm, albeit rather embarrassing welcome. The soldiers who

14 Ibid. The quotation is from Act III of Shakespeare's "Romeo and Juliet."
15 The comment was reported by Furay in the *Cincinnati Daily Gazette*, 29 May 1863.

witnessed the affair thereupon reached the conclusion that the Alexanders were at least half "secesh."[16]

After breakfast, the participants waited rather impatiently for Colonel McKibbin and Major Wiles to return. The two Union officers, meanwhile, encountered considerable difficulty in arranging for the transfer. The Confederate captain who had charge of the pickets expressed a reluctance to let Vallandigham enter his lines and he insisted upon first contacting his immediate superiors. Since his superiors were still asleep and he did not wish to disturb them, McKibbin and Wiles had to wait two hours, pacing to and fro impatiently. It seemed more like two days than two hours.

Finally the unnamed captain and Colonel James D. Webb of the Fifty-first Alabama Regiment appeared, and the two Union officers again explained their mission. Colonel Webb, in turn, refused to accept Vallandigham on his own; he wanted the consent or approval of General Braxton Bragg, the Confederate commander, whose headquarters were in Shelbyville. The two Union officers argued convincingly that Colonel Webb should accept Vallandigham under a flag of truce. Webb, however, remained adamant, refusing to accept the exile "in any official manner." While the two Union officers pondered their next move, they noticed that quite a number of men and children, Tennessee residents wanting "the protection of the Union army," passed between the lines under flags of truce.

Rebuffed in their attempt to arrange an official exchange, Major Wiles then sought Colonel Webb's permission to conduct Vallandigham close to the Confederate pickets and "dump" him there "unofficially." Colonel Webb could hardly say "No." If the prisoner were put down in no-man's land and he approached Confederate pickets, seeking the protection of the Confederate flag, he would be received.

Colonel McKibbin and Major Wiles mounted their horses and dashed off toward the Alexander house to get their prisoner and conduct him toward the Confederate pickets. The two Union officers said nothing to Vallandigham about the reluctance of the Confederates to receive him. In fact, they misled him into be-

16 *Louisville Daily Journal,* 3 June 1863; *Hamilton True Telegraph,* 18 June 1863; *Cincinnati Daily Gazette,* 26, 29 May 1863; *Dayton Daily Journal,* 26, 27 May 1863.

lieving that he would be welcomed with open arms. While McKibbin remained at the Alexander house to have breakfast, Wiles and Captain Goodwin conducted their notorious prisoner near a Confederate picket, unloaded his trunk and carpetbag, and hoped the transfer could be completed without incident.

As an orderly from Colonel Webb's staff approached the trio, Vallandigham got ready to recite a statement he had memorized, intended to counteract President Lincoln's effort to stigmatize him by exiling him to the Confederacy. Addressing himself to a Confederate soldier and calling upon Captain Goodwin to witness the ceremony, the would-be exile recited his piece: "I am a citizen of Ohio, and of the United States. I am here within your lines by force and against my will. I therefore surrender myself to you as a prisoner of war."[17]

Visibly relieved, yet fearful that the Confederates might change their minds, Wiles and Goodwin said a hurried farewell to their onetime prisoner and galloped away to rejoin their fellow officers at the Alexander house. Then reforming their "procession," they led the way back to Murfreesboro and Rosecrans's headquarters. They had no intention of letting the Northern public know that the Confederates were most reluctant to receive the exile. By suppressing some of the facts and distorting others, they contributed to the legend that Vallandigham, as an exile in the Confederate States of America, was really "among friends." Wartime propaganda very often is based upon distortion, suppression, and fabrication.

The Confederate soldier to whom Vallandigham surrendered "as a prisoner of war" seemed greatly perplexed how to address his prisoner or whether to treat him as a friend or foe. He guided the exile to Colonel Webb's headquarters and turned him over to some aides. Colonel Webb meanwhile waited for in-

[17] W. D. Kendall to his parents, 31 May 1863, William D. Kendall Papers, Huntington Library; Merritt Miller to "Br. Clement," 30 May 1863, Merritt Miller Papers, in possession of V. L. Rockwell, Union Grove, Wisconsin; report, Wiles to Brig. Gen. James A. Garfield, 25 May 1863, Citizens' File, 1861-1865, War Department Collection of Confederate Records; *Official Records*, ser. 2, 5: 705-6; *Cincinnati Daily Gazette*, 29 May 1863; *Louisville Daily Journal*, 3 June 1863; *Chattanooga Daily Rebel*, 28 May 1863; *Dayton Daily Journal*, 26-28 May 1863; and S. F. Nunnelee, "How Vallandigham Crossed the Lines," in *Under Both Flags: A Panorama of the Great Civil War, Written by Celebrities of Both Sides* (St. Paul, 1896), pp. 316-17.

structions from General Bragg, some sixteen miles away. While awaiting word as to his fate and future, Vallandigham had a chance to spend several hours in solitude. "These were hours," Vallandigham said in the postwar years, ". . . calmly spent—the bright sun shining in the clear sky above me, and faith in God and the future burning in my heart."[18] Yet he must have realized the novelty and irony of the situation. His fate hinged on the wishes of others, not his own. He could not go back, and he did not know, as yet, whether he could go forward.

About noon, Webb received a message from Bragg's headquarters instructing him to send the exile to Shelbyville. Webb immediately provided Vallandigham with an escort which had instructions to go directly to Bragg's headquarters. The exile and his escort arrived in Shelbyville about dusk. Since Bragg was out in the field and not expected to return until late that night, one of his aides conducted Vallandigham to the home of a Mrs. Eakin, where a spacious and pleasant room had been reserved for him.

A correspondent for the *Chattanooga Daily Rebel* witnessed Vallandigham's arrival at Bragg's headquarters. Mixing observation with propaganda, he wrote, "Mr. Vallandigham is cheerful and seems to breathe freer on escaping from Lincoln's despotism. He very properly desires to avoid all public demonstrations, and only asks that he may find a quiet refuge in our midst, until such time as the people, relieved from the despotic influence, shall call him back again to their midst. He seems fully to realize the embarrassment of his position, and will, beyond a doubt, be equal to its responsibilities. . . ."[19]

Exhausted from the day's ordeal and knowing he would be conducted into General Bragg's presence next morning, Vallandigham decided to retire early. "I retired at once," he later wrote to a friend, "having slept but half an hour since Saturday night, and was awakened early the next morning by the rays of a bright Southern sun piercing the eastern window of my room. There were no sentinels at the door and I walked out unchallenged."[20]

18 Speech of 24 October 1867, in full in *Crisis,* 30 October 1867.
19 *Chattanooga Daily Rebel,* 28 May 1863.
20 Quoted in Vallandigham, *Vallandigham,* p. 300-301.

14

UNWELCOME GUEST:
VALLANDIGHAM IN DIXIE

THE PRESENCE OF Clement L. Vallandigham in Dixie proved embarrassing to both General Bragg and Jefferson Davis. Since Southerners were fighting for their independence, they could not welcome with open arms a man who wanted compromise and reunion. He was truly an unwelcome guest, yet Southern newspapers tried to squeeze propaganda value out of his presence.

Bragg accepted Vallandigham's presence as a *fait accompli*, and dutifully took responsibility for not turning back the Union detail affecting the transfer. He also felt obligated to be a gracious host in the Southern tradition. When Vallandigham visited Bragg's headquarters on the morning of May 26, the general congratulated the exile upon his arrival in a "land of liberty" and told his guest that he would find freedom of speech and conscience in Dixie. Vallandigham curtly denied that he sought citizenship or rights and freedom in Dixie, insisting that he was a prisoner of war. Somewhat surprised, Bragg told Vallandigham he could be his guest until instructions relative to the exile came from Richmond. The exile, in turn, asked for a pass so that he might visit former friends or travel to a seaport to arrange for passage on a blockade runner.[1]

General Bragg, like a responsible commander, wrote a letter to formalize his relationship with the exile. After congratulating Vallandigham again upon his arrival in a land of liberty, he stated that the exile's freedom, of necessity, would have some boundaries or restrictions. He could give Vallandigham a pass "within the Department," not for travel elsewhere. Such permission would have to come from officials of the Confederacy.[2]

The next day, somewhat belatedly, Bragg reported Vallandigham's presence to Confederate authorities in Richmond and accepted the responsibility for permitting the exile to come within his lines. He had received the exile "with the courtesy due any unfortunate exile seeking a refuge from tyranny." Vallandigham, Bragg added, wanted to go to Georgia—evidently to run the blockade out of Savannah—and he had granted him oral permission for that purpose. Meanwhile, he awaited instructions from Richmond.[3]

On the same day that Bragg reported Vallandigham's presence to Richmond, the exile wrote again to his wife. He was well and had faith in the future. He had been received "very kindly." Instead of "threats and insults," officers and citizens whom he had met were ready "to sit down and argue the question." He added a sentence or two for political effect: "My position in favor of a restoration of the Union is well known here, . . . my opinions and hopes as to a future settlement remain unchanged, and indeed are strengthened."[4]

Southern newspapers developed considerable propaganda value from Vallandigham's presence in Dixie. It seemed to substantiate Confederate contentions that Lincoln was a despot, that civil rights had evaporated in the North, and that secession had saved the Southern states from Lincolnian tyranny. "The incarceration and condemnation of Vallandigham," wrote John Moncure Daniel of the *Richmond Examiner,* "marks the last step of despotism— there is nothing now to distinguish the politics of the North from that of Austria under Francis, and that of Naples . . . under 'King Bomba' [Ferdinand I]."[5] The editor of the *Richmond Sentinel* wrote in a like manner: "The trembling Chinaman prostrates himself no more submissively before the 'celestial' sovereign, who eats rice with chop-sticks, than they [Northerners] will henceforth before the majestic ABRAHAM, the joker."[6]

[1] Charles Martin, an intimate friend during Vallandigham's college days, was a professor at Hampden-Sidney College in 1863.

[2] 26 May 1863, copy in Vallandigham Papers, Western Reserve Historical Society, Cleveland. Also in the Vallandigham Papers is a pass dated 26 May 1863 and signed by Bragg. It reads: "Mr. Vallandigham, the bearer, a citizen of the State of Ohio, is permitted to pass as a citizen of the Confederacy, within the limits of this department."

[3] Bragg to Adjutant General [Samuel Cooper], 27 May 1863, copy in Vallandigham Papers.

[4] 27 May 1863, published in part in *Dayton Daily Ledger,* 27 May 1863.

[5] 20 May 1863.

[6] 18 May 1863.

Most Confederate editors, on the other hand, recognized that anyone, exile or otherwise, who preached the doctrine of reunion was an "enemy" to their dream of independence. The *Richmond Sentinel* stated that Vallandigham was not welcome if he insisted that his loyalty was to the United States. "Unless he intends to renounce his allegiance to our enemies," stated the editor of the *Sentinel*, "he owes it to himself and us not to stay here." By leaving Southern soil and heading for Canada, he could well counter the "cunning and tyranny" of Lincoln and Seward.[7] Daniel of the *Richmond Examiner* was even more outspoken against granting Vallandigham hospitality. The exile was no friend. He had opposed the establishment of the Confederacy; he was, in fact, "an earnest agent for its political annihilation." Since he was really "an alien enemy," he might well be imprisoned in Richmond until the next exchange of prisoners, under a flag of truce, was arranged at City Point. If the Federals refused to receive him, then he should "be forced to leave the Confederacy."[8] The same line of argument appeared in the *Chattanooga Rebel.* "We do not wish to be inhospitable," wrote its editor, "but we do not recognize the right of any power or court to send its convicts here as in Botany Bay. The South is not the proper place for political hermits, however dignified, or popular, or noble."[9]

President Jefferson Davis and his secretary of war, James A. Seddon, also recognized that they dared not welcome an exile who still claimed his loyalty was to the United States. Furthermore, a friendly welcome would play into Lincoln's hands and give him a chance to say that Vallandigham was among "friends," thus stigmatizing all antiwar Democrats. This, of course, was exactly what Vallandigham and Confederate officials wanted to prevent.

President Davis, therefore, wanted a formal statement of Vallandigham's intent and status. He instructed his secretary of war to make the necessary inquiry of General Bragg. "If the Honorable C. L. Vallandigham has come or been forced within

[7] Ibid., 29 May 1863.
[8] *Richmond Daily Examiner*, 30 May 1863.
[9] *Chattanooga Daily Rebel*, 29 May 1863.

your lines," Secretary Seddon wrote to Bragg, "ascertain and report on what character and under what circumstances he stands. If he claims to be a loyal citizen of the United States, he must be held in charge or on parole as an alien enemy. He may be allowed on parole to proceed to Wilmington, and then to report to General [William H. C.] Whiting."[10]

Seddon's telegram embarrassed Bragg and caused him to retreat from the independent measures he had taken earlier. He asked his "guest" to return the pass given him on May 26 and to put into writing his "status" and "intentions." Vallandigham complied. He had come into the Confederate lines, he wrote, under compulsion and against his consent and in pursuance of a military order of the president of the United States, executed by force. "My most earnest desire," he added, "is for a passport, if necessary, and permission to leave as soon as possible through some Confederate port, or by way of Matamoros, for Canada, where I can see my family, and as far as possible, transact my business unmolested. I am still a citizen of Ohio, and of the United States, recognizing my allegiance to both, and retaining the same opinions and position which I have always held at home."[11]

When Vallandigham learned that blockade runners were going to and from Wilmington, North Carolina, "almost with the regularity of packets,"[12] he decided to go there rather than risk the tedious trip to Matamoros, Mexico. Confederate authorities, too, recognized that Vallandigham's easiest way out of Dixie would be from Wilmington. After General William H. C. Whiting had assumed command of the military district of Wilmington, he had made the Cape Fear River the best haven for blockade runners in the South, and had fortified Fort Fisher at the mouth of the river, making it a near impregnable fortress.

When Bragg received Vallandigham's "formal statement" of May 31, he again reported to Richmond authorities. He not only summarized the exile's statement but added the suggestion that

[10] 30 May 1863, *Official Records*, ser. 2, 5: 963.

[11] Bragg to Vallandigham, 31 May 1863, and Vallandigham to Bragg, same date, Vallandigham Papers.

[12] Vallandigham, in a postwar speech of 24 October 1867, published in *Dayton Daily Ledger*, 30 October 1867.

Adjutant General Samuel Cooper or "a confidential agent" interview Vallandigham.[13]

President Davis liked Bragg's suggestion. One telegram instructed Bragg to send Vallandigham "as an alien enemy under guard of an officer" to Wilmington "where further orders await him."[14] A second asked his secretary of war to arrange a meeting of Vallandigham with Colonel Robert Ould, Confederate commissioner for the exchange of prisoners, in Lynchburg, Virginia. After the interview Ould should conduct his "guest" to Wilmington.[15]

Bragg immediately carried out President Davis's instructions, adding a penciled note to the president's telegram so it could also serve as a pass: "Upon Mr. Vallandigham's earnest request, he was permitted to go this morning to Lynchburg to confer with a distinguished friend [Ould] of Virginia. He reports from there on parole to the War Department."[16]

Seddon complied with Davis's orders by writing a note to Ould, asking him to meet Vallandigham in Lynchburg and then assume "direction and control over his future movements." In part, Seddon's directive read:

> You will see that he is not molested or assailed or unduly intruded upon, and extend to him the attentions and kind treatment consistent with his relation as an alien enemy. After a reasonable delay, with him at Lynchburg to allow rest and recreation from the fatigue of his recent exposure and travel, you will proceed with him to Wilmington, N. C., and there deliver him to the charge of Major-General Whiting, commanding in that district, by whom he will be allowed at an early convenient opportunity, to take shipping to any neutral port he may prefer, whether in Europe, the Islands, or on this Continent. More full instructions on this point will be given General Whiting, and your duty will be discharged when you shall have conducted Mr. Vallandigham to Wilmington and placed him at the disposition of that commander.[17]

13 Bragg to Samuel Cooper, 1 June 1863, *Official Records*, ser. 2, 5:965.

14 Davis to Bragg, 2 June 1863, Vallandigham Papers.

15 The instructions of Davis to Seddon are not included in the *Official Records*. Seddon's instructions to Ould, however, indicate that Davis ordered his secretary of war to interview Vallandigham; see *Official Records*, ser. 2, 5:968.

16 The penciled note is on the Davis-to-Bragg telegram of 2 June 1863, Vallandigham Papers.

17 Seddon to Ould, 5 June 1863, *Official Records*, ser. 2, 5:968.

As an "alien enemy," Clement L. Vallandigham waited in Shelbyville for instructions to proceed. He passed most of the time in seclusion, although he took a brief walk daily. Several newspaper correspondents sought him out, anxious to provide a description of the exile for subscribers and readers. "Mr. Vallandigham," wrote a correspondent for the *Richmond Examiner,* "is about fifty years of age, five feet eight inches high, brown short hair, slightly grey, a large twinkling blue eye, aquiline Roman nose, full face, ruddy complexion, rather stout, has a very affable, pleasant manner, and smiles most graciously, exhibiting a white set of teeth, but has one of the incissors [*sic*] out at the left corner of his mouth. He is what may be called a good looking man, with a very prepossessing, popular manner, and admirably adapted to electioneering and stump speaking."[18]

A second reporter, also favorably impressed with Vallandigham, wrote an even fuller description of the exile: "His manner has nothing studied or affected; he speaks without effort or hesitation, and his face bears a permanent expression of good humor and friendship. His eyes are blue, full, and look right into yours; whilst they beam with vivacity and intelligence, there is an honesty in them which has won your regard and admiration before you know it. His complexion is florid, his nose rather hooked, chin and lips well chiselled and firm, teeth strong and white, hair and whiskers dark chestnut, and close trimmed, height about 5 feet 10. His frame is robust, compact, and graceful. Altogether he is certainly a man of extraordinary mental and physical vigor. . . . A man of great natural abilities, improved by cultivation, combining impulse with deliberation, and enthusiasm with remorseless determination of purpose."[19]

Reporters and correspondents who came to Shelbyville after June 1 missed an opportunity to observe or interview the noted exile. On that day General Bragg gave instructions to Vallandigham to proceed to Wilmington via Lynchburg and report on parole to General Whiting. Bragg detached an officer from his staff to accompany Vallandigham, and John DeWitt Atkins, who had served in Congress before the war and considered himself a friend, also received permission to travel part of the way. Both

18 *Richmond Daily Examiner,* 8 June 1863.
19 *Atlanta Confederacy* (n.d.), quoted in *Chattanooga Daily Rebel,* 3 June 1863.

Atkins and Vallandigham had attended the Democratic National Convention when it met in Cincinnati in 1856, one representing Ohio and the other Tennessee. As a member of the Thirty-fifth Congress, Atkins had helped the Ohio Democrat gain Lewis D. Campbell's seat in 1858. The crisis which developed after that year strained their friendship and the start of hostilities caused each to go his own way. In 1861 Atkins accepted a colonelcy in the Confederate army. After winning election to the Confederate congress in 1862, he sheathed his sword and returned to the political arena. Fate played strange tricks upon the two friends of prewar years. One was now an exile, the other his traveling companion.

As Vallandigham, Atkins, and Bragg's aide passed through the camps to the Shelbyville depot, crowds of Confederate soldiers gathered along the route. Some expressed their sympathy for the exile through cheers and "friendly demonstrations," but Confederate officers took steps to suppress the demonstrations, quite embarrassing to Vallandigham.[20]

The three travelers arrived in Chattanooga early in the afternoon of June 2. Citizens of that city knew of Vallandigham's arrival and a large number of the city's residents assembled at the depot to see a man who was exiled because he had the courage to speak out and criticize the Lincoln administration.

Edward M. Bruce, a member of the Confederate congress from Kentucky, met the arrivals at the railway depot and conducted the three to the Crutchfield House, the finest hotel in town. There Bruce presented the exile to Judge Robert L. Caruthers and other distinguished citizens of Tennessee. After the exchange of pleasantries and a brief visit, Vallandigham was taken to his room. He spent the rest of the day visiting with strangers in the lobby of the hotel or with old acquaintances in the privacy of his room.[21]

The next morning, Vallandigham and the officer who had him in charge left for Knoxville. There was a long delay between trains in the largest city of eastern Tennessee, for provision and troop trains monopolized the main line. Later in the day Vallandigham's train proceeded toward Lynchburg via Abingdon,

---

[20] *Richmond Daily Examiner*, 8 June 1863.
[21] *Chattanooga, Daily Rebel*, 3 June 1863.

but did not arrive until Wednesday evening, June 5. In Lynchburg the officer in charge conducted the parolee to the Norvell House and instructed him to rest and relax until Colonel Robert Ould arrived to interview him.

Southerners, meanwhile, continued to treat Vallandigham with civility, as befitted "an alien enemy." Editors and others stated time and again that he was "a mortal enemy," but felt some hope that the exile might learn that the South wanted independence, not compromise and reunion. The South would never accept peace "without independence." If Vallandigham supposed that Southern states would return to the Union if concessions were belatedly offered, they declared, he was mistaken and "badly deluded." No, reunion could never occur until "the terrible past" was "wiped out" and sinking into oblivion, or "until the many thousands who had been slain should be brought back to life" and the many "outrages" committed upon the Southern people undone.[22]

Southern editors advanced three reasons why Vallandigham ought to leave Dixie and go to Bermuda or Canada. In the first place, if he stayed in the South for a year or two, it would give "a color of probability" to the innuendoes which stamped him as a traitor to the Northern government. Republican propagandists could claim that the exile enjoyed the company of his "friends." In the second place, Vallandigham's position on peace and reunion conflicted directly with the objectives of the Southern war for independence. "So odious to us has the idea of reunion with the North become," stated the editor of the *Richmond Sentinel*, "that we denounce the party of which Vallandigham is chief" as bitterly as Lincoln's supporters. Some Southerners evidently regarded peace-and-compromise men like the exile as "most dangerous enemies," to be abhorred as much as Thaddeus Stevens or Charles Sumner. In the third place, it was likely that Vallandigham would receive his party's gubernatorial nomination at the Ohio State Democratic Convention of June 11. It would be more expeditious for him to conduct his campaign from Canada rather than from the Confederacy. Ex-

---

[22] *Richmond Daily Examiner*, 2 June 1863; *Chattanooga Daily Rebel*, 2 June 1863; entry of 6 June 1863, in Kate Cummings, *Kate: The Journal of a Confederate Nurse*, Richard Harwell, ed. (Baton Rouge, 1959), p. 108.

pediency, then, dictated that Vallandigham shake Southern dust from his soiled shoes and leave the Confederacy as soon as possible.[23]

While Southern editors were urging Vallandigham to leave Dixie, Colonel Robert Ould arrived in Lynchburg for his interview with the exile. Ould, on assignment as "special interrogator" for the Confederate government, had a long and friendly discussion with Vallandigham. Never a shrinking violet and at times quite garrulous, the exile answered Ould's queries frankly and often at great length. If the Confederates held out for fifteen months the peace party in the North would sweep "the Lincoln dynasty" out of political existence. An invasion of the North by Confederate armies, on the other hand, would "unite all parties" and strengthen Lincoln's hand. It might, in fact, enable him to crush all political opposition and trample even more upon the constitutional rights of the people.

Vallandigham offered the opinion that the Southern cause was crumbling or "sinking," and that the peace movement in the North would also collapse "if Northern arms triumphed." Northerners, whether radical Republicans or peace Democrats, had the same final objective—reunion. The Democracy wanted reunion through conciliation and concession; radical Republicans sought reunion through coercion and conquest. Any reconstruction which was not voluntary on the part of the South could not be permanent; it would be followed by another separation and a worse war than the present.

If reunion could not be effected through either compromise or coercion, Vallandigham continued, the Northern government would be compelled to recognize the independence of the South, albeit reluctantly. In any event, Vallandigham reiterated, he had not changed his views since the beginning of the war. Compromise could have prevented the war; compromise should be the means to restore "the Union as it was."[24]

23 *Richmond Sentinel,* 6 June 1863; *Petersburg* (Va.) *Daily Express,* 8 June 1863; *Richmond Daily Examiner,* 4 June 1863; *Wilmington* (N.C.) *Daily Journal,* 5 June 1863.

24 Ould's memorandum, which summarized Vallandigham's views and gave an account of the interview, seems to be lost. John B. Jones's statement of what Ould had reported (Jones saw the memorandum in the Confederate War Department files) is summarized in Jones, *A Rebel War Clerk's Diary* (New York, 1958), pp. 229-30. Jones's entry of 22 June 1863 also appeared in the *Dayton Daily*

After completing his interview with the exile, Ould escorted him to Wilmington via Petersburg. It was necessary to change trains again in Petersburg. No reception was given Vallandigham in that city and the two left as quietly as they had come.[25]

In Wilmington, Colonel Ould turned the parolee over to Gen. Whiting and headed back to his desk and his many duties in Richmond. General Whiting secured passage for Vallandigham on a blockade runner, the *Lady Davis*, previously called the *Cornubia*, owned by Secretary of War James A. Seddon. Through Seddon's influence, Vallandigham received a priority rating on the passenger list.

It took several days to unload the cargo which the *Lady Davis* had brought in from Bermuda, to reload the 600-ton, two-masted side-wheeler with cotton bales, and to ready her for another game of hide-and-seek with Yankee ships of the blockading squadron. On June 17, Captain Richard H. Gayle directed the passengers to file aboard and instructed the pilot to take the 210-foot ship, with a reputation for being "very fast," to a position behind the New Inlet bar, not far from the mouth of the Cape Fear River. While they waited for darkness, the firemen stoked the furnaces until the flames flashed over the tops of the smokestacks. After darkness set in, Captain Gayle ordered the *Lady Davis* headed for the high seas. The side-wheeler ran the blockade successfully and headed for St. George's harbor, Bermuda. The trip, evidently without incident,[26] ended

Journal, 8 May 1866. Jones mentioned that Jefferson Davis endorsed Ould's memorandum and added a note that Vallandigham's views regarding a Northern reaction to an invasion by Lee's army were in error.

[25] *Augusta* (Ga.) *Chronicle,* undated clipping in Vallandigham Folder, New York Historical Library, New York City.

[26] Vallandigham, *Vallandigham,* pp. 314-15, recounts an incident which has all the earmarks of a myth. While the *Lady Davis* was on the high seas it was approached by a U.S. warship, a faster steamer than the *Lady Davis*. Captain Gayle, in panic, rushed to Vallandigham's cabin to seek help and advice. After being apprised that a number of British uniforms were aboard, Vallandigham advised Captain Gayle to have his men don the British uniforms and parade up and down the deck, so as to produce the impression that the steamer was an English transport with troops aboard. Captain Gayle followed Vallandigham's advice and the ruse worked like "a charm." Vallandigham's ingenuity thus saved the day and the cargo.

The story seems quite improbable. In the first place, it is unlikely that any Union warship was fast enough to catch or even approach the *Lady Davis* on the high seas. In the second place, a seasoned blockade runner like Captain Gayle would hardly panic and run to a landlubber's cabin to seek advice. If

some eighty-two hours later, and Vallandigham left the *Lady Davis* and set foot on British soil.[27]

Most Confederates seemed happy to see Vallandigham's twenty-four-day stay in their country come to an end. "We are glad that Vallandigham has gone," wrote the editor of the *Augusta Chronicle*, "for his presence in the Confederacy was a source of perplexity to the Government, and general uneasiness to the people."[28] The editor of the *Richmond Sentinel* also expressed satisfaction with the way the Confederate officials had handled the Vallandigham case. "We are glad, indeed," he wrote, "that the matter was managed as it was . . . [in a way] most likely to frustrate Lincoln's amiable designs."[29]

Captain Gayle had carried British uniforms to fool Yankee blockade captains, he would have known when to use them. Furthermore, when the *Lady Davis* was captured on November 8, 1863, after having run aground off South Inlet, all contents were seized and inventoried. The list fails to mention any British uniforms.

[27] *Bermuda Royal Gazette*, 27 June 1863, quoted in *Daily Ohio State Journal* (Columbus), 4 July 1863; *Official Records of the Union and Confederate Navies in the War of the Rebellion*, 26 vols. (Washington, D.C., 1894-1922), ser. 1, 9: 274, 277-78; ibid., ser. 2, 1: 66.

[28] Undated clipping in Vallandigham Folder, New York Historical Library.

[29] 25 June 1863; see also *Bermuda Royal Gazette*, 23 June 1863, quoted in *Crisis*, 8 July 1863.

15

ASYLUM IN CANADA

CLEMENT L. VALLANDIGHAM's plans were now clear, even if seemingly insurmountable barriers stood in the way. He intended to go to Canada, secure housing near Niagara Falls, and renew his campaign for the governorship of Ohio.

He had to wait several days before a Halifax-bound steamer came into St. George's harbor, Bermuda. Time hung heavy on the exile's hands, for he was most anxious to get on with his campaign. Every day that passed was a day lost. Finally, on July 2, Vallandigham boarded the *Harriet Pinckney*, bound for Halifax with 600 bales of cotton.

While the *Harriet Pinckney* plowed through the waves, Vallandigham had time to think about the past and plan for the future. He had gained his party's gubernatorial nomination while waiting in Wilmington to board a blockade-runner. His bid for martyrdom had given him the party's nomination—this he had expected. He hoped to realize the second half of his dream on October 13, when he faced the Union Party nominee at the polls. He had reason to be optimistic. Popular demands for peace had never been higher than in the closing months of June 1863. The public reaction to his arrest, trial, and exile seemed to become more intense with each passing week. Democratic dreamers hoped that the public reaction might put Vallandigham in the governor's chair and sweep the Lincoln administration from power.

As the ship was approaching Halifax, two portentious events elsewhere affected the exile's roseate dreams. General Ulysses S. Grant captured Vicksburg and cut the Confederacy in two. Then, in a dramatic climax, the Army of the Potomac turned back the rebel challenge and General Lee's best troops on the slopes at Gettysburg. These two titanic victories helped to squelch the peace movement, to make the Lincoln administration respectable again, and to make many citizens forget the treatment Clement L. Vallandigham had received at the hands of General Burnside and President Lincoln.

Although Vallandigham arrived unannounced in Halifax, he received a friendly greeting, for he symbolized opposition to the Lincoln administration. Several Halifax merchants had invested heavily in blockade-runners, and two of their ships had been captured by Yankee warships a short time before. Then, too, several days before the *Harriet Pinckney* arrived in Halifax, a Yankee gunboat had visited the port to take on coal. The captain and his crew received a hostile reception from the local citizens. As the unpopular Yankee captain took his gunboat out to sea, he heard the crowd on the wharf give three resounding cheers for Jefferson Davis and the Southern Confederacy.[1]

As soon as Vallandigham arrived in Halifax, he booked passage on the *Daniel P. King*, scheduled to leave next day for Pictou with mail and a general cargo. After securing hotel accommodations for the night, he hurried down to the telegraph office to inform his friends and his wife that he had arrived safely in Halifax and to instruct them to meet him at the Clifton House, Niagara, Canada West, on July 14. Finally he went down to the express office to send $170 to Mrs. Jonas P. Levy of Philadelphia, wife of an imprisoned Union captain who had given him the money for safe-keeping. Later that evening the exile wrote a long letter to his wife and several shorter ones to friends in Dayton.[2]

The American consul in Halifax dutifully reported Vallandigham's arrival to the State Department. Playing the detective, he noted with whom the exile talked and walked. "His intimate associates here," the concerned consul wrote, "were the most violent secessionists and supporters of the Confederate cause." He also reported on Vallandigham's departure from Halifax and his plans. "Vallandigham left this morning via St. Johns, N. B., for Canada," he added, "where he designs to remain and await the results of the Ohio election."[3]

[1] *Nova Scotian* (Halifax), 1, 3, 13 July 1863; *Montreal Gazette*, 21 July 1863.

[2] C.L.V. to Hon. H. M. Phillips, 24 October 1863 (asking about the $170 he had sent from Halifax on July 5), Simon Gratz Papers, Historical Society of Pennsylvania, Philadelphia; Mrs. Thomas O. Lowe to her husband, 14 July 1863, Thomas O. Lowe Papers, Dayton and Montgomery County Public Library.

[3] Melville M. Jackson to William H. Seward, 7 July 1863, Consulate Files, State Department Section, National Archives. Jackson erred in believing Vallandigham's

The trip to Pictou was uneventful. When the *Daniel P. King* arrived, Vallandigham was lucky to find the *Lady Head* in port being readied for a trip to Quebec, and he quickly made arrangements for passage. After the transfer of mail to the *Lady Head*, the passengers filed aboard and the ship raised anchor. Wearisome stops at Shediac, Chatham, Newcastle, Dalhousie, Paspebiac, and Gaspé tested the patience of the passengers and delayed the arrival of the 168-ton steamship in Quebec Bay.[4]

Early on the morning of July 11 the *Lady Head* finally arrived in Quebec. Vallandigham disembarked and walked up Palace Street to the Russell Hotel to secure a room and inquire about train transportation to Niagara. Several Cincinnati citizens happened to be staying at the luxurious hotel, so the exile had a chance to inquire about the reaction to his arrest and the chances of his election as governor. He also announced his intention to hurry on to Niagara and take up residence at the Clifton House.[5]

Charles S. Ogden, the excitable U.S. consul stationed in Quebec, sent a terse telegram to Secretary of State Seward: "C. L. Vallandigham is here."[6] Ogden, who thought a consul's chief responsibilities were to act as spy and clip local newspapers, made a determined effort to keep track of the exile's activities. He noticed that prominent Quebec residents called upon Vallandigham at his hotel and gave him a warm reception. It galled Ogden to have to report that Edward W. Watkin, prominent London financier linked to various Canadian railroad and commercial interests, and Charles J. Brydges, superintendent of the Grand Trunk Railroad and a member of the elite Stadacona Club, escorted Vallandigham about the city to look at scenic spots and to visit places of historical interest.[7]

---

ship would go to St. John. Instead, the ship sailed eastward, along the coast of Nova Scotia, through the Straits of Canso, and on to Pictou, at the eastern end of Northumberland Strait.

[4] *Nova Scotian*, 13 July, 5 October 1863; *Quebec Morning Chronicle*, 13 July 1863.

[5] *Courrier du Canada* (Quebec), 13 July 1863; *Journal de Québec*, 12 July 1863; *Quebec Morning Chronicle*, 13 July 1863. The Cincinnati residents, evidently not friends of Vallandigham, were Mr. and Mrs. H. A. Bowman and Mr. and Mrs. G. M. Hand.

[6] 13 July 1863, William H. Seward Papers, Rush Rhees Library, University of Rochester.

[7] Ogden to Seward, 15 July 1863, Consulate Records, State Department Section.

Watkin and Brydges convinced Vallandigham to tarry a
day in Quebec so they could give a dinner in his honor at the
Stadacona Club. Although the exile was anxious to hurry on
to Niagara, he consented to stay over for the hurriedly planned
affair. Quite a number of notables attended the dinner, including John A. Macdonald, former head of the Canadian government. Watkin, entrepreneur extraordinary, presided. Neither
he nor other Canadians who spoke briefly made any mention
of the American civil war nor indicated by what they said that
their sympathies were with the South. They viewed the dinner
as "mere hospitality to a refugee" who had arrived in Canada
"in distress." Eventually, Watkin invited the noted guest to say
a few words.

Vallandigham began his short speech with an apology for
appearing in a wrinkled suit and for the poverty of his dress.
"I can only explain," he stated with an apparent bid for sympathy,
"that I am standing in the clothes I was allowed to put on, after
being taken out of my bed, in my own house, without warning
and without warrant, and have not the means to clothe myself."
Then, in a few appropriate sentences, Vallandigham thanked his
hosts for their kindness and their country for extending him
rights and liberties which the Lincoln administration had denied
him.[8]

Later that evening Watkin and Brydges escorted C.L.V. down
to the Grand Trunk Railroad depot. Watkin, who held the
presidency of the railroad, offered Vallandigham "a friendly
loan," though the exile declined the gesture of good will. Brydges
then offered him "a free railroad pass," which he accepted.
Vallandigham thanked his friends and expressed a wish to return
to Quebec at some future date for another visit. But he was
anxious to get to Niagara for a rendezvous with Ohio political
friends and a reunion with his family.[9]

[8] Quoted in Edward W. Watkin, *Canada and Her States: Recollections, 1851-
1866* (London, 1887), p. 455.
[9] Ibid., pp. 455-56; *Buffalo Commercial Advertiser*, 14 July 1863. Both the
Quebec Mercury, 13 July 1863, and Charles S. Ogden (report, Ogden to Seward,
15 July 1863, Consulate Records) reported that Vallandigham left Quebec via a
special train, a courtesy of Brydges and Watkin. On the other hand, Watkin
later wrote that Vallandigham "accepted a free pass to Niagara." Another
passenger, one who recognized Vallandigham, offered evidence substantiating

Vallandigham's presence in Canada received less newspaper space than he had expected, for the Canadian papers were filled with news of the climactic battles of Gettysburg and Vicksburg. Yet Vallandigham received the sympathy of many Canadians. In the first place, the English practice of extending hospitality to exiles had rubbed off on the Canadians. In the second place, Canadians were tempted to view the exile as a martyr to free speech and the traditional rights of Englishmen. Then, too, Joshua R. Giddings, United States Consul General in Canada, had alienated public opinion by suggesting that the Reciprocity Treaty of 1854, drafted for a ten-year period, be terminated as "a lesson" to Canadian and British commercial and maritime interests and had shown even poorer judgment by talking of annexation of Canada by the United States. Rumors continued to persist that the United States armies would march northward and conquer Canada after the collapse of the Confederacy. It was not surprising, therefore, that some Canadian newspapers expressed editorial sympathy for Vallandigham.[10]

Despite Giddings' foolish comments, the late summer of 1863 witnessed the development of a "tranquil period" in United States-Canadian relations. Economic prosperity, due in part to the needs of the American civil war, helped soothe ruffled feelings. Time had healed the injury to United States-British relations caused by the *Trent* affair and other incidents of 1861-1862. Most Canadian newspapers supporting the John Sandfield Macdonald ministry favored rapprochement with the United States and felt obligated to discredit Vallandigham and belittle his presence. George Brown of the *Toronto Globe*, for example, was critical of Vallandigham, and this influential politician-newspaperman gave the cue to other newspapers supporting the Macdonald government.

After an exhausting journey, Vallandigham arrived at the

Watkin and contradicting Ogden. The American consul, even at best, was a most inept reporter. He even credited Mr. William Walker, who had died two months earlier, with being at the Quebec dinner in Vallandigham's honor. Robin Winks, *Canada and the United States* (Baltimore, 1960), p. 143, states that Vallandigham traveled from Quebec to Niagara in "a special coach." Winks also has the deceased Walker attending the dinner.

[10] *Quebec Morning Chronicle*, 11 July 1863; *Nova Scotian* (Halifax), 13 July 1863; *Journal de Québec*, 16 July 1863.

Niagara railroad depot in the early hours of July 15.[11] After
securing a room at the Clifton House, he retired to get some
rest. Later on the fifteenth he met members of the welcoming
party who had gathered across the border, some of whom had
grown rather impatient awaiting the exile's arrival. The Hon.
Daniel W. Voorhees, Indiana congressman and a bold critic
of the Lincoln administration, had arrived on the thirteenth and
secured a room at the Stephenson House. The Hon. Richard T.
Merrick, a self-styled "peace man" from Illinois, had arrived on
the fourteenth, bearing a message from the crusty editor of the
Chicago Times. Joseph Warren, editor of the *Buffalo Courier,*
had crossed the border to greet Vallandigham and write copy
for his newspaper. Then there were some friends from Dayton
and Cincinnati. Altogether they comprised a good-sized reception committee.[12]

After members of the party finished the hand-shaking and
greetings, they turned to the subject of the gubernatorial campaign in Ohio. The exile pulled a copy of another "Address to
the Democracy of Ohio" out of his pocket. Dated July 15, 1863,
this document formally accepted the nomination tendered him
on June 11 by the Democratic State Convention. It enumerated
the basic issues of the campaign and wrapped the cloak of
martyrdom around the exile. It criticized President Lincoln for
trampling upon civil rights, for trespassing beyond constitutional bounds, and for establishing a military despotism. Vallandigham's address referred to Lincoln and his agents as
"usurpers" and "weak despots." It also referred somewhat
vaguely to peace and reunion, expecting both to be achieved
"through compromise."[13]

In effect, the newest address served as Vallandigham's personal
political platform. It stated his case admirably, without any
apparent rancor or trace of bitterness. It also revealed the exile's
firm faith in the future, for it repeated C.L.V.'s favorite phrase
that time would vindicate him and incriminate his enemies.

[11] Vallandigham, *Vallandigham,* p. 316, errs in transferring the Stadacona Club
dinner from Quebec to Montreal. Winks erroneously states that C.L.V. received
a public reception in Montreal. Neither Giddings, the consul general in Montreal,
nor any Montreal newspaper mentions Vallandigham's stopping in the city.
[12] *St. Catharines Evening Journal,* 15 July 1863; *Toronto Daily Leader,* 16,
17 July 1863; *Buffalo Morning Courier,* 16 July 1863.
[13] Dated 15 July 1863, published in *Cincinnati Daily Enquirer,* 20 July.

After Warren and Merrick completed their visit with Vallan-digham, they shuffled off to Buffalo, the first to his newspaper office and the latter to the telegraphic headquarters. While Warren started to set Vallandigham's address in type, Merrick tried to relay it over the telegraph to the *Chicago Times*. The Republican-minded telegraph operator, however, considered Vallandigham's address a treasonable and mischievous document and refused to send it over the wires. Merrick, somewhat in-dignant, put the address back in his pocket, hurried to the rail-road depot, and took the next train to Cleveland. The telegrapher in Cleveland also acted as a censor and refused to transmit the document. Even more indignant now, Merrick caught the next Chicago-bound train and personally delivered Vallandigham's address to the *Times*'s editorial office. The incident was indicative of the obstacles Vallandigham faced. Telegraph operators not only acted as censors, but also circulated rumors and outright lies about the exile who sought the governorship of Ohio. Val-landigham's friends believed that the telegraphers, the Lincoln administration, and Ohio Republicans constituted an unholy al-liance to defeat C.L.V.[14]

In the weeks that followed, the exile had hundreds of visitors. Mrs. Vallandigham and her ten-year-old son hurried to Niagara as soon as they received word that the exile had arrived at the Clifton House. The Dayton party also included Mrs. Vallan-digham's sister, Dr. Jefferson A. Walter, and Judge Harvey A. Blanchard. Those who had heard reports that Mrs. Vallandigham was "not well" were pleasantly surprised that she was once more self-composed, personable, and quite cheerful. "Mrs. V. is a comely, pleasant-looking lady," wrote one Canadian observer, "and betrays no evidence of insanity or even unhappiness." The same observer noticed that young "Master Charlie" was "a bright lively youth of ten summers" and possessed of Young America proclivities.[15]

Ohio Democrats occasionally visited Vallandigham at his Canadian retreat to discuss political strategy or to refill their

[14] *Buffalo Morning Courier*, 16 July 1863; *Buffalo Morning Express*, 18 July 1863; *Chicago Daily Times*, 18 July 1863; report of A. Stager to Stanton, 15 July 1863; published in *Official Records*, ser. 2, 5:122; *Illinois State Register* (Spring-field), 19 July 1863.

[15] *Toronto Daily Globe*, 28 July 1863; *Crisis* (Columbus), 15 July 1863; *Daily Ohio State Journal* (Columbus), 4 August 1863.

cup of hope. George E. Pugh, campaigning for the lieutenant-governorship, took time out from speech-making to visit the exile and discuss their chances of winning the October 13 election. Even some Pennsylvania Democrats called to pay their respects and to express a wish for victory at the polls. Judge John C. Fulton of New York led a party of pilgrims from Erie County to the Clifton House. After imbibing Canadian whiskey "in frequent and ponderous potations," they talked of hanging Lincoln, Seward, "and other abolitionists." They took their turns visiting "the great Martyr," perhaps embarrassing him by their conduct, and left Niagara to make room for other callers. Occasionally visitors from the States fell afoul of the law because of their liking for Canadian whiskey. (A high excise tax made the price of United States whiskey prohibitive.) Several visitors from Cleveland got drunk after visiting Vallandigham, were arrested, and spent the night in jail. Next morning, after paying a fine, they headed back home, poorer and perhaps wiser. An observant Canadian newsman wrote, "Yankees can't stand Canadian whiskey. There is too much fight in it."[16]

Canadians who stopped at the Clifton House were anxious to see the fellow who had stirred up such a fuss in his own country and who styled himself a martyr to free speech. The sympathetic editor of the *Toronto Leader* had a lengthy visit with Vallandigham and left most favorably impressed, finding him "exceedingly intelligent, . . . amiable in disposition, . . . [and] refined in manner and language."[17]

Vallandigham's growing popularity galled George Brown of the *Toronto Globe*. Earlier he had criticized those Canadians who had feted Vallandigham in Quebec, "fawning over him" and paying him homage. Now he sought to undermine Vallandigham's popularity by depicting him as an enemy of Canada. The tradition of civility to exiles should be practiced, Brown wrote, but the right of asylum did not require fussing over them or courting them. He insisted that during the crisis over the *Trent*, Vallandigham had tried to bring on war with England. His "scurrilous tongue" and "anti-British tirades" of

[16] *St. Catharines Evening Journal*, 31 July 1863; *Toronto Daily Globe*, 28 July 1863.
[17] 25 July 1863.

earlier years ought to convince Canadians that he deserved neither sympathy nor honor. "If it had been possible to bring on a war between England and America," Brown concluded, "Vallandigham is the man who would have done it."[18]

Vallandigham resented Brown's attack and wrote a letter to defend himself. This anonymous letter, signed "An American," chided Brown for misquoting Vallandigham and for quoting out of context to pervert meaning. The letter also accused the editor of taking the side of Lincoln and the abolitionists and of assailing a man of courage who was a martyr for civil liberties.[19]

Brown refused to retreat. He restated his contention that the exile should not be "feted, caressed, and petted." Then he quoted extensively from Vallandigham's speeches in Congress of December 1861 and January 1862. He dropped quotation marks within one of Vallandigham's statements in order to make a better case against him, crediting the Ohio congressman with a quotation from somebody else. "He is a well-known Anglophobiac," editor Brown insisted, "who never missed a chance of libelling Great Britain, until he had to fly to her dominions for safety."[20] Other pro-government papers joined the *Globe* in trying to discredit the exile and undercut his popularity. The editor of the *Chatham Patriot*, for example, wrote that Vallandigham should have shown his true colors by enlisting in the Confederate army and admitting publicly that he was lined up on the side of secession, slavery, and Satan.[21]

Vallandigham tried to counter with still another anonymous letter. Having secured a printed copy of the speeches he had given in Congress a year and a half earlier, C.L.V. wrote his rebuttal. With his sources at his elbow, he conclusively proved that Brown and the *Toronto Globe* had been guilty of unfair practices—misrepresenting, omitting quotation marks, and selecting words and phrases out of context. These practices, the exile wrote, "created prejudices" against a stranger and an exile who had sought no more than the protection of a foreign flag.[22]

---

[18] 21 July 1863.
[19] C.L.V. to editor of the *Toronto Daily Leader*, 21 July 1863, published 25 July.
[20] *Toronto Daily Globe*, 27 July 1863.
[21] 30 July, 13 August 1863; *London Free Press*, 28 July 1863.
[22] Letter to editor of the *Toronto Daily Leader*, 7 August 1863, signed "An American," published 11 August.

Vallandigham's argument reflected unfavorably upon Brown of the *Globe,* and several antigovernment editors seized the opportunity to rebuke one of Canada's most powerful political figures. The editors of the *Toronto Patriot* and *St. Catharines Journal* lauded the exile for pinning Brown to the mat. The *Globe,* they said, had been guilty of untrue statements and grossly unfair to a helpless exile who wore well the halo of martyrdom.[23]

Brown neither apologized to Vallandigham nor retracted his statements. Instead, he continued to insist that Vallandigham deserved neither favor nor respect. He ended his effort at self-justification with several parting shots. Vallandigham, Brown stated dogmatically, was "a traitor to his own people" as well as "a bitter enemy of England."[24]

While Vallandigham was carrying on his feud with Brown and the *Globe,* he decided to seek new quarters. He and the owner of the Clifton House had had several heated exchanges. Too many callers drifted into the noted hotel, some to visit Vallandigham and express their admiration for his courage, others to gape at him as if he were a monkey in a cage and to see if he possessed the horns and the forked tail which some Republicans attributed to him. Sometimes these pilgrims drank too much liquor and embarrassed both Vallandigham and the proprietor. Then, too, it was reported that Lord Lyons, British ambassador to the United States, and Secretary of State William H. Seward planned a joint visit to Niagara Falls and Toronto. The proprietor hoped that Lord Lyons and Seward might be his guests, but it was unthinkable that Seward and Vallandigham would stay under the same roof.[25]

On August 1 the unwanted tenant and his family moved from the Clifton House to the Table Rock Hotel, an inn and curio shop operated by Saul Davis on the outskirts of Niagara. The exile, however, was not fully satisfied with his new quarters and decided to investigate Windsor as a possible place of residence.

[23] *St. Catharines Evening Journal* (n.d.), quoted in *Toronto Daily Leader,* 8 August 1863; *Toronto Patriot,* 19 August 1863; *Journal de Québec,* 24 August 1863.

[24] *Toronto Daily Globe,* 12 August 1863.

[25] *Montreal Daily Transcript,* 27 August 1863; *New York Daily News* (n.d.), quoted in *Crisis,* 12 August 1863; *St. Catharines Evening Journal,* 31 July, 1 August 1863; *Toronto Daily Globe,* 28 July 1863.

He took a hurried trip to Windsor, opposite Detroit, and decided that he would move his base of operations to that community of about 3,000 inhabitants.[26]

Early in August, Vallandigham had an opportunity to meet and mingle with some of the most famous Canadians of his day and to be where dreams for a "new" Canada were being discussed. Edward W. Watkin, the entrepreneur who had co-sponsored the famous dinner for Vallandigham in Quebec, evidently arranged for the gathering of notables at the Clifton House. Watkin's contingent from Quebec included Charles J. Brydges and Thomas D'Arcy McGee, an expatriated Irishman who had parlayed excellence in literature, oratory, and politics into a remarkably successful career. When the Quebec trio arrived in Niagara, Canada West, they found Alexander G. Dallas, once chief factor of the Hudson's Bay Company but now governor of Prince Rupert's Land, awaiting them. Professor Henry Y. Hind, whose reports on the land between Winnipeg and the Rockies had stirred the imagination of all Canadians, had not yet arrived from Toronto. Nor had Charles Mackay, correspondent for the *London Times*, yet arrived from New York City. The real purpose of the get-together was to acquaint Mackay with several "new schemes," including one to transfer the Hudson's Bay Company's extensive land holdings to Canada. Watkin and McGee wanted Mackay to use his pen and position to prepare Englishmen for the transfer of lands and for the promotion of a Canadian federation.[27]

While awaiting the arrival of Hind and Mackay, Watkin, Brydges, and McGee paid a social call upon Vallandigham at the Table Rock Hotel. Watkin and Brydges renewed their acquaintance while the talkative McGee expressed his views on the American civil war and asked Vallandigham dozens of questions. McGee, who had edited newspapers in Boston and New York before moving to Canada, asked about Irish-Americans in Ohio and the upper Midwest. He had a younger brother serving in the Union army, and he knew that most Irish-Ameri-

[26] *Buffalo Morning Courier*, 1 August 1863; *Hamilton Evening Times*, 8 August 1863; *Milwaukee Sentinel*, 15, 26 August 1863; Vallandigham to Manton Marble, 2 August 1863, Manton Marble Papers, Library of Congress.

[27] *Hamilton Evening Times*, 6 August 1863; Watkin, *Canada and Her States*, pp. 455-56.

cans in the States voted the Democratic ticket, opposed Lincoln's emancipation policy, and sympathized with Vallandigham. Watkin and McGee intended to visit a Canadian political rally next day near Drummondville and invited Vallandigham to accompany them. He readily agreed.[28]

The next morning Watkin, McGee, and Dallas called for Vallandigham in a carriage and the four drove to Drummondville to attend a rally sponsored by the "Clear Grits," critics of the Macdonald government. They saw 2,000 carriages and wagons, some decorated and bearing huge signs or slogans, take part in a three-mile-long procession which ended in Kerr's Grove. McGee and Vallandigham shared places of honor on the speakers' platform and listened with interest as several antigovernment men recited the shortcomings of the Macdonald ministry. After the speech-making, they heard a dozen bands and enjoyed a sumptuous barbecue.[29] Perhaps the affair reminded the exile of happier days, when he had so often been the lion of the occasion at political rallies in Ohio.

The next day Vallandigham had a chance to meet and visit with Charles Mackay, the *Times* correspondent. Mackay developed a favorable impression of the exile, but noticed that United States spies, both amateur and professional, were "as thick as flies" in the area. They hung around the hotels, some sitting "Yankee fashion," leaning backward and balancing on their chairs. They jotted down the names of those with whom Vallandigham talked or with whom he took his walks. They also took down the description of those he dined with, and they relentlessly sought the name of everyone who came within ten feet of the exile.[30]

Watkin and his compatriots called upon Vallandigham after their get-together and urged him to accompany them on the return trip. He declined the invitation but promised to visit Quebec later during the month.

Since his gubernatorial campaign seemed to be progressing

---

[28] Vallandigham's stay in Canada is treated in Frank L. Klement, "Vallandigham as an Exile in Canada, 1863-1864," *Ohio History* 74 (Summer 1965): 151-68; and idem, "Exile across the Border: Clement L. Vallandigham at Niagara, Canada West," *Niagara Frontier* 11 (Autumn 1964): 69-73.

[29] *St. Catharines Evening Journal*, 6 August 1863; *Chatham Weekly Patriot*, 20 August 1863.

[30] Charles Mackay, in *London Times*, 24 August 1863.

satisfactorily, C.L.V. arranged for a leisurely trip down the St. Lawrence to while away the hours which imprisoned his patience. The party included Mrs. Vallandigham, young Charlie, Miss McMahon, and Irving S. Vallandigham, a great uncle from Newark, Delaware. There were also some friends from Dayton and Cincinnati, including Mr. and Mrs. George H. Pendleton. The rugged rocks along the shoreline and the expansive green forests entranced the travelers, taking them out of the harsh world of reality. The trip proved relaxing and the delightful scenery and pleasant conversation made it seem much shorter than it actually was.

The travelers arrived in Quebec on the evening of August 18 and secured comfortable quarters at the St. Louis Hotel. The exile soon had a call from Thomas D'Arcy McGee, who invited him to attend a parliamentary session as his guest the next day. He accepted the invitation with alacrity.

On the evening of August 19 Vallandigham occupied a seat on the floor of the Legislative Assembly, to the left of the Speaker. He witnessed a long and lively session, one which had begun at three o'clock in the afternoon and would continue until after midnight. McGee had challenged the ministry relative to a contested election in Essex. In presenting his case for the opposition, McGee made one of the finest speeches of the entire session. Cheers, laughter, and applause punctuated his oratorical effort, and shouts of "No! No!" or "Hear! Hear!" came more often than usual. Despite McGee's ardent effort, Macdonald's party successfully postponed action on the question.[31] Perhaps Vallandigham's thoughts drifted back to 1856-1858 when he had contested an election and had run into delay after delay before he finally gained a seat in the Thirty-fifth Congress.

The next day Vallandigham again visited the Legislative Assembly as McGee's guest. This time the exile heard McGee defend him and castigate his Canadian critics. Earlier McGee had written to the editor of the *Montreal Gazette* about rumors of an invasion plot in the United States. He was fully aware that the *New York Herald* had engaged in fist-shaking at Canada and that the United States seemed to be in an unusual hurry

[31] *Quebec Morning Chronicle,* 20 August 1863; *Toronto Daily Leader,* 20 August 1863; report, Charles S. Ogden to William H. Seward, 19 August 1863, Consulate Records.

to complete Fortress Montgomery at Rouse's Point, only forty-five miles south of Montreal. McGee's letter to the *Gazette* brought the rumors above board. "The plan contemplated at Washington for the invasion of Canada," the articulate Irishman had written, "is to march 100,000 men up to the district of Montreal to cut the connection between Upper and Lower Canada . . . and to force a separation of the provinces." McGee's chief motive for airing the rumor was really to embarrass the government and to pressure the ministry to reconsider the Militia Bill, the very measure upon which the Macdonald ministry had fallen the previous May. George Brown, who had repeatedly used the *Toronto Globe* to prop up the government and defend the ministry, had seized upon McGee's letter to the *Gazette* to ridicule and lambast the letter-writer and to take another hefty slap at Vallandigham. Brown had sarcastically suggested that the exile must have served as McGee's chief informer and rumor monger. Did Vallandigham possess a surreptitious pipeline to Washington, D.C.?[32]

With the exile sitting at his elbow in the legislature McGee explained why he had written his letter of August 8 to the *Gazette*. Next he stated that his "informer" was "a minister in the cabinet of the government"—*not Vallandigham*. The intent speaker turned to pay his respects to "the honorable exile" sitting nearby. And finally McGee spanked George Brown and the *Toronto Globe* for violating the time-honored principles of "hospitality and decency." The *Globe,* McGee asserted, was guilty of an "unfair, ungenerous attack upon a stranger seeking a secure and quiet refuge in Canada." "He has come within our gates," the orator told his audience, "asking only a peaceful home which his country had denied."[33] It must have been sweet music to the exile to hear one of the most brilliant orators who ever graced Canadian public life befriend and defend him.

McGee's friends and some antigovernment newspaper editors took the cue, scolding Brown and criticizing the *Globe*. "*Il ressort*

---

[32] McGee to editor of the *Montreal Gazette*, 8 August 1863, published 11 August; *Montreal Daily Transcript*, 14 July, 12 August 1863; *Toronto Daily Globe*, 19 August 1863.

[33] "Proceedings of the Legislative Assembly of August 20, 1863," published in *Toronto Daily Leader*, 21 August 1863. McGee later identified his "informer" in the cabinet as Luther H. Holton.

Clement L. Vallandigham, 1862. Reproduced from a
carte de visite made by Thomas W. Cridland, Dayton,
Ohio.

The Curtis Hotel, Mt. Vernon, Ohio, before which Vallandigham made the speech that led to his arrest.

The Hirons House, Windsor, Ontario, where Vallandigham stayed during part of his Canadian exile. The site is now occupied by the British-American Hotel.

Vallandigham's desk and study in his Dayton home.
Courtesy of Lloyd Ostendorf, Dayton, Ohio

Vallandigham's home, 323 First Street, Dayton, no longer standing.

Courtesy of Lloyd Ostendorf, Dayton, Ohio

A pumpkin (Vallandigham) among the Canadian thistles.
Cartoon in *Harper's Weekly*, October 31, 1863.

"The Copperhead Party—In Favor of a Vigorous Prosecution of Peace!"
Cartoon in *Harper's Weekly*, February 28, 1863.

Jeff Davis and Lincoln playing "Shuttlecock." Cartoon in *Frank Leslie's Illustrated Newspaper*, June 20, 1863.

McClellan and Pendleton, the Democratic team in the presidential contest of 1864. Cartoon in *Harper's Weekly*, October 8, 1864.

donc de tout cela," wrote McGee's friend who edited *Le Journal de Québec, "que M. Vallandigham n'est pas un délateur et que le Globe est un calomniateur."*[34]

After his public vindication, Vallandigham and his party headed for Windsor, the small city he had selected as his new Canadian base, and arrived there early in the evening of August 24, unheralded and almost unnoticed. With carpetbag in hand and accompanied by his wife, son, sister-in-law, and the Pendletons, he walked to the Hirons House, less than a block south of the small depot. A Canadian editor who recognized Vallandigham and happened to witness his arrival in Windsor described him as "an ordinary looking fellow," one whom a phrenologist would have judged to possess little "caution, conscientiousness, or veneration. . . . On the whole," the inquisitive editor wrote, "Vallandigham looks more the foreigner than the Yankee."[35]

The exile found Windsor to be a friendly city. Its proximity to Detroit meant that Michigan Democrats would come to call; and its nearness to Toledo gave Ohio Democrats a chance to communicate readily with him. He rented a two-room suite on the second floor of the Hirons House. His reception room faced the river, affording a splendid view of Detroit. He could see the *U.S.S. Michigan,* a gunboat, moored in the middle of the river. The warship's shotted Dahlgren seemed to bear upon the windows of his suite. The *Michigan* symbolized the armed might of the United States, bent upon keeping him from setting foot again upon his country's soil.

Vallandigham's arrival in Windsor alarmed federal authorities assigned the task of watching the Michigan-Canadian border. Military authorities in Detroit excitedly asked their superiors what to do if the exile crossed the river onto United States soil. "If Vallandigham crosses," replied one superior, "he is to be at once arrested and sent under strong guard direct to Fort Warren." "Get all the information you can about Vallandigham's move-

[34] "It is evident, therefore, that Mr. Vallandigham is not an informer and that the *Globe* is a slanderer." *Journal de Québec,* 24 August 1863. Also see *Toronto Daily Leader,* 22 August 1863, and *Toronto Patriot,* 26 August 1863.
[35] *Chatham Weekly Planet,* 3 September 1863; *Rochester* (N.Y.) *Union & Advertiser,* 27 August 1863. The Hirons House stood at the corner of Sandwich and Ouellette streets. Sandwich Street was later renamed Riverside Drive. The British-American House now occupies the ground where the Hirons House stood.

ments," another superior ordered, "and communicate it to General Burnside."[36]

Some of the bolder Democrats of the Midwest wanted Vallandigham to defy Federal authorities and return to Ohio to claim the rights and privileges to which he was entitled. By tarrying in Canada and failing to claim his rights, wrote Wilbur F. Storey of the *Chicago Times,* he really forfeited the support of the Ohio Democracy. After consulting with a number of Ohio Democrats, including George E. Pugh, the exile decided to ignore Storey's advice and stay in Canada. He renewed his campaign for the governorship of Ohio and decided to await the election returns of October 1.[37] If he won the office he would return and Lincoln's legions dared not challenge the wrath of Ohio Democrats.

[36] Telegrams, Col. B. H. Hill to Gen. James B. Fry, 27 August 1863, W. P. Anderson to J. R. Smith, 27 August 1863, J. R. Smith to Burnside, 27 August 1863, and Fry to Hill, 27 August 1863, in *Official Records,* ser. 2, 5:231-32.

[37] *Chicago Times* (n.d.), quoted in *Dayton Daily Journal,* 24 October 1863.

16

THE GUBERNATORIAL CAMPAIGN OF 1863

THE OHIO GUBERNATORIAL campaign of 1863 was clothed in irony and contrasts. A popular reaction had put Vallandigham at the head of the Democratic ticket despite the opposition of most party leaders, whereas the nomination of John Brough was carefully contrived by Republican wire-pullers, who bowed to expediency and ignored the grass-roots sentiment in their party. It pitted a candidate in exile, unable to contribute much to the contest, against an able stump-speaker and a hearty campaigner. It matched a well-read if intransigent theorist against a very practical man capable of changing his mind or trimming his sails. In a sense it was a contest between the old and the new, for Vallandigham still envisioned the re-creation of a federal union while Brough accepted the changes which the war had brought to his country. The former looked backwards and dreamt while the latter looked forward and readjusted. Vallandigham's supporters saw him as a symbol of states' rights, civil liberties, and peace; Brough's devotees saw him as a symbol of patriotism, fidelity, and the new nation. Both sides were dead-sure they were right, their opponents wrong and self-deluded. It was a campaign in which there was no middle ground, and emotional loyalties colored the thinking of both Democrats and Republicans. And never in American history was a Democratic gubernatorial candidate more scorned, more misrepresented and misquoted, more vilified than Vallandigham.

Although Republican vilification preceded C.L.V.'s nomination at the Democratic State Convention of June 11, the campaign of abuse reached a new level in the days that followed. "It is a burning disgrace upon the country to allow such a man to run for constable," wrote one Republican businessman when he heard of Vallandigham's nomination, "let alone for governor of the great State of Ohio."[1] "Shame! Shame! upon the professed Union men," wrote another Ohio patriot, "who permitted such a convention in their midst, desecrating by its unhallowed breath the fair escutcheon of a noble state (and at a time too when thousands of her sons are writing the story of her glory in their blood). I can only express my feelings in big resounding 'cuss' words . . . ."[2] Inability to spell correctly did not prevent one soldier from denouncing Vallandigham as "a Treble tounged, Hidra headed, Cloven footed, Heaven forsaken, Hell begotten, Pucilanimous curse."[3]

Despite Republican indignation and malice, Vallandigham's candidacy won considerable support in many circles during the remaining days of June. The heavy losses suffered by General Joseph Hooker at Chancellorsville the previous month helped to convince many that the Confederacy could not be defeated and that the continued sacrifice of life and treasure was most foolish. The countryside wanted peace and the exile-candidate took on the appearance of a prophet. Then, too, the reaction to the Emancipation Proclamation had not been fully erased nor the army yet fully abolitionized. "I think it advisable for us folks in the service to whip the rebels as soon as possible," wrote a soldier of Democratic antecedents, "and then come home and take the miserable, cowardly abolitionists in hand and learn them a little sense." The dissatisfied soldier added, "It's a poor reward for the men in the field to think that they are expending their time, treasures, blood, and everything to purchase a country for a pack of fanatics and madmen that don't appreciate it."[4]

Moreover, General Burnside's arbitrary practices helped to transform the politician Vallandigham into a symbol. "The great Democratic party love the Union," wrote a young Dayton lawyer who worshipped at Vallandigham's feet, "but they are determined that the rebellion might succeed a thousand times before they will surrender their constitutional privileges of writing, speaking, [and] voting . . . subject only to the restraints which duly enacted

---

[1] A. Pierce to his wife, 12 June 1863, published in *McArthur* (O.) *Register* (n.d.), clipping in the John Sherman Papers, Library of Congress.

[2] James A. Connolly to his wife, 12 June 1863, published in Paul Angle, ed., *Three Years in the Army of the Cumberland: The Letters and Diary of Major James A. Connolly* (Bloomington, Ind., 1959), pp. 88-89.

[3] Clemens L. Clendenen to "Dear Sister," 16 September 1863, Clendenen Family Papers, Huntington Library.

[4] Henry Coffinberry to "Dear Folks," 29 May 1863, Marcia D. Coffinberry Papers, Western Reserve Historical Society, Cleveland

laws impose."[5] In other words, if all civil rights were lost, the Union was not worth saving.

Democrats who glorified civil rights depicted Vallandigham's nomination as a rebuke to the Lincoln administration. Those who viewed the exile as their champion interpreted the summary treatment accorded him as "persecution for opinion's sake."[6] One of his apostles composed a ten-stanza poem entitled "Vallandigham: the Bastiled Hero," and the rather crude verses made the rounds of the Democratic newspapers. The first stanza read:

> They bore him to a gloomy cell,
> And barred him from the light,
> Because he dared to tell
> The people what was right.

The concluding stanza suggested that the election of Vallandigham to the governorship might break the chains of persecution:

> Lift up thy head, O martyred brave,
> Thy chains shall broken be,
> Thy people come their friend to save—
> Look up, thou shall be free.[7]

Had the election taken place in late June of 1863, it is likely that Vallandigham would have won the governor's chair. But the election was not scheduled until October 13, and the Republicans, aided by Union victories at Gettysburg and Vicksburg, succeeded in checking the Democratic tide. Time became a Republican ally, and Lincoln's supporters seized upon the opportunity to discredit and destroy Vallandigham.

After the exile reached Canada and issued his "Address to the Democracy of Ohio" of July 15, Republicans lit into the document and its author with a vengeance. Isaac Jackson Allen of the *Ohio State Journal* characterized the partisan document as "a pronunciamento," quite like the pronouncements emanating from the mouths of Mexican factionalists. For good measure he defined it as "a weak, bombastic, and maudlin" product of

---

[5] Thomas O. Lowe to his brother William, 14 June 1863, Thomas O. Lowe Papers, Dayton and Montgomery County Public Library.
[6] John Law to Samuel S. Cox, 18 June 1863, Samuel S. Cox Papers (microfilm), Hayes Memorial Library, Fremont, Ohio.
[7] *Hamilton True Telegraph*, 18 June 1863.

"a most violent and malignant passion."[8] Edwin Cowles of the
Cleveland Leader depicted the address as rank treason and its
author as a black-hearted traitor. He thought Vallandigham's
friends in Dixie's capital city would be delighted with the
document. Confederates, Cowles contended, might agree with
those sections of the address which referred to Lincoln's "unconstitutional and despotic acts." Cowles also criticized Vallandigham for misunderstanding the mind of the South, and
argued that the rebels scorned compromise and desired independence. Evidently Cowles was right. Vallandigham had
learned nothing from his twenty-four-day sojourn in Dixie. There
was little sentiment for peace and reunion in the Confederacy—
Lincoln's emancipation policy had effectively quashed the Union
movement. "We are sure we have conversed with many more
Southerners than he [Vallandigham] ever did," wrote one Richmond editor, "and we never heard the first one yet speak of
reunion."[9]

Vallandigham's arrival in Canada coincided with the New
York anti-draft riots of July 13-16. Imaginative Republicans saw
a link between the two. Some Republican editors even made
the wild charge that Vallandigham had connived with Confederate agents to bring about the riots. Lacking any evidence
to give substance to the charges, one Republican editor devised
a forged letter which gave a semblance of respectability to the
rumor that the exile had helped to plan the riots. It was a dishonest and dastardly tactic, but highly effective. Bigots are
likely to practice the axiom that the end justifies the means.

This lie was matched by others as preposterous and as
fantastic. Some Republicans claimed that Lee's invasion of the
North, ending on the battlefield of Gettysburg, had been suggested and encouraged by Vallandigham when he was an exile
in Dixie. They circulated the same kind of reports about General
John H. Morgan's raid into Indiana and Ohio, July 8-26, even
claiming that the exile had helped to plan the daring expedition.
More than that, Republican propagandists contended that
Morgan's excursion was intended to serve as a signal for an
uprising by Vallandigham's supporters and ultimately lead to

[8] 20 July 1863.
[9] *Richmond Daily Dispatch* (n.d.), quoted in *Toronto Daily Globe*, 17 August
1863.

the creation of a "Northwest Confederacy." Republican-concocted reports that General Morgan instructed those whom he captured and paroled to vote for Vallandigham and against Brough also received considerable circulation in the partisan press. The lie linking Vallandigham to the Morgan raid had still another variation which held that the Knights of the Golden Circle, at Vallandigham's insistence, had invited the rebel raider to come into Indiana and Ohio to give help to the promoters of a "Northwest Confederacy."[10] Those who invented and circulated the tales linking Vallandigham to the Morgan raid contributed to a myth which grew popular in the postwar years.[11]

Certainly Morgan's horse-stealing expedition into Indiana and Ohio hurt Vallandigham's election campaign. It brought the war closer home to the residents of Ohio and made some lethargic citizens realize that the rebels were their enemies, not their friends. The same was true of Lee's invasion of Pennsylvania. It too awakened patriotism and bestirred some to whom the war was half dream and half reality. In later years, Vallandigham always felt that these two military events affected his election adversely, especially since they gave Republicans an opportunity to intensify their propaganda campaign against him. He was right in more ways than one. Morgan's defeat and the Union victories at Gettysburg and Vicksburg pushed back the Copperhead movement, nullified the crusade for peace and compromise, and brought some respectability to the Lincoln administration.

Vallandigham, of course, expressed indignation at the stories linking him to Lee's invasion and Morgan's raid. He termed the tales "ridiculous" and claimed they were "desperate" measures of desperate men. He pointed out how ironic it was that General Morgan was captured within six miles of New Lisbon, his birthplace, and reminded his friends of a statement he had made six months earlier in Newark, New Jersey. "If they invade us," he had said, "we will write for them precisely the same history they

10 *Dayton Daily Journal*, 15, 16 July 1863; *Cleveland Leader*, 30 July 1863; *Buckeye State* (New Lisbon), 13 August 1863; *Bucyrus Weekly Journal*, 14 August 1863; *Daily Ohio State Journal*, 20 July 1863; *Buffalo Morning Express*, 18 July 1863.

11 The myth is perpetuated in such popular works as James D. Horan, *Confederate Agent: A Discovery in History* (New York, 1954), and debunked in Frank L. Klement, "Carrington and the Golden Circle Legend in Indiana during the Civil War," *Indiana Magazine of History* 61 (March 1965): 31-52.

have written for us for two years, & give them 'Bull Runs' upon our own soil."[12]

In the months that followed, Republicans in Ohio marshaled all their forces to defeat Vallandigham and the Democrats in the October 13 election. To them, Vallandigham symbolized treason, and they rallied to save the honor of Ohio. Since campaign money was plentiful, Republicans flooded the state with dozens of tracts and propaganda pamphlets. They distributed 100,000 copies of Brough's "patriotic" speech of July 4, 1863, and reprinted and circulated thousands of copies of Judge Leavitt's decision to deny Vallandigham a writ of habeas corpus, which gave a semblance of legality to Burnside's treatment of the Dayton Democrat. They reprinted Lincoln's able and effective reply to the Committee of Nineteen. A speech which John Sherman had given in Delaware, Ohio, and in which he had manhandled Vallandigham, proved an effective campaign document. They also prepared three pamphlets especially for the '63 campaign. One of the three, entitled *The Echo from the Army*, contained anti-Vallandigham statements extracted from generals' speeches and soldiers' letters. Some of the quotations were genuine, others fabricated. A sixteen-page pamphlet entitled *The Peace Democracy, alias the Copperheads* developed the theme that Vallandigham was a traitor and that his congressional record proved he was a friend of the rebels. It also contained the interesting allegation that the exile's gubernatorial nomination had actually been "arranged" by the rebels. The third pamphlet, far and away the most effective and most popular, bore the title *A Short Catechism for the People*. It too helped to convince the unwary that Vallandigham deserved the treatment he had received at Burnside's hands. The so-called catechism opened with the question, "Who is the noted disloyal candidate of the peace party in Ohio?" The answer: "C. L. Vallandigham."[13]

---

[12] Vallandigham to Manton Marble, 2 August 1863, Manton Marble Papers, Library of Congress.

[13] *A Short Catechism for the People* (Columbus, 1863) and *The Peace Democracy, alias the Copperheads* (Columbus, 1863) were prepared and circulated by the Republican State Central Committee of Ohio. The document entitled *Echo from the Army: What Our Soldiers Say about the Copperheads* (New York, 1863) was published and distributed by the Loyal Publication Society, a propaganda arm of the Union League.

The Republicans disseminated their campaign propaganda through postmasters and the Union Leagues. Since every postmaster was a Republican—often the Republican editor in the village or the city, too—he had a vested interest in Vallandigham's defeat. Postmasters furnished the Republican State Central Committee with the names of residents or carefully passed out the bundles of pamphlets put in their charge. The Union Leagues had proved themselves an effective propaganda agency in the April 1863 election, and Republicans used the reading rooms maintained by these allied organizations to distribute partisan pamphlets and convert unwary citizens to their cause. Serving as the strong right arm of the Republican party, the Leagues made a major contribution to the political campaign in the fall of 1863.[14]

Republicans also used the churches to influence public opinion against Vallandigham. Since some church leaders regarded the exile as a traitor and believed it their duty to support the government, they convinced synods, conferences, and sessions to adopt anti-Vallandigham resolutions or statements. The Ohio Congregational Conference, for example, took a strong stand on the issues relevant to the gubernatorial campaign of 1863. The conference adopted resolutions defending the Lincoln administration, championing "the righteousness of the war," and condemning "the factious spirit" of the Democratic critics of war policy. It bemoaned the disunity and "insubordination" which undermined the war effort and played into the hands of the Confederates.[15] Backed by the resolutions of their conference, Congregationalist clergymen used their pulpits to preach patriotism, call Copperheads aides of Satan, and compare Vallandigham to Cain or Judas.

The Methodist Episcopal Church took just as strong a stand in behalf of patriotism, the Lincoln administration, and Brough's

14 Canvass Books of Cuyahoga County, Western Reserve Historical Society; *Buckeye State* (New Lisbon), 2 April 1863; Harvey Reid to "Dear Sarah," 18 September 1863, Harvey Reid Papers, State Historical Society of Wisconsin. Guy Gibson, "Lincoln's League: The Union League Movement during the Civil War" (Ph.D. dissertation, University of Illinois, 1957), views the League as a patriotic organization. Clement M. Silvestro, "None But Patriots: Union Leagues in Civil War and Reconstruction" (Ph.D. dissertation, University of Wisconsin, 1959), recognized that the Leagues were a Republican propaganda agency.

15 *Daily Ohio State Journal*, 20 June 1863.

candidacy. The *Western Christian Advocate*, the influential Methodist weekly, gave open support to Brough and ignored the Christian dictum to love one's enemies. Charles Kingsley, the paper's strong-minded editor, had denounced Vallandigham in harsh language long before he became an exile and the Democratic nominee for governor. During the election contest of 1863 he distilled the issues into a simple formula: truth and patriotism *vs.* heresy and treason. The Reverend Granville Moody, one of Ohio's best known Methodist revivalists, preached the same doctrine in all corners of the state. Moody accused Vallandigham of "poisoning" the minds of the people, "almost equaling the audacity of Satan himself." Although occasional Democrats viewed Moody's sermons as political tirades, most Ohio Methodists accepted the point of view promoted by him and the *Western Christian Advocate*.[16]

Most Ohio Mennonites also lined up on the side of Brough and patriotism. The *Religious Telescope*, published in the exile's home town as the organ of the Church of the United Brethren, took an anti-Vallandigham position quite like that of the *Western Christian Advocate*. The *Telescope's* editor endorsed the Lincoln administration, gave strong support to emancipation, pleaded for full support of the war, and encouraged its subscribers to vote for Brough.

Although the Presbyterian Church in Ohio drafted no statement concerning the war for its communicants, most of its clergymen used the pulpit to endorse the war, condemn Copperheadism, and criticize Vallandigham and other apostles of peace. Several Presbyterian ministers who had befriended Vallandigham earlier and who had joined the peace crusade found themselves shunned by their colleagues and could find no pulpits from which to preach dissenting doctrine. The pastor of the First Presbyterian Church of Dayton openly supported the Union Leagues, the Republican party, and Brough's candidacy. Even the church of which Vallandigham had once been a pew-paying member turned its back on him and declared that the issue was really patriotism *vs.* treason.

16 *Western Christian Advocate* (Cincinnati), 29 April 1863; *Cincinnati Gazette*, 7 August 1863. The role of Methodism in the 1863 gubernatorial contest is treated in Bruce C. Flack, "The Attitude of the Methodist Episcopal Church in Ohio toward the Civil War, 1861-1865" (master's thesis, Ohio State University, 1962).

Although almost all Irish-Catholics and German-Catholics belonged to the Democratic party and sympathized with Vallandigham, several prominent Catholic churchmen tried to dissuade their flocks from voting for him and taking part in the Copperhead movement. Archbishop John B. Purcell of Cincinnati, for instance, encouraged his Catholic subjects to join the Union Leagues, vote the Union ticket, and reject "the false prophets" who taught "insubordination" and preached the gospel of Copperheadism. The *Catholic Telegraph*, edited by Archbishop Purcell's brother, the Reverend Edward Purcell, waged a constant war against slavery, the peace crusade, and Vallandigham. Although most Irish-Americans and German-Catholics opposed emancipation and feared its consequences, the Purcell brothers viewed slavery as "a monstrous crime." "It corrupts heart and soul," wrote the resolute editor of the *Catholic Telegraph*, "and we have no respect for the Christianity of any person who, now that the evil is dying out, would wish to see it restored."[17] The efforts of the Purcells in behalf of Brough received the enthusiastic support of Purcell's coadjutor, Bishop Sylvester H. Rosecrans. Perhaps the fact that the bishop's brother, Major General William S. Rosecrans, sought honor on the nation's battlefields, accentuated the enthusiasm for the Union cause which characterized the archbishop's office.[18]

Even Rabbi Isaac M. Wise of Cincinnati found outside pressures irresistible. This nationally known Jewish leader started out by advocating Vallandigham's election and endorsing his crusade for peace and compromise. Before long, however, the trustees of his temple and prominent businessmen of his congregation convinced him that none of the Ten Commandments justified his pro-Vallandigham views. Silenced by self-styled patriots, Rabbi Wise retired to the sidelines to sit out the campaign as a spectator. His defection, Archbishop Purcell's preachments, and the pro-Brough stand taken by prominent Ohio Protestants convinced some of Vallandigham's followers that "organized religion" was directing all its resources to keep the exile from obtaining the governor's chair.

17 N.d., quoted in *Bucyrus Weekly Journal*, 14 August, 18 September 1863.
18 Archbishop Purcell's contributions to the war effort are discussed in Anthony Deye, "Archbishop John Baptist Purcell and the Civil War" (Ph.D. dissertation, Notre Dame University, 1944).

Although the clergy, the pamphleteers, and the Union Leagues gained some converts for Brough's candidacy, the most effective work in the political vineyards was done by the Republican orators and editors. "Honest Johnny" Brough carried more than his share of the load. He was a superb stump-speaker possessing a booming voice and a wry humor mixed with spontaneous sincerity. His effectiveness as a speaker brought smiles to the faces of the Republican strategists who had insisted that Brough could serve their cause better than David Tod. He always made a patriotic appeal, relighting fires that had flickered and died in many breasts. Ohio had a glorious history, Brough said again and again, and proud Ohioans would never let "a convicted traitor" occupy the State House. It was the duty of men to support the war and be loyal to their country. "For I tell you," Brough once shouted, "there is a mighty mass of men in this State whose nerves are strung like steel, [and] who would never permit this dishonor to be consummated in their native State."[19]

Brough had capable support from Colonel Charles Anderson, candidate for lieutenant-governor on the Union party ticket. The fact that Major Robert Anderson of Fort Sumter fame was a brother made Charles a bit of a celebrity. Furthermore, Charles Anderson was a most effective speaker and a hard-working campaigner. Since Anderson, like Vallandigham, claimed Dayton as his home and since he had won honors on several battlefields, it was easy for the efficacious colonel to talk about patriotism and propriety.

All prominent Ohio politicos took to the hustings. David Tod, still distressed because Republican wire-pullers had denied him honors he thought due him, kept his promise to work hard to elect Brough and the rest of the ticket. General Schenck, excused from field service to campaign against Vallandigham, added his voice to the chorus. He could crow that he had retired Vallandigham from Congress, and he too waved the banner inscribed "Patriotism" at every rally. "Bluff Ben" Wade, still incensed because Vallandigham had once called him a liar on the floor of the House of Representatives, left his desk in the Senate to define treason, indict Vallandigham, and advocate Brough's

---

[19] Quoted in the *Dayton Daily Journal*, 6 July 1863; *Ohio Daily Statesman* (Columbus), 9 September 1863.

election. Even Salmon P. Chase, secretary of the treasury, left his busy office in the nation's capital to convince Ohioans that Brough was an honorable man and Vallandigham a renegade. No prominent Ohioan, however, made a greater impression upon his audiences than United States Senator John Sherman. Several of Sherman's speeches evolved into pamphlets which were widely distributed and often quoted. Dayton Republicans invited him to give a major address in the exile's home town. Sherman removed his gloves and treated Vallandigham roughly. Every vote for the candidate-in-exile, he said, would be an insult to the soldiers—those who had died for the holy cause and those still willing to offer the supreme sacrifice. Vallandigham was "a convicted traitor"; he deserved no martyr's halo. He was guilty of the same offense as Confederate General John H. Morgan, although in a different sort of way. Vallandigham's record in Congress, Sherman added, proved him to be sympathetic to the South. He was really a hypocrite, prattling about civil rights while trying to destroy the very government designed to protect and preserve them.[20]

Other notables joined the parade. General Thomas Meagher, who had gained fame as the commander of the "Irish Brigade" of the Army of the Potomac, hurried to Ohio to woo the Irish-Americans so reluctant to desert Vallandigham.[21] General Franz Sigel visited the state to instruct German-Americans to vote for Brough rather than Vallandigham. Governors Richard Yates of Illinois and Oliver P. Morton of Indiana each accepted several speaking engagements in Ohio to urge citizens to vindicate their state's honor. Even Zachariah Chandler of Michigan came down to recite a patriotic piece. And there were others, criss-crossing the state and singing the same tune. All in all, it was a rare array of oratorical talent which invaded Ohio for a single purpose—to keep Vallandigham out of the governor's mansion.[22]

Ohio's Republican editors also made a major contribution to

[20] *Dayton Daily Journal*, 27 August 1863. John Sherman's Delaware, Ohio, speech appeared as a pamphlet entitled *Valandigham's [sic] Record Reviewed: A Political Traitor Unmasked* (Dayton, 1863). It came off the press of the *Dayton Daily Journal*.

[21] Thomas Francis Meagher to John Jay Janney, 8 September 1863, John Jay Janney Papers, Indiana University Library, Bloomington.

[22] *Cleveland Leader*, 16, 25 September 1863; *Dayton Daily Journal*, 27 August, 14 September, 1, 2 October 1863.

the effort to discredit Vallandigham. They published the addresses of Republican speakers, extracts from anti-Vallandigham pamphlets, and the patriotic resolutions adopted at local rallies. They wrote lengthy editorials advocating Vallandigham's defeat, circulated rumors and lies which damaged his candidacy, coined new epithets for the exile, and tried to create a schism in Democratic ranks.

Editor Isaac Jackson Allen of the *Ohio State Journal* took the lead in trying to convince influential Democrats that they had "an unwanted candidate" on their hands. He chided them for supporting a traitor who could not possibly win the election. He urged them to repudiate their candidate-in-exile, follow their consciences, and offer a more worthy nominee. Allen publicly supposed that the exile would refuse to withdraw no matter what pleas were made, whether in the name of party unity or party welfare. The "unwanted candidate," Allen wrote, would rather be "a live jackass than a dead lion."[23]

Failing to convince Vallandigham to withdraw from the contest or to effect a noticeable schism in the Democratic party, Republican editors then made a concerted effort to develop the notion that the words "Vallandigham" and "Treason" were synonymous. They organized rallies at which the exile was hung in effigy, and gave state-wide circulation to the chant:

Hurrah for Brough and Abraham
And a rope to hang Vallandigham.

They encouraged readers to recite anti-Vallandigham verses, sing anti-Vallandigham songs, and believe anti-Vallandigham propaganda. Cloaking themselves in patriotism, some editors even justified efforts to disrupt Democratic rallies, intimidate Vallandigham's supporters, and wreck Democratic newspaper offices.

Republican zealots examined Vallandigham's personal life and his public career to find items they might use for political effect. They found surprisingly little. Oh yes, he had held a brigadiership in the Ohio militia *before* the war. He could best be characterized, the editor of the *Dayton Journal* wrote, as "Invincible in peace, invisible in war."[24]

23 20 July, 19 August 1863.
24 *Dayton Daily Journal*, 14, 21 August 1863.

Republican editors also made good use of the fact that Vallandigham's mother had received "support money" of $100 annually from a Presbyterian Church fund for "needy widows . . . of deceased ministers" during the 1850s and 1860s after the death of her husband, a fact disclosed by the Republican treasurer of the fund. The report that Vallandigham's mother was "a needy widow" made the rounds of the Republican press. The exile must be a "wretched son" if he failed to support a mother who was in need. "Ingratitude," one Republican editor wrote, "is one of the meanest acts that a person can commit, and the name of one guilty of such a thing, should be branded with infamy. He is unfit to occupy any position of importance, much less that of Governor of this great State."[25] Republicans located a Biblical verse they believed relevant to the issue: "He who provideth not for his own household is worse than an infidel." Editor William F. Foster of the *Wellesville Union* concocted a verse which received state-wide circulation:

> Vallandigham, he will not vote
> A dollar for our army;
> But if they make him Governor
> He will support his mammy.[26]

Since they found so little of a personal nature to use against the Democratic candidate, Republican editors resorted to the old game of misrepresenting and fabricating. It was common practice to quote out of context and misrepresent what Vallandigham had earlier said. They again claimed that his four-section scheme of early 1861 was a proposition to divide the nation into four separate confederacies instead of a clumsy device to save the Union. They revived Vallandigham's oft-denied contention that Northern troops going southward to fight the rebels would have to pass over his dead body. They misrepresented Vallandigham's hopes for peace and compromise as a "peace-at-any-price" proposition.

Vallandigham and his supporters resented the misrepresentation as a disgraceful and unethical practice. "The disunion [Republican] newspapers of Ohio," complained one of the exile's

25 *Wellesville Union*, 10, 24 September 1863.
26 Ibid.

friends, "are filling their columns with garbled and mutilated extracts from the speeches of Vallandigham in order to deceive the people."[27]

In addition to repeating the charges that Vallandigham was indelibly linked to the New York anti-draft riots, Morgan's raid, and Lee's invasion of Pennsylvania, Republicans concocted and circulated other lies. One concerned the Knights of the Golden Circle, a mythical subversive society supposedly widespread in the upper Midwest. This serpentine society, Republican editors reported, worked day and night to bring about Vallandigham's election. The dark-lantern organization was said to be involved in a number of sordid and "deep and desperate schemes." The rumor-mongering editor of the *Cincinnati Commercial* claimed that one of the schemes involved "importing" 50,000 Kentuckians to vote for Vallandigham. Joseph Medill of the *Chicago Tribune,* who had once advised an aspiring politician to "Go in boldly, strike straight from the shoulder—hit *below* the belt as well as above, and kick like thunder,"[28] embroidered upon the Golden Circle tale. He wrote that it was "reliably reported" that 10,000 Illinois members of the Knights of the Golden Circle intended to invade Ohio the week before the election in order to vote for their idol and fellow-member, Clement L. Vallandigham.[29]

Other reports also linked the Knights of the Golden Circle to Morgan's and Lee's movements. A scoundrel stepped forward to testify that he was in Richmond when Vallandigham was there to call on Jefferson Davis and that the exile was closeted with the president of the Confederacy, begging for invasions of the North.[30] Although Vallandigham actually had bypassed Richmond, this story became popular with Republican newspaper editors, and it too became a postwar legend.[31]

[27] *Dayton Daily Empire,* 22, 31 August 1863. Examples of misrepresentation can be found in the *Dayton Daily Journal,* 9 September 1863, and the *Cleveland Leader,* 17 August 1863.

[28] Joseph Medill to Lincoln, 10 September 1859, Robert Todd Lincoln Papers, Library of Congress.

[29] *Daily Ohio State Journal,* 18 July, 31 August 1863; *Cleveland Leader,* 17 September 1863; *Cincinnati Daily Commercial* (n.d.), quoted in *Daily Ohio State Journal,* 27 August 1863; *Chicago Tribune,* 1 October 1863; *Bucyrus Weekly Journal,* 4 September 1863.

[30] *Detroit Free Press,* 14 September 1863. They gave the name of the informant as Henry Reinish.

[31] The manufacture of lies was a common political practice. John Sherman's secretary, who later became a noted Ohio newspaperman, wrote to a friend,

Some of the falsehoods took the shape of forgeries. Perhaps the most widely circulated of the forgeries was the so-called Vallandigham-Inshall letter, supposedly written by Vallandigham while he was an exile in Dixie. Allegedly it came into the hands of Northern editors after its recipient, a colonel of the Eighth Alabama Regiment, was captured by Union troops. In the letter Vallandigham called himself "a friend of the South," and expressed sympathy with her in her struggle for "freedom." He detested "the hated and tyrannical government of the North" and "prayed and hoped" that the Confederacy would achieve her goals—his "heart bled for Dixie." The letter made the rounds of the countryside despite Democratic insistence that it was an out-and-out forgery. Some Republican newspapers, such as the *Cincinnati Gazette,* published the Vallandigham-Inshall letter on election eve, so that denials could not be made before the voters marched off to the polls.[32]

Vallandigham's supporters did not stand by idly while Republicans told their lies, circulated rumors, and generated nationalism. They attacked Brough with a vengeance, giving tit for tat. They called him a "renegade," "fool," and "nigger-lover." Samuel S. Cox, who rather reluctantly supported the Democratic ticket, characterized Brough as "a flailing Falstaff" and a "fat Knight of the corps d'Afrique."[33] Democrats ridiculed his roly-poly appearance, putting their scorn in words:

> If flesh is grass as people say,
> Then Johnny Brough's a load of hay.[34]

Vallandigham's supporters liked to depict Brough as an Othello in the hands of cunning Iago—he would discover too late that he had been deceived. They repeatedly referred to the Republican party or the Union party as the "Abolition party" or to

---

"... when I get home [from Washington], I will get up some stories to tell about your opponent whoever he is. I don't know him, and it is not necessary that I should in order to tell a few big lies about him." (James B. McCullogh to William Henry Smith, 31 May 1864, William Henry Smith Papers, Ohio Historical Society, Columbus.)

[32] *Cincinnati Gazette,* 12 October 1863; *Daily Ohio State Journal,* 10 October 1863.

[33] Quoted in *Dayton Daily Empire,* 24 September 1863.

[34] William W. Armstrong, "Personal Recollections," in *Cincinnati Daily Enquirer,* 20 March 1886.

Republicans as "Black Republicans." When Republicans called Vallandigham "a branded traitor," Democrats replied that Brough was "a brandied patriot." When Republicans shouted "Copperheads!" Democrats retorted "Blowsnakes!" When Republicans chanted "Hurrah for Brough and Abraham, And a rope to hang Vallandigham," Democrats responded:

> May every Buckeye—smooth or rough,
> Denounce the renegade Jack Brough;
> May every woman, child and man,
> Pray Heaven to bless Vallandigham.[35]

Besides practicing name-calling, Democrats developed half a dozen arguments in Vallandigham's behalf. They insisted that the country wanted peace and that the exile symbolized the peace movement. Samuel Medary and William M. Corry, an out-and-out antiwar man, appealed to the war-weary and the faint at heart. Democrats also linked Vallandigham's name with civil rights; many still considered him a martyr for freedom of speech and civil liberties. George Pugh and George L. Converse contended that civil rights could be salvaged by rebuking "the military despotism in Washington" and giving Vallandigham "a flood of votes." "Every vote cast for Vallandigham is a vote for Liberty," wrote one Democratic editor, "and every vote cast for Brough is a vote for Despotism."[36] The latent spirit of sectionalism so widespread in the upper Midwest was a rallying point. Democrats resented New England's efforts to impose her moral, cultural, and political views upon their section. They decried New England's ascendancy in business and politics, her wish to hold the West in bondage. They ranted against the tariffs, against high railroad rates, and against the excise tax on whiskey. They pointed out that both Brough and Tod were railroad presidents and "tools" of "the monopolists, speculators, and army contractors."[37]

Democratic spokesmen seemed to regard emancipation as one of the chief issues; at least they made a strong appeal to Negrophobia. Anti-Negro banners and slogans predominated at most

---

[35] *Mount Vernon Democratic Banner*, 11 July 1863; *Hancock* (O.) *Courier* (n.d.), quoted in *Dayton Daily Empire*, 25 August 1863.
[36] *Crisis* (Columbus), 9, 23 September 1863.
[37] James M. Robbins to Samuel S. Cox, 19 August 1863, Cox Papers.

Democratic rallies, the legend "Protect us from Negro Equality" being the most popular. God's laws regarding race and climate, some Democrats contended, could not be "repealed" by the "nigger-worshipping Republican party." Democrats still blamed abolitionism for the war and for stifling the peace movement. "If Abolition were dead and buried beyond resurrection," wrote one Democratic dreamer, "in less than thirty days hereafter, we could have a Union which all the fanatics in Christendom could not disrupt."[38] "The 'irrepressible conflict' between white and black laborers," wrote another of Vallandigham's defenders, "will be realized in all its vigor upon Ohio soil if the policy of Lincoln and Brough is carried."[39] Democrats circulated a pamphlet entitled *The Results of Emancipation*[40] among Irish- and German-Americans who feared the influx of cheap, competitive labor. One Democratic racist wrote:

> Let every vote count in favor of the *white* man, and against the Abolition hordes, who would place negro children in your schools, negro jurors in your jury boxes, and negro votes in your ballot boxes! . . . Down with the flag of Abolition; mount the flag of the WHITE MAN upon the citadel.[41]

In the absence of Vallandigham, George Pugh served as the color-bearer of the Democratic party. He followed a punishing speaking schedule, crossing the state time and again. At times his voice gave out or he suffered from fatigue. His theme did not vary. Vallandigham was a martyr for free speech, and the rights of citizens were disappearing. Emancipation was both a crime and a disgrace. Republicans had brought on the war. The nation could be restored only by peace and compromise. A Democratic victory at the polls on October 13 would recall Vallandigham from Canada—the Lincoln administration would not dare defy the wishes of the people of Ohio.

Pugh received invaluable help from Samuel Cox, Allen G. Thurman, George Pendleton, and George Converse, all Democratic congressmen. Even old Samuel Medary, whose pen wrote such vituperative editorials for the *Crisis*, took to the stump to

---

[38] *Dayton Daily Empire*, 21 August 1863.
[39] *Cincinnati Daily Enquirer*, 7 September 1863.
[40] This booklet was published in New York in 1863, by Samuel F. B. Morse's propaganda agency, the Society for the Diffusion of Political Knowledge.
[41] *Dayton Daily Empire*, 21 August, 12 October 1863.

polish his rusty voice and to fulminate against John Brough and Abraham Lincoln. The venerable William Allen came out of political retirement to speak out for "Vallandigham and Liberty." George W. Morgan, who had resigned his general's commission because of a dispute with Major General William T. Sherman, returned to Ohio to throw himself into the election with a vengeance. Unexpected help came from the brother of the Union (Republican) party candidate for lieutenant-governor. Resentment replaced brotherly love as William A. Anderson praised Vallandigham's courage, endorsed his views, and labeled his brother "a political apostate." Even the unpredictable William M. Corry campaigned for Vallandigham. Since Corry had called for "peace with separation," publicly proclaimed secession "a sound principle," and advocated recognition of the Confederacy, his support embarrassed most Democrats and probably did more harm than good.[42]

Some prominent Democrats, however, sat out the campaign and refused to raise a finger to help Vallandigham's candidacy. Hugh Jewett, who had lost the nomination to the exile, sulked on the sidelines. So did Rufus P. Ranney and Henry B. Payne, each previously a Democratic gubernatorial candidate. Some lesser lights also stayed at home, accepting the Republican definition of treason and rejecting Vallandigham's contention that peace and reunion were reasonable goals.

From his Canadian base, the Democratic candidate did his best to instill the hope of victory into a dispirited party. He wrote letters to be read at political rallies or published in the party press. He tried to assure Ohio Democrats that abolition was a curse to the country and that liberty was endangered. Continued war might mean the loss of all civil rights! He wrote personal letters to his friends, urging them to carry on the good fight or complaining about the lack of party unity.[43]

Occasionally Ohio Democrats visited Vallandigham in Canada to discuss party strategy or report on election trends. Samuel

[42] *Crisis*, 16 September 1863; *Circleville Democrat*, 1 September 1863; *Ohio Daily Statesman*, 27 August 1863; William A. Anderson, quoted in *Mount Vernon Democratic Banner*, 5 September 1863.

[43] Vallandigham to Thomas Dunlap and others, 31 July 1863, published in *Mount Vernon Democratic Banner*, 15 August 1863; Vallandigham to Alexander S. Boys, 1 September 1863, Alexander S. Boys Papers, Ohio Historical Society, Columbus; Vallandigham to Samuel L. M. Barlow, 8 August 1863, Samuel L. M. Barlow Papers, Huntington Library.

Medary of the *Crisis* wrote that he found "the gallant exile" in excellent health and in "remarkably good spirits. . . . Buoyed up by his love of country—pledged to constitutional liberty and the personal freedom of his fellow citizens," Medary wrote, "he enjoys a confidence in the future which no tyrant can feel, no sycophant appreciate."[44] In mid-September George Pugh took a hurried trip to Windsor to visit the candidate and get a few days' leave from speech-making. He too found Vallandigham optimistic and hopeful. The crowds at Democratic rallies were large and enthusiastic, leading Pugh and Vallandigham to substitute dreams for reality.

One of the more memorable rallies took place in the exile's home town on September 7. Thousands gathered for the affair, knowing that they were the cynosure of Ohio eyes. Every township in Montgomery County had a good-sized delegation, and even the threat of rain failed to dampen the enthusiasm of those who repeated again and again:

> We want our rights;
> We must be free—
> Vallandigham and Liberty.

Some delegations had journeyed to Dayton singing songs from the *Vallandigham Songbook*, published especially for the campaign of 1863. Each delegation found its prescribed area, and joined the four-mile-long procession, with Mayor Gillespie as chief marshal. Several brass bands provided music for the marchers and spirited horses pulled the many wagons decorated as floats. The first wagon, drawn by half a dozen horses, carried a huge banner with the words "Vallandigham, Pugh, and Peace." The second float carried thirty-four young ladies dressed in white —one representing each of the states. On each side of the wagon was a large sign which said: "Fathers and Brothers, protect us from Despotism and Negro Equality." The third wagon, filled with young ladies wearing white dresses, blue sashes, and fancy red rosettes, bore a banner with the slogan "The Union as it was, the Constitution as it is." One wagon carried a wooden cage, with some handcuffed men inside; its banner spelled out "LINCOLN'S BASTILE" in large capital letters.

44 19 August 1863.

There were hundreds of other wagons and signs. Some of the banners read: "Peace," "Equal and Exact Justice for All Men," "Vallandigham, the People's Friend and Tyrant's Foe," "Vote for Val and Liberty," "Vallandigham, Martyr to Freedom of Speech," "Vallandigham, Our Friend and Hero," and "Down with Tyranny." In all, two hundred wagons and buggies, and 2,314 people took part in the procession.

After reaching the fairgrounds, the crowd gathered around the half dozen speakers' stands to hear Lincoln and Brough denounced and Vallandigham and Pugh praised. Vallandigham had written a long letter, intended to be read at the rally, but it failed to arrive on time. Sponsors of the rally, nevertheless, pronounced the affair highly successful and claimed that 35,000 people had attended—an estimate which Republicans termed "a gross exaggeration."[45]

Another of the more interesting Democratic rallies took place in New Lisbon, Vallandigham's boyhood town. Columbiana County Democrats collected "an immense throng" to pay their respects to the exile and to participate in the rally. There were old and bewhiskered men who had cheered for Thomas Jefferson six decades earlier, and there were young yeomen, dressed in butternut-dyed jeans, full of hope and insolence. There were wrinkled-faced women, some in butternut shawls, and there were dimpled young girls, exhilarated by the excitement of the hour. The procession, held under a clear sky, was most impressive. Two dozen bands participated, mixing noise and music. There were hundreds of wagons and carriages, many decorated with bunting, hickory branches, and banners bearing slogans or mottoes. The procession began under a huge banner, eighteen feet long, strung across the street and bearing the slogan "Resistance to Tyrants is Obedience to God." The long procession, set in motion at ten o'clock in the morning, wound its way down the streets of New Lisbon and past the old Vallandigham homestead. A plain white muslin sheet, bearing the words "VALLANDIGHAM'S BIRTHPLACE," hung over the gateway, and nearby on a grassy knoll stood the gray and aged mother of the exile. As bands, footmen, horsemen, carriages, and wagons passed by,

[45] *Dayton Daily Journal,* 18 September 1863; *Dayton Daily Empire,* 18, 19 September 1863.

many stopped to give three cheers for Vallandigham. "What must have been her feelings," wrote a sympathetic newspaperman, "when that great procession of freemen, as they passed, set forth hearty huzzahs in honor of her exiled and persecuted son!" Three hours later, the procession reached the outlying picnic grove, and after lunch the participants gathered around the speakers' stand to applaud an array of orators who praised their candidate and damned his political enemies.[46]

As political rallies nurtured enthusiasm and dogmatism, the excitement became so intense in many communities that partisans severed social and business relations. Many arguments developed over the wearing of Vallandigham badges, Butternut emblems, and Union League pins. Soldiers home on leave took special pleasure in insulting Vallandighamers and defying Democrats. The exile's home town witnessed several tragic incidents. Once some young Democrats tested the temper of soldiers lounging in the public square by hurrahing for Vallandigham. Several soldiers chased the impolitic Copperheads and assaulted them. One of the Vallandighamers pulled a gun and fatally wounded a soldier. Another incident occurred two weeks later, proving that political tempers prevented Daytonians from learning their lesson. Frederick Brown, a moulder by trade and a Democrat by choice, entered the Montgomery House, a popular eating place. As he came in the door he gave a "Hurrah" for Vallandigham. An army lieutenant home on leave challenged the entrant, demanding, "What right have you to hurrah for a damned traitor?" Brown answered, "Vallandigham is no more a traitor than you are." The irate lieutenant rushed at Brown, seized him by the throat, pushed him toward the door, and felled him with a right smash. Brown, raising himself on his left elbow, pulled a pistol out of his right pocket and fired twice at his attacker. The lieutenant quickly drew his own pistol and shot his fellow-townsman dead.[47]

Even the feminine sex argued over badges, emblems, and

[46] Ohio Patriot (New Lisbon), 25 September 1863; Wellesville Patriot (n.d.), quoted in Henry Howe, Historical Collections of Ohio: An Encyclopedia of the State, 2 vols. (Norwalk, O., 1898), 1: 438.

[47] Dayton Daily Empire, 3, 18 September 1863. Harold L. Naragon, "The Ohio Gubernatorial Campaign of 1863" (Master's thesis, Ohio State University, 1934) contains the statement (p. 42) that the campaign was "comparatively free from violence."

Vallandigham. Young women pulled each other's hair, tore dresses, or scratched faces. Once a rather plump young lady, wearing a Butternut emblem, was sitting on a log listening to a speaker praise Vallandigham and condemn Brough and Lincoln. A tall and gaunt young lady wearing a Brough badge quietly approached the stout girl and snatched her Butternut emblem. The angry young lady eyed her tormentor, lunged at her, and swung a closed fist in an awkward fashion, striking the Brough girl under the chin and knocking her flat on her back. Eyes snapping fire, freckles aflame, and arms akimbo, like a bantam rooster spreading his wings, she crowed, "I can whip any damn Brough girl on the grounds."[48]

In mid-September of 1863 the tide began to turn against the exile. Effective campaigning by Brough and his advocates helped. So did war prosperity, which visited Ohio in that year. The Union victories at Vicksburg and Gettysburg cast long shadows, giving the lie to Democratic contentions that the war was a failure. The Union Leagues and the churches functioned effectively, convincing the wavering to vote for Brough and the dear old flag. Fear that Vallandigham's election might bring war to Ohio—a threat which Brough constantly reiterated—led the faint at heart to rationalize that it was best to vote for the Union party candidates. Republicans recognized that they would win, but they continued to work hard to make the victory margin "as overwhelming as possible."[49]

Vallandigham, meanwhile, busied himself as best he could. He continued to write letters to be read at Democratic rallies. He hoped his friends could convince Brough that he should withdraw from the canvass so the Ohio Democracy could present a "one and indivisible front" against abolition and despotism. "He [Brough] knows I was nominated first and by the regular Democratic convention as a 'life-long' Democrat," wrote the exile, "and he has no right to 'bolt.' "[50] C.L.V. continued to spend

[48] Related in Armstrong, "Personal Recollections," in *Cincinnati Daily Enquirer*, 20 March 1886. The controversy over badges and emblems is discussed, in part, in Carl M. Becker, " 'Disloyalty' and the Dayton Public Schools," *Civil War History* 11 (March 1965): 58-68.

[49] Whitelaw Reid, report to *Cincinnati Gazette*, 12 October 1863, in William Henry Smith Papers, Ohio Historical Society, Columbus.

[50] Vallandigham to Alexander S. Boys, 1 September 1863, Boys Papers.

much time receiving visitors, even finding it necessary to lock his doors occasionally in order to get some time to rest or relax.[51]

Once the exile seriously considered returning to Ohio, even selecting a rally in Lima as the site of his "re-appearance." But the more conservative Democrats in Ohio feared that rioting and bloodshed might follow his re-arrest and affect the election adversely. Vallandigham bowed to the wishes of his friends. Still, however, he deluded himself as to his chances to win the election. "My friends everywhere are *extremely confidant* [*sic*] of carrying the State, & by a considerable majority," he wrote just nine days before election. "By 'carrying the State,' we mean the *home* vote; although there is a fair prospect of carrying the election straight over all. . . . Our strength is in the country, and we will beat them—my friends *all* say—*badly*."[52] Vallandigham was evidently deceived by his friends, too many of whom were sycophants and blind partisans.

The eyes of the nation turned toward Ohio on election day. Residents of Canada and of the Confederacy also expressed an interest in the returns. Every Ohio Republican working at a desk in the nation's capital took time out to return home to vote for Brough, holding it a duty to help defeat Vallandigham.[53] President Lincoln repeatedly expressed his concern about the Ohio election. Republicans everywhere regarded Brough's election as "an absolute necessity."

Election day, October 13, dawned bright and clear. A radiant sun clothed the countryside in beauty as rural residents walked or drove to the polling places. In the cities, too, voters turned out in record numbers, some who had not voted for years trudging to the polls. In Cincinnati, the venerable Archbishop Richard Purcell voted for the first time in twenty-five years. He let everybody know that he was voting "an open Union ticket." In the nation's capital President Lincoln paced to and fro, despite assurances that all was well. "The President says he feels nervous," wrote a member of Lincoln's cabinet.[54] On the high seas, aboard

51 *Crisis*, 30 September 1863; *Cleveland Plain Dealer*, 29 September 1863.
52 Vallandigham to Manton Marble, 4 October 1863, Marble Papers.
53 Whitelaw Reid's report to *Cincinnati Gazette*, 12 October 1863, in William Henry Smith Papers.
54 Entry of 13 October 1863, Howard K. Beale, ed., *Diary of Gideon Welles*, 3 vols. (New York, 1960), 1: 469-70.

the blockade-runner the *Lady Davis,* a Confederate sailor wrote a brief entry: "October 13, Tuesday—Sea quite smooth. Ohio election comes off today; hope C. L. Vallandigham will be elected."[55]

But October 13 proved to be an unlucky day for Vallandigham, who went down to defeat by 100,000 votes. Brough received 61,752 more "home" votes than Vallandigham, and the "soldier vote" (collected in the field) added nearly 40,000 more to that majority. All in all, it was an astounding victory for Brough, a devastating defeat for Vallandigham.[56]

The Republicans celebrated the election returns, crowing lustily. Secretary of War Edwin M. Stanton sent a congratulatory telegram to the victorious candidate: "Your election is a glorious victory, worthy of the rejoicing which will greet it."[57] Secretary of the Treasury Salmon P. Chase sent a more original note: "Count every ballot a bullet fairly aimed at the heart of the rebellion."[58]

Lincoln, more "anxious" about the Brough-Vallandigham election than he had been about his own in 1860,[59] stayed up very late to read the progress reports from Ohio. It was after midnight when Governor David Tod telegraphed to Lincoln: "God be praised. Our majority on the home vote cannot be less than 30,000. Advise Sec'y Stanton."[60] Lincoln, jubilant, supposedly wired back: "Glory to God in the highest; Ohio has saved the Union."[61]

Ohio Republican editors gloried in Vallandigham's decided defeat. "The dark and evil cloud that hung over us," wrote the ecstatic editor of the *Ohio State Journal,* "has been dispersed and the sunshine of coming peace, honor, and prosperity is rising

---

[55] Entry of 13 October 1863, in T. J. Gordon, "Private Notebook," published in *Official Records of the Union and Confederate Navies in the War of the Rebellion,* 26 vols. (Washington, D.C., 1894-1922), ser. 1, 9: 278.

[56] Brough received 247,216 "home" votes to C.L.V.'s 185,464. He carried fifty-four counties to Vallandigham's thirty-one. Brough carried Montgomery County (Val's home county) by a 5,092 to 5,052 margin and Dayton by 1,920 votes to 1,747.

[57] Quoted in *Dayton Daily Journal,* 17 October 1863.

[58] Quoted in *Indianapolis Daily State Sentinel,* 16 October 1863.

[59] Entries of 13, 14 October 1863, Beale, *Diary of Gideon Welles,* 1: 370.

[60] 14 October 1863, Robert Todd Lincoln Papers, Library of Congress.

[61] This telegram seems to be nonexistent and some of the foremost Lincoln scholars doubt that he sent Tod such a message. It is repeated, nevertheless, in many Ohio histories.

upon our horizon. . . .".[62] The editor of the *Cleveland Leader*, more vindictive, wrote, "The allies of Jeff Davis are overthrown, dispersed, and driven sneaking to their hiding places," their poisonous fangs plucked out.[63] "To have been a Tory in the Revolution," wrote the clairvoyant editor of the *Cincinnati Gazette*, "will seem a light thing in the years that come, besides having been a Vallandigham leader in the Great Rebellion."[64] Perhaps the editor who put words from Milton's "Paradise Lost" into Vallandigham's mouth showed the least charity of all:

> Me miserable!
> Which way shall I fly? Which way I fly is Hell.
> My self is Hell. And in the lower deeps, a lower deep,
> Still opening wide, threatens to devour me,
> To which the Hell I suffer seems a Heaven.[65]

Dayton Republicans sponsored "a gigantic Union jollification." The transparencies and banners bore legends intended to rub salt into Democratic wounds. One transparency depicted a coffin with a sign saying "Copperhead remains—please forward to Winsor" [*sic*]. A second bore a picture of a dejected Vallandigham, surrounded by a cordon of battered copperhead snakes. Another banner read, "Ohio Stands by her Soldiers!" There were others, some clever, some crude. After the cheers and speeches ended, the celebrants lit an enormous bonfire.[66] While the bonfire licked at the skies and victorious Republicans yelled themselves hoarse, all was very, very quiet at 323 First Street. A dim and flickering light burned in Mrs. Vallandigham's window. Perhaps it reflected the gloom in her heart.

Every other large city in Ohio sponsored its own victory celebration. Sometimes the celebrants destroyed Democratic property or went out of their way to insult Vallandighamers. "The Abolish," wrote a dejected Democrat living in Springfield, Ohio, "had an illumination here last night. Such a time! I never want to see the like again. The *negroes* and *whites* together visited the houses of prominent Democrats, hissed, groaned, and

---

[62] Isaac Jackson Allen, 19 October 1863.
[63] 16 October 1863.
[64] 14 October 1863.
[65] Quoted in *Buffalo Commercial Advertiser*, 16 October 1863.
[66] *Dayton Daily Journal*, 17 October 1863.

throwed stones thro the windows. They broke all the large windows in Dr. Wallace's Drug Store, and many others. . . . Their conduct would have shamed devils out of hell. This is a terrible place, Cox. I am sick at heart, and will not punish my 'flesh and spirit' by publishing another campaign [paper]. The labor seems all lost."[67]

While Republicans celebrated their victory, Democrats offered a variety of excuses, none convincing, for their defeat. Some, such as Samuel Medary of the *Crisis* and Dr. John McElwee of the *Hamilton True Telegraph,* closed their eyes to the facts and blamed the defeat upon forthright frauds—"imported voters," "ballot-stuffing," "floods of greenbacks," "arbitrary power," and outright intimidation.[68] Most Democrats recognized that Republicans had abolitionized the army, transforming soldiers into anti-Vallandigham men. Only one regiment (the Fifty-seventh Ohio, from Auglaize County) cast a majority of its votes for the exile.

Some Democrats, seeking a scapegoat, held Vallandigham responsible for their party's defeat. He had "foisted" his "peculiar views" upon the party, contrary to the wishes of the majority of Ohio Democrats and in opposition to the wishes of the people.[69] In a sense these dissenting Democrats were right. The country did not want peace in October of 1863. "The nation is for war," a Canadian observer concluded after studying the election returns, "and he who represents it must be warlike. His [Vallandigham's] decided expressions of a desire for peace at any price, were utterly repugnant to the American mind."[70] Thomas O. Lowe, one of Vallandigham's most devoted disciples, also interpreted the election returns as a repudiation of "the peace policy." "The people have voted in favor of the war and the way it is at present conducted," young Lowe wrote, "and it has to go on of course. The case went to the jury and they

[67] C. M. Gould to Samuel S. Cox, 15 October 1863, Cox Papers.
[68] *Crisis,* 14, 21 October 1863; *Hamilton True Telegraph,* 16, 22, 23 October 1863; *Ohio Daily Statesman,* 21 October 1863; *Cincinnati Daily Enquirer,* 15 October 1863; *Dayton Daily Empire,* 26 January 1864.
[69] J. N. Baldwin to Manton Marble, 14 October 1863, Marble Papers; C. M. Gould to Samuel S. Cox, 15 October 1863, Cox Papers; *Ohio Daily Statesman,* 30 October 1863.
[70] *Toronto Daily Globe,* 17 October 1863.

have rendered their verdict, and I am not disposed to move for a new trial."[71] The editor of the *Dayton Empire* seemed to hold a like view when he wrote, "The people of Ohio, by their votes, have decided for war, taxation, conscription, and despotism."[72]

Vallandigham seemed to accept his defeat in good grace; he did not blame it upon frauds nor did he exhibit any bitterness. He showed enough good sense to write a post-election letter addressed to the "Democrats of Ohio." He thanked all for their efforts in his behalf, for their votes, and for their sympathy. He asked his fellow-Democrats not to be discouraged by the election returns, but to retain their faith in the time-tested Democratic principles. "Our defeat will soon be forgotten," he wrote, "but the glory of having rescued free discussion and a free ballot will be remembered for ages—even though we should lose them at last." Then, with his usual self-righteousness, he added, "The highest political boast, some years hence, of any man, will be 'I was a soldier in the Grand Army of Constitutional Liberty in 1863.'"[73] Evidently, the exile still refused to believe that his views were anathema to most Ohioans and that the majority views of 1863 would be written into history as the true views.[74] Intransigent as ever, he still believed that time and future historical events would vindicate him, polishing his halo and praising him for courage, foresight, and perseverance. "As to the future," he wrote to his dejected wife, "*posterity will vote for me,* and there will be neither chance nor motive for violence and fraud."[75] He continued to exhibit the single-mindedness which characterizes the self-deluded martyr. "I am myself just as firm & *perservering,*" he wrote to a friend in Philadelphia, "as I was six years ago in the case of *Vallandigham vs. Campbell;* and I mean to win again in the end."[76]

Vallandigham could well have found some solace in several aspects of the election. He had received more votes than any

71 Thomas O. Lowe to his brother William, 26 October 1863, Lowe Papers.

72 *Dayton Daily Empire,* 14 October 1863.

73 14 October 1863, published in *Ohio Daily Statesman,* 20 October 1863.

74 C.L.V. to Samuel S. Cox, 28 October 1863, Marble Papers.

75 14 October 1863, published in part in Vallandigham, *Vallandigham,* pp. 335-36.

76 Vallandigham to Hon. H. M. Philips, 24 October 1863, Simon Gratz Papers, Historical Society of Philadelphia.

other defeated gubernatorial candidate in Ohio history. More than that, aside from Brough, he had received more votes than any other victorious candidate. In defeat, he won more votes than Salmon P. Chase had in victory in 1857. "Vallandigham defeated," wrote one Democratic editor, "had more friends in the State than Chase when he was elected."[77] Vallandigham could also have found some solace in the fact that Democratic party discipline was magnificent even in defeat. Despite all the propaganda and pressure, most Irish-Americans and German-Catholics voted for Vallandigham and so did the much-abused Butternuts of the backwoods.[78] The fact that the Ohio vote reflected a national trend—Republicans swept Pennsylvania as well as every Midwestern state which held an October or November election in 1863—may have offered some consolation, too.

The Republican trend of 1863 enabled Vallandigham to claim that his peace views did not contribute to his defeat.[79] He therefore continued to rationalize that he really represented basic principles and he sought courage by worshipping in the Democratic chapel which Thomas Jefferson had erected.

Once, when some sympathetic students from the University of Michigan came to call, he felt compelled to give them a lengthy speech. He talked of morality and virtue. He asked them to study hard and to take advantage of their opportunities—to taste the sweets of knowledge. Although he referred infrequently to politics, he did say that a statesman must be guided by principles rather than expediency, as a mariner is guided by a compass. "It is easy to be a politician or a demagogue," the exile told the attentive students; "it is easy to sail with the wind or float with the current."[80] In part, the speech was a justification of his own inflexibility and self-righteousness—of his conviction that he was *right* and the country *wrong*.

[77] *Dayton Daily Empire,* 14 October 1863.

[78] Armstrong, "Personal Recollections," published in *Cincinnati Daily Enquirer,* 20 March 1886. In Columbus, the Ninth Ward, in which Irish-Catholics who attended St. Patrick's Church predominated, Vallandigham received 240 votes, Brough but 91. The Sixth Ward, peopled largely by German-Americans who attended Holy Cross Catholic Church, gave Vallandigham 435 votes, Brough only 77. Also see Francis P. Weisenberger, *Columbus during the Civil War* (Columbus, 1963), p. 26.

[79] Vallandigham to H. M. Philips, 24 October 1863, Gratz Papers.

[80] Quoted in *Detroit Free Press,* 15 November 1863.

17

POLITICAL MANEUVERING
AND VALLANDIGHAM'S RETURN

THE CLOSING MONTHS of 1863 were lonely ones for Vallandigham. His defeat in the October 13 elections had wounded his pride and tested his belief that time would vindicate him. The election returns also slammed the door on his hopes to return to Ohio triumphant and vindicated. The Canadian press lost interest in him, for he was no longer an important émigré. When the disheartened Ohioan looked out of the window of his hotel suite, he could see the *U.S.S. Michigan*, still serving as a grim reminder that military and naval authority could be used to keep him in exile.

Then, too, he was beset by financial problems late in 1863, being dependent upon money sent him by George Pugh and Samuel Cox.[1] Since the exile was a proud man, it depressed him to play the beggar. Furthermore, he was concerned about the health of his wife, who had returned to Dayton after a brief visit to Windsor. Her emotional instability plagued Vallandigham and he feared that his prolonged absence and the circumstances surrounding it might result in her nervous breakdown. In these months the martyr's halo which C.L.V. imagined he wore lost much of its glow. He spent a lonely Christmas in his quarters at the Hirons House. The Christmas message, "Peace on earth, goodwill to men," seemed to have a hollow ring for the troubled exile.

When word of Vallandigham's financial needs reached Ohio, friends rallied to his support. Samuel Medary of the *Crisis* organized a "Vallandigham Fund," begging subscribers of Democratic newspapers to give a dime or a dollar, and collecting money at party rallies. The success of the scheme thrilled Medary and eased the exile's financial woes. By mid-January of 1864 Vallandigham could write, "Money I have now all that I shall need for some time."[2] The "Vallandigham Fund" netted the exile about $20 thousand, perhaps more.[3]

Many of Vallandigham's Ohio friends also visited him in Windsor, some dropping in nearly every weekend. Furthermore, several residents of Detroit and Windsor transformed acquaintances into friendships. "I have some excellent friends here and in Detroit," the exile wrote to his brother James, ". . . and what time I am not occupied with them . . . I devote to my books."[4]

Books furnished an escape from the harsh world of reality. Dayton friends brought some from his own library, and he bought or borrowed others. He reviewed history and political philosophy, seeking justification for his own inflexible views. He dipped again into "the ancient classics," taking notes and extracting quotations which he might incorporate into letters or speeches. He had the time and the opportunity to don the mantle of a scholar. "Indeed, scarce ever in my life have I had so fine a chance to study," he wrote, "and I am improving it to the utmost."[5]

Vallandigham built up a false hope when he learned that the Supreme Court would hear his case on January 22, 1864. George Pugh, who occasionally visited Windsor, had applied for a writ of certiorari in the exile's behalf, arguing that military commissions had limited uses and that General Burnside's panel of army officers should not have tried a citizen "unconnected with the armed forces." Pugh then asked the court to annul the exile's sentence on grounds of illegality; he did not ask the court to judge if Vallandigham's criticism of General Burnside and the Lincoln administration bordered on treason.[6]

Judge Advocate General Joseph Holt responded for the government. He argued that the court could be called upon to

---

[1] Cox to Samuel L. M. Barlow, 21 November 1863, Samuel L. M. Barlow Papers, Henry E. Huntington Library, San Marino, California.

[2] C.L.V. to his brother James, 16 January 1864, published in part in Vallandigham, *Vallandigham*, p. 346.

[3] This estimate is based on reports published periodically in the *Crisis* and the *Dayton Empire*. The *Dayton Daily Empire*, 20 April 1864, reported that the "Vallandigham Fund" increased by $5,046.68 during the two-week period 4-18 April. Earlier the *Hillsborough Weekly Gazette*, 7 April 1864, stated that the fund had passed the $10,000 mark "by the end of March."

[4] 16 January 1864, published in part in Vallandigham, *Vallandigham*, p. 346.

[5] Ibid.

[6] *Ex Parte Vallandigham* 68 U.S. (1 Wallace) 243-54 (1864).

restrain the proceedings of Congress by injunction with as much propriety as it could to reverse the proceedings of military authority by certiorari in time of war. The laws providing for common defense and public safety, Holt maintained, recognized courts martial.[7]

Had Vallandigham known that eighty-six-year-old Chief Justice Roger B. Taney was too ill to hear Pugh's arguments, he would have been less optimistic. In Taney's absence, the judges decided not to paralyze the hand of the military and they ruled against the exile. Justice James M. Wayne delivered the opinion for his colleagues on February 15, 1864. The decision, which incorporated Holt's arguments as well as his phraseology, denied the court's right of jurisdiction. The nation's highest judicial body ruled that it could not "originate a writ of certiorari to review . . . the proceedings of a military commission." The judges refused the writ on the grounds that, even if the arrest, trial, and punishment were illegal, the court still had no authority to grant relief in this mode and that there was no law by which any appeal, or proceedings in the nature of an appeal, could be taken from a military commission to the Supreme Court.[8] Hiding behind legal jargon, the Supreme Court simply believed it inexpedient to challenge military authority during the war.

Republicans applauded the court's decision. President Lincoln, Attorney General Edward Bates, and General Burnside breathed sighs of relief. Some Republican editors seemed to believe that the court's refusal to accept jurisdiction proved Vallandigham guilty of treason. William D. Bickham of the *Dayton Journal* deceived his readers by maintaining that the court had refused to intervene because the exile was guilty of the charges made by General Burnside. He turned to literature for an analogy to chide the hapless exile: "His Satanic Majesty is reported to have exclaimed when he was plunged into the infernal regions: 'Miserable me! Which way shall I fly!'"[9]

Democrats, on the other hand, attacked the Supreme Court's timidity and lack of integrity, claiming the judges had bowed

[7] Ibid.
[8] Ibid. David M. Silver, "The Supreme Court during the Civil War" (Ph.D. dissertation, University of Illinois, 1940), proves conclusively that Justice Wayne leaned heavily upon Holt's brief, paraphrasing large sections of it.
[9] 16 February 1864.

to expediency. The editor of the *Dayton Empire*, for example, wrote that the court was guilty of "a cowardly evasion of a question which it was the duty of the Court to decide."[10] One angry and perceptive Democratic editor stated his views even more bluntly: "The Supreme Court has no jurisdiction in matters of individual liberty, unless the party claiming redress can prove he was outraged *according to law*."[11]

Although an exile, Vallandigham was intensely interested in political developments in the United States. Since 1864 was a presidential election year, the political pot began to boil early. Lincoln's friends introduced resolutions in various state legislatures endorsing his reelection. Neither the Missouri nor the Ohio legislature, however, gave Lincoln the vote of confidence which he wanted, for radical Republicans in those states preferred John C. Frémont or Salmon P. Chase. Democrats, aware that explosive forces operated within the Republican party, hoped that a schism might develop and give their party a chance to win the election.

All Democrats agreed that Lincoln did not deserve a second term. "That Abraham Lincoln is ruining our country to perdition," Samuel Medary stated in the *Crisis*, "—destroying 'life, liberty, and the pursuit of happiness,' everybody not crazy with 'negro on the brain' knows, and knows it well."[12] Although Democrats were united in their opposition to the reelection of Lincoln, they could agree on nothing else. They disagreed over the efficacy of peace and compromise, some giving it priority, others viewing it as impractical and unrealistic. Some styled themselves "Peace Democrats" while others called themselves "War Democrats." Many Midwestern Democrats, including Medary and Vallandigham, viewed themselves as Western sectionalists and they resented the efforts of August Belmont and Erastus Corning, both of New York, to take over the party hierarchy. Defeated nearly everywhere in the '63 elections and torn by dissension, the Democracy had degenerated into an ineffectual organization, without a positive program and without vibrant leadership.

[10] 16, 29 February, 1 March 1864.
[11] *Detroit Free Press*, 26 February 1864.
[12] 27 January 1864.

Aware that neither Millard Fillmore nor Franklin Pierce retained any political magic, Democratic strategists studied the credentials of prominent generals. Samuel Cox, who had criticized Vallandigham on occasion while befriending him at other times, took the lead in promoting General George B. McClellan's candidacy—the controversial general could envision himself in the White House and he made himself most available. Cox was sure that even Vallandigham could be brought around to support McClellan and that other peace men would fall in line. "We can get the Peace men for McClellan," Cox wrote. "They are the fiercest disciplinarians," he added, "& they dare not bolt."[13]

Cox knew he had Vallandigham over a barrel. He had campaigned for him assiduously in 1863 even though he did not endorse his extreme peace views. He had gone out of his way to testify in Vallandigham's behalf before Burnside's military commission, even claiming as his own some remarks which the proscution attributed to the prisoner. More than that, Cox had reached deeply into his own pocket in the exile's hours of greatest need and had encouraged his New York friends to do likewise. Having accepted Cox's money and assistance, C.L.V. would hardly dare to repudiate his colleague's candidate, unless he was willing to be called an ingrate or a self-centered snob. Cox did not expect Vallandigham to abet the McClellan boom, but he was sure that once McClellan had gained the nomination, the exile would accept the facts of political life.[14]

While Cox was busy promoting McClellan's candidacy, some Midwestern peace men took steps to impose their views upon the party. Harrison H. Dodd of Indiana tried to revive the Sons of Liberty, a secret Democratic organization he had attempted to launch in 1863, as a vehicle to unite Peace Democrats and prevent McClellan's nomination.

A handful of Midwestern peace men accepted the invitation of Fernando Wood and James A. McMaster of the *Freeman's Journal* to meet secretly in New York on February 22 to discuss ways and means to stop the McClellan boom. On their way to New York City, Amos Green of Illinois and Dr. James A. Barret of Missouri passed through Windsor, stopping to visit Vallan-

---

[13] Cox to Samuel L. M. Barlow, 21 November 1863, Barlow Papers.
[14] Ibid.

digham and exchange views. They told the exile of their hope to create a widespread Democratic secret society, one that would effectively counter the work of the Union Leagues and help nominate and elect a peace man as president. They asked Vallandigham to head this association, appealing to his vanity by telling him that his name would draw many Democrats into the society. Green and Barret also insisted that they intended to reorganize and revitalize Dodd's dormant association in New York City—selling their bill of goods to eastern peace men.

The exile stated his opposition to secret political associations. He endorsed the tenet preached by Charles H. Lanphier of the *Illinois State Register:* "True democracy works in the light of day."[15] But Green and Barret assured Vallandigham that the motives of the society's founders were pure and that such action was necessary to meet the secret Union League on its own ground. When C.L.V. stopped protesting, Green and Barret took it for granted that he had acquiesced.[16]

Two other Midwestern Democrats, Dr. Thomas C. Massey of Ohio and Harrison H. Dodd of Indiana, stopped in Windsor on March 1, on their way home from the peace conclave in New York City. Vallandigham had a slight acquaintance with Massey. The two callers told the exile that he had been elected "Supreme Grand Commander" of the Sons of Liberty at the New York meeting and showed him the partly drafted constitution and ritual. Vallandigham crossed out much of the hocus-pocus and some of the ritual and added selections from the Virginia and Kentucky Resolutions of 1798 as "lessons of the Inner Temple." Then he agreed to serve as "Supreme Grand Commander" for a year.[17] Pleased that Vallandigham had lent his name to the organization, Dodd and Massey returned home, each bearing the self-selected title of "Grand Commander" for his state.

A handful of Peace Democrats gathered in Vallandigham's suite in the Hirons House in mid-April. Although their eyes were upon the exile, their thoughts dwelt on the Democratic National Convention of July 4 in Chicago, as they groped for

[15] 24 February 1863.
[16] Testimony of Vallandigham before the Cincinnati Military Commission, 29 March 1865, published in the *Cincinnati Daily Enquirer*, 30 March 1865.
[17] Ibid.

ways to prevent McClellan's nomination and to revive the peace-and-compromise crusade. As a result of the discussion, Vallandigham agreed to write an "open letter" emphasizing the need for compromise and the advisability of nominating a peace man at Chicago.[18]

After the meeting some of those present discussed the status of the Sons of Liberty. S. Corning Judd, a gubernatorial candidate in Illinois, reported on conditions in his state. Democrats there, Judd asserted, would not give up their rights without a struggle—they would insist upon free elections and all constitutional rights. Harrison H. Dodd reported on affairs in Indiana. He was bitter about Governor Oliver P. Morton's arbitrary and partisan practices and he stated that the Sons of Liberty would save civil rights and elect peace men. Massey then discussed the situation in Ohio, and the exile bent an interested ear. The Ohio Democracy, Massey said, had not yet fully recovered from its resounding defeat in the gubernatorial contest of the previous fall. Antiwar sentiment, however, seemed to be gaining favor; Samuel Medary continued to chant "Peace! Peace! Peace!" in the *Crisis*, and the new editors of the *Dayton Empire* simplified the issue by claiming it was either peace or pandemonium. Vallandigham's leadership of the Sons of Liberty, Massey added, should draw many into the society and make it a more effective political force.

Affairs in Missouri were then discussed by Charles L. Hunt. As a close personal friend of Phineas C. Wright, who had organized a handful of dissidents into the Order of American Knights, Hunt brusquely stated that Missouri peace men preferred the American Knights to the Sons of Liberty. Hunt further riled Vallandigham by advocating an immediate armistice and suggesting giving aid to the Southern rebels. Visibly angry, Vallandigham interrupted Hunt and gave him a severe castigation. He averred that he would have nothing to do with the Missouri "outfit!" There was a difference, the exile bluntly asserted, between being a critic of the government and a traitor. He would never be the latter! While ill feelings still smoldered, James A. McMaster of the *Freeman's Journal* had his say. As the inactive "Grand Commander" in New York, McMaster spoke

[18] Ibid.

vehemently against President Lincoln and shocked some of those present by openly endorsing secession. Vallandigham forthrightly dissented and so did Judd. On the other hand, Hunt hurried to McMaster's defense and sparks flew.[19]

Because of the disagreements among those trying to set policy for the Sons of Liberty, the organization died "aborning." It became again merely a paper organization and a pretense. As "Supreme Grand Commander," Vallandigham never issued an order or directive and never called a meeting of the "Grand Commanders" of the several states. The exile held only a title, not an office. The quarrelsome Peace Democrats returned home to their respective states, quite disheartened. They knew that their paper-based organization could not serve as an effective antidote to the Union Leagues. It could not protect the civil rights of dissenters and preserve states' rights. Nor could it prevent General McClellan from gaining the Democratic presidential nomination. In fact, when ex-President Millard Fillmore, Manton Marble of the *New York World*, and Wilbur F. Storey of the *Chicago Times* threw their support to Cox's candidate, McClellan's nomination was all but assured.[20]

Vallandigham's Dayton and Ohio friends, however, refused to accept Cox's contention that McClellan had the nomination in the bag. They assured the exile that they would put his name forward as a delegate-at-large to the Democratic National Convention, scheduled to meet in Columbus on March 23. Loyal supporters of Vallandigham believed that if he showed up at the Chicago convention as a duly elected delegate, President Lincoln would hardly dare order his arrest. "If he is chosen as a delegate," avowed an adamant supporter of Vallandigham, "the Democracy of Ohio will see that he attends the Chicago Convention"[21]—even if 100,000 Democrats had to march to Windsor and escort him to the convention.

Heartened by the loyalty and promises of his friends, Val-

---

[19] Testimony of S. Corning Judd and Vallandigham before the Cincinnati Military Commission, 29-31 March 1865, published in the *Cincinnati Daily Enquirer*, 30, 31 March 1865. The testimony of the two, given on different days, agreed on what was said at the conference in Vallandigham's room.

[20] Fillmore to McClellan, 24 March 1864, George B. McClellan Papers, Library of Congress; Thomas O. Lowe to his brother William, 2 April 1864, Thomas O. Lowe Papers, Dayton and Montgomery County Public Library.

[21] John A. Trimble to David A. Houk, 4 April 1864, Alexander S. Boys Papers, Ohio Historical Society, Columbus.

landigham took steps to refurbish his reputation. He helped collect a stack of his speeches, addresses, and letters and waited impatiently while Jefferson A. Walter arranged for their publication in book form.[22] He wrote letters of encouragement to his friends in Hamilton and Dayton. He must have regained some hope and confidence when the Montgomery County Democracy adopted a statement which read: "Resolved, That the Patriot and Statesman, Clement L. Vallandigham, is the first choice of the Democracy of Montgomery County for the next President of the United States."[23] Perhaps the halo of the martyr regained some of its glow.

While Vallandigham sought to refurbish his reputation with one pen, he inadvertently damaged it with another, writing a letter while angry and indignant. Upon hearing that the editorial offices of several Democratic newspapers, including the *Dayton Empire* (in which he still had a financial interest), had been "mobbed" or destroyed, Vallandigham endorsed "the law of retaliation" and promised reprisals. His letter, written to the editor of the *Empire* and evidently intended for publication, regretted that Dayton mobsters had not received "the complete punishment"—lead from the defenders' guns. To prevent future mob action against their persons or property, Democrats must let Republicans know that they would fight fire with fire—*"instant, summary and ample reprisals upon the persons and property* of those who, by language or conduct, incited the outrages."[24]

Every Daytonian knew that Vallandigham was thinking of William D. Bickham and his newspaper, the *Dayton Journal*. Earlier Bickham had intimated that threats and violence were proper means to transform dissenters and would-be traitors into

22 Twenty thousand copies were published under the title *Speeches, Arguments, Addresses, and Letters of Clement L. Vallandigham* (New York, 1864).

23 "Resolutions of the Montgomery County Democracy, March 19, 1864," published in the *Dayton Daily Empire*, 31 March 1864.

24 C.L.V. to "Messrs. Hubbard," 1 March 1864, published in *Dayton Daily Empire*, 12 March. Even George W. Manypenny, known as a moderate Democrat editor, endorsed the reprisal doctrine, writing that if his office or printing plant was destroyed, the *Ohio State Journal* (the Columbus Republican newspaper) would go down at the same time and by the same means, whether mob or fire. See *Daily Ohio Statesman* (Columbus), 17 February 1864. Marcus Mills "Brick" Pomeroy of the *LaCrosse Democrat* stated the law of reprisal more bluntly: "Matches are cheap. If fanatics and fools seek mob law and anarchy, by all means let them have it. . . . for every dime of property destroyed by political opponents, destroy a dollar's worth in return" (1 February 1864).

patriots. When Vallandigham's reprisal letter was published, Bickham's ears burned. He denounced Vallandigham and his "mischievous teachings." For good measure, Bickham restated an earlier contention, that Vallandigham was as much a traitor as Benedict Arnold and that he wanted to plunge the country into anarchy and civil war.[25]

Vallandigham's absurd reprisal letter brought him notoriety again. Even the editor of the *New York Tribune* censured the exile for "casting aside the practices of civilization and advocating the law of the jungle." Reprisal policy, Greeley suggested, would popularize burglary, arson, and murder. Perhaps Vallandigham's "manifesto," Greeley added, was intended to help "his friend," Jefferson Davis.[26]

Reprisal doctrine, coming from Vallandigham's mouth, had a strange sound for he had constantly claimed he was devoted to law, order, and constitutionalism. Now he seemed to revive John Brown's tactics. The law of retaliation contradicted all of what Vallandigham had preached or written previously. It contradicted his claim that he was essentially a conservative who loved law and order and liberty. Even indignation was no excuse for writing another letter which was effective ammunition for his enemies.

While friends and foes discussed the merits of the exile's reprisal letter, they immersed themselves in politics, for 1864 was a presidential election year. Ohio Democrats favorable to McClellan's candidacy worked night and day to prevent the selection of peace Democrats as delegates to the Chicago convention. Above all, they did not want Vallandigham named as a delegate-at-large. Such prominent Ohio Democrats as Samuel Cox and George Manypenny, having pitched McClellan's presidential tent on the state's soil, regarded peace men like Vallandigham as "misguided warriors" and did not want the state convention to damage their chief's chances in Chicago. Nor did such political realists as Allen G. Thurman and Rufus P. Ranney want Vallandigham's "dead weight" to pull their party down to defeat.[27]

[25] *Dayton Daily Journal*, 14 March 1864.
[26] *New York Tribune*, 13 March 1864.
[27] *Daily Ohio Statesman* (Columbus, n.d.), quoted in the *Dayton Daily Empire*, 31 March 1864.

On March 23 all eyes turned toward Columbus, where Democrats gathered to adopt resolutions and name four at-large delegates to the party's national convention. Those who called themselves War Democrats expressed disappointment when the convention wrote Vallandigham's views into the resolutions. The first lauded Jeffersonian doctrine "as expressed in the Virginia and Kentucky Resolutions." The second characterized the Lincoln administration as "an abject failure." The third (the controversial peace-and-compromise resolution) asked for "the immediate inauguration of peaceful means" to end the war and restore "the Union under the Constitution." Although Vallandigham and most of the delegates approved this resolution, radicals like Alexander Long and William M. Corry favored the immediate cessation of hostilities and the withdrawal of troops from the South. The fourth and last resolution denounced the "mob spirit" so prevalent throughout the country and laid the blame for it at Lincoln's door. "The tyranny of the present Administration," the last sentence of the resolution read, "has sown seeds from which we are now reaping a harvest of crime."[28] It was typical of the law-and-order pleas expressed by conservatives throughout the Civil War.

After approving and applauding the resolutions, the representatives turned to the task of naming the state's four delegates-at-large to the national convention. Three McClellan men received enough first-ballot votes to gain the necessary plurality: William Allen of Chillicothe, Allen G. Thurman of Columbus, and George H. Pendleton of Cincinnati. Rufus P. Ranney finished fourth, Vallandigham fifth, and Samuel Medary sixth on the first ballot, but each failed to receive the quota of votes set by the convention rules.

As the convention prepared for the second ballot, Medary arose, withdrew his name, and asked his friends to vote for Vallandigham. The exile's friends, many no more than spectators, sent up a cheer that shook the rafters and caused Cox to turn pale. After the second ballot had been cast, the tellers tallied the votes: Ranney, 216⅔; Vallandigham, 211⅓; and William M. Corry, 1. When the presiding officer declared Ranney elected,

[28] "Resolutions adopted at the Democratic State Convention, March 23, 1864," published in the *Daily Ohio Statesman* (Columbus), 24 March 1864.

Vallandigham's supporters created an uproar. The scene defied description. The Vallandighamers denounced the presiding officer, the tellers, and their opponents generally. A dozen of them sought the floor, gesticulating violently and shouting at the president of the convention. Several in the bellicose Hamilton County delegation squared off as if to fight. After their fury had been spent in vain, the presiding officer stated that the tallies had been rechecked and recounted, with the results the same as first announced. When all "had been proven fair," John A. McMahon, made "a very handsome speech" in favor of party harmony, asking the defeated delegates to accept the results as befitted loyal party men. Since McMahon was Vallandigham's nephew and confidant, the discontented delegates stopped acting like street urchins who had lost their candy. Dr. Edson B. Olds, a well-known peace man, also asked for party harmony and good sportsmanship. Someone then moved to make the election of the four delegates-at-large "unanimous." The motion carried, although a handful of discontented Vallandigham supporters showed their ill-will be shouting "Nay!" Before adjourning, the convention gave three cheers for the Constitution and three more for the Union.[29]

McClellan's Ohio supporters were elated at Vallandigham's defeat, interpreting it as a victory for "Little Mac." "Altogether," one McClellan man wrote, "it may be considered that we have gained a great triumph."[30]

After their disappointment at Vallandigham's defeat had worn off, his disciples realized that they had not walked away from the table empty-handed. They claimed that the party platform, in the form of the four resolutions, was quite satisfactory—more than crumbs at the political feast. Vallandigham, informed of his defeat at the convention, felt compelled to deny that he had sought a delegateship, even stating that his name had been presented "against his express consent."[31] He even implied that he could have been elected if he had so wished and the editors

[29] A. Benning Norton to Samuel L. M. Barlow, 25 March 1864, Barlow Papers; John A. Trimble to David A. Houk, 4 April 1864, Boys Papers; *Dayton Daily Journal,* 25 March 1864; *Crisis,* 25 March 1864.

[30] George Morgan to McClellan, 28 March 1864, McClellan Papers; A. Benning Norton to Samuel L. M. Barlow, 25 March 1864, Barlow Papers.

[31] *Detroit Free Press,* 26 March 1864.

of the Democratic newspapers in his home town put the same contention into print.[32] It was another case of sour grapes. The exile still had a second chance—he could be elected one of the two delegates from the Third Congressional District. Vallandigham's friends in Dayton announced they intended to nominate him at the district convention, scheduled to meet in Hamilton on June 15. Ground lost at Columbus might be regained there and some of his friends urged him to put in an appearance at Hamilton in mid-June. Such bold action might throw the balance in his favor and give him the delegateship he wanted more than words could tell.

Meanwhile, Republicans were engaged in a family fight. Both Salmon P. Chase and John C. Frémont wanted the Republican nomination, and each had the support of some radicals in the party. Outwitted and out-maneuvered by Lincoln, Chase felt compelled to renounce his presidential ambitions. Frémont, however, stayed in the field and his friends issued a call for "a special convention" to meet in Cleveland on May 31—a week before the Republican convention was slated to meet in Baltimore. The Cleveland convention, as expected, nominated Frémont but failed to intimidate Lincoln's supporters or stampede the Republican party. The party steamroller nominated Lincoln at Baltimore on June 7, calling the gathering the National Union Convention and drafting Andrew Johnson as the running mate. Frémont, however, kept his hat in the ring and radical Republicans pushed the Wade-Davis Bill through Congress, thereby declaring war on Lincoln's reconstruction program. The fight between Lincoln and the radicals of his own party gave heart to Vallandigham and the Democrats. They hoped it was a fight between two Kilkenny cats.[33]

Democrats failed to exploit the Republican schism. Ohio Democrats were more guilty of feuding than were those of other states. Alexander Long, William M. Corry, and Samuel Medary tried to foist their extreme peace views upon the party. Long wanted an armistice and even advocated his views on the floor of the House of Representatives in the nation's capital. "If the

---

[32] *Dayton Daily Empire*, 28 March 1864.

[33] The story of the Republicans and the presidential election of 1864 is related in William Frank Zornow, *Lincoln and the Party Divided* (Norman, Okla., 1954).

time ever was when the Union could be restored by war," he declared dogmatically, "it has since been disspelled by emancipation, confiscation . . . and like proclamations."[34] Party spokesmen such as Samuel Cox and George Manypenny, on the other hand, urged Democrats to put patriotism before partisanship. They arduously advocated the nomination of McClellan and accused peace men in the party of trying to lead the Democracy down the road of self-destruction.[35]

At his Canadian retreat, meanwhile, Clement L. Vallandigham mulled over possible courses of action. He grew more restless with each passing month, fully aware of his waning influence in Ohio politics. Continued exile consigned him to oblivion, while his ego required publicity and attention. Furthermore, he was tired of the long separation from his family; word from Ohio indicated his wife was not well and his mother was gravely ill. Dr. John McElwee, editor of the *Hamilton True Telegraph* and one of Vallandigham's closest personal friends, urged the exile to cross the border, appear at the Third District Convention on June 15, and get back into the public limelight. He even promised to escort Vallandigham from Windsor to Hamilton.

There were other considerations. Wilbur F. Storey of the *Chicago Times* had practically called him a coward for not returning to the U.S. to claim rights to which he was entitled. In addition, the peace movement, which Vallandigham had led before his arrest and exile, gathered new life in 1864. Grant's murderous assaults against Lee's lines in the Wilderness (May 5-6), at Spotsylvania (May 8-12), and at Cold Harbor (June 3) gained little ground and resulted in Union losses of 55,000. The blood baths gave impetus to the peace crusade, and Vallandigham would like to have been in Ohio aiding the groundswell.[36]

Then too, Confederate agents in Windsor embarrassed him and gave his critics an excuse to say he was among friends.

---

[34] *Congressional Globe,* 38 Cong., 1 sess., p. 1500.

[35] *Daily Ohio Statesman* (n.d.), quoted in the *Dayton Daily Empire,* 29 April 1864; Manton Marble to James W. Wall, 30 March 1864, Manton Marble Papers, Library of Congress.

[36] Edward C. Kirkland, *The Peacemakers of 1864* (New York, 1927), once regarded as a classic, needs considerable revision. Elbert J. Benton, *Movement for Peace without Victory during the Civil War* (Cleveland, 1919) and J. N. Hofer, "Development of the Peace Movement in Illinois during the Civil War," *Journal of the Illinois State Historical Society* 24 (April 1931): 119-28, are also outdated.

Jacob Thompson, a Confederate commissioner serving his country in Canada, visited Vallandigham in Windsor, perhaps to seek his aid to achieve Confederate aims. They discussed the question of peace and compromise but disagreed on the basic issue: Vallandigham desired peace, compromise, and reunion; Thompson wanted peace and Southern independence. The Confederate commissioner asked about the Sons of Liberty—the order's size and objectives. Vallandigham bluntly told Thompson that he would give no information to a nonmember. Embarrassed by the rebuff, Thompson tactfully turned the conversation to such topics as reconstruction and the election of 1864.[37] Thompson's visit to Vallandigham and the presence of an ever-increasing number of draft dodgers and Confederate agents in Windsor gave Republicans ample opportunity to concoct anti-Vallandigham propaganda.

All of these facts caused Vallandigham to grow more and more restless. Perhaps returning to Hamilton might insure his election as a delegate to the Democratic national convention. If he was elected, would President Lincoln dare defy the wishes of the Democracy of the Third District?

Vallandigham finally decided that the game was worth the candle. To put federal agents off the track, he stated aloud his intention to attend the Chicago convention of July 4. Four friends[38] from Hamilton arrived in Windsor on June 14 to escort

[37] Testimony of Vallandigham before the Cincinnati Military Commission, 29 March 1865, published in Cincinnati Daily Enquirer, 30 March 1865. At a later date Jacob Thompson claimed that Vallandigham had initiated him into the Sons of Liberty. Historians are faced with the problem of weighing Vallandigham's word against Thompson's. Vallandigham was under oath when he testified at Cincinnati and he had a reputation for veracity even with his enemies. Thompson's reputation, on the other hand, was tarnished by charges of corruption while he was in public office. (Perhaps a word should be said about the Cincinnati Military Commission, before which Vallandigham testified regarding his association with the Sons of Liberty. Early in 1865, the Commission tried a handful of men arrested and accused of being implicated in the "Chicago Conspiracy" or the "Northwest Conspiracy." It was charged that a group of conspirators wanted to release Confederate prisoners held in Camp Douglas, outside Chicago, overthrow federal authority, and establish a "Northwest Confederacy." Vallandigham testified willingly, seeing it as a chance to clear himself of reports and rumors that he also was involved. S. Corning Judd, the leader of the Sons of Liberty in Illinois and a well-known Democratic politician, also testified at Cincinnati; his testimony corroborated much of Vallandigham's.)

[38] The four were Dr. John McElwee, David W. Brant, Jacob Troutman, and Edward Dalton. Vallandigham, Vallandigham, p. 352, states that no one in Hamilton or elsewhere knew of the exile's return until he appeared on the stand

the exile back home. After darkness had enveloped the city, Vallandigham donned his disguise—false whiskers and a cape. The five crossed the Detroit River on the ferry boat, walked to the Detroit railroad station, entered a sleeping car on the Toledo train, and tossed sleeplessly in their berths as they considered the possible consequences of their action.

The night ride was uneventful. The train passed through Dayton on its way southward and no one there dreamed that Vallandigham had taken steps to end a year's exile. It chugged into Hamilton early on the morning of the fifteenth. As the train slowed down near the depot, the five weary travelers stepped off the cars. Two in the party conducted Vallandigham to the home of a farmer two miles north of Hamilton. There he planned his dramatic reentry into public life. After leaving Vallandigham near the depot, Dr. McElwee hurried to his print shop to set up handbills announcing the exile's return and stating that Vallandigham would speak from the central platform at three o'clock. By that time the scheduled speakers should have had their say.

At his farm hideout, Vallandigham wrote a note to his nephew, John McMahon, representing Montgomery County at the Third District Convention. The note stated that C.L.V. was "two miles from Hamilton" and "would speak at three o'clock." Vallandigham anticipated that the Montgomery County delegates would meet in caucus that morning to consider appropriate resolutions and endorse candidates to represent the district at the Chicago convention.

Vallandigham's note reached McMahon's hands at eleven o'clock, just after Montgomery County representatives met in caucus. When McMahon showed the note to others, an air of excitement pervaded the room. Some were surprised, most were elated, and all stated their intent to work for Vallandigham's election. They convinced themselves that they would witness an historic event that afternoon.[39]

---

at the convention of June 15. An observer and participant, however, refutes this story and lists the four who escorted Vallandigham to Hamilton. See Stephen D. Cone, *A Concise History of Hamilton, Ohio*, 2 vols. (Middletown, O., 1901), 2: 231.

[39] *Dayton Daily Empire*, 16 June 1864; *Cincinnati Daily Commercial*, 16 June 1864; *Dayton Daily Journal*, 16, 17 June 1864; *Hamilton True Telegraph*, 23 June 1864; Vallandigham, *Vallandigham*, pp. 352-53; Cone, *A Concise History of Hamilton*, 2: 230-32.

Representatives of the Third District Democracy convened at one-thirty in the afternoon, electing Chris Hughes of Hamilton as chairman. They adopted a set of radical resolutions, some far to the left of Vallandigham's position on peace, compromise, and reunion. The most controversial resolution asked for an "immediate cessation of hostilities" and the inauguration of measures to secure "a just and lasting peace." The resolution offered evidence that defeatism and war-weariness were rampant and that the prayer for peace was on a thousand lips. Another resolution thanked Alexander Long for his propeace speech of April 8 in Congress—it was a speech which had brought him censure and nearly resulted in his expulsion from the House of Representatives. Other resolutions repeated the usual line: one blamed the Republicans for bringing on "the unnecessary war," and another condemned the Lincoln administration for its "many arbitrary acts."[40]

After convention action on the resolutions, Chris Hughes read the handbill which stated that Clement L. Vallandigham was back and would address the gathering at three o'clock. "The whole crowd," wrote a reporter who was present, "joined in one prolonged, furious, and overwhelming yell that lasted for several minutes."[41] When the presiding officer finally restored order, the convention named its two delegates to the Chicago National Convention. The selection fell upon Clement L. Vallandigham and Chris Hughes. Vallandigham's supporters, jubilant and defiant, again rent the air with cheers and shouts.

At three o'clock, when the former exile walked onto the platform, his appearance electrified the crowd. "He came unheralded from his exile," a devotee later recalled, "and his sudden appearance was like an apparition from the clouds."[42] Excited Democrats mixed calls for "Vallandigham! Vallandigham!" with hurrahs and applause. "The cheers and excitement was [sic] beyond anything we ever witnessed," wrote another disciple of the exile, adding, "It was a most touching and inspiring spectacle. The hold Mr. Vallandigham has upon the popular heart is a very striking and wonderful fact."[43]

[40] *Dayton Daily Empire*, 16 June 1864.
[41] Ibid.
[42] Stephen D. Cone, *Biographical and Historical Sketches: A Narrative of Hamilton and Its Residents from 1792 to 1896*, 2 vols. (Hamilton, O., 1896), 1: 198.
[43] *Dayton Daily Empire*, 16 June 1864.

Vallandigham seemed to be his old confident self. He spoke deliberately, often half-reading from a carefully prepared manuscript, as the audience strained to catch every word. He denied he was guilty of any crime, adding that he was willing and ready to answer any charges in civil courts. He called the 186,000 Democrats who had voted for him on October 13, 1863, his "sureties." He asserted that he had the right to be critical of Republican policies and the Lincoln administration. He also had the right to protection under the Constitution's guarantees. "I am here," he said with a voice ringing with sincerity, "for peace, not turbulence; for quiet, not convulsions; for law and order, not anarchy." Yet his plea for law and order was shaded with the suggestion that his supporters should riot and rebel if he was again arrested and denied his rights.[44] It was the kind of boldness that Wilbur F. Storey of the Chicago Times would have admired and applauded.

Then the speaker felt compelled to explain his link to the Sons of Liberty and to deny Republican contentions that it was a subversive society, organized to aid Southern rebels and formed to bring a Northwest Confederacy into being. It was no more, Vallandigham asserted, than "a lawful Democratic society" interested in countering the work of the Republican-sponsored Union Leagues and in winning the coming presidential contest. He pretended that the organization was extensive, evidently thinking that the administration would be less inclined to rearrest him, interfere with free elections, and trample upon the rights of Democrats if Republicans believed the Sons to be as numerous as the leaves on the trees.[45]

A detective, sent out by the provost marshal general of the Department of the Missouri to investigate rumors that Vallandigham would return from exile, happened to be in the audience at Hamilton on June 15, watching the crowd reaction and listening to the speakers. He scribbled scrupulously in a little black book and listened for statements he believed traitorous. He was disappointed, for he found no taint of treason attached to Vallandigham's varied comments. Later, the agent presented himself to Vallandigham as a reporter for the Chicago Times and

44 Ibid.
45 Ibid.

asked him about his future plans. But neither Vallandigham nor his immediate friends trusted the garrulous fellow; they surmised that he was a spy and evaded answering his questions.[46]

Later that afternoon Vallandigham, his nephew, and most of the Montgomery County delegates to the convention entrained for Dayton, arriving early in the evening and without fanfare. The former exile took a carriage to his home at 323 First Street.

Next day excited Daytonians spread the word that Vallandigham was back. Many called at his home to receive a warm handshake, exchange pleasantries, and guess what the future held. In the afternoon, accompanied by Mayor Gillespie, C.L.V. walked down Main Street and on to the *Empire* Building. There, as in days of old, he received a warm welcome. In the evening some four hundred Dayton Democrats serenaded Vallandigham at his home. A hastily organized band played several numbers, including the "Vallandigham Polka." The serenaders then formed a semi-circle around the front porch and called for "Valiant Val" to come out and give a short speech. His face wreathed in a smile of appreciation, he soon appeared on the front porch. He spoke briefly, saying he had come home to be with his family and to claim and enjoy the civil rights to which he was entitled. He publicly warned Dayton Republicans that if they sought to "interfere" with his rights, they might feel "the hand of wrath." If any military commander came to arrest him, he supposed that Dayton Democrats would make "the persons and properties of his enemies" serve as "hostage" for him. Evidently he hoped to intimidate Dayton Republicans and expected them to use their influence to prevent his rearrest.[47]

Governor Brough, excited at the news of Vallandigham's return, promptly asked military authorities to arrest him. Colonel John H. Potter, provost marshal general of Ohio, ordered four companies of federal troops readied to assist in the arrest, but Major General Samuel P. Heintzelman, commanding the department,[48]

---

[46] "Report of William Taylor," 18 June 1864, in John P. Sanderson Papers, Ohio Historical Society. Taylor was one of a dozen detectives whom Colonel John P. Sanderson sent out to scour the Midwest. Sanderson was General Rosecrans's provost marshal general in the Department of the Missouri, headquartered in St. Louis.

[47] *Dayton Daily Empire*, 17, 18 June 1864; *Dayton Daily Journal*, 17 June 1864.

[48] Heintzelman succeeded Burnside in command in the region north of the Ohio River. War Department orders, dated 12 January 1864, brought an end to the

stalled for time and sought advice from Indiana's governor, Oliver P. Morton, with whom he happened to be closeted when he heard of Vallandigham's return and Brough's orders. Morton urged Heintzelman to rearrest Vallandigham, but the general procrastinated. He was reluctant to act without orders from Washington. Furthermore, he resented Brough's and Potter's instructions, for he questioned their right to give orders to his troops. Heintzelman escaped the pressure which Governors Brough and Morton sought to apply by getting lost on his return trip from Indianapolis to Columbus—he boarded the wrong cars at Xenia, ended up in Springfield next morning, and spent most of that day finding his way back to Columbus.[49]

Although frantic partisans, such as Edgar Conkling of the *Cincinnati Gazette*, threatened to organize a posse and make a citizens' arrest if federal or state authorities failed to act, more rational Republicans advised state and military authorities to ignore Vallandigham. "Say for me, if you please, to the Governor [Brough]," wrote the influential Murat Halstead, "that it would be a great mistake *now* to arrest Vallandigham. . . . Sensible Republicans without exception say the best thing to do is to let him alone."[50]

Horace Greeley, always free with advice, asked President Lincoln to ignore the returned exile. "Better let him alone," Greeley advised the president. "He will do good here. His running for Governor last year was worth fifty thousand votes to the Unionists of Ohio. Can't we get him on the Copperhead ticket as Vice-President?"[51]

Lincoln decided to follow the policy of watchful waiting. He wrote a letter to Brough and Heintzelman, asking them to consult together and to watch Vallandigham "closely." If there was "any palpable injury, or imminent danger to the Military," they should arrest the former exile and all others implicated. Showing irresolution and vaccilation, Lincoln added, "Otherwise do not

old Department of the Ohio, which Burnside had commanded, created the Northern Department (composed of Ohio, Indiana, Illinois, and Michigan), and put Heintzelman in command. These orders listed Columbus rather than Cincinnati as headquarters for the new department.

[49] Entries 15, 16 June 1864, Samuel P. Heintzelman Papers, Library of Congress.

[50] Murat Halstead to William Henry Smith, 21 June 1864, William Henry Smith Papers, State Historical Society Library, Indianapolis.

[51] *New York Tribune*, 17 June 1864.

arrest him without further orders; meanwhile report the signs to me from time to time."[52] Changing his mind again, the president never sent the letter, letting it gather dust upon his desk. Privately he wryly stated that he had no official knowledge of Vallandigham's return and that he would know nothing until the Ohioan was guilty of some objectionable acts.[53]

In the days that followed, Vallandigham lived quietly in Dayton, making no public speeches and even failing to reopen his old law office. Nor did he take any out-of-town trips, fearing arrest if he left the friendly confines of his city. He did not even go to New Lisbon to visit his mother, lying on her deathbed. "But while I feel perfectly secure *here*, I think the Administration would be but too glad to find me at a distance from home," he wrote on July 7.[54] His mother never read the letter, for she died before it reached her. Nor did he go to New Lisbon for his mother's funeral. He felt guilty for staying away and he put the blame on others rather than himself. "Words cannot express the feelings of my heart," he wrote with a heavy pen, "at the thought that I have not been in a position to be with her and with you all. But it is part of the evil times upon which we have fallen. . . . Though I could not see her in death, I rejoice that she lived to see my return to my own country and my home."[55]

Vallandigham approved the postponement of the Chicago convention to August 29, believing that new draft calls and more military failures might seal the doom of the party in power. The onetime exile and other doves talked of "the high price of blood." They pointed to Sherman's heavy losses at Kennesaw Mountain and added his casualties to those resulting from Grant's campaign before Richmond. Dr. John McElwee, for example, demanded that the government "STOP THIS WAR!", asked Lincoln "to call off his dogs of war," and ended a propeace editorial with the assertion, "This murderous crusade has gone far enough."[56]

While the peace crusade gathered momentum during June and July of 1864, a Republican-minded army colonel prepared an

[52] Lincoln to Brough and Heintzelman, 20 June 1864, Robert Todd Lincoln Papers, Library of Congress. The envelope contains the endorsement "Not Sent."
[53] *Detroit Free Press*, 17 July 1864.
[54] Vallandigham Papers, Western Reserve Historical Society, Cleveland.
[55] Vallandigham to his brother James, 10 July 1864, published in part in Vallandigham, *Vallandigham*, p. 364.
[56] *Hamilton True Telegraph*, 16 June 1864.

extraordinary piece of political propaganda. This "mare's nest," entitled "Conspiracy to Establish a Northwest Confederacy,"[57] claimed that a subversive society called the Order of American Knights aimed to "overthrow the Federal Government," create "a Northwestern Confederacy," and aid in the election of a Democratic president. Colonel John P. Sanderson, author of the exposé, claimed that Clement L. Vallandigham commanded the northern half of the serpentine society and that Confederate General Sterling Price headed the southern half.[58]

Vallandigham, viewing Sanderson's handiwork as pure poppycock, refused to dignify the story with any comments. His Democratic colleagues, however, turned their wrath upon the storyteller and his revelations. They characterized the report, which Republican newspapers broadcast over the country, as "pure humbuggery" and "a fantasy full of contradictions and inconsistencies." "A greater lot of trash and falsehood," wrote one indignant Democratic editor, "was never concocted for the telegraph wires. It is one of the old 'Lincoln dodges' to affect the Chicago Convention and elevate the falling stock of the administration party."[59]

While denying the O.A.K. revelations, the Democrats set their sights on the Chicago convention. Vallandigham and other Peace Democrats gloried in the ever-growing peace movement, hoping to draft a propeace platform and nominate a peace candidate. The heady wine misled them to believe their dream might become a reality.

[57] John P. Sanderson, "Report," 22 June 1864, Sanderson Papers. This manuscript varies slightly from the draft in the Records of the Office of the Judge Advocate General, National Archives. The latter appears in *Official Records*, ser. 2, 7: 314-36.

[58] Space does not allow extensive treatment of this strange story, which Sanderson concocted out of a few facts and much conjecture. An account of the exposé is found in Frank L. Klement, *The Copperheads in the Middle West* (Chicago, 1960), pp. 175-87.

[59] *Dayton Daily Empire*, 29 July 1864; *Detroit Free Press*, 2 August 1864; *Chicago Times*, 30 July 1864; *New York Journal of Commerce* (n.d.), clipping in the Sanderson Papers.

18

THE DEMOCRATIC NATIONAL CONVENTION
AND THE ELECTION OF 1864

DEMOCRATS HAD EVERY REASON to be optimistic during the dog days of August 1864. Union battle losses from January to August stunned the North, nurtured both the peace crusade and defeatism, and gave Democrats new rays of hope. Secretary of State Seward candidly told Lincoln that he could not be reelected, and others close to the president expressed the same fear. Greeley, whose views changed with his moods, headed an abortive Republican movement to shove Lincoln aside and put a prominent general in his stead on the presidential ticket. Caught up in the gloom surrounding him, Lincoln wrote that famous memorandum of August 23, supposing that he would not be reelected and promising to cooperate with the president-elect.

Samuel Cox, meanwhile, worked night and day to convince Midwestern Democrats that McClellan had the best chance to gain the nomination and defeat Lincoln. Cox, McClellan's "chief manager," was so successful in his efforts that astute observers conceded that the aspiring general had the nomination in hand.

Although he was personally indebted to Cox, Vallandigham and other Peace Democrats refused to jump aboard McClellan's bandwagon. The onetime exile spoke at a Dayton "peace rally" at which he publicly stated his opposition to McClellan and demanded that a "peace man" be nominated in Chicago. If McClellan gained the presidency, Vallandigham said, the war would drag on and more blood would be shed. Still advocating peace *and* reunion, he hoped peace petitions signed by two million Americans would be placed on Lincoln's desk.[1]

Vallandigham also felt bold enough to leave the confines of Dayton and take a train trip to New York. He shared the platform at a Syracuse peace rally with Fernando Wood of New York City. Both made a public plea that Democrats nominate a peace man at Chicago.[2] Wood promised Vallandigham that he would stop in Dayton on his way to the Democratic National Convention.

When Wood arrived in Dayton on August 24, Vallandigham's friends and followers gave him a "grand reception" at the depot and turned out *en masse* for the rally that evening. Mixing history and conjecture, Wood made a good case for conciliation and reunion. He must have spoken convincingly, for next day one of Vallandigham's young admirers wrote, "You may rely upon it that the masses of the people are tired of the war and want it stopped at once *on the best terms we can get*. Whoever is nominated at Chicago must stand on the platform of an armistice and Convention of the States for the settlement of all difficult questions—otherwise there will be a fourth candidate [Frémont was still in the field] who will be elected. The people have at length become appalled and disgusted with blood and carnage and demand cessation."[3] Evidently many Peace Democrats, afflicted with defeatism, had a way of deceiving themselves and misjudging the public mood.

Vallandigham and Wood entrained for Chicago on August 26 to attend their party's national convention. They found the "Windy City" seething with excitement; gamblers were giving four-to-one odds that McClellan would gain the nomination on the first ballot. Each faction employed strategy to further its goals. War Democrats held a preconvention caucus, usurping the name "Conservative Union National Convention" for their gathering, and recommended the nomination of McClellan. Peace Democrats organized some preconvention peace rallies which featured prominent antiwar speakers. Both Vallandigham and Wood had a chance to air their views.

The Daytonian, introduced as "the Honorable Exile and Patriot," proved he had not forgotten how to persuade an audience and gain their applause. First he lauded the historic role of the Democracy in America. Then he attacked the Lincoln administration, reciting its sins. He had returned from exile,

[1] Thomas O. Lowe to his brother William, 14 August 1864, Thomas O. Lowe Papers, Dayton and Montgomery County Public Library; *Dayton Daily Journal*, 15 August 1864.

[2] *Dayton Daily Empire*, 17 August 1864.

[3] Thomas O. Lowe to his brother William, 25 August 1864, Lowe Papers.

he said, to claim his rights. Next he spoke at length on the peace-and-compromise theme, criticizing those who had misrepresented his views. Finally, he felt compelled to talk again about the Sons of Liberty and convince his audience that its purpose was to counteract the Union League, protect rights which Lincoln's "minions" and "the reign of terror" threatened, and elect Democrats to office. Yes, the order was involved in a "conspiracy" as Republican propagandists charged, but this "conspiracy" consisted of no more than using the ballot boxes to defeat the administration. The leader of that "conspiracy," Vallandigham added with a twinkle in his eye, would be made known when the Democratic National Convention selected its presidential candidate.[4]

Political maneuvering characterized the evening of August 28. Cox visited as many delegations as he could, trying to convince or cajole members to support McClellan. The divided New York delegation, meeting in caucus, debated the general's candidacy long after midnight. Peace Democrats gathered informally in Vallandigham's room; the door was never locked and friends and delegates walked in and out constantly. Such Ohioans as Chris Hughes of Hamilton, Dr. Edson B. Olds of Lancaster, and Alexander Long of Cincinnati wanted Peace Democrats to support Governor Horatio Seymour of New York even though he had publicly endorsed McClellan. Several viewed Thomas Seymour of Connecticut as a possibility although no one expected he could effectively challenge McClellan for the nomination. Other callers, including Harrison H. Dodd of Indiana and S. Corning Judd of Illinois, talked of making the Sons of Liberty a potent political force. Later, propagandists characterized this informal, open meeting in Vallandigham's room as a conclave of the Sons of Liberty to promote a conspiracy. Even General Heintzelman, commanding the Northern Department, called at Vallandigham's room to visit with Democratic leaders, smoke cigars, and engage in political banter.[5]

Ill-found rumors made the rounds. One was that Peace Democrats would bolt the convention if McClellan gained the nomina-

---

[4] *Chicago Times*, 27, 28 August 1864; *Dayton Daily Empire*, 27 August 1864.
[5] Entries of 27-29 August 1864 in "Diary," and 30-31 August, 1 September 1864 in "Journal," Samuel P. Heintzelman Papers, Library of Congress.

tion. Another was that treason-minded Democrats might use the Chicago convention as a means or opportunity to establish a "Northwest Confederacy"—the O.A.K. exposé of July contributed considerably toward convincing the credulous that many Democrats conspired behind locked doors.

The meeting in Vallandigham's room broke up rather belatedly. It proved that the Sons of Liberty was little more than a paper organization and that Vallandigham, despite a year spent in exile, had a host of friends and sympathizers. And it proved that Peace Democrats were disorganized and divided, lacking a national leader. The meeting broke up without a single resolution being adopted or a single peace candidate endorsed.[6]

Next morning the forty-two Ohio delegates met in caucus. They named Chris Hughes to represent Ohio on the Committee on Organization and Vallandigham to represent the state on the Committee on Resolutions. These two appointments were clear concessions to the peace men. Cox spoke out boldly for McClellan. Many dissented. Some of the dissenters said they favored Horatio Seymour despite his forthright statement that he was not a candidate. Long and Olds spoke out in behalf of Thomas Seymour. After a round of argument, the chairman called for a preferential poll. The tally indicated that 17 favored McClellan, 4, Horatio Seymour, and 21 (including Vallandigham), Thomas Seymour. Cox expressed his disappointment, both at the lack of McClellan support and at the intensity of peace sentiments in Ohio. The caucus adjourned, but Cox badgered Vallandigham and insisted he promise support of the convention's nominee, whoever it might be. In time, Cox and Samuel L. M. Barlow gained such a private pledge from both Vallandigham and Wood, in return for reasonable concessions regarding the party platform.[7] It was easier to make the bargain, though, than to carry it out.

After Vallandigham and Wood returned to their quarters at the Sherman House, a crowd gathered outside and called for a speech. The two stepped out on a balcony and each spoke briefly. Vallandigham demanded that the party platform include

[6] Testimony of Vallandigham before the Cincinnati Military Commission, 29 March 1865, published in the *Cincinnati Daily Enquirer,* 30 March 1865.

[7] *Dayton Daily Empire,* 29 August 1864; Barlow to Manton Marble, 21 August 1864, and Cox to Marble, 7 August 1864, Manton Marble Papers, Library of Congress.

a peace-and-compromise plank and pledged himself to support the nominee of the convention. Wood parroted what Vallandigham had said. Perhaps Cox was right when he characterized Peace Democrats as the "fiercest disciplinarians" whose loyalty to party would make them swallow any medicine, no matter how bitter it might be.[8]

Late in the morning, delegates and visitors drifted over to the convention hall, soon filled to overflowing. Vallandigham received considerable applause as he walked down the aisle toward his seat. He mixed and talked with other members of the Ohio delegation.

At twelve-thirty the temporary chairman banged his gavel for order. After some of the preliminaries, Cox asked that Amos Kendall, a Democrat whose political prominence dated back to Jackson's day, be given permission to report on the recommendations of the "Conservative Union National Convention" which had met several days earlier. When Kendall read the resolution recommending McClellan's nomination, many delegates stamped their feet and tried to stampede the convention in the general's favor. Cox, pleased with the noise and cheers, cleverly and quickly moved that Kendall's report be referred to the Committee on Resolutions.

The Kendall-Cox stratagem caught Vallandigham and the peace men by surprise. After a very brief huddle, Dr. Edson B. Olds protested against the technique used in bringing McClellan's name forward before the convention was formally organized. He said that "another body," Democrats organized as the Sons of Liberty, then "in session in Chicago," would also have a recommendation to make to the convention. If Kendall's resolution went into the minutes, so should the recommendation of the Sons of Liberty—even though the "communication" from that body was neither ready nor formalized. Pressed for further information, Dr. Olds, caught bluffing, retreated and said he would drop the matter.[9]

While Horatio Seymour, who had been chosen to preside over the convention, was making the opening speech, the Committee

---

[8] Cox to Barlow, 21 November 1863, Samuel L. M. Barlow Papers, Henry E. Huntington Library, San Marino, California; *Dayton Daily Empire*, 30 August 1864.
[9] *Chicago Times*, 30, 31 August 1864; *Dayton Daily Empire*, 29, 30 August 1864.

on Resolutions held its organizational meeting in a side-room. James Guthrie of Kentucky gained the chairmanship, getting twelve votes to Vallandigham's eight, with three scattering. Guthrie asked members to submit proposals for the platform, then the committee recessed and its members filed back into the main hall to hear the rest of Seymour's address.

After the applause ceased, Seymour asked Guthrie when his committee expected to have its report ready. Guthrie answered that he expected the committee would finish its work before four o'clock and that "industry" and "harmony" would bear early fruit. Vallandigham arose to disagree, emphasizing that the committee faced a difficult assignment. Perhaps it would be best, the dissenter added, if the convention did not meet again until next morning. Guthrie, fearful that the anti-McClellan forces might use the overnight recess to advantage, insisted that his committee should and would finish its work by four o'clock. Vallandigham said no more, but he and other antiwar men recognized that the pro-McClellan crew was using urgency as an ally.

Guthrie then asked the members of the Committee on Resolutions to follow him to the assigned room. Walking side by side, Guthrie and Vallandigham led the other members down the aisle and through the rear door of the main hall. Guthrie wasted no time in putting his committee to work. Since the committee membership of twenty-three might slow down progress, Guthrie suggested that he name a subcommittee of seven to get the job done, and named Vallandigham to this subcommittee.

Most of the resolutions were routine and produced little disagreement. Only one, the so-called Second Resolution, tested the temper of the subcommittee. This resolution, framed by Vallandigham and Dr. John McElwee, declared that the Lincoln administration had failed to restore the Union by "the experiment of war" and that "justice, humanity, liberty, and public welfare" necessitated making "immediate efforts . . . for a cessation of hostilities, with a view to an ultimate convention of the States." It was a watered down version of Vallandigham's peace-compromise-reunion views. William Cassidy, editor of the *Albany Argus* and an avowed McClellan man, led the attack upon Vallandigham's resolution. Others had their say, some for and others against the controversial plank. In the end Vallandigham's obstinacy, abetted by able arguments, carried the questionable resolution through the subcommittee—it was endorsed by a majority vote.

Vallandigham faced a more difficult task in convincing the twenty-three-member Committee on Resolutions to accept his handiwork. Cassidy again led the fight against the Second Resolution, providing a "most desperate [and] persistent opposition." He offered several substitutes, always gaining the support of several other McClellan men. But none of the substitutes received more than three votes. Time and again, Vallandigham valiantly defended his resolution. He succeeded in carrying it through the full committee as he had earlier pushed it through the subcommittee. He had, in effect, scored a personal triumph.[10]

When the convention reassembled at four o'clock, Seymour called upon the chairman of the Committee on Resolutions to present the party's platform. Guthrie arose to read the resolutions. The first, which lauded the Constitution and asked that it be a "guidepost" for all executive and legislative action, brought nods of approval from the hushed assemblage. Vallandigham's so-called Second Resolution, however, produced considerable audible dissent and angered some McClellan supporters. Guthrie, ignoring the dissension, finished reading the resolutions.

Actually, Vallandigham's peace plank pleased neither the War Democrats nor the peace-at-any-price men. Alexander Long, one of the best known of the latter group, gained the floor and condemned the Second Resolution, saying it was too vague and too compromising. He asked for a more forthright statement, one that would demand an immediate cessation of hostilities, the recognition of the Southern confederacy, and the incorporation of the Virginia Resolves of 1798 into the party platform. He then offered a substitute resolution expressing his own extreme views. War Democrats, who thought the Second Resolution already too much of a concession to the peace men, had to defend a plank they did not really favor lest Long's proposal prevail. Samuel Cox, a master of parliamentary maneuvers, cut

---

[10] C.L.V. to editor of the *New York News,* 22 October 1864, published in *Dayton Daily Empire,* 29 October 1864; *Chicago Times,* 28-31 August, 1 September 1864; *Missouri Republican* (St. Louis), 28-31 August, 2 September 1864.

off debate and prevented a vote on Long's substitute measure. The presiding officer then put all of the resolutions which Guthrie had read to a voice vote. Only four delegates (Long was one of them) cast negative ballots against the resolutions which came to be known as the Chicago Platform. Vallandigham's controversial peace plank thus won a reluctant acceptance, although it pleased neither the War Democrats, such as August Belmont and Manton Marble, nor the extreme peace men of the stripe of Alexander Long, William M. Corry, or Samuel Medary of the *Crisis*. Even the mildest war men viewed Vallandigham's peace plank as left of center.[11]

With the platform out of the way, the delegates turned to the task of naming their presidential candidate. As the clerk called the roll of the states, it was obvious that McClellan had gained strength. Astute observers awaited the announcement of Ohio's forty-two votes: McClellan, 17; Thomas Seymour, 21 (including Vallandigham's); and Horatio Seymour, 4.

Later, as McClellan's vote approached the majority mark, Ohio asked for recognition and an opportunity to change her vote. Vallandigham and other realistic delegates had decided to bow to the inevitable and put expediency above principle. Ohio's revised vote read: McClellan, 30 (including Vallandigham's), and Thomas Seymour, 12. Scattered applause greeted the announcement, while Long and the extremists groaned.

When all the votes were in, Vallandigham capped his fence-straddling by moving that McClellan's nomination be declared unanimous. The motion carried in spite of the protests of Long, Corry and several other peace-at-any-price delegates. Then the delegates completed their work by naming George H. Pendleton, an Ohio peace man, as the vice-presidential nominee, another sop thrown to the Vallandigham faction. The newspaperman who had predicted that the Democratic convention would "nominate a Peace Democrat on the war platform, or a War Democrat on a peace platform"[12] proved to be a good prophet.

McClellan's nomination pleased most of the delegates, except the few of the Alexander Long stamp. "Everybody," one dele-

---

[11] *Missouri Republican,* 31 August 1864; *Dayton Daily Empire,* 31 August 1864.
[12] Noah Brooks, *Washington in Lincoln's Time* (New York, 1895), p. 180; Samuel Cox to Manton Marble, 6 September 1864, Marble Papers.

gate recorded in his diary, "seems satisfied."[13] But there was considerably less enthusiasm for the Chicago Platform. Vallandigham's Second Resolution chilled the optimism and ardor of the "conscientious War Democrats," many of whom viewed it as a millstone around McClellan's neck. Nevertheless, the delegates left for home hoping that McClellan's star was rising and Lincoln's setting.

As the Democratic presidential nominee, McClellan found that a political campaign was beset by as many problems as a military one. He disapproved of the peace plank in the Chicago Platform, regarded it as a barrier to his election, and listened to War Democrats who urged him to repudiate it when accepting the nomination.[14]

When Vallandigham heard rumors of the advice McClellan was receiving, he seized his pen to exhort the general not to acquiesce. "Do not listen to your Eastern friends, who, in an evil hour, may advise you to *insinuate* even a little war in your letter of acceptance," Vallandigham begged. For good measure he added a threat, "If anything implying war is presented, two hundred thousand men in the West will withhold their support, and may go further still."[15] Did he mean that Peace Democrats might then nominate their own candidate?

McClellan chose to ignore Vallandigham's advice as well as his threat. In his letter of acceptance he threw the peace plank overboard and raised a war flag over the pilot house. Most Democratic editors expressed satisfaction with "Little Mac's" letter, some declaring that it was composed of noble ideas, golden words, and stirring phrases—"beautiful and appropriate."[16]

Alexander Long and other ultras, however, were furious. A handful of dissidents sponsored a meeting in Cincinnati in October to consider launching a new party with a peace platform

13 Entry of 1 September 1864, "Diary, 1864," George B. Smith Papers, State Historical Society of Wisconsin, Madison.

14 William H. Aspinwall to McClellan, 4 September 1864, and George T. Curtis to McClellan, 1 September 1864, George B. McClellan Papers, Library of Congress; Col. Durbin Ward to Samuel S. Cox, 2 August 1864, Samuel S. Cox Papers (microfilm), Hayes Memorial Library, Fremont, Ohio.

15 4 September 1864, McClellan Papers.

16 Entry of 9 September 1864, "Diary, 1864," Smith Papers; *New York World*, 8 September 1864. See Charles R. Wilson, "McClellan's Changing Views on the Peace Plank of 1864," *American Historical Review* 38 (April 1933): 498-510.

and a peace candidate. The movement fizzled, but several of the malcontents went home vowing to sit out the campaign. Samuel Medary typified the Peace Democrats who complained that the nomination of McClellan was "a sell-out" to Wall Street and the Rothchilds and the revised platform a "fraudulent sale," not binding in law.[17]

McClellan's letter of acceptance proved especially embarrassing to Vallandigham. After returning from Chicago, he had spoken at two McClellan ratification rallies, one in Dayton, one in Hamilton. At each he had dwelt at length on the Chicago Platform and explained that the alternative to McClellan would be four more years of taxation, confiscation, conscription, and despotism. It was evident, however, that Vallandigham felt uneasy about boosting McClellan while preaching peace.

Shortly after this, the telegraphic wires carried the news that McClellan had repudiated the peace plank. The report struck Vallandigham like a thunderbolt. Not only had "Little Mac" discarded Vallandigham's peace plank, but he had also disregarded his personal advice. Furious and frustrated, Vallandigham engaged in some "tall cussing." He told Cox he had been hoodwinked and insulted. He would not raise a finger in McClellan's behalf. In fact, he would cancel all of his speaking dates and thus repay McClellan for the public insult.[18]

Washington McLean, the "big boss" of the Hamilton County Democracy and co-owner of the *Cincinnati Enquirer*, personally intervened to get the sulking Daytonian out of his tent and back in the battle line. He convinced Vallandigham to come down to Cincinnati on September 10 to meet with some of "the party faithful." Still angry at McClellan, Vallandigham bluntly told the meeting that he had already cancelled all his speaking engagements scheduled by the Democratic State Central Committee. Members of McLean's clan tried to reason with Vallandigham, but to no avail—he remained caustic, critical, and belligerent. In answer to a plea of cooperation, he threatened to bolt the party, joining Medary and Long on the sidelines. Someone in the group cut the dissenter short with the bald

[17] *Crisis* (Columbus), 8 September 1864.
[18] Cox to Manton Marble, 6 September 1864, Marble Papers; *Dayton Daily Journal*, 10 September 1864; *Dayton Daily Empire*, 7, 9 September 1864.

assertion that a Vallandigham-led bolt would help the party and enhance McClellan's election chances—it would purge the party of its evil genius. Vallandigham fumed, then threatened to take the stump against McClellan. One of the quick-witted, sharp-tongued listeners offered to pay Vallandigham's expenses if he carried out his threat, for such action would aid the Democratic party and McClellan's candidacy. Just when it seemed that the meeting might blow up, Washington McLean deftly applied some salve to Vallandigham's wounds. Before the evening ended, the ruffled peacock agreed to support the McClellan-Pendleton ticket. Jubilant, McLean reported his success in effecting a rapprochement to Manton Marble of the *New York World* in a terse telegram: "Difficulties all arranged. Vallandigham all right. Have no fears."[19]

In mid-September, George H. Pendleton, the vice-presidential nominee, quietly slipped into Dayton to visit Vallandigham and verify McLean's assumption. Yes, the onetime exile stated, he would speak out openly for McClellan when the opportunity presented itself, despite injured pride and the "unpalatable letter of acceptance."

To prove his conversion to the cause, Vallandigham arranged for a serenade for his house-guest. The ever-serving *Dayton Empire* urged Democrats to participate in the rally. In the evening a good-sized crowd gathered at the Vallandigham residence and sent up a chant for Pendleton. The distinguished visitor, with his smiling host at his side, appeared at the front door. Pendleton spoke briefly, thanking the serenaders for their "sentiment" and "hospitality." Pendleton then called upon his host to speak, giving the author of the peace plank a chance to profess publicly his loyalty to the party and its official nominees.

It was a rather awkward situation for Vallandigham. Some in the audience had heard him condemn McClellan several days earlier, even promising not to lift a finger in behalf of the nominee. He justified his support with such phrases as "party loyalty" and "practical necessity." He praised the Chicago Platform, saying it still expressed his true sentiments. Then he turned to the main theme of his talk—the historic role of the

19 13 September 1864, Marble Papers.

Democratic party in the nation's history. He laid tributes to Thomas Jefferson, Andrew Jackson, and Stephen A. Douglas on the Democratic altar. He eulogized the party's principles, its record, and its history. He exhorted his fellow Democrats to be faithful to their party, too, and prayed that God might give the Democracy success at the polls in November.[20]

Republican editors and cartoonists had a field day caricaturing Vallandigham's dilemma. Dayton Republicans, especially, enjoyed their fellow townsman's discomfiture. The caustic editor of the *Dayton Journal* ridiculed him for "selling out" his principles under "pressure"—Vallandigham had "crawled upon his belly" like a snake and had "eaten dirt at McClellan's feet" like a worm.[21]

During the remaining days of September, Vallandigham gave half a dozen speeches in Ohio for the McClellan-Pendleton ticket, so that McLean could not accuse him of sulking in his tent. Unsavory incidents occurred frequently. In some places, local War Democrats shied away from him. In others, local Republican rowdies or furloughed soldiers threatened, intimidated, and insulted him or disrupted rallies while Vallandigham was speaking. At Sydney, for example, a regiment of soldiers from a nearby camp lined the road and gave "three hefty groans" when Vallandigham, at the head of a Democratic procession, passed by.[22]

During the closing weeks of September the Democratic tidal wave began to ebb. Republicans healed their party schism; John C. Frémont withdrew from the presidential sweepstakes as a result of a backstage bargain.[23] Union military victories undermined defeatism and made the Lincoln administration respectable again. "The success of Sherman at Atlanta, following on that of Farragut at Mobile," Gideon Welles wrote in his diary, "has very much discomposed the opposition."[24] General Sheridan contributed two victories. "Phil Sheridan has made a speech in

---

[20] *Dayton Daily Empire,* 16 September 1864.

[21] *Dayton Daily Journal,* 17 September 1864.

[22] *Dayton Daily Empire,* 24 September 1864. The refusal of John Hough James to share a platform with C.L.V. is related in William E. and Ophia D. Smith, *Buckeye Titan* (Cincinnati, 1953), p. 516.

[23] Zachariah Chandler to his wife, 24 September 1864, Zachariah Chandler Papers, Library of Congress.

[24] Howard K. Beale, ed., *Diary of Gideon Welles: Secretary of the Navy under Lincoln and Johnson,* 3 vols. (New York, 1960), 2:140.

the Shenandoah Valley," one jubilant Republican wrote, "more powerful and valuable to the Union cause than all the stumpers in the Republic can make—our prospects are everywhere heightening."[25] Economic prosperity, "so enormous as to challenge disbelief," also helped quash discontent. Bounteous crops and high farm prices brought smiles back to the faces of Midwestern farmers. Prosperity served as "the lance of Achilles, healing by its touch the wounds of war and desolation." "Nothing is strange," an English newspaperman noted, "nothing is unusual, nothing is unconstitutional, nothing is wicked to people who are prospering upon the war."[26]

Encouraged, Republican editors and orators attacked McClellan, Vallandigham, and the Democracy with new vigor. They repeated old lies and invented new ones. Horace Greeley, for example, averred that the Chicago Platform was "concocted by Rebels in Richmond, . . . agreed to by disloyal politicians at the North in a conference with Rebels at Niagara Falls," and "taken to Chicago and adopted by a convention expressly chosen to adopt it."[27] One respected Republican editor claimed that Jefferson Davis had much to do with the writing of the platform,[28] while others embroidered the tale by claiming that Vallandigham had helped Davis write the cursed document while he was in exile in the Confederacy.[29]

Vallandigham, of course, came in for more than his fair share of the abuse. Some Republican speakers railed against Vallandigham more than against McClellan. Was not a vote for McClellan really a vote for Vallandigham, anarchy, and treason? One wag suggested that Vallandigham would become secretary of war if McClellan won the presidency. A liar named Émile Boulier claimed he had seen Vallandigham in Richmond, closeted with Jeff Davis and other rebel leaders and pledging himself to the Confederate cause. Boulier's "Startling Revelations" circulated as propaganda and made the headlines in most Republican newspapers. The popularity of Boulier's tall tale prompted

25 James A. Garfield to his wife, 23 September 1864, James A. Garfield Papers, Library of Congress.
26 William H. Russell, in *London Times*, 17 March, 24 September 1864.
27 *New York Tribune*, 22 September 1864.
28 *Boston Daily Journal*, 29 September 1864.
29 *Dayton Daily Journal*, 1 September 1864.

Vallandigham to write an open letter and nail Boulier's hide to the wall. "I did not see Jefferson Davis, Seddon, or Benjamin, or any other member of the Southern Cabinet," the onetime exile wrote in a card published in the *Cincinnati Enquirer*. "I was never 'closeted' with any of them anywhere, never was a visitor or had any 'conferences' with Mr. Benjamin, and in short, *was not in Richmond at all*—as the fellow asserts."[30]

Republican editors and orators ignored Vallandigham's denials. They were using treason as a campaign issue and gaining popular support. Traitorous blood, one imaginative Republican asserted, flowed in McClellan's as well as Vallandigham's veins. They were brother traitors, the only difference being that the Daytonian's treason was "more open and noisy"; McClellan's was "just as real and earnest."[31]

The first election tests occurred in early October, for half a dozen states held gubernatorial and congressional contests at that time. Republicans won every test, disheartening Democrats everywhere. In Ohio, Samuel Cox lost his bid for reelection. "It is evident," wrote one despairing Democrat, "that there is no use in trying to save Ohio [in the presidential contest]."[32]

Heartened by the October election returns, Republicans intensified their effort to keep McClellan out of the White House. Propaganda agencies such as the Union Congressional Committee and the Loyal Publication Society ground out new campaign documents. Even the secretary of war had a hand in the production of a propaganda piece. Judge Advocate General Joseph Holt, on instructions from Edwin M. Stanton, investigated "subversive secret societies" and produced a report that linked the Sons of Liberty and the Order of American Knights to perfidy and treason: encouraging the peace movement in the North,

[30] Émile Boulier to "Members of the Union League, Philadelphia" [1864], in William P. Palmer Papers, Western Reserve Historical Society, Cleveland; report, Clement C. Clay to Hon. Judah P. Benjamin, 12 September 1864, published in *Official Records*, ser. 4, 3:637-38; *Dayton Daily Journal*, 24 September 1864; C.L.V. to editors of the *Cincinnati Daily Enquirer*, 21 September 1864, published 24 September.

[31] Gerritt Smith, *Gerritt Smith on McClellan's Nomination and Acceptance* (New York: Loyal Publication Society, 1864), p. 12; George H. Otis to Lucius Fairchild, 10 September 1864, Lucius Fairchild Papers, State Historical Society of Wisconsin, Madison. Also see William Frank Zornow, "Treason as a Campaign Issue in the Re-election of Lincoln," *Abraham Lincoln Quarterly* 5 (June 1949): 348-63.

[32] Samuel L. M. Barlow to Cox, 15 October 1864, Cox Papers.

abetting Southern independence, resisting the draft, and establishing a "Northwest Confederacy." Vallandigham, Holt insisted, commanded the Northern half of the subversive organization while General Sterling Price headed the Southern half. Although Holt's report borrowed heavily from Sanderson's exposé of the Order of American Knights, he succeeded in dragging McClellan's name into his fairy tale. He ended his 14,000-word report with a literary flourish: "Judea produced but one Judas Iscariot, and Rome, from the sinks of her demoralization, produced but one Cataline; and yet, as events prove, there has arisen in our land an entire brood of traitors, all animated by the same parricidal spirit, and all struggling with the same ruthless malignity for the dismemberment of the Union."[33]

Holt's handiwork, published as a Republican campaign document,[34] damaged McClellan's presidential ambitions. It also maligned Vallandigham, portraying him as a "conspirator" and "traitor." Vallandigham felt compelled to make explanations and denials. In two public speeches he talked at length about the Sons of Liberty and its objectives as he understood them. Its aims, he said, were to counteract the Union Leagues, to "promote Jeffersonian doctrine," and to "protect individual rights." It was, he added, "a militant Democratic group" within the great national [Democratic] party" and he compared it to the Sons of Liberty of pre-Revolutionary War days.[35]

Vallandigham also wrote the editor of the *New York News* to debunk Holt's composition and some fantastic comments which Greeley had published in the *New York Tribune:* "As to the charges of 'conspiracy' set forth in Judge Advocate Holt's pamphlet and the eleven specifications summed up by Horace Greeley, I have only to say that, as far as I am concerned, they are absolute falsehoods and fabrications from beginning to end. They are false in the aggregate, and false in detail. More than that, they are [as] preposterous and ridiculous as they are without foundation; and all this Mr. Judge Advocate Holt . . . and Mr.

[33] Report, Joseph Holt to Edwin M. Stanton, 8 October 1864, published in *Official Records,* ser. 2, 7: 930-53.
[34] *Report of the Judge Advocate General on "The Order of American Knights," alias "The Sons of Liberty": A Western Conspiracy in Aid of the Southern Rebellion* (Washington: Union Congressional Committee, 1864).
[35] *Chicago Times,* 22 October 1864; *Dayton Daily Empire,* 7 November 1864.

Horace Greeley know very well."[36] In a large measure, Vallandigham was correct. The report was compounded of lies, conjecture and political malignancy, designed solely to discredit Vallandigham and McClellan and help reelect Lincoln. Democratic editors joined Vallandigham in denouncing Holt's report. They characterized the author as "a deliberate and atrocious liar," "a modern Titus Oates," and "a man who is ready to commit any folly to please his employer." They labeled his report "a conglomeration of falsehoods," "a precious pottage cooked in the cauldron of his imagination," "an electioneering document," and "a cold-blooded piece of campaign propaganda, printed and circulated at public expense."[37] They were right on most counts, but their denials and disapprovals had little effect either in checking the circulation of Holt's report or in undermining public credulity as to its contents. "The exposé of the Sons of Liberty," wrote a jubilant Republican, "is tearing the ranks of the Democracy all to flinders. McClellan stock is not quoted at all."[38]

Democrats who feared the worst from the November 8 election returns found their fears realized. Lincoln defeated McClellan by 400,000 votes and grabbed 212 electoral votes to McClellan's 21. Lincoln received the electoral vote of every Northern state, losing only the border states of Kentucky, Delaware, and New Jersey, although his margin in New York State was less than 7,000 votes out of 730,000 cast.

Democrats held election post-mortems, tried to console each other, and grasped at straws. Some blamed their defeat upon fraud, forgeries, threats, and intimidation. Others suggested that "blind fanaticism," stirred up by Republican propaganda, prevented the people from knowing the truth. Men like Alexander Long blamed party delegates for ignoring the wishes of the people who wanted peace, nominating McClellan rather than a Peace Democrat. Still others believed that Vallandigham's

[36] 22 October 1864, undated clipping in "O.A.K. Scrapbook," John P. Sanderson Papers, Ohio Historical Society. The letter was published in the *Dayton Daily Empire*, 29 October 1864.

[37] *Cincinnati Daily Enquirer*, 16, 20 October 1864; *Detroit Free Press*, 23 October 1864; *Illinois State Register* (Springfield), 18, 21 October 1864.

[38] William H. H. Terrell to John T. Wilder, 6 October 1864, John T. Wilder Papers, Indiana Division, Indiana State Library.

presence at the Democratic National Convention had stigmatized the party and given Republicans a chance to make treason a campaign issue. Those looking for a scapegoat pointed their fingers in Vallandigham's direction.

Chastized but not chastened by the election returns, Vallandigham returned to his law practice. He nevertheless retained his interest in national affairs. Generally, he backed Lincoln in his quarrel with radical Republicans over reconstruction policy. He did not, however, favor the Thirteenth Amendment, viewing it as another step toward centralization of the government and "another deadly blow at the rights solemnly reserved to the States."[39]

Grant's defeat of Lee's army and the capture of Richmond forced Vallandigham to give up his stubbornly held views of compromise-and-peace. C.L.V. then wrote to Greeley, urging him to take the lead in promoting a liberal reconstruction policy, one free of confiscation, execution, and subjugation. A vindictive policy, Vallandigham asserted, would bring "ages of mischief and agitation."[40]

For once, Vallandigham and Lincoln saw eye to eye on an issue. Lincoln's advocacy of a moderate reconstruction policy made him grow in Vallandigham's esteem. Suddenly, like an electric shock, the news that Lincoln had been assassinated reached Dayton. Vallandigham characterized the act as "the worst public calamity which could have befallen the country." He praised Lincoln's "liberal and conciliatory" reconstruction policy. And he said that those who did not shudder because of "the most horrible of all crimes" were really "no better than the assassin."[41]

Midway in the war Vallandigham had viewed Lincoln as a blind partisan and had even convinced himself that Lincoln sought the despot's scepter. Yet before the war's end he had gained some respect for the president. Certainly Lincoln's feud with the radical Republicans and his advocacy of a reasonable reconstruction policy convinced the Dayton Democrat that Lincoln was not the evil genius he had pictured him to be.

[39] Dayton Daily Empire, 25 January 1865.
[40] 11 April 1865, Horace Greeley Papers, New York Public Library.
[41] Dayton Daily Empire, 16 April 1865.

Perhaps the fact that Lincoln had not ordered his rearrest affected Vallandigham's point of view. The public's reaction to the assassination certainly mellowed and molded his once rigid anti-Lincoln views. C.L.V.'s persistent belief that time would vindicate him, however, prevented him from accepting the contention that the Civil War transformed Lincoln the politician into Lincoln the statesman. Nor could he agree with the prophecy, written by a radical Republican critic of the president: "This murder, this oozing blood . . . opens to him immortality."[42]

[42] Count Adam Gurowski, *Diary . . . from March 4, 1861, to November 10, 1865*, 3 vols. (Washington, 1862-1866), 3:398.

19

STORMY PETREL
OF THE POSTWAR YEARS

LEE'S SURRENDER AND Lincoln's assassination did not bring an end to the Civil War era. The fruits of the war appeared on the mangled tree of reconstruction as the country tried to solve problems arising from the fratricidal conflict. Clement L. Vallandigham was as controversial a figure during the reconstruction era as he had been during the war years. His efforts to attain vindication and a seat in the United States Senate were adversely affected by his wartime record and the Republican practice of "waving the bloody shirt." Personal animosities which had developed during the war years plagued him during the reconstruction era and helped to make him the stormy petrel of Ohio politics.

Vallandigham had strong convictions in regard to reconstruction policy and he presented them publicly at every opportunity. He wanted the Southern states brought back into the Union without rancor or revenge, without penalties or punishment, without test-oaths and trials for treason. He did not want an army dictatorship imposed upon the South, nor years of probation before normality prevailed. He accepted emancipation as a *fait accompli,* but he did not want the newly freed to have any political and social rights. He abhorred the doctrine of "Negro equality" as much during the reconstruction years as he had during the war, proving he was still a racist, for he advocated rights for the white man which he would deny the black man.[1]

At various party rallies or public meetings Vallandigham urged his fellow Democrats to give full support to President Johnson's reconstruction policies, regarding them as moderate and reasonable. He shuddered at the demands of radical Republicans, for he believed it a simple choice between order and chaos, moderation and malevolence, reunion and continued conflict.[2]

He played an important part in the Democratic State Convention of August 24, 1865. As temporary chairman, he had a chance to make a speech and he talked about reconstruction. Democrats were the true Unionists, he asserted, because they sought to readmit the Southern states quickly and quietly, without imposing undue penalties or causing undue suffering. After defending President Johnson, he restated his racist views—he opposed social and political rights for all blacks, whether they resided in Ohio or in the Southern states.[3] Later he endorsed the resolutions, tainted with racism,[4] which the convention adopted, and he applauded the selection of George W. Morgan as the party's gubernatorial candidate.

Vallandigham campaigned extensively for Morgan, a close friend of his boyhood days in New Lisbon. He recognized that Morgan's election and the selection of a Democratic legislature might further his political rehabilitation. Simply stated, Vallandigham wanted John Sherman's seat in the United States Senate, and that wish could not be realized if Republicans won the October elections. Not only did the onetime exile want the honor, but he craved the vindication the office would bring. He believed that political enemies had heaped "obloquy, persecution and wrong" upon him undeservedly and that a man of lesser character and fortitude would have broken under the "excessive pressures." His insatiable desire for the senate seat made him rationalize; he convinced himself that the Ohio Democracy owed him the honor.[5]

The election returns of October 10 doomed Morgan's hopes to serve his state as governor and deferred Vallandigham's desire to sit in the senate. The Republican-controlled state legislature, meeting in early January 1866, returned John Sherman to the

---

[1] C.L.V. to Horace Greeley, 20 April 1865, Horace Greeley Papers, New York Public Library; Vallandigham to Young Men's Democratic Association of Lancaster, Pennsylvania, 5 May 1865, published in *Dayton Daily Empire*, 24 May; *Dayton Daily Journal*, 8 June 1865.

[2] *Cleveland Herald* (n.d.), quoted in *Dayton Daily Journal*, 21 August 1865.

[3] *Daily Ohio Statesman* (Columbus), 25 August 1865.

[4] One resolution stated that the government ought to be run "by and for the white man" and that Negroes should be denied the right to vote both in Ohio and in the Southern states. Another resolution called upon the Ohio legislature to pass laws which would prevent or discourage Negroes from emigrating into Ohio.

[5] Vallandigham to James W. Wall, 25 November 1865, in Vallandigham Folder, New York Historical Society, New York City; *Dayton Daily Journal*, 8 October 1865.

senate for another six-year term. Vallandigham, consequently, had to reset his sights and aim for Ben Wade's seat. His chance of replacing Wade, of course, depended in part upon the election returns of 1867 as well as the support of his party's hierarchy.

As time passed by, national politics became more complex, more confused, and more emotional. President Johnson and the radical Republicans drifted farther apart; Johnson's veto of the Freedmen's Bureau Bill and the Civil Rights Bill widened the rift. Some of the president's supporters, such as Henry J. Raymond, editor of the *New York Times*, and James R. Doolittle, senator from Wisconsin, took steps to effect a coalition of conservatives, whether Republicans or Democrats. They arranged for a national convention in Philadelphia on August 15 to rally public support for President Johnson's reconstruction policies and affect the elections of October and November. The call for the convention, however, simply stated that its purpose was "to hold counsel together upon the state of the Union."

Ohio Democrats disagreed as to the desirability of sending delegates to the Philadelphia convention. Should they encourage the split developing within the Republican party? Would the Democracy be swallowed up in the fusion movement? Should not straight-laced Democrats boycott the Philadelphia meeting? After wrangling among themselves, Ohio Democrats, encouraged by Vallandigham, decided to endorse the election of delegates to Philadelphia.

The controversial Dayton Democrat actively sought to be named one of the two delegates from the Third Congressional District. Hugh J. Jewett and Lewis D. Campbell, on the other hand, openly opposed his selection. Jewett and Campbell claimed that Vallandigham had flirted with treason during the war, helping to taint the Democracy in the eyes of the nation. His very presence at Philadelphia, Campbell contended, would stigmatize the fusion movement and discredit the convention. Still claiming to be a Republican, Campbell insisted that C.L.V. watch the fusion movement from the sidelines. "We must *squelch* him," Campbell wrote to another conservative Republican, Orville H. Browning. "He means mischief. . . . He is a dangerous man and must be watched. His motto is 'rule or ruin'—particularly the ruin part. I know him well. He is as full of pure cussedness as an egg is of meat."[6] Evidently Campbell had not yet forgiven Vallandigham for depriving him of a seat in Congress eight years earlier and for preaching Copperhead doctrine during the war.

Yet C.L.V.'s strength in the party was such that his critics could not deny him a delegateship from the Third District. It was ironic that the fusionists of this district named Lewis D. Campbell as their second delegate. The two were strange bedfellows, neither having any personal respect for the other. Their political rivalry had degenerated into personal animosity bordering on contempt. Yet they traveled together to Philadelphia to boost Johnson's political stock, undermine radical Republican reconstruction policy, and serve conservative interests. The wheel of fortune took strange turns indeed!

Vallandigham had little opportunity to partake in political maneuvering on the eve of the Philadelphia convention. After arriving in the "City of Brotherly Love," he went to bed in his room at the Girard House, felled by a violent attack of dysentery, plus choleric symptoms. Later in the evening, however, he felt well enough to receive visitors. A steady stream of callers poured into his room, some concerned with his health and some with his politics. Philip Hoyne of Illinois and Montgomery Blair of Maryland called to ask Vallandigham not to claim his seat in the next day's convention—he could stay in bed and offer an excellent excuse for missing the meeting. Hoyne told his host that many delegates intended to deny him his seat and that the fusion movement might collapse if an open fight developed over his presence. Blair, assigned to convince Vallandigham to withdraw, added his arguments to those of Hoyne, but he failed to secure a commitment from the bed-ridden delegate. Blair enlisted the aid of Benjamin F. Perry and Governor James L. Orr of South Carolina. They visited Vallandigham's room and had a lengthy visit, but also came away empty-handed.[7]

Later that night, Vallandigham felt well enough to lock his suite and hunt up the committee room where the Ohio delegation was in caucus. As he entered the room and walked toward an

[6] 31 July 1866, Orville H. Browning Papers, Illinois State Historical Library, Springfield.

[7] Benjamin F. Perry, *Reminiscences of Public Men* (Greenville, S.C., 1889), pp. 298-302.

empty chair, he realized that the delegates were discussing a resolution asking him "not to present himself to the Convention." The argument was hot and heavy. A timid man would have excused himself and walked out, somewhat embarrassed. Vallandigham, rather brazenly, took a chair to listen to the discussion and insist upon his rights. The heated discussion lasted a full hour and produced only more discord. The caucus adjourned late at night without the resolution being put to a vote and with the question of Vallandigham's participation in the next day's convention still unresolved.

Seeking solace, Vallandigham drifted to Room 32 of the Girard House. There Samuel Cox and several guests were enjoying viands and cigars while debating the merits of fusion and the future of their party. Vallandigham's entry served as an excuse for Cox to shift the discussion to a more practical question. Should not Vallandigham, in the interests of harmony and expediency, withdraw as a delegate? Cox bluntly asked the Daytonian to withdraw, occasionally pounding a table for effect. Others, including Benjamin Wood and James E. English, once a prominent Connecticut Copperhead, added their pleas and their arguments to those of Cox. James W. Wall of New Jersey, on the other hand, argued that Vallandigham was entitled to sit in the convention—certainly he had more right to a seat than out-and-out ex-Confederates or ex-rebels. Cox, who later characterized Vallandigham as "selfish as a mink and as stubborn as a mule,"[8] bore down upon his latest caller as sparks flew. Vallandigham, of course, defended his right to sit in the convention and insisted that his conscience was clear. In time, Vallandigham ceased defending himself, but listened intently to the arguments and counterarguments of the others. The discussants consumed the last bottle of claret at about three o'clock in the morning and the informal gathering broke up. Although Vallandigham had made no pledge, Cox gained the impression that he would not seek his seat in the convention.

Early the next morning, most of the Ohio delegates, Vallandigham being one of the absentees, met again in a prebreakfast conference. Since the controversial Daytonian had failed to

[8] Quoted in the *New York Times*, 16 August 1866.

formalize his removal from the convention, the assembled delegates adopted "a ripping vote of censure," accusing him of "sowing seeds of disharmony." Word of the censure reached Vallandigham, still sleepy-eyed and thick-headed after the night's ordeal. After shaking out the cobwebs, the Daytonian hunted up George W. McCook, a member of the Ohio delegation and a longtime friend. He asked McCook if there was any question of the legality of his election as a delegate. McCook replied that there was none. Vallandigham next asked if he could have a ticket to the convention hall. "Certainly," said McCook, reaching into his vest pocket, "take mine." It was a clever retort, one that left Vallandigham hanging in mid-air.[9]

Vallandigham decided to capitulate, saving what honor he could. By withdrawing, he would make some Ohioans indebted to him; he would need their help in future years to get that coveted senate post. He concluded a backstage bargain with William S. Groesbeck, chairman of the Ohio delegation. If the Ohio delegates would rescind their censure resolution and adopt one complimenting him for his voluntary action, he would write a "letter of withdrawal."

Groesbeck hurriedly rounded up the Ohio delegates to carry out his half of the bargain. A delegate introduced a measure which withdrew the censure resolution and incorporated one which read: "*Resolved*, That we recognize the right of the Hon. Clement L. Vallandigham . . . to hold a seat in the Convention . . . yet for the sake of harmony and good feeling . . . we consent to his withdrawal from a seat in the Convention, if, in his judgment, his duty to his constituents shall justify such a withdrawal."[10] Groesbeck then sent the revamped resolution up to Vallandigham's room.

The unwanted delegate then sent his "letter of withdrawal" to Groesbeck. Instead of addressing it to the chairman of the

[9] This story of Vallandigham and the Philadelphia Convention is a composite of accounts in the *Cincinnati Daily Enquirer*, 15, 16 August 1866; *New York World*, 15, 16 August 1866; *Dayton Daily Journal*, 15, 16, 18 August 1866; *Dayton Daily Empire*, 16-20 August 1866; *Philadelphia Inquirer*, 16 August 1866. For an excellent scholarly summary of the convention see Thomas Wagstaff, "The Arm-in-Arm Convention," *Civil War History* 14 (June 1968): 101-19.

[10] *Cincinnati Daily Enquirer*, 16 August 1866; *Dayton Daily Journal*, 16 August 1866.

Ohio delegation, however, the foxy Daytonian addressed it to the "Chairman of the National Union Convention, Philadelphia,"[11] making it nearly mandatory that his letter be read before the entire convention.

By retreating, Vallandigham gained more publicity than he would have if the delegates had allowed him to take his seat without a fuss. His action gained some stature for him. In addition, he made new friends, made some Ohioans indebted to him, and gave the impression that he had surrendered personal wants for the public good. He saw himself as a martyr to harmony, contributing immeasurably to the success of the Philadelphia convention.

Ohio Republican editors claimed to find considerable pleasure in the fact that Vallandigham had had his face slapped at Philadelphia. "It is worse to be booted out of the house of a friend," wrote Murat Halstead of the *Cincinnati Commercial*, "than kicked out of the house of an enemy."[12] William D. Bickham also rubbed salt in Vallandigham's wounds. "After all his blatherings and gasconade," Bickham stated, "Vallandigham suffered himself to be ignominiously kicked out of the Philadelphia convention."[13]

Other Republican critics were able to gauge Vallandigham's withdrawal more realistically. Whitelaw Reid of the *Cincinnati Gazette* supposed that the recalcitrant delegate had gained stature, not lost it. He labeled the convention "Vallandigham's triumph."[14] In a sense Reid was correct. Certainly, Vallandigham had outwitted and outmaneuvered his detractors in Philadelphia. Republicans also recognized the irony of the situation. Ex-Confederates, military officers in the rebel army, or civil leaders in the Confederacy, had been welcomed with open arms at the convention. Yet Vallandigham's presence there embarrassed some convention leaders. If Vallandigham had raised a regiment and fought for the Confederacy, Joseph Medill of the *Chicago Tribune* stated, he would have been welcomed, feted, and ap-

---

11 Dated 15 August 1866, published in *Dayton Daily Journal*, 16 August. Also see the *Nation*, 23 August 1866; *Philadelphia Inquirer*, 16 August 1866; *New York Times*, 16 August 1866.

12 20 August 1866; *Dayton Daily Journal*, 21 August 1866.

13 *Dayton Daily Journal*, 16 August 1866.

14 29 August 1866.

plauded. Ex-rebels, he added, were more welcome at "the rene-gades' convention" than ex-Copperheads.[15]

After returning home from Philadelphia, Vallandigham leaped into the maelstrom of Ohio politics. He campaigned extensively in the Third District for Durbin Ward, Democratic nominee for Congress, and criss-crossed the state to speak in defense of the Democracy and a moderate reconstruction policy.

Both of Vallandigham's causes went down to defeat in the election of 1866, and it was time again for the defeated to seek explanations for failures. C.L.V. concluded that Democrats must discuss the current issues, face the future, and shut the trapdoor upon the past. The Civil War had imposed a veritable revolution upon the country—freeing the slaves, centralizing the government, and putting captains of industry and masters of capital in control of affairs. Times had changed, Democrats had not. The Democracy might as well bury the states' rights principles of Jefferson and Calhoun and cease blaming Republicans for the Civil War. Since they regarded themselves as law-and-order men, Democrats must accept the Thirteenth Amendment and recognize the ascendancy of the Industrial Revolution. Only by introducing new issues could Democrats nullify the Republican practice of winning elections by "waving the bloody shirt." *"The past,"* Vallandigham argued, *"must be forgotten, antecedants ignored,* and the great issues of the hour be made the sole test of present fellowship and cooperation."[16]

Certainly no one had more to gain by shutting out the past than Vallandigham. If he could get Republicans to discuss such issues as Greenbackism, reform, monopoly, transportation, and agricultural surpluses, Democrats might score better at the polls. If Vallandigham could get Republicans to ignore his record as a Copperhead and forget the story of his arrest and exile, he too might effect a political rehabilitation. No Democrat had more to gain by asking the party faithful to look toward the rising sun rather than the setting sun, advocating a policy later desig-nated the "New Departure." In a way it was strange that a man who had so often gloried in the historic role of the Democracy

[15] 20 August 1866.
[16] C.L.V. to George W. Morgan, 11 December 1866, Vallandigham Papers, Western Reserve Historical Society, Cleveland.

and in the deification of Jefferson and Jackson should ask his party to cease arguing old issues and seek out the new. As a disciple of Burke he had favored evolutionary change, but the revolution which had occurred within the Civil War was very real. In seizing the distaff of the prophet, however, he was also proving himself an opportunist. In helping his party to emphasize the present and forget the past he was also helping himself. The more he reviewed the past and assayed the future the more he wanted Ben Wade's seat. His desire was evolving into an obsession.

Vallandigham again took to the hustings during the gubernatorial campaign of 1867, partially to strengthen his claim to a seat in the senate if the Democrats gained control of the state legislature. He advocated the election of Allen G. Thurman, a rival within the party, over Rutherford B. Hayes, the Republican candidate. He invariably stated his opposition to the proposed Fifteenth Amendment, denounced Republican corruption and Yankee cupidity, condemned the harsh reconstruction policy of the radicals, and railed against Wall Street and "the money monopoly."[17] He gave eighty speeches in all during the two-month campaign, keeping old friends and making new ones.

In the October election, the Democrats lost the governorship by a narrow margin—Hayes edged Thurman by 2,983 votes out of 484,227 cast, but captured control of the state legislature. Vallandigham immediately cast his eye on Wade's senate seat, and his supporters sponsored rallies or wrote editorials advancing his claims. The Democratic newspaper of Dayton spearheaded the move to put Vallandigham in Wade's place. It would, stated the sympathetic editor, be "a fitting rebuke to the many who had abused him so long."[18]

Vallandigham even took the train to the state capital to lobby in his own behalf when the state legislature met in January 1868. He buttonholed old friends and unabashedly advanced his claims to new members. Members of the party hierarchy, however, thought that Thurman merited the post. The Democratic caucus considered the claims of both contenders and chose Thurman

---

[17] *Crisis* (Columbus), 4 September 1867; *Dayton Daily Journal*, 19 August 1867.
[18] *Dayton Daily Ledger*, 17 October 1867. In a reorganization, the *Ledger* replaced the *Empire*.

over Vallandigham, 51 votes to 24. The next day the state legislature ratified the decision of the Democratic caucus and Thurman took Wade's seat in the senate.[19]

When Vallandigham returned to Dayton he made no effort to hide his deep disappointment. He proved himself a poor loser by refusing to attend a Columbus reception in Thurman's honor. Republican editors noticed Vallandigham's bad political manners and personal pique. "He loves and hates with intensity," wrote Murat Halstead of the *Cincinnati Commercial,* "concentrating his love upon himself and hating all who do not approve or uphold him." With obvious delight, Halstead added, "Vallandigham, with diminished proportions, his comb cut and tail feathers pulled out, roosts low on the sour apple tree."[20]

Vallandigham continued to sulk for more than a month, finding time, meanwhile, to rebuild his law practice. He also helped to reorganize the faltering Democratic newspaper in Dayton, acquiring a half-interest in the financial enterprise and full control of the editorial policy. Immersed in newspaper and law work, he even announced that he would not seek to represent his state or the Third District at the Democratic National Convention in New York City in July.[21]

As the meeting-date of the national convention approached, however, C.L.V. became restless and decided to renege on his promise. He headed for the convention as "an observer," not a delegate. He soon reached the conclusion that Salmon P. Chase ought to be his party's presidential choice and he quit observing and engaged in behind-the-doors arguments in behalf of the chief justice. Vallandigham argued that some of Chase's decisions on the court proved that he had returned to the Democratic fold, and that only a candidate who could cut into the Republican vote had a chance to be elected. Chase, Vallandigham argued, was the only possible nominee who might beat Grant, named earlier by the Republicans as their presidential choice.

On the fourth day of the convention four Ohio delegates resigned to return home and Vallandigham was one of several "observers" who then became delegates. Vallandigham still favored Chase while Winfield S. Hancock, Thomas J. Hendricks,

[19] *Daily Ohio Statesman,* 9 January 1868; *Dayton Daily Ledger,* 9 January 1868.
[20] 22 January 1868.
[21] *Dayton Daily Ledger,* 24, 31 January, 2 February, 7 March 1868.

and George H. Pendleton remained as favorites. When it became apparent that none of the three favorites could gain the necessary two-thirds majority, Vallandigham evolved a scheme to swing the convention to Chase. Horatio Seymour would be put in nomination to drive off the three favorites, and when the New Yorker declined again, Chase's candidacy would be pressed actively "and carried through with a whirl."[22]

The first step proceeded according to plan. The Ohio delegation nominated Seymour and dozens of delegates stepped into line, developing a boom for the New Yorker. But the plan backfired when Seymour's ardent supporters refused to let him withdraw his name, and in the end the reluctant candidate received the nomination "amidst the wildest enthusiasm" on the twenty-second ballot. Vallandigham and his fellow plotters were left holding an empty Chase bag. He had tried to play the kingmaker, but had bungled the job.[23]

Soon after, Vallandigham experienced the same frustrations as Seymour. Without his knowledge and against his wishes, Democrats of the Third District drafted the controversial Daytonian to oppose Robert C. Schenck, the Republican nominee, in the congressional contest. At New York, Vallandigham had urged Seymour to put the wishes of the convention ahead of personal considerations. Now others used the same arguments to prevent the onetime exile from declining to run for congress.

Rather reluctantly, Vallandigham hit the campaign trail. But applause, friendly handshakes, and the thrill of the chase soon made his blood stir anew and relit the old spark. He talked of the problems of the present and the challenges of the future, advocating his "New Departure" policy. He tried to make Republicans discuss problems then facing the electorate. But the Republicans were too wise to play Vallandigham's game; they "waved the bloody shirt" vigorously, reminding the gullible that Southern rebels and Northern Copperheads were brethren of the same principles, and they used their treason charges effectively. William D. Bickham of the *Dayton Journal*, for example, argued that the '68 contest was one between treason and perfidy, represented by Vallandigham, and patriotism and honor, repre-

---

[22] William W. Armstrong, "Personal Recollections," published in *Cincinnati Daily Enquirer*, 20 March 1886.
[23] Ibid.

sented by Schenck. Vallandigham could not be trusted in 1863; he should not be trusted in 1868. In fact, the former exile's candidacy was "a direct challenge to the patriotism of all who fought for, labored for, and prayed for the salvation of the Union during its recent struggle for self-preservation."[24]

The '68 election returns brought little comfort to Vallandigham. Schenck defeated him by 475 votes in October and Grant handily whipped Seymour in November—214 electoral votes to 80.[25] Yet he found some solace in the fact that he had polled 1,100 more votes in his congressional district in October than Seymour did a month later. The more he mulled over the matter the more his spirits rose, his ego spurring him on. He believed he was reestablishing himself in Ohio politics, regaining popularity with the people. Once again he cast his eye upon John Sherman's senate seat and dreamt of a favorable election in 1871. He still wanted the vindication which would go with his election to the senate. Like a true martyr, he still thought his party owed him the favor for the wrongs he had suffered during the war.

After the election post-mortems, Vallandigham again concentrated upon the law. In December 1869, he formed a practice with Daniel A. Haynes, who had served as Montgomery County's judge of the Superior Court since its creation in 1855. The new team proved to be "one of the best and ablest in the West."[26] Both were excellent lawyers; no one knew how to apply precedent better than Haynes, and no one researched a case better than Vallandigham. The latter had an excellent law library and possessed the knack of anticipating the arguments of opposing lawyers. He had few peers in Ohio when it came to convincing a jury, for he was eloquent, charming, and persuasive in court, possessing that intangible quality called charisma. He could charm a jury, amuse or solemnize them as the occasion required, and simplify complex points of law.

Vallandigham's ability at the bar sometimes led to the miscarriage of justice. The firm of Haynes & Vallandigham won nearly every criminal case in which it was involved. At times villains gained their freedom when they deserved the noose, or, conversely, men paid the full penalty when justice demanded a

---

[24] 19 August, 1 September 1868.
[25] The popular vote was 3,012,000 for Grant, 2,703,000 for Seymour.
[26] *Dayton Evening Herald,* 30 December 1869.

lesser penalty. One case which attracted statewide attention concerned Eli A. Lecklider, an 81-year-old farmer who had let his uncontrollable temper get out of hand and shot his son in an argument. The Republican attorney general of the state employed Vallandigham to prosecute the charges against Lecklider in one of the most notable murder trials ever held in Darke County. The trial lasted for eleven days, with the courtroom always filled to overflowing. In his final plea Vallandigham was so persuasive that he had most of the jurymen in tears. He sealed the doom of an old man who had already paid in remorse, and the hangman's noose claimed another life. It was a questionable victory for the state. There was no question, however, that the jury's verdict was a personal triumph for Clement L. Vallandigham.[27]

In 1871 friends of Thomas McGehan, a Hamilton rowdy accused of murder, asked Vallandigham to take over his defense. Because feeling against McGehan ran so high in Hamilton, C.L.V. requested a change of venue, and the court set the trial in Lebanon, Warren County, for June 6.

The trial lasted a full two weeks and public interest was so extensive that several dozen Ohio newspapers published nearly complete transcripts of the testimony. Attorneys for the state tried to prove that McGehan, with a pistol in his right-hand coat pocket, had shot Tom Myers while the two were but a few feet apart during a barroom brawl. Vallandigham, on the other hand, contended that Myers, in drawing his pistol out of his pocket while trying to rise from a kneeling position, had actually shot himself. Defense witnesses contradicted prosecution witnesses, and under Vallandigham's persistent questioning prosecution witnesses contradicted themselves.[28]

After the court adjourned about three o'clock on the afternoon of June 16, Vallandigham and a fellow lawyer took a brief walk in the country to check at what distance and to what degree

27 *Dayton Daily Journal*, 8 November 1869, 2, 3 March 1870; *Dayton Evening Herald*, 11 March 1870.

28 *Life and Trials of Thomas McGehean* (Cincinnati, 1874) was written anonymously by McGehan. He used the ruse of misspelling his name in an effort to hide his identity. Some of the information in this and succeeding paragraphs is based upon William E. VanHorne, "The Strange Deaths of Clement L. Vallandigham and Thomas McGehan," an unpublished manuscript in the hands of the author at 1576 Guilford Road, Columbus, Ohio, 43221.

powder marks were visible when a pistol was fired at a piece of cloth at close range—a point of contention in the trial. After the experiment, Vallandigham returned to his room at the Lebanon Hotel and placed his revolver, with three bullets still in the chamber, alongside a similar but empty pistol, on the bureau. During a conference with his fellow lawyers later in the evening, Vallandigham stated that he would demonstrate to the jury next day just how Tom Myers had accidentally shot himself while drawing a pistol as he tried to arise from the floor. Pretending he was Myers, Vallandigham took a pistol from the bureau and put it in his right trouser pocket, not realizing that he had taken the loaded one by mistake. Then he slowly pulled it out, cocking it as he drew it forth. When the muzzle cleared the pocket, he tried to place it in the exact position which he believed Meyers's weapon would have assumed at the moment when it was discharged. "There, that's the way Myers held it," Vallandigham said, "only he was getting up, not standing erect." At that moment he pressed the trigger. There was a flash and the half-suppressed sound of a shot. "My God, I've shot myself!" Vallandigham exclaimed in shocked dismay as he reeled toward the wall and tried to hold himself up.[29]

Consternation reigned in the hotel. Hurried telegrams to Dayton brought Vallandigham's sixteen-year-old son and the family physician, Dr. J. C. Reeves, to the wounded man's bedside. Dayton friends arrived to join in the bedside vigil. Even Thomas McGehan, handcuffed and escorted by the jailer, visited the death room and shed tears freely before he was led away.[30]

After twelve hours of pain, at about nine-thirty the next morning, life ebbed away. There was a sudden movement of the body, stretched full length, and a few gasps of the fast-failing breath; the lower jaw dropped, and the iris disappeared, leaving only the white of the eye to be seen. Clement L. Vallandigham, Ohio's most controversial politician, "departed with life."[31]

[29] Testimony of A. G. McBurney, published in Vallandigham, *Vallandigham,* p. 525. The *Dayton Daily Journal,* 17 June 1871, reported that Vallandigham exclaimed, "Oh, Murder! O what a blunder!"

[30] *Lebanon Weekly Star,* 22 June 1871.

[31] The *Dayton Evening Herald,* 19 June 1871, gives a detailed and vivid account of Vallandigham's death. Also see *Lebanon Weekly Star,* 22 June 1871; *Cincinnati Daily Commercial,* 17, 18 June 1871; and *Cincinnati Daily Enquirer,* 17, 18 June 1871.

Vallandigham's nephew, John A. McMahon, took charge of the funeral arrangements. He had the corpse, packed with ice,[32] conveyed to Dayton. He had trouble contacting Mrs. Vallandigham, who had gone to Cumberland, Maryland, to attend the funeral of her brother, John Van Lear McMahon. He asked Masonic friends of the deceased to conduct the burial rites. The same shop which brought forth the *Dayton Journal* printed 1,000 handbills announcing the funeral plans and these were circulated in the community.[33] During the war William D. Bickham's *Journal* had persecuted Vallandigham mercilessly, even publishing forged documents to help destroy his reputation. Now the *Journal* publicized the funeral and helped to bring out a huge crowd.

The controversial Daytonian was buried on June 20, 1871, in the shade of a sturdy oak tree in Woodland Cemetery. Mrs. Vallandigham, brought back to Dayton after attending her brother's funeral in Cumberland, missed the ceremonies, being confined to her bed in "a state of collapse."[34] But many of Ohio's notable sons and thousands of her citizens came from far and near to pay their respects. Salmon P. Chase journeyed to Dayton from Washington to help bury the man who tried to make him president in 1868. The Honorable Samuel S. Cox, who had moved to New York City, arrived to pay his respects to Vallandigham the man, whom he liked much more than Vallandigham the politician. George W. McCook, boyhood friend and political colleague, came from Steubenville to pay tribute to the deceased. Allen G. Thurman, a rival within the Ohio Democracy, came from Chillicothe to honor the man who wanted to be a United States senator more than words could tell. George E. Pugh, who had fought many political battles at Vallandigham's side, came for one last look at his courageous friend. Then there were the

[32] Bills for the ice, for "soiled bedding & extras," and for shipping the body to Dayton are included in Packet No. 9875, Probate Records, Montgomery County Court House, Dayton.
[33] Bickham's bill of $3.75 for "printing and distributing" the handbills, as well as other funeral expenses, can also be found in Packet No. 9875.
[34] Mrs. Louisa A. Vallandigham survived her husband by less than two months, dying on August 13 in Cumberland, where she was being cared for by her sister. Son Charles tried to follow in his father's footsteps, studying law and entering politics. He was elected to the state legislature during the 1880s. Appointed to a clerkship in the state capitol, he moved to Columbus and deserted the city indelibly linked with his father's name.

thousands from the countryside who, as Butternuts during the Civil War, had developed an admiration for their idol which even death could not efface. Workingmen in Dayton, Hamilton, and country villages took a day off from work to honor a man they regarded as their champion. It took the funeral procession a full hour and twenty minutes to pass the Court House steps where Vallandigham had often stood, preaching his conservative brand of politics.

Under a soft summer sky and amidst the tears of his relatives and friends, they lowered his silver-trimmed rosewood coffin into the newly dug grave. After the band played its final dirge, the crowd dispersed and left the stormy petrel of Ohio politics to his eternal sleep. His friends wondered whether the fifty-one-year-old politician would have gained the senate seat he coveted if he had lived and whether, with the aid of time, he might have fully erased the stigma that partisan Republicans, aided by the patriotic fervor which the Civil War engendered, had linked to his name.[35]

There were the usual eulogies. "I thank God," said George Pendleton, "he has lived long enough to see that Time, the Avenger in whom he had such unwavering faith, has commenced her work, and that many who maligned him most, were beginning to see their error and to do him justice."[36] Some eulogists spoke of his abilities as a lawyer and said that Vallandigham had indeed given his own life to save that of a client[37]—a rascal hardly worth saving. Others praised him for his eloquence as an orator, for his ability to evolve empathy with an audience, and for the depth and breadth of his scholarship. A few partisans recalled his unflinching devotion to the Democratic party and to the political principles of Thomas Jefferson. But most spoke of his courage, the sincerity of his convictions, and his willingness to fight for what he believed right, regardless of the cost. He was no reed bowing to the wind; rather, he was a sturdy oak defying the winds of change and the storms of passion. It was

[35] *Dayton Evening Herald,* 20 June 1871.
[36] Quoted in Vallandigham, *Vallandigham,* p. 365.
[37] After three separate trials, McGehan was discharged. This enabled Vallandigham's friends to say that he had saved McGehan's life by sacrificing his own. McGehan was assassinated by an unknown assailant on June 11, 1875, four years after Vallandigham's death.

appropriate that his grave lay in the shadow of a sturdy oak tree.

He read history with the devotion of the true scholar, having one of the finest personal libraries in Ohio.[38] His nine copies of Burke contained well-worn pages. Like Burke, he could recite historical events and repeat historical quotations by the hour, and his recollections could be trusted implicitly. Yet he knew little of the lessons of history. He never understood the power and influence of that psychological phenomenon called nationalism. And he never learned the lesson that those who swim against the current and test the limits of dissent—especially in wartime—fail to win the plaudits of posterity.

[38] Inventory of his library, in Packet No. 9875, Probate Records.

20

IN RETROSPECT

CLEMENT L. VALLANDIGHAM, like most controversial persons, was a complex individual who could fit no single mold. Although he was a conservative in thought and action most of the time, he occasionally spoke like a radical or a reactionary.

Certainly his contemporaries regarded his defiance of General Burnside as a radical act. He used radical means (arrest and martyrdom) to bolster his sagging political fortunes in 1863. As a gadfly in the Thirty-seventh Congress, he made some radical statements and even introduced a resolution calling for the arrest of President Lincoln if the rights of citizens continued to be violated. Those who gave property rights the highest priority were shocked when Vallandigham endorsed the radical doctrine of retaliation and retribution after Republican soldiers and civilians mobbed the offices of the *Dayton Empire* and the *Crisis* (Columbus) early in 1864.[1] Eastern bankers and Wall Street spokesmen thought his advocacy of Greenbackism during the late 1860s made him a dangerous radical.

On occasion, however, Vallandigham talked and acted like a liberal. He knew the Kentucky Resolutions of 1798 by heart and claimed they were part of his political creed. He regarded himself as a disciple of Jefferson, frequently quoting the sage of Monticello upon such subjects as freedom, rights, and liberties. Like Jefferson, he would leave the individual as unrestricted as possible in his search for self-expression and self-fulfillment. During the Civil War years no one spoke out more boldly than Vallandigham against executive usurpation and arbitrary arrests and in behalf of civil rights. Like so many of the English liberals of his day he espoused free trade, except on the one occasion when he sought protection for the flax growers of his congressional district. When he tried to abolish capital punishment in Ohio or insisted that rabbis should have the right to serve as regimental chaplains, he took stands which stamped him as a liberal. It seemed at times that Vallandigham was the congenital champion of the underdog.[2] Then, too, his advocacy of "New Departure" practices put him at the head of a small group anxious to reform and revitalize the Democratic party.

On most issues, however, and especially during the war years, Vallandigham was essentially a conservative. His early exposure to Calvinism, his training in law, and his devotion to Edmund Burke helped shape that conservatism. He resisted the changes which the revolution operating within the Civil War was imposing upon the country. He opposed the ascendancy of industrialism, viewing himself as the champion of farmers and workingmen. He was the idol of the Butternuts, backwoods farmers who regarded themselves as Jacksonian egalitarians, though they never dreamed that such a term might be applied to them. Vallandigham also opposed the centralization of the government and the dissipation of states' rights, recognizing that Lincoln and the war were destroying federalism and transforming the character of the government. Then, too, he opposed the enlargement of the war aims, especially the addition of emancipation as governmental policy. He objected to Lincoln's proclamation of emancipation and the Thirteenth Amendment, and to the Fourteenth and Fifteenth amendments during the postwar years. Like Burke he believed changes should be evolutionary and not revolutionary and that the deep roots of the past should be continually cultivated.

There were times—few and far between—when C.L.V. talked more like a reactionary than a conservative. Even after emancipation became official policy he talked of turning the calendar back, espousing the restoration of "the Union as it was" before the Civil War—*with states' rights and with slavery.* His endorsement of racism, his belief that the white man should have all the rights and the black man none, put him in a class with the plantation owners of antebellum days.

1 C.L.V. to "Messrs. Hubbard," 1 March 1864, published in the *Dayton Daily Empire,* 12 March. Other Ohio Democratic newspapers mobbed in early 1864 included: *Ottawa County Democrat* (Port Clinton), *Ohio Eagle* (Lancaster), and the *Mahoning Democratic Press.*

2 Bertram W. Korn, "Congressman Clement L. Vallandigham's Championship of the Jewish Chaplaincy in the Civil War," *American Jewish Historical Quarterly* 53 (December 1963): 188-91, has high praise for the Ohio Copperhead's efforts to eliminate discrimination against rabbis.

Vallandigham's personality was as complex as his political and socioeconomic views. He could be most pleasant, charming, and friendly—graciousness personified. He attracted devotees and friends whose loyalty knew no bounds, and many working-men and yeoman farmers regarded him as their champion. On the other hand, he could be petty, vindictive, and stubborn. In his own personal life he believed he practiced self-discipline and self-control; he had contempt for those who wore their feelings on their sleeves and for the wishy-washy fellow incapable of making up his mind. Vallandigham was ambitious, more for political honor and prestige in law than for vast property holdings or a fat bank account.

He was keen, well-read, and very knowledgeable, and he was wont to believe his views and ideas superior to those of others; he tended to be egotistical and conscious of his own rectitude, believing that time would vindicate him. His self-confidence sometimes led him to have naught but scorn for those who opposed him and there was a certain intransigence in his views. In short, he possessed those qualities which characterize the dissenter and the martyr: strong convictions, a degree of inflexibility, consciousness of his own rectitude, and courage— defined as the quality of mind which allows one to face dangers and threats without fear. His belief that he was right helped strengthen his convictions that his party owed him political compensation in the form of a seat in the United States Senate for the wrongs he had suffered during the war and for his martyrdom. He believed that the public reaction to his arrest and imprisonment had helped save civil rights which were endangered by the Washington-based despotism and the arbitrary practices of military commanders like General Burnside.

Had he confined his considerable talents to law, he might have become one of the great lawyers of his generation. But his desire for attention, publicity, and applause drew him into public life. Having once heard the siren call of politics, he could not resist. "If I had sense enough to let politics alone and attend to my professional business," he once remarked to a friend, "I might easily make $15,000 a year."[3] Actually, politics brought him

[3] Quoted in *Dayton Daily Ledger*, 3 October 1866.

more disappointments than successes. He won only two of eight bids for a seat in the lower house of Congress, and he never gained that senate seat he wanted so badly in the postwar years.

Probably the aspect of Vallandigham's life that is most significant for the contemporary reader is his role as a dissenter during the war, when the limits of dissent were vague and undefined. Dissension, most certainly, was no new phenomenon in American history. During the Revolutionary War, when "Patriots" held the reins of power, dissenters (the self-styled "Loyalists") were numerous and paid a heavy penalty for their devotion to the Crown; the Patriots not only intimidated the Loyalists but confiscated their estates and drove them into exile—"to hell, Hull, or Halifax." Patriots defined a Loyalist as "a thing whose head is in England, whose body is in America, and [whose] neck ought to be stretched."[4] After the war, Patriots wrote their own definitions of justice, honor, and treason into history.

Those who opposed the War of 1812 also found themselves treated with contempt in the years that followed. It was generally believed that if those who attended the Hartford Convention of 1814 had not courted treason, they had at least flirted with it. "The federalist party, from its apparent sympathy with the Hartford Convention," wrote a reputable historian more than a hundred years later, "received a death blow from which it did not recover."[5] The nationalistic surge which followed the War of 1812 prompted Americans to view that questionable conflict as "a fight for a free sea" and "a crusade in defense of national honor," and to characterize the Hartford Convention as "an ugly incident."[6] Historians justified the war, even claiming that it had "given strength and splendor to the chain of the Union."[7] Conversely, they felt compelled to treat dissenters of the 1812-1816 era as men guilty of disloyalty.

Those who opposed the Mexican War, whether on political or

---

[4] Quoted in Merle Curti and others, *An American History*, 2 vols. (New York, 1950), 2:159.

[5] John Spencer Bassett, *A Short History of the United States* (New York, 1921), p. 338.

[6] S. E. Foreman, *Our Republic* (New York, 1924), p. 215.

[7] Christopher R. Greene, *An Oration Delivered in St. Michael's Church, on Tuesday, the Fourth of July, 1815* (Charleston, 1815), p. 11, quoted in Merle Curti, *Growth of American Loyalty* (New York, 1946), p. 152.

moral grounds, also suffered at the hands of posterity. The spirit of Manifest Destiny, centered in a belief in the nation's greatness, helped to evolve the doctrine that dissenters during the Mexican War had played "an ignoble role" and that the contest had strengthened the fibers of the country. Flag-waving historians went so far as to argue that wars were often the only means of advancing civilization and that support of a war was a plain patriotic duty.[8]

Civil War dissenters—and here Vallandigham stands at the head of the list—have also been treated critically by historians. During the postwar years, especially the 1885-1900 era, a nationalistic revival swept the United States. Nationalism became a religion; even Walt Whitman defined the nation as a living organism and the instrument through which citizens could best realize and express their divine sense of fellowship. Nationalism underwrote the big navy policy, fostered the dream of empire, introduced United States history into high schools, furnished a setting for the Columbian Exposition of 1892-1893, and laid the base for Frederick Jackson Turner's "frontier thesis." It also promoted the apotheosizing of Lincoln and helped Americans accept Republican opinions and contentions of Civil War days as fact. Copperheads, consequently, emerged as men whose hearts were black, whose blood was yellow, and whose minds were blank.

Many Republicans who had manufactured political propaganda during the Civil War put their partisan views into print as "history" in the postwar years. Whitelaw Reid, who edited the *Cincinnati Gazette* and accused Vallandigham of disloyalty, wrote a two-volume work, *Ohio in the War*,[9] which became the standard text on wartime politics for half a century. Horace Greeley, who sometimes called a spade a plow in the *New York Tribune*, wrote a book which mixed fact and partisanship in a readable ratio. Greeley's book, *The American Conflict*, accused Vallandigham of cooperating with the rebels and heading a secret society engaged in treasonable activities.[10] Reid and Greeley were but two

[8] Nahum Capen, *The Republic of the United States* (Boston, 1848), pp. 37-38.

[9] (Columbus, 1869.) Reid treated Vallandigham as a traitor. No one during the war did more than Reid to develop "Copperhead" as a smear term.

[10] Two vols. (Hartford, Conn., 1867.) This book typifies the "history" written by Republican participants.

of the many[11] whose partisan contentions muddied the stream of history.

Although postwar propagandists and historians sincerely believed that Clement L. Vallandigham had overstepped the limits of dissent, federal courts failed to substantiate their contentions. Furthermore the courts failed to lay down specific boundary lines between loyalty and treason; students of the law could not agree among themselves to what extent citizens should give up traditional rights in the interest of national unity in time of war and when citizens should bow to patriotic conformism.

The question of wartime rights received consideration in three well-known court cases which had Civil War settings—two of the decisions were in Vallandigham's favor. The first case, *Ex Parte Merryman* (1861), involved an arrested Maryland secessionist whom President Lincoln refused to release, even under a writ of habeas corpus from Chief Justice Taney, sitting on circuit duty. When military officials failed to honor Taney's writ, he prepared a carefully worded opinion which denounced military defiance of judicial powers, insisting that any suspected treason should have been dealt with by judicial process. He accused the president of usurping power and put the responsibility of maintaining constitutional guarantees squarely upon Lincoln.[12] Vallandigham always believed Taney's decision a victory for civil rights and a reprimand of the Lincoln administration.

In Vallandigham's own case, two different courts were involved and both retreated from the forthright stand taken by Taney in *Ex Parte Merryman*. Judge Humphrey H. Leavitt, sitting in the U.S. circuit court at Cincinnati, evaded an answer to the question of civil rights in wartime in order to prevent a clash between civil and military officials. Leavitt, trying to stay in the good graces of General Burnside and the Lincoln administration, ignored Taney's ruling and wrote a decision which made champions of civil rights gasp. "The sole question," Judge

---

[11] Other "histories" include: Berry R. Sulgrove, *History of Indianapolis and Marion County* (Philadelphia, 1884); John Moses, *Illinois, Statistical and Historical*, 2 vols. (Chicago, 1889); Logan Esarey, *History of Indiana from 1850 to the Present* (Fort Wayne, 1918); and William H. H. Terrell, *Report of the Adjutant General of Indiana*, 8 vols. (Indianapolis, 1869).

[12] *Ex Parte Merryman*, 17 Federal Cases 144 (1861).

Leavitt stated, "is whether the arrest was legal, and . . . its legality depends on the necessity . . . for making it, and of that necessity . . . this court cannot judicially determine."[13]

When Vallandigham's case went up to the United States Supreme Court on a writ of certiorari, those august judges also found an excuse to avoid defining the limits of dissent in wartime and ruling on the Daytonian's constitutional rights. The judges used the lame excuse that the court's authority, as derived from the Constitution and the Judiciary Act of 1789, did not extend to the proceedings of a military commission.[14] Although the high court's evasive tactics and timidity may have pleased President Lincoln and General Burnside, Democrats who glorified the rights of citizens protested in chorus. They pointed out that, in essence, the Supreme Court had said that if one's rights were not ravaged according to law, one had no recourse to justice in the courts.[15]

The third important civil rights case of the Civil War period came out of Indiana and paralleled Vallandigham's in many ways. Lambdin P. Milligan and several other prominent Indiana Democrats were arrested by military authorities at Governor Oliver P. Morton's request shortly before the fall elections of 1864 and tried by a military commission. The indictment stated that Milligan *et al.* were involved in a vague plan to release Confederate prisoners from several Northern prison camps and had plotted to establish a "Northwest Confederacy." Found guilty by the military commission, Milligan and two others were sentenced to be hanged. Friends of the condemned men secured a postponement of the death penalty pending an appeal to the Supreme Court. Ignoring the action of the court in *Ex Parte Vallandigham,* the judges this time accepted jurisdiction and rendered an opinion sometimes characterized as "one of the bulwarks of American civil liberty."[16] Judge David Davis read the court's opinion in *Ex Parte Milligan* and advanced the principle that a military trial in an area where the civil courts were open and functioning was both extraordinary and illegal. "Martial

---

[13] 28 Federal Cases 923 (1863). Leavitt's decision was later published in *Official Records,* ser. 2, 5:575-76.

[14] *Ex Parte Vallandigham,* 68 U.S. (1 Wallace) 243-54 (1864).

[15] *Detroit Free Press,* 26 February 1864; *Dayton Daily Empire,* 16, 19 February, 1 March 1864.

[16] James G. Randall, *The Civil War and Reconstruction* (Boston, 1937), p. 398.

law can never exist where the courts are open, and in the proper and unobstructed exercise of their jurisdiction," Judge Davis stated, ". . . the Constitution of the United States is a law for rulers and people, equally in war and peace, and covers with the shield of its protection all classes of men, at all times, and under all circumstances."[17]

While the Radicals attacked the court because *Ex Parte Milligan* seemed to threaten the system of military government which they were planning for the South, Clement L. Vallandigham and most Democrats applauded the decision. Not only did the onetime exile believe that Davis's decision had vindicated him, but he claimed that the court had "convicted" Lincoln and his "agents" of "high crimes against the Constitution." He also took a trip to New York City and Washington, D.C., to investigate the desirability of instituting a damage suit against ex-Governor David Tod and General Ambrose E. Burnside in order to gain a measure of public revenge.[18]

Although *Ex Parte Milligan* challenged the right of military commissions to deprive citizens of their rights, the court made no attempt to set the limits of dissent—to specify when criticism of the Lincoln administration gave aid and comfort to the enemy and bordered on treason. Whereas Republicans equated dissent with treason, Vallandigham insisted upon practicing the same rights during the war that he exercised in times of peace. He refused to accept the principle that the character of every act depended upon the circumstances in which it was committed. He also refused to believe that wartime restrictions on rights, whether partial or arbitrary, were essentially a part of the trend toward enforced unity which total war demanded.

Although no court case arising out of the Civil War defined the limits of dissent, a later court continued to wrestle with the question of wartime rights. One case came out of World War I and bore the designation *Schenck v. United States* (1919). The decision justified governmental restriction upon the rights stated in the

---

[17] *Ex Parte Milligan*, 71 U.S. (4 Wallace) 1-143 (1866).

[18] Vallandigham to Marcus Mills Pomeroy, 3 January 1867, published in *Dayton Daily Empire*, 15 January 1867; *Dayton Daily Journal*, 7 May 1866; *Dayton Daily Empire*, 27 December 1866. The passage of a special habeas corpus bill which protected army officers from suits when they were executing orders of their military superiors, prevented Vallandigham from instituting a suit for damages against Tod and Burnside.

First Amendment during time of war. "When a nation is at war," the court's decision read, "many things that might be said in time of peace are such a hindrance to its effort that their utterance will not be endured so long as men fight and that no Court could regard them as protected by any constitutional right." If an actual obstruction of the recruiting services could be proved, liability for words which produced that effect might be enforced. The most stringent protection of free speech, the opinion continued, would not protect one who falsely shouted "Fire!" in a theatre, thereby causing a panic.[19]

If the *Schenck* v. *United States* decision had been given during Vallandigham's lifetime, he probably would have dissented. On the other hand, he would have heartily endorsed the dissenting opinion written by Justice Oliver Wendell Holmes in *Abrams et al.* v. *United States* (1918). In this case Holmes attempted to deal with a fundamental issue—the meaning of "loyalty" and "disloyalty" in a democracy. He stated that the government was justified in interfering in the realm of ideas *only* if the nature of the specific utterance of the ideas and the circumstances in which they were uttered were such as to give rise to a clear and present danger of overt actions which a state might legitimately forbid.[20] Clement L. Vallandigham, dissenter extraordinary of Civil War days, would have applauded Justice Holmes, dissenter in the Abrams case.

Despite the fact that the Supreme Court occasionally dealt with the conflict between the principles of *civil liberty* and *national security*, it evolved no formula and never set the limits of dissent in wartime. This question, in fact, still confronts every democracy in time of war, with the practical results too often dependent upon the restraint and wisdom of the individuals in power. United States citizens, during the later stages of the Vietnam War, continued to disagree over questions of "loyalty" and "disloyalty"—whether antidraft rallies and moratorium marches were merely exercised rights or acts which gave aid and comfort to the enemy. Do these "allegedly disloyal activities" imperil the government and blunt its military objectives? In what way and to what extent? To what extent may a government

[19] *Schenck* v. *United States* 249 U.S. 47 (1919).
[20] Holmes, dissenting opinion in *Abrams et al.* v. *United States* 250 U.S. 616, 624-63 (1918-1919).

restrict rights to achieve an enforced unity? These questions, essential to a definitive appraisal of Vallandigham's role as a dissenter in the Civil War, remain unanswered a hundred years later.[21]

President Lincoln recognized that influential critics like Vallandigham posed a difficult problem. "Must a government of necessity be too strong for the liberties of its people, or too weak to maintain its own existence?" he asked. He sincerely believed that Vallandigham's statements and speeches encouraged desertion, discouraged enlistments, and hampered the war effort. "Must I shoot a simple-minded soldier boy who deserts," he inquired, "while I must not touch a hair of a wiley [sic] agitator who induces him to desert?"[22] The president evidently believed that his administration and the government were synonymous terms—that the administration *was* the government. He denied that there was a no-man's land between loyalty and treason and he believed that the Dayton critic had trespassed beyond the limits of dissent.

Vallandigham, on the other hand, denied that the Lincoln administration and the government were one and the same. He claimed he was loyal to the government and the Constitution and that every effort of Republicans to confine loyalty to a single pattern, to constrain it to a single formula, was disloyalty to the Constitution and American tradition. He believed the concept of loyalty as conformity a false one and he questioned whether radical Republicans (whom he believed guilty of mockery of the Bill of Rights) had the right to impose their definition of loyalty upon the country.

But Vallandigham's quarrel with Lincoln was more than a dispute over the meaning of loyalty and disloyalty. It was also a quarrel between the nation's leader, who recognized coercion

21 Those interested in the question of loyalty and disloyalty can pursue the subject further in: Arthur M. Schlesinger, Jr., "What Is Loyalty? A Difficult Question," *New York Times Magazine*, 2 November 1947; Henry Steele Commager, "Who Is Loyal to America?" *Harper's Magazine* 195 (September 1947): 193-99; Alan Barth, *The Loyalty of Free Men* (New York, 1951); and John C. Wahlke, ed., *Loyalty in a Democratic State (Problems in American Civilization)*, (Boston, 1965).

22 Lincoln to "Hon. Erastus Corning & others," 12 June 1863, Robert Todd Lincoln Papers, Library of Congress. The original letter has not been located. Revisions were made, evidently, before Lincoln sent the letter to Corning and released it to the press. (It was published in the *New York Tribune*, 15 June 1863.)

as the only practical means of saving the Union, and a visionary who misjudged the mood and mind of the South. Furthermore, it was a controversy between a pragmatic president who added new dimensions to the war, furthering the revolution within it, and a conservative Democrat who opposed the direction of events and chanted the slogan "The Constitution as it is, the Union as it was." It was a controversy between a president who was flexible and who believed that a government must be a viable, dynamic organism responsive to the changing times, and an inflexible Copperhead who rejected change, opposed the wishes of the majority, and became entrapped by his own principles.

Clement L. Vallandigham always believed that time would vindicate him and posterity would adjudge him a prophet. But time vindicated Lincoln, not Vallandigham.

Bibliographical Essay

James L. Vallandigham began to collect material to write a biography of his brother shortly after Clement was buried in Woodland Cemetery, Dayton. The would-be biographer inserted notices in the *Dayton Herald* (successor to the *Empire* and *Ledger*) and in the *Crisis*, asking all who had any information, whether letters or other items, to contact him. He borrowed letters which C.L.V. had written to his mother, wife, son, brothers, and friends. He perused the columns of the *Dayton Empire* for speeches and news notes. He also leaned heavily upon two autobiographical accounts which his deceased brother had published to enhance his political aspirations: *The Record of Hon. C. L. Vallandigham on Abolition, the Union, and the Civil War* (Columbus, 1863), and *Speeches, Arguments, Addresses, and Letters of Clement L. Vallandigham* (New York, 1864). James, whose name was also tainted with charges of treason, had at his elbow a sixty-four-page booklet, *Biographical Memoir of Clement L. Vallandigham by His Brother* (New York, 1864), which he had published seven years earlier, soon after the exile's return from Canada to Ohio.

James L. Vallandigham, *A Life of Clement L. Vallandigham* (Baltimore, 1872), appeared within a year after the death of the subject. It was a laudatory version, depicting the controversial Daytonian as a statesman of the first order. It presented brother Clement as a true gentleman, possessing ability and self-control, persecuted by bigots and fanatics. James included many of C.L.V.'s speeches and letters, in whole or in part, and practiced selection and omission in order to whitewash him. He omitted speeches, or sections thereof, which proved his brother petty and personal. He also left out paragraphs or sentences without using ellipsis marks to indicate omissions. This was true with regard to letters as well as speeches.

Some of the stories which James L. Vallandigham incorporated into his one-sided biography have all the earmarks of sheer fiction. Yet, *A Life of Clement L. Vallandigham* is an invaluable work, for most of the letters published in part or in entirety seem to have been lost or destroyed.

Almost all of the letters in the Vallandigham Papers at the Western Reserve Historical Society, Cleveland, were written to Clement L. Vallandigham's paternal and maternal grandfathers. Only a dozen of the 219 items are in C.L.V.'s hand. Perhaps fifty letters written by Vallandigham are available to scholars. Two dozen were "cards" or letters published in the *Dayton Daily Empire* and the *Cincinnati Daily Enquirer*. The Manton Marble Papers (Library of Congress) contain eleven Vallandigham-written letters. The Alexander S. Boys Papers (Ohio Historical Society, Columbus) and the Horace Greeley Papers (New York Public Library) contain three each. The Franklin Pierce Papers (Library of Congress), the Francis Lieber Papers (Henry E. Huntington Library, San Marino, California), and the Simon Gratz Collection (Historical Society of Pennsylvania, Philadelphia) each contain two. Others are scattered here and there.

Several other manuscript collections are important to the Vallandigham story. The Thomas O. Lowe Papers and the Daniel L. Medlar "Journal," kept from September 1, 1859 to April 30, 1862 (both in the Dayton and Montgomery County Public Library), make frequent references to Dayton's best-known citizen and are rich in detail about Dayton and "war fever." The George B. McClellan Papers (Library of Congress) are important for dealing with the presidential election of 1864, while the James Buchanan Papers (Historical Society of Pennsylvania, Philadelphia) are important for the prewar era. The Samuel S. Cox Papers (originals in the Brown University Library, Providence, Rhode Island, and microfilm copies in the Hayes Memorial Library, Fremont, Ohio) are essential to any study of Ohio politics during the Civil War years. The extensive Alexander Long Papers (Cincinnati Historical Society) reveal the mind of a peace-at-any-price Copperhead. The Daniel Read Larned Papers (Library of Congress) contain some interesting information about Vallandigham's arrest in 1863. The Samuel P. Heintzelman Papers (Library of Congress) are quite important because General Heintzelman commanded the Department of the Ohio for a time during the Civil War. The Benjamin Tappan Papers throw light upon Ohio politics, as do the Samuel Medary Papers (both at the Ohio Historical Society, Columbus). Every student of Civil War politics should also use the Samuel Finley Breese Morse Papers, the Benjamin F. Wade Papers, the Salmon P. Chase Papers, the John Sherman Papers, and the Joseph Holt Papers—all in the Library of Congress.

The National Archives house several collections most important to any study of Vallandigham and the Civil War. The Lafayette C. Baker-Levi C. Turner Papers (Adjutant Generals' Records, War Department Files), stored in eighty steel boxes, contain information regarding the "investigations of fraud, examinations of civilian and military prisoners, and other matters pertaining generally to subversive activities in connection with the Civil War." The Civil War Political Prisoners' Records (State Department Files) contain information about Vallandigham's arrest, trial, and exile. The George W. L. Bickley Papers (Records of the Judge Advocate General) fail to link Vallandigham to the Knights of the Golden Circle. The Consulate Records, 1862-1865 (State Department Files) contain several reports on the dissenter as an exile in Canada.

The absence of a collection of Vallandigham's personal papers accentuates the need for extensive newspaper research. The Dayton and Montgomery County Public Library holds almost complete files of the *Dayton Journal* and the *Dayton Empire* for the twenty-five years Lincoln's best-known critic lived in Dayton. The *Journal* presented the Republican viewpoint, the *Empire*, the Democratic. Samuel Medary of the *Crisis* (Columbus) usually defended Vallandigham, and his weekly newspaper criticized Lincoln, opposed the war, and expressed pro-Western views. Dr. John McElwee, a personal friend of Vallandigham, edited the *Hamilton True Telegraph* and gave his subscribers a one-sided account of the news. James J. Faran of the *Cincinnati Enquirer* was a partisan as Medary and McElwee, but more discreet. The *Ohio Statesman* (Columbus), edited by George W. Manypenny, often differed with the Dayton dissenter as to means and objectives. It was the official voice of the Ohio Democracy. The Democratic-oriented *Detroit Free Press* occasionally reported on C.L.V. while he resided across the river in Windsor, Canada West. The observant critic will notice that other Democratic newspapers, such as the *Indianapolis State Sentinel*, the *Chicago Times*, the *Stark County Democrat* (Canton), the *Cleveland Plain*

Dealer, the *Mount Vernon Democratic Banner,* the *Ohio Patriot* (New Lisbon), and the *New York World* are also cited in the footnotes and deserve special mention.

A dozen Republican newspapers provided most of the source for anti-Vallandigham quotations incorporated into the text. The *Dayton Journal,* edited first by William F. "Deacon" Comly and later by William D. Bickham, waged a constant war of words against the controversial Copperhead. The *Ohio State Journal* (Columbus) defended the Lincoln administration and preached Republican doctrine. Murat Halstead of the *Cincinnati Commercial* and Whitelaw Reid of the *Cincinnati Gazette* criticized Vallandigham and bluntly labeled him a traitor. Horace Greeley of the *New York Tribune* always presented the Dayton "Peace Democrat" in an unfavorable light, and so did other Republican newspapers, such as the *Cleveland Leader,* the *Chicago Tribune,* the *Buckeye State* (New Lisbon), and the *Indianapolis Journal.*

The *Toronto Globe* and the *Toronto Leader* contained more about Vallandigham while he lived in exile than did other Canadian newspapers. I used two dozen Southern newspapers, typified by the *Richmond Examiner* and the *Chattanooga Rebel,* to trace the movements of the exile in Dixie.

It was necessary to comb the *Congressional Globe* for Vallandigham's record in the House of Representatives. Much on the arrest and trial of the Daytonian can also be culled from *The War of the Rebellion: A Compilation of the Official Records of the Union and Confederate Armies* (128 vols., Washington, D.C., 1880-1901).

Several dozen secondary accounts provide an essential background for any study of Vallandigham and the 1850-1870 era. Eugene H. Roseboom summarized the period well in *The Civil War Era* (Columbus, 1944), volume 4 in *The History of the State of Ohio,* edited by Carl Wittke (6 vols., Columbus, 1940-1944). Whitelaw Reid, *Ohio in the War* (2 vols., Cincinnati, 1868), saw everything through his well-worn Republican spectacles. George H. Porter presented the era in a more scholarly fashion in his doctoral dissertation, published under the title *Ohio Politics during the Civil War Period* (New York, 1911).

Wood Gray, *The Hidden Civil War* (New York, 1942), and George Fort Milton, *Lincoln and the Fifth Column* (New York,

1942), both depict Copperheads as men tainted with treason. My own book, *The Copperheads in the Middle West* (Chicago, 1960), indicates that political, sectional, and socioeconomic causes underwrote Midwestern opposition to the Lincoln administration. It also debunks the secret society and conspiracy stories which Gray and Milton incorporate into their books. V. Jacque Voegeli, *Free But Not Equal: The Midwest and the Negro during the Civil War* (Chicago, 1967), and Leonard P. Curry, *Blueprint for Modern America: Nonmilitary Legislation of the First Civil War Congress* (Nashville, 1968), are both thoroughly researched and deserve a prominent place on Civil War bookshelves. William Frank Zornow, *Lincoln and the Party Divided* (Norman, Okla., 1954), provides excellent background for the presidential election of 1864, while Charles H. Coleman, *The Election of 1868* (New York, 1933), is still the standard work on the Grant-Seymour contest. Three prominent Ohioans, all critics of Vallandigham, are dealt with in Donnal V. Smith, *Chase and Civil War Politics* (Columbus, 1931), Hans L. Trefousse, *Benjamin Franklin Wade: Radical Republican from Ohio* (New York, 1963), and Harold Hyman, *Stanton: The Life and Times of Lincoln's Secretary of War* (New York, 1962). Winfield S. Kerr, *John Sherman, His Life and Public Service* (2 vols., Boston, 1908), is badly outdated. David Lindsey, *"Sunset" Cox, Irrepressible Democrat* (Detroit, 1959), deals with one of Vallandigham's colleagues; it should be supplemented with Cox's autobiographical account, *Union— Disunion—Reunion: Three Decades of Federal Legislation* (Providence, Rhode Island, 1888). Other biographies of Vallandigham's fellow Democrats include Reginald C. McGrane, *William Allen, 1803-1879* (Columbus, 1925), and William E. and Ophia D. Smith, *Buckeye Titan* (Cincinnati, 1953); the latter deals with John H. James, who once refused to share a platform with Vallandigham.

Two books deal with the Negro in Ohio or with white racial attitudes in the state. Charles T. Hickok, *The Negro in Ohio, 1820-1870* (Cleveland, 1896), is badly outdated. Francis U. Quillen, *The Color Line in Ohio: A History of Race Prejudice in a Typical Northern State* (Ann Arbor, 1913), contains some excellent insights and interesting generalizations. Charles H. Wesley, *Ohio Negroes during the Civil War* (Columbus, 1962), is a booklet which provides a superior summary of its topic.

Of the three dozen doctoral dissertations I used, three proved invaluable. John L. Stipp, "Economic and Political Aspects of Western Copperheadism" (Ohio State University, 1942) recognizes that the movement contained socioeconomic aspects and contends that the Copperhead country of Ohio was characterized by poorer soils, smaller homesteads, and more widespread illiteracy than the non-Copperhead counties. Charles R. Wilson, "The *Cincinnati Daily Enquirer* and Civil War Politics" (University of Chicago, 1934), thoroughly examines the editorials of a paper which invariably endorsed Vallandigham's views. John S. Hare, "Allen G. Thurman: A Political Study" (Ohio State University, 1933), traces the career of a rival of Vallandigham. It was Thurman who secured the Senate seat in 1869 which the Daytonian had coveted.

A score of masters' theses touched upon topics directly related to the story of Clement L. Vallandigham and Ohio politics during the Civil War. Irving L. Schwartz, "Dayton, Ohio, during the Civil War" (Miami University, Oxford, 1949), and Florence E. Boyd, "Dayton, Ohio, during the Civil War" (Ohio State University, 1939), depended largely upon newspaper files and cited neither the Thomas O. Lowe Papers nor the Daniel L. Medlar "Journal." Christena M. Wahl, "The Congressional Career of Clement Laird Vallandigham" (Ohio State University, 1938), is both ill-organized and superficial. Harold L. Naragon, "The Ohio Gubernatorial Campaign of 1863" (Ohio State University, 1934), gives a rather good analysis of the election which Vallandigham lost to Brough. William D. Murdock, "The Ohio Gubernatorial Election of 1859" (1938), William J. Ulrich, "Ohio and the Election of 1862" (1948), and Elizabeth F. Yager, "The Campaign of 1864 in Ohio" (1925)—all masters' theses at Ohio State University—deal with elections in which Vallandigham was actively involved. Thomas H. Smith, "The Peace Democratic Movement in Crawford County, Ohio, 1860-1865" (Ohio State University, 1962), shows an excellent grasp of wartime issues. This thesis, somewhat revised, has been published under the title "Crawford County 'Ez Trooly Dimecratic,'" in *Ohio History* 76 (1967): 33-53. Mildred O. Wertman, "The Democracy of Pickaway County in the Civil War (Ohio State University, 1932), and Lester J. DeFord, "Mercer County, Ohio, during the Civil War" (Ohio State University, 1948), deal with two counties which gave Vallandigham a majority over Brough in the 1863 election contest. Bruce C. Flack, "The Attitude of the Methodist Episcopal Church in Ohio toward the Civil War, 1861-1865" (Ohio State University, 1962), reveals the pressures of patriotism and conformity. Ruth Wood Gold, "The Attitude of Labor in the Ohio Valley toward the Civil War" (Ohio State University, 1948), explores an interesting facet of Midwestern Copperheadism. William Young, "Soldier Voting in Ohio during the Civil War" (Ohio State University, 1948), discusses a political stratagem Republicans used to win some wartime elections. Elden R. Young, "Arbitrary Arrests during the Civil War" (Ohio State University, 1924), is badly outdated and wholly inadequate. Harry C. Harnish, "The Activities of the Copperheads in Ohio during the Civil War" (Western Reserve University, 1930), incorporates legends as facts and offers a rather shallow summary.

Hundreds of historical articles have a bearing upon Vallandigham, Midwestern Copperheadism, and the Civil War. I myself have dealt with Vallandigham as an exile in three different articles: "Clement L. Vallandigham's Exile in the Confederacy, May 25-June 17, 1863," *Journal of Southern History* 31 (May 1965): 149-63; "Exile across the Border: Clement L. Vallandigham at Niagara, Canada West," *Niagara Frontier* 11 (Autumn 1964): 69-73; and "Vallandigham as an Exile in Canada, 1863-1864," *Ohio History* 74 (Summer 1965): 151-68, 208-10. I have also treated Midwestern Copperheadism in a series of articles: "Economic Aspects of Middle Western Copperheadism," *The Historian* 14 (Autumn 1951): 27-44; "Middle Western Copperheadism and the Genesis of the Granger Movement," *Mississippi Valley Historical Review* 38 (March 1952): 679-94; and "Midwestern Opposition to Lincoln's Emancipation Policy," *Journal of Negro History* 49 (July 1964): 169-83.

Carl M. Becker has thoroughly researched a number of topics concerned with Dayton history. Three are especially relevant to the Vallandigham story: "'Disloyalty' and the Dayton Public Schools," *Civil War History* 11 (March 1965): 58-68; "Picture of a Young Copperhead [Thomas O. Lowe]," *Ohio History* 72 (January 1962): 3-23; and "The Death of J. F. Bollmeyer: Murder Most Foul?" *Bulletin of the Cincinnati Historical Society* 24 (July 1966): 249-69.

Before and after completing his doctoral dissertation, "The

Re-election of Abraham Lincoln" (Western Reserve University, 1952), William F. Zornow mined it for two dozen articles, many of which relate to Vallandigham. Several of the more important are: "Clement L. Vallandigham and the Democratic Party in 1864," *Bulletin of the Historical and Philosophical Society of Cincinnati* 19 (January 1961): 21-37; "McClellan and Seymour in the Chicago Convention of 1864," *Journal of the Illinois State Historical Society* 43 (Spring 1951): 282-95; and "Treason as a Campaign Issue in the Re-election of Lincoln," *Abraham Lincoln Quarterly* 5 (June 1949): 348-63.

Ollinger Crenshaw, "The Speakership Contest of 1859-1860," *Mississippi Valley Historical Review* 29 (December 1942): 323-38, deals with an event in which Vallandigham was a participant. Eugene H. Roseboom, "Southern Ohio and the Union in 1863," *Mississippi Valley Historical Review* 39 (June 1952): 29-42, effectively disproves the myth that all the pro-Vallandigham country bordered the Ohio River. Kenneth B. Shover, "Maverick at Bay: Ben Wade's Senate Re-election Campaign, 1862-1863," *Civil War History* 12 (March 1966): 23-42, endorses the untenable thesis that the Union Party was an actual political entity rather than a wartime cloak behind which Republicans hid. Benjamin F. Prince, "The Rescue Case of 1857," *Ohio State Archaeological and Historical Quarterly* 16 (April 1907): 292-309, deals with litigation in which Vallandigham had much more than a passing interest. Bertram W. Korn, "Congressman Clement L. Vallandigham's Championship of the Jewish Chaplaincy in the Civil War," *American Jewish Historical Quarterly* 53 (December 1963): 188-91, suggests that the controversial Daytonian was the champion of the underdog. Mary Land, "John Brown's Ohio Environment," *Ohio State Archaeological and Historical Quarterly* 57 (January 1948): 24-47, contains some interesting detail and explains why Vallandigham was interested in "Old Brown's" career.

Wartime events in Ohio have been treated in several historical articles. Eugene H. Roseboom, "The Mobbing of the *Crisis*," *Ohio State Archaeological and Historical Quarterly* 59 (April 1950): 150-53, is too brief and is more a narrative than an analysis. J. R. Vance, "Holmes County Rebellion—Fort Fizzle," *Ohio State Archaeological and Historical Quarterly* 40 (January 1931): 30-51, raises as many questions as it answers. Wayne Jordan, "The

Hoskinsville Rebellion," *Ohio State Archaeological and Historical Quarterly* 47 (October 1943): 319-54, shows how molehills sometimes evolve into mountains.

Vallandigham's interest in compromise is revealed in David Lindsey, " 'Sunset' Cox, Ohio's Champion of Compromise, in the Secession Crisis of 1860-1861," *Ohio State Archaeological and Historical Quarterly* 62 (October 1953): 348-67. R. Alton Lee, "The Corwin Amendment in the Secession Crisis," *Ohio History* 70 (January 1961): 1-26, also deals with efforts at compromise in early 1861.

Russel B. Nye states that Vallandigham "stained his own name with treason in defense of his principles" in his sketch of the Daytonian in a collective biography entitled *A Baker's Dozen: Thirteen Unusual Americans* (East Lansing, 1956), pp. 185-208. Edward N. Vallandigham, "Clement L. Vallandigham, 'Copperhead,' " *Putnam's Monthly* 2 (August 1907): 590-99, is a nephew's eulogy. W. H. Van Fossan, "Clement L. Vallandigham," *Ohio State Archaeological and Historical Society Publications* 23 (Columbus, 1914): 256-67, is mostly dross and hardly worth reading. Louis W. Koenig, "The Most Unpopular Man in the North," *American Heritage* 15 (February 1964): 12-15, 81-88, warms up the Copperhead for public consumption and helps perpetuate some of the Vallandigham myths.

Footnotes cite or mention other sources than those listed in the preceding paragraphs. Readers who check the footnotes will see that the present book is based mainly upon primary sources, especially manuscript collections and contemporary newspapers.

INDEX

Abingdon, Va., 208
abolitionists: criticized by C.L.V., 9, 17, 19, 26, 40, 44-45, 55, 62, 86, 89-91, 100, 103, 105, 117, 124, 129, 250, 315; Comly brothers, as, 11; Democrats oppose, 14, 36, 39, 68, 89-90, 97, 100, 106-08, 119, 120, 143-44, 160, 186, 230, 243-45, 247-48, 260; denounced by Douglas, 21; and John Brown, 23, 24; in Congress, 25, 52, 89-90; blamed for dissension, 44-45, 163-64; blamed for war, 67, 74, 124, 143; linked to Union party movement, 82, 112, 243-44, 253-54; disappointed with Lincoln's message, 87; opposed by Irish-Americans, 107-08; opposed by German-Catholics, 107-08; identified with New England, 107; opposed by Butternuts, 108; repudiated by 1862 elections, 112; helped defeat C.L.V. in 1862, 112, 113; reaction to, 230; and 13th Amendment, 305. *See also* Brown, John; emancipation
Abrams et al. v. *United States* (1919), 322
"Address of the Democratic Members of Congress to the Democracy of the United States," 97-98, 100
African slave trade, 21
Albany, N. Y.; Democratic conference (March 1863), 135-36; protest rally (16 May, 1863), 180-81. *See also* "Albany Resolves"
Albany Argus, 284
"Albany Resolves," 181, 188, 189
Aldrich, Cyrus, 78
Allen, Isaac Jackson: criticized C.L.V., 127, 150, 164, 231-32, 240; quoted, 127, 231-32, 240; editor of *Ohio State Journal*, 150; urged C.L.V.'s arrest, 150; and Francis Hurtt, 152; endorsed arrest of C.L.V., 164; on C.L.V.'s defeat, 252-53
Allen, William: endorsed war, 64; campaigned for C.L.V., 246; named delegate-at-large, 267

American party: and Speakership contest of 1859-1860, 24-25, 28
Anderson, Col. Charles, 238
Anderson, Maj. Robert, 61, 238
Anderson, William A.: campaigned for C.L.V., 246
Antietam, Battle of, 105
Antislavery Standard (New York), 181
arbitrary arrests: criticized in Congress, 89; denounced by C.L.V., 89, 117, 121, 124, 134-35; denounced by Democrats, 89, 100, 103; in Ohio in 1862, 108-09; reaction to, 108-09, 230-31; repudiated by 1862 election returns, 112; resolutions regarding, 117; defended by Lincoln, 182. *See also* Kees, John W.; Mahony, Dennis A.; McMaster, James A.; Olds, Dr. Edson B.; Reeves, Henry
Armstrong, William W.: secretary of state (Ohio), 138-39; critical of Vallandigham's ambitions, 138-40; quoted, 139
Army Bill (1862), 91-92
Army Deficiency Bill, 91-92
Army of the Cumberland, 190
Ashland (Ohio) *Union*, 178
Ashley, James M., 126, 132
Ashtabula County, Ohio, 5-6
Ashtabula Sentinel, 144
Atkins, John DeWitt, 207-08
Atlanta, Ga., 290
Auglaize County, Ohio, 254
Augusta Chronicle: quoted, 212

Baltimore, Md., 65, 78, 93; site of Democratic National Convention, 1860, 36; riots in, 65
Baltimore & Ohio Railroad, 3
Baltimore Clipper, 92
Barber, George, 161-62n
Barlow, Samuel L. M., 282
Barret, Dr. James A., 261-62
Bates, Attorney General Edward, 258
Beer, Thomas, 136
Bell, John, 36

336

344